OXFORD ENGLISH MONOGRAPHS

General Editors

NANDINI DAS   SANTANU DAS   PAULINA KEWES
MATTHEW REYNOLDS   FIONA STAFFORD   MARION TURNER

Modernist Parody

Imitation, Origination, and Experimentation in Early Twentieth-Century Literature

SARAH DAVISON

OXFORD
UNIVERSITY PRESS

Great Clarendon Street, Oxford, OX2 6DP,
United Kingdom

Oxford University Press is a department of the University of Oxford.
It furthers the University's objective of excellence in research, scholarship,
and education by publishing worldwide. Oxford is a registered trade mark of
Oxford University Press in the UK and in certain other countries

© Sarah Davison 2023

The moral rights of the author have been asserted

All rights reserved. No part of this publication may be reproduced, stored in
a retrieval system, or transmitted, in any form or by any means, without the
prior permission in writing of Oxford University Press, or as expressly permitted
by law, by licence or under terms agreed with the appropriate reprographics
rights organization. Enquiries concerning reproduction outside the scope of the
above should be sent to the Rights Department, Oxford University Press, at the
address above

You must not circulate this work in any other form
and you must impose this same condition on any acquirer

Published in the United States of America by Oxford University Press
198 Madison Avenue, New York, NY 10016, United States of America

British Library Cataloguing in Publication Data
Data available

Library of Congress Control Number: 2022951491

ISBN 978–0–19–284924–3

DOI: 10.1093/oso/9780192849243.001.0001

Printed and bound in the UK by
Clays Ltd, Elcograf S.p.A.

Links to third party websites are provided by Oxford in good faith and
for information only. Oxford disclaims any responsibility for the materials
contained in any third party website referenced in this work.

To my mum, Penny, and my dad, John

Acknowledgements

Many students, colleagues, and other scholars too numerous to name have enlarged my understanding of modernism in ways that have shaped this book, and my thanks go to all of them. I owe an enormous and lasting debt of gratitude to Ann Pasternak Slater for her wonderful generosity and kindness, and the care and critical attention with which she supervised the thesis on which this book is loosely based. Heartfelt thanks are also due to Lynda Pratt for being such an unfailingly supportive mentor and colleague. I want to thank Chrissie Van Mierlo for her research assistance on 'Intertextual Joyce' (a project funded by a British Academy Small Research Grant that yielded lots of information on the genesis of the 'Oxen of the Sun' episode of *Ulysses*) and Christopher Wait, Permissions Editor at New Directions Publishing Corporation, for his expert guidance and assistance on matters copyright.

Various parts of this book build on articles published elsewhere. I am grateful to *Textual Cultures* for permission to reproduce my reading of Max Beerbohm's parody of Henry James 'The Mote in the Middle Distance' from 'Max Beerbohm's Altered Books', *Textual Cultures* 6(1) (spring 2011), 48–75. Insights from 'An "Atmosphere of Parody": Ezra Pound and Imagism', in Catherine Morley and Alex Goody, eds., *American Modernism: Cultural Transactions* (2009), 143–64, appear in Chapters 3 and 4 of this book with the permission of Cambridge Scholars Publishing. I am also grateful to *Genetic Joyce Studies* for permission to incorporate materials from 'Oxtail Soup: Dialects of English in the Tailpiece of the "Oxen of the Sun" Episode of *Ulysses*', *Genetic Joyce Studies* 14 (2014) in the discussion of Joyce's use of sea slang and regional dialect in Chapter 6.

Finally, I want to take this opportunity to express my love and thanks to my husband Bram Mertens, who made it possible for me to write this book.

Permissions

Excerpts from Richard Aldington's 'The Egoist', 'Vates, the Social Reformer', and *Life for Life's Sake* reproduced by kind permission of the Estate of Richard Aldington c/o Rosica Colin Limited, London.

From *The Dialogic Imagination: Four Essays* by M. M. Bakhtin, edited by Michael Holquist, translated by Caryl Emerson and Michael Holquist, copyright © 1981. Courtesy of the University of Texas Press. Excerpts from *A Christmas Garland*, 'A Defence of Cosmetics', 'A Letter to the Editor', *Last Theatres, Letters of Max Beerbohm, Max Beerbohm: Collected Verse*, and *The Works of Max Beerbohm, with a Bibliography by John Lane*, by Max Beerbohm, copyright of the Estate of Max Beerbohm. Courtesy of Berlin Associates.

From T. S. Eliot's draft notes for *Selected Poems* (1928), quoted in Humphrey Carpenter, *A Serious Character: The Life of Ezra Pound*, copyright © 1988, by Humphrey Carpenter. Reprinted by permission of Faber & Faber. From 'John Dryden' by T. S. Eliot in *The Complete Prose of T. S. Eliot: The Critical Edition, Volume 2, The Perfect Critic, 1919–1926*, ed. Anthony Cuda and Ronald Schuchard, copyright © 2014, by the Estate of T. S. Eliot. Reprinted by permission of Faber & Faber. From 'Parodies of Publisher's "Blurbs" Composed by T. S. Eliot for the Firm of Faber & Faber', typescript (1937), Papers of the Hayward Bequest of T. S. Eliot Material HB/P9, King's College, Cambridge, by T. S. Eliot. Copyright by the Estate of T. S. Eliot. Reprinted by permission of Faber & Faber. From 'Old Possum's Book of Practical Cats &c. Typescript by the Author [T. S. Eliot] with Early Drafts of Two Poems, & Unpublished Material. Including His Old Possum's Letter to the Publishers and Parodies of Readers' Reports Ascribed to Members of the Firm of Faber & Faber Ltd', typescript, n.d., Papers of the Hayward Bequest of T. S. Eliot Material HB/V9, King's College, Cambridge, by T. S. Eliot. Copyright by the Estate of T. S. Eliot. Reprinted by permission of Faber & Faber. In the world (excluding the United States) from *The Letters of T. S. Eliot: Volume 1: 1898–1922*, rev. edn, ed. Valerie Eliot and Hugh Haughton, all writings by T. S. Eliot, introductions and editorial material © Set Copyrights Limited 1988, 2009, all writings by Vivien Eliot © Valerie Eliot, 1988, 2009, and *The Letters of T. S. Eliot: Volume 3, 1926–1929*, ed. Valerie Eliot and John Haffenden, all writings by T. S. Eliot, introductions and editorial material © Set Copyrights Limited 2012, all writings by Vivien Eliot © Valerie Eliot, 2012. Reprinted by permission of Faber & Faber. In the United States, from *The Letters of T. S. Eliot: Volume 1: 1898–1922*, rev. edn, ed. Valerie Eliot and Hugh Haughton (New Haven, CT: Yale University

viii PERMISSIONS

Press, 2011), all writings by T. S. Eliot, introductions and editorial material © Set Copyrights Limited 1988, 2009, all writings by Vivien Eliot © Valerie Eliot, 1988, 2009, and *The Letters of T. S. Eliot: Volume 3, 1926–1929*, ed. Valerie Eliot and John Haffenden (New Haven, CT: Yale University Press, 2012), all writings by T. S. Eliot, introductions and editorial material © Set Copyrights Limited 2012, all writings by Vivien Eliot © Valerie Eliot, 2012. Reprinted by permission of Yale University Press. From 'Reflections on Contemporary Poetry', by T. S. Eliot, *Egoist* VI(3) (July 1919). Reprinted by permission of Faber & Faber. From 'Sweeney Erect', by T. S. Eliot, in *T. S. Eliot, Collected Poems*, by T. S. Eliot, copyright © 1925, 1936, 1963 by T. S. Eliot. Reprinted by permission of Faber & Faber. In the world (excluding the United States, its dependencies, and the Philippines), from *The Waste Land: A Facsimile and Transcript of the Original Drafts*, ed. Valerie Eliot, all writings by T. S. Eliot, copyright © 1971 by Valerie Eliot. Reprinted by permission of Faber & Faber.

Excerpts by James Joyce from *A Portrait of the Artist as a Young Man, Finnegans Wake, Joyce's 'Ulysses' Notesheets in the British Museum, Letters of James Joyce, Occasional, Critical, and Political Writing, Stephen Hero, Ulysses*, and '*Ulysses*: Episode 12: part I' in *Little Review* VI(7), copyright the Estate of James Joyce. Quoted by kind permission of Seán Sweeney.

Excerpts by Wyndham Lewis from *The Apes of God, Blast: Review of the Great English Vortex* I, *Blasting and Bombardiering, Men without Art*, and *Time and Western Man* quoted by permission of the Wyndham Lewis Memorial Trust (a registered charity).

Excerpts by Ezra Pound, from *ABC of Reading*, copyright © 1934 by Ezra Pound. Reprinted by permission of New Directions Publishing Corp. From 'Redondillas, or Something of that Sort', 'Aria', 'Donzella Beata', 'Epigraph to *A Lume Spento*: Make-strong old dreams . . . ', 'Fifine Answers', 'Histrion', 'L'Art', 'La Fraisne', 'Note Precedent to "La Fraisne"', 'Pax Saturni', 'Piazza San Marco', 'Piccadilly', 'Revolt: Against the Crepuscular Spirit in Modern Poetry', 'Salve O Pontifex!/To Swinburne; an hemichaunt', 'Scriptor Ignotus', 'Song in the Manner of Houseman', 'The Decadence', 'To Hulme (T. E.) and Fitzgerald (A Certain)', 'Translations from Heine', 'Und Drang', 'In Tempore Senectutis (An Anti-stave for Dowson)' by Ezra Pound, from *Collected Early Poems*, copyright ©1926, 1935, 1954, 1965, 1967, 1976 by the Ezra Pound Literary Property Trust. Reprinted by permission of New Directions Publishing Corp. Various excerpts by Ezra Pound, from *Ezra Pound and Dorothy Shakespear*, copyright © 1976, 1984 by the Trustees of the Ezra Pound Literary Property Trust. Reprinted by permission of New Directions Publishing Corp. Various excerpts by Ezra Pound, from *Ezra Pound to His Parents*, copyright © 2010 by Mary de Rachewiltz and the Estate of Omar S. Pound. Reprinted by permission of New Directions Publishing Corp. From 'A List of Books: "Others"', 'A Rejoinder', '"Abel Sanders" [Ezra Pound], The Reader Critic: This Approaches Literature!', 'Kongo Roux', 'L'Art', 'Prolegomena', 'The Approach to Paris', 'The Reader Critic: The Hoax of the "Spectrics"', various excerpts, 'Vortex. Pound', by Ezra Pound, from *Ezra Pound's Poetry and Prose: Contributions to Periodicals* (Garland Press), copyright © 1991 by the Trustees of the Ezra Pound Literary Property Trust. Reprinted by permission of New Directions Publishing Corp. From 'Vorticism', by Ezra Pound, from *Gaudier-Brzeska*, copyright © 1980 by New Directions Publishing Corp. Reprinted by permission of New Directions Publishing Corp. From 'A Retrospect', 'A Retrospect: A Few Don'ts', 'Cavalcanti', 'Hell', 'How To Read', 'Joyce', 'Notes On Elizabethan Classicists', 'The Serious Artist', 'Irony, Laforgue, and Some Satire', 'Swinburne Versus his Biographers', 'Troubadours—their Sorts and Conditions', by Ezra Pound, from *Literary Essays of Ezra Pound*, copyright © 1935 by Ezra Pound. Reprinted by permission of New Directions Publishing Corp. From 'Ulysses', by Ezra Pound, from *Literary Essays of Ezra Pound*, copyright © 1973 by the Estate of Ezra Pound. Reprinted by permission of New Directions Publishing Corp. From 'Homage to Ford Madox Ford', by Ezra Pound, from *New Directions in Prose and Poetry*, No. 7, copyright ©1942 by New Directions Publishing Corp. Reprinted by permission of New Directions Publishing Corp. The words 'chançons ithyphallique' on the back of an envelope postmarked 11 January 1915, quoted in *The Poems of T. S. Eliot: Volume II*, by Ezra Pound, from New Directions Pub. acting as agent, copyright © 2015 by Mary de Rachewiltz and the Estate of Omar S. Pound. Reprinted by permission of New Directions Publishing Corp. From unpublished letter from Pound to H. Monroe quoted in Ellen Williams, *Harriet Monroe and the Poetry Renaissance: The First Ten Years of Poetry, 1912–22*, by Ezra Pound, from New Directions Pub. acting as agent, copyright ©1976 by the Trustees of the Ezra Pound Literary Property Trust. Reprinted by permission of New Directions Publishing Corp. From '"To R. B." [prose reflections/journal]', by Ezra Pound, from New Directions Pub. acting as agent, copyright © 1985 by the Trustees of the Ezra Pound Literary Property Trust. Reprinted by permission of New Directions Publishing Corp. 'Previously unpublished writings as quoted in *A Serious Character: The Life of Ezra Pound*', by Ezra Pound, from New Directions Pub. acting as agent, copyright © 1988 by the Trustees of the Ezra Pound Literary Property Trust. Reprinted by permission of New Directions Publishing Corp. From 'Have I Not, O Walt Whitman' [unpublished typescript], Ezra Pound Papers, Yale Collection of American Literature, Beinecke Rare Book and Manuscript Library, 'To R. B.' [unpublished typescript], Ezra Pound Papers, Yale Collection of American Literature, Beinecke Rare Book and Manuscript Library, by Ezra Pound, from New Directions Pub. acting as agent, copyright © 1995 by the Trustees of the Ezra Pound Literary Property Trust. Reprinted by permission of New Directions Publishing Corp. From Pound's corrections, additions, and marginal comments on *The Waste Land*, by Ezra Pound, from New Directions Pub. acting as agent, copyright © 2015 by Mary de Rachewiltz and the Estate of Omar S. Pound. Reprinted by permission of New Directions Publishing Corp. In the United States, its dependencies, and

X PERMISSIONS

the Philippines, from annotations of Ezra Pound's and of Vivien Eliot's, and notes of Valerie Eliot's from *The Waste Land: A Facsimile and Transcript of the Original Drafts Including the Annotations of Ezra Pound*, by T. S. Eliot, edited and with an introduction by Valerie Eliot, Copyright © 1971 by Valerie Eliot, preface, annotations and extracts from letters and poems by Ezra Pound, copyright © by Ezra Pound. Used by permission of HarperCollins Publishers. From 'In Praise of the Masters', Ezra Pound Papers, Beinecke Rare Book and Manuscript Library, YCAL MSS 43, box 86, folder 3712, 'Med', typescript, n.d., Ezra Pound Papers, Beinecke Rare Book and Manuscript Library, YCAL MSS 43, box 89, folder 3809, 'Mr. K', typescript, n.d., Ezra Pound Papers, Beinecke Rare Book and Manuscript Library, YCAL MSS 43, box 89, folder 3809, 'Pagentry', typescript, n.d., Ezra Pound Papers, Beinecke Rare Book and Manuscript Library, YCAL MSS 43, box 88, folder 3778, by Ezra Pound, from New Directions Pub. acting as agent, copyright © 2022 by Mary de Rachewiltz and the Estate of Omar S. Pound. Reprinted by permission of New Directions Publishing Corp. For world electronic rights and world print rights excluding UK and the British Commonwealth but including Canada, from 'A Pact', 'Come My Cantilations', 'Commission', 'Dance Figure', 'Epitaphs', 'Homage to Sextus Propertius', 'In A Station of the Metro', 'Mesmerism', 'Monumentum Ære, Etc.', 'Ortus', 'Poems of Alfred Venison: Alf's Second Bit', 'Prefatory Note to the Complete Poetical Works of T. E. Hulme', 'Salutation', 'Salutation the Second', 'Salutation The Third', 'Tenzone', 'The Condolence', 'The Garret', by Ezra Pound, from *Personae*, copyright © 1926 by Ezra Pound. Reprinted by permission of New Directions Publishing Corp. For UK and British Commonwealth (excluding Canada) print rights, from 'A Pact', 'Come my Cantilations', 'Commission', 'Epitaphs', 'In a Station of the Metro', 'Monumentum Ære, Etc.', 'Mesmerism', 'Tenzone', 'The Garret', 'Salutation', 'Salutation the Second', 'Salutation the Third', 'Song in the Manner of Housman', by Ezra Pound, from *Personae: Collected Shorter Poems*, copyright © 1926 by Ezra Pound. Reprinted by permission of Faber & Faber. Various excerpts, by Ezra Pound, from *Pound/Joyce: Letters and Essays*, copyright © 1967 by Ezra Pound. Reprinted by permission of New Directions Publishing Corp. Various excerpts, by Ezra Pound, from *Selected Letters 1907–1941 of Ezra Pound*, copyright © 1950 by Ezra Pound. Reprinted by permission of New Directions Publishing Corp. From Timothy Materer, ed., *Selected Letters of Ezra Pound to John Quinn*, copyright © 1991 by the Trustees of the Ezra Pound Literary Property Trust. Reprinted by permission of New Directions Publishing Corp. From 'I Gather the Limbs of Osiris', 'What I Feel about Walt Whitman', by Ezra Pound, from *Selected Prose 1909–1965*, copyright © 1973 by the Estate of Ezra Pound. Reprinted by permission of New Directions Publishing Corp. By Ezra Pound, from *The Spirit of Romance*, copyright ©1968 by Ezra Pound. Reprinted by permission of New Directions Publishing Corp.

Works by J. C. Squire are quoted by kind permission of Roger Squire.

Works by Tristan Tzara are quoted by kind permission of Marie Thérèse Tzara.

Lines from Emile Verhaeren, *Poems*, selected, translated, and introduced by Will Stone, with a preface by Patrick McGuinness, are quoted by kind permission of Tony Ward.

From 'Kora in Hell: Prologue' by William Carlos Williams, from *Imaginations*, copyright ©1970 by Florence H. Williams. Reprinted by permission of New Directions Publishing Corp.

Contents

Abbreviations	xiii
Introduction	1
1. Parody: History and Theory	7
2. Pasticherie: Ezra Pound's Apprenticeship from His College Verses to *Canzoni*	43
3. 'An Atmosphere of Parody': Imagism and *Blast*	78
4. Mocking Modernisms: Parody in Little Magazines	117
5. 'A *Moqueur* to the Marrow': T. S. Eliot, Parody, and the Writing of *The Waste Land*	147
6. A 'Bawd of Parodies': James Joyce's Practices as a Parodist from His Early Writings to *Ulysses*	190
7. Parodists of History: Ford Madox Ford, Virginia Woolf, Wyndham Lewis, and James Joyce	232
Bibliography	254
Index	274

Abbreviations

BTA	Virginia Woolf, *Between the Acts,* ed. Frank Kermode (Oxford: Oxford University Press, 1998)
C	Ezra Pound, *Canzoni* (London: Elkin Mathews, 1911)
CEP	Ezra Pound, *Collected Early Poems of Ezra Pound,* ed. Michael John King (London: Faber & Faber, 1977)
Con	Ezra Pound, 'Contemporania', *Poetry: A Magazine of Verse* II.1 (April 1913), 1–12.
DI	Ezra Pound et al, *Des Imagistes: An Anthology* (New York: Albert and Charles Boni, 1914)
ECS	Austin Dobson, *Eighteenth Century Studies* (London: Dent, 1914)
FW	James Joyce, *Finnegans Wake,* ed. Seamus Deane (London: Penguin, 1992); references are given in the form: *FW* page number, line number
HWR	Else von Freytag-Loringhoven, 'Thee I call "Hamlet of the Wedding Ring", Criticism of William Carlos William's "Kora in Hell" and why . . .' Part I, *Little Review* VII(4) (1921), 48–55; Part II, *Little Review* VIII(1) (1921), 108–11
JJA XII	*James Joyce: Ulysses: Notes & 'Telemachus'—'Scylla and Charybdis': A Facsimile of Notes for the Book & Manuscripts & Typescripts for Episodes 1–9,* ed. Michael Groden, James Joyce Archive, vol. XII (New York: Garland, 1978)
LE	Ezra Pound, *Literary Essays of Ezra Pound,* ed. T. S. Eliot (London: Faber & Faber, 1954)
LEP	Ezra Pound, *The Letters of Ezra Pound: 1907–1941,* ed. D. D. Paige (London: Faber & Faber, 1951)
LJJ	James Joyce, *Letters of James Joyce,* vol. I, ed. Stuart Gilbert (London: Faber & Faber, 1957; vols. II and III, ed. Richard Ellmann (London: Faber & Faber, 1966)
LTSE	T. S. Eliot, *The Letters of T. S. Eliot: Volume 1: 1898–1922,* rev. edn, ed. Valerie Eliot and Hugh Haughton (New Haven, CT: Yale University Press, 2011)
MB	Ford Madox Ford, *Mister Bosphorus and the Muses, or A Short History of Poetry in Britain, Variety Entertainment in Four Acts, Words by Ford Madox Ford: Music by Several Popular Composers: with Harlequinade, Transformation Scene, Cinematograph Effects, and Many Other Novelties, as well as Old and Tried Favourites, Decorated with Designs Engraved on Wood by Paul Nash* (London: Duckworth & Co., 1923)

xiv ABBREVIATIONS

N	James Joyce, *Joyce's 'Ulysses' Notesheets in the British Museum*, ed. Phillip F. Herring (Charlottesville: University Press of Virginia, 1972); references to individual notesheet entries are given in the form: *N* notesheet number, line number. Otherwise, references are to page numbers
O	Virginia Woolf, *Orlando: A Biography*, intro. Peter Ackroyd and Margaret Reynolds (London: Vintage, 2000)
PP	Richard Aldington, 'Penultimate Poetry: Xenophilometropolitania', *Egoist* I(2) (1914), 36
R	Ezra Pound, *Ripostes of Ezra Pound: Whereto are Appended the Complete Poetical Works of T. E. Hulme, with Prefatory Note* (London: Stephen Swift & Co., 1912)
SR	Ezra Pound, *The Spirit of Romance: An Attempt to Define Somewhat the Charm of the Pre-Renaissance Literature of Latin Europe* (London: J. M. Dent & Sons, 1910)
TDI	M. M. Bakhtin, *The Dialogic Imagination: Four Essays by M. M. Bakhtin*, ed. and trans. Michael Holquist and Caryl Emerson (Austin: University of Texas Press, 1981)
TWLFT	Valerie Eliot, ed., *The Waste Land: A Facsimile & Transcript of the Original Drafts including the Annotations of Ezra Pound* (London: Faber & Faber, 1971)
U	James Joyce, *Ulysses*, ed. Hans Walter Gabler, Wolfhard Steppe, Claus Melchior, afterword Michael Groden (London: Bodley Head, 2002); references are given in the form: *U* episode number, line number

Introduction

The hybrid European—all in all, a tolerably ugly plebeian—simply needs a costume: he requires history as a storage room for costumes. To be sure, he soon notices that none fits him very well; so he keeps changing. Let anyone look at the nineteenth century with an eye for these quick preferences and changes of the style masquerade; also for the moments of despair over the fact that 'nothing is becoming'. It is of no use to parade as romantic or classical, Christian or Florentine, baroque or 'national', *in moribus et artibus*: it does not look good. But the 'spirit', especially the 'historical spirit', finds its advantage even in this despair: again and again, a new piece of prehistory or a foreign country is tried on, put on, taken off, packed away, and above all *studied*: we are the first age that has truly studied 'costumes'—I mean those of moralities, articles of faith, tastes in the arts, and religions—prepared like no previous age for a carnival in the grand style, for the laughter and high spirits of the most spiritual revelry, for the transcendental heights of the highest nonsense and Aristophanean derision of the world. Perhaps this is where we shall still discover the realm of our *invention*, that realm in which we, too, can still be original, say, as parodists of world history and God's buffoons—perhaps, even if nothing else today has any future, our *laughter* may yet have a future.[1]

In *Beyond Good and Evil* (1886), Friedrich Nietzsche inveighed against the loss of substantive identity and authenticity in a modern culture over-endowed with a historical sense, where the costumes, attitudes, and poses of the past could be borrowed and discarded at the drop of a hat. He was thinking particularly of the nineteenth-century fashion for Shakespearean fustian, which he viewed as a symptom of decadence and cultural decline, despairing at the superficial relativism of a detached eclecticism and hollow imitation of manner and belief. The commonplace nineteenth-century remedy for such a complaint was for art to return to the naive, the natural, or the local, but for Nietzsche parochialism was no cure.

---

[1] Friedrich Nietzsche, *Beyond Good and Evil: Prelude to a Philosophy of the Future*, ed. and trans. Walter Kaufmann (New York: Vintage Books, 1989), 150, §223, Nietzsche's italics.

Modernist Parody. Sarah Davison, Oxford University Press. © Sarah Davison (2023).
DOI: 10.1093/oso/9780192849243.003.0001

2 MODERNIST PARODY

Nietzsche's ironic point was that a culture in thrall to the historical spirit might only discover true *invention* in parody, the seeming opposite of original creation. His tone is wry and almost incredulous, yet he also raises the distinct possibility that parody's laughter—its capacity for nonsense, derision, and buffoonery— might give future consequence to that otherwise decadent and motley carnival of style by facilitating a newly self-aware mode of historical sensibility that thrives on ironic, knowing fabrications of the past.

So far as Nietzsche was concerned, tragic ages (ages of morality or religion that seek to account for life's meaning in serious, purposeful terms) must ultimately give way to comic ages, when only laughter can make sense of things. Or, as he put it in the preface to the second edition of *The Gay Science* (1887), 'Incipit tragoedia, we read at the end of this awesomely aweless book. Beware! Something downright wicked and malicious is announced here: *incipit parodia*, no doubt.'[2] By this he meant that the beginning of tragedy is also the beginning of parody, unless, that is, 'the pampering spiritual diet' of romanticism is to prevail.[3] It should therefore come as no surprise that Nietzsche made extensive use of parody in his philosophical writings and his poetry.[4] Indeed, the appendix of songs that concludes *The Gay Science* includes two obvious parodies: 'To Goethe' parodies the end of *Faust* and 'The Poet's Call' parodies Edgar Allan Poe's 'The Raven.'[5]

This book contends that parody's laughter had a brighter future than even Nietzsche foresaw, and that future was modernism. This is not to say that the modernists were not serious about their art. Indeed, critical formulations foregrounding their aesthetics of detachment, difficulty, and fragmentation have long emphasized the high seriousness of modernism's struggle with the crisis of belief that proliferated into all areas of European life and culture. The focus on the modernists' solemnity has made it hard to perceive their comic turns. In fact, the jauntiness, verve, and daring of experimental modernism is fundamentally parodic, and not just at the extreme avant-garde with the antics of Dada. The parody of modernism was ubiquitous and wide-ranging. It was not confined to mischievous skits on contemporaries' foibles, or pranks, hoaxes, and jokes. At the level of formal experimentation, parody became programmatic. It enabled the modernists to situate themselves within and beyond historical narratives, cultivating a modern sensibility that distinguished their work from that of mere revivalists. It was the technique by which modernist writers learned their craft, sharpened their historical sense, defined themselves as post-Victorian, and let their imaginations run

---

[2] Friedrich Nietzsche, *The Gay Science: With a Prelude in Rhymes and an Appendix of Songs*, ed. and trans. Walter Kaufmann (New York: Random House, 1974), 33.

[3] Nietzsche, *Gay Science*, 33.

[4] Sander L. Gilman has written extensively on parody in Nietzsche's works. See his *Nietzschean Parody: An Introduction to Reading Nietzsche*, 2nd edn (Aurora: Davies Group, 2001).

[5] Nietzsche, *Gay Science*, 351–5 (see Johann Wolfgang von Goethe, *Goethe's Faust*, ed. and trans. Walter Kaufmann (New York: Doubleday, 1961), 503, and Edgar Allan Poe, 'The Raven', in *The Raven and Other Poems* (New York: Wiley & Putnam, 1845), 1–5).

INTRODUCTION 3

while composing. It provided a ready method to spike enemies, transgress literary convention, and violate social decorum. Chopping and changing between parodies of historical modes of expression and contemporary dialect, the modernists creatively refashioned items from wardrobes past and present, and paraded them in a carnival of the grand style, discovering a spur for invention and originality sufficient to proclaim a new era for art.

It is a measure of Nietzsche's prescience that some of the most formally innovative modernist works literalize the terms of his extended metaphor. Examples include: Ezra Pound's attempt to compile 'a chronological table of emotions' from Provençal to the present day in *Canzoni* (1911); the parodies of historicized styles paraded by James Joyce in the 'Oxen of the Sun' episode of *Ulysses* (1922); the pageant play where villagers put on homespun costumes to perform scenes from their national history in Virginia Woolf's novel *Between the Acts* (1941); and Wyndham Lewis's satire on London's literary scene, *The Apes of God* (1930).[6] Richard Huelsenbeck was even more explicit about Dada's fundamentally Nietzschean response to its sense of its own historicity, its transience, but also its timeliness. He quoted the very same passage from *Beyond Good and Evil* in his 'Introduction' to the *Dada Almanach* (1920), explaining that Dada has discovered that realm of invention of which Nietzsche speaks, having made itself into a parodist of world history and God's buffoon, but that Dada had not exhausted itself: 'Dada does not die of Dada. Its laughter has a future.'[7]

Nietzsche seized on parody because it has a critical purchase on the non-identity and inauthenticity that is inscribed into its very form. To put it simply for now, parody is amusing because it purports to be one thing when what it actually means is quite another. The indeterminacy arising from parody's ironic fusion of irreconcilable perspectives provided a language and structure that could give expression to and even transcend the modernists' paradoxical situation in history. As self-conscious parodists, they could assert *themselves* to be original, authentic, and above all *modern*, precisely because they were knowingly derivative, disingenuous, and transhistorical. In parody's inbuilt insistence that literature is historicized language in unstable play before it is representation, modernist writers found a ready means to counter naive mimesis and even confront the crisis in aesthetic representation that motivated their break with established artistic conventions. In the face of its unstable and counterpoised perspectives, parody's

---

[6] Ezra Pound to Dorothy Shakespear, 16 July 1911, in Omar Pound and A. Walton Litz, eds., *Ezra Pound and Dorothy Shakespear: Their Letters 1910–1914* (New York: New Directions, 1985), 37.

[7] Richard Huelsenbeck, 'Einleitung', *Dada Almanach* (Berlin: Erich Reiss Verlag, 1920), 7; 'Dada hat das Reich der Erfindung entdeckt, von dem Friedrich Nietzsche in jenen oben angeführten Zeilen spricht, es hat sich zum Parodisten der Weltgeschichte und zum Hanswurst Gottes gemacht—aber es ist nicht an sich gescheitert. Dada stirbt nicht an Dada. Sein Lachen hat Zukunft.' [Dada has discovered the realm of invention that Friedrich Nietzsche speaks of in those lines quoted above, it has made itself the parodist of world history and the buffoon of God—but it did not fail. Dada does not die of Dada. Its laughter has a future.] Huelsenbeck, 'Einleitung', *Dada Almanach*, 8.

formal acknowledgement that meaning must be socially negotiated by its readers gave the modernists the satirical leverage for their writing to comment on the real world. Presented thus, parody becomes central to the whole modernist project.

The parody practised by the modernists had many guises—it could be flamboyant or surreptitious, momentous or nonsensical, mordant or gay—but the technique's long-standing association with low seriousness has led to its being significantly overlooked and under-theorized in criticism of high modernism. The case for parody as a primary reflex of modernism has not been helped by the way that the technique confounds and crosses many of divisions on which so much of our understanding of the movement still depends, particularly the line between high and low. Admitting minor genres of writing such as unpublished juvenilia, occasional verses, and even hoaxes and practical jokes into the canons of modernism and setting them alongside major works is one of the ways in which this book seeks to restore the mischievous spirit of parody to modernist literature.

Of course, the modernists were not the first writers to use parody innovatively. Parody is as old as literature itself. It is also one of the most equivocal and elusive literary modes. The chequered history of the term needs to be unpicked in relation to dominant practices to be able to appreciate why modernist parody has been so underestimated, and to distinguish the theory that can best illuminate what makes it special and characteristic. Chapter 1 provides a historical overview of parody as it has been practised and theorized. It identifies parody's salient qualities, examines fluctuations in reputation, and sets these in relation to the curious critical silence concerning its pervasive presence in modernism. Chapter 2 explores the modernists' apprentice experiments in imitative writing, focusing particularly on Pound's early poetry. It tells the story of Pound's evolution as a poet from the poor pastiche of his college verses and of *A Lume Spento* (1908) up to and including *Canzoni* (1911), a series of exercises in historical styles that also form a self-conscious record of Pound's own progress as an imitator who aspires to produce poetry that is original and, above all, contemporary.

Pound would remain an active parodist throughout his career, partly because he saw what could be done with it as a literary mode and partly because he just could not help himself. He features as a central and unifying case study in this book for his irrepressible parodic impulses, his role as a modernist impresario who made it his business to be up to date, his close working relationships with other important modernist writers, and the synergy between his critical writings and creative practices. This is not to position Pound as magisterial, but to affirm the complexity of his rise to prominence and influence and the extent of his entanglements with other contemporary writers, including his opponents.

As the book progresses, it opens out to consider the practices of a range of writers, some close to Pound, some in stark opposition. Chapter 3 explores how Pound's journey of discovery with parody shaped the course of Imagism, focusing particularly on 'Contemporania' (1913) and *Des Imagistes* (1914). It

INTRODUCTION 5

examines his efforts to inaugurate an 'atmosphere of parody' so that the new school might flourish under the same conditions that had animated recent European avant-gardes. It also investigates the parody that sustained the contradictions inherent in *Blast* (1914–15), the magazine of what was to be the first English avant-garde movement, Vorticism. Chapter 4 investigates the culture of parody in little magazines, where parody was used to conduct ideological debates concerning the aesthetic qualities and moral probity proper to modern literature. It begins by exploring the extent to which parodies of modernism defined the popular understanding of the movement, before opening out to consider the Spectra hoax, where parodies of modernist writing were passed off as genuine articles to a credulous public. Contestations between Pound and Beatrice Hastings and also between Pound, William Carlos Williams, and Elsa von Freytag-Loringhoven then provide case studies that attest to the intensity of the ideological battles fought through parody and its creative role as an engine that could drive further experimentation forward.

While parody was enmeshed in modernist thinking from its earliest stages, it was not until high modernism that the full, multilayered, philosophical, and literary applications of parody came to the fore as a palimpsestual means towards a complex historical critique. Chapter 5 focuses on T. S. Eliot, whom Lewis described as 'a *moqueur* to the marrow'.[8] It explores Eliot's career as a parodist, starting with his parodies of different genres and voices in early comic writings such as 'Effie the Waif', his 'Brilliants', and the King Bolo verses. It proceeds to evaluate the shaping role that Pound and Eliot's ideas about parody, imitation, and historicity played in the composition of *The Waste Land*, setting Eliot's use of parody in the light of the practices of writers such as Jules Laforgue, Tristan Tzara, James Joyce, John Dryden, and Alexander Pope. It concludes with reflections on the *jeux d'esprit* Eliot wrote to amuse his friends in later life and the perils of self-parody.

Chapter 6 concentrates on Joyce, whose use of parody is well recognized. It examines the early and middle stages of his evolution into a 'bawd of parodies' (to use the language of *Finnegans Wake*), which is to say a bard whose works are promiscuously parodic, who, like a bird of paradise, 'a parody's bird', shows his borrowed plumes in ritual display.[9] It focuses on Joyce's use of parody up to and including the 'Cyclops', 'Nausicaa', and 'Oxen of the Sun' episodes of *Ulysses*, accounting for the ways in which his activities as a parodist intensified precisely to highlight and potentially overcome the problem that style is never neutral but brings with it perspectives that ultimately compromise the illusion of mimesis and the facticity of historical narratives. It investigates Joyce's use of parodic stylization

---

[8] Wyndham Lewis, *Blasting and Bombardiering* (London: Eyre & Spottiswoode, 1937), 2nd rev. edn (Berkeley: University of California Press, 1967), 283.
[9] *FW* 296.7, 11.9.

6 MODERNIST PARODY

to interrogate the distorting discourses that contour Dubliners' views on their national life and sense of self, from the influence of revivalist historiographies on the male public sphere in 'Cyclops' to the influence of mass-market publications and improving literatures on the female public sphere in 'Nausicaa'. It then proceeds to scrutinize Joyce's wholesale parody of the English literary canon in 'Oxen of the Sun', in which parody is explicitly figured as the principle of textual genesis that drives the ongoing progress of literature itself. Acting on the implicit invitation 'Oxen' extends to examine how it was written, it investigates the precise use Joyce made of the various literary and linguistic sources that he consulted, revealing patterns that complicate and enrich our understanding of the most difficult episode of *Ulysses*. So far as Joyce was concerned, the English of the present was so much more than the sum of its parodies of its past. Genetic analysis reveals that 'Oxen' liberates English from history, remaking the language anew as a live and ever-evolving entity that draws on the past but is invigorated by regional and racial dialects, loanwords, and Englishes spoken at the fringes of the anglophone world.

While the other chapters primarily focus on materials up to and including that modernist *annus mirablis* of 1922, Chapter 7 reflects on the ways in which modernist writers felt compelled to respond to the parody that had come to define high modernism, having reached its apotheosis in *Ulysses* in general and 'Oxen of the Sun' in particular. It examines works by Ford Madox Ford, Woolf, and Lewis that reckon with the achievements of Joyce and other authors by presenting versions of their contemporary literary culture as culminating moments that are defined by their parodies of the past. The chapter concludes by exploring how Joyce surpassed the parody of *Ulysses* in *Finnegans Wake*, showing how parody is not only fundamental to the genesis of modernist literature but also its sense of its historical situatedness and paradoxical modernity.

1

Parody

History and Theory

Parody originates in παρῳδία, from the Greek παρά, meaning 'alongside of', and ἀείδω, the transitive verb 'to sing'.[1] It is first recorded in Aristotle's *Poetics*, where Hegemon the Thasian (late fifth century BC) is referred to as 'the inventor of parodies', from which it has been inferred that the term was first used for 'a narrative poem of moderate length, in epic metre, using epic vocabulary, and treating a light, satirical, or mock-heroic subject'.[2] Aristophanic scholiasts later broadened its meaning to embrace any device for comic quotation. The etymologically precise metaphor of 'singing alongside of' is complicated by the ambiguity surrounding παρά, which admits a range of evaluative intention from closeness to derivation, transformation, and opposition. Speaking very generally, parody conjures an image of its model(s) that is available to be read alongside its actual text. Parody has therefore been understood to be a mode of transformative imitation that distorts its model(s) in ways that are incongruous and therefore amusing yet preserves the resemblance in such a way that the model(s) might be inferred. It drifts between tribute and travesty, being of its model(s) and yet distinct. Where the emphasis might fall in any given reading—which is, after all, also a form of rereading— is therefore delicately reliant on the audience's taste, the wider literary context, and the author's presumed intent. The protean nature of parody has led to diverse attempts to define its workings and effects, with commentators striving to keep pace with the changing preoccupations and techniques of practitioners. This history provides important theoretical models and contexts for the parody that is deeply rooted in modernist writing and from which its sense of its own stylishness and panache proceeds.

Parody made its English debut in the final lines of Ben Jonson's comedy *Every Man in His Humour* (1616 folio), reflecting the fashion for parodic redactions and the kind of rivalry between playwrights that resulted in the so-called War of the Theatres. The accusation 'A *parody*! A *parody*! With a kind of miraculous gift, to make it absurder than it was' is levelled by a justice at an ambitious but

---

[1] Henry George Liddell and Robert Scott, *Greek–English Lexicon*, 9th rev. edn, ed. Henry Stuart Jones (Oxford: Clarendon Press, 1968), παρῳδία.

[2] S. H. Butcher, *Aristotle's Theory of Poetry and Fine Art with a Critical Text and Translation of the Poetics*, 4th edn (London: Macmillan, 1927), 11; Fred W. Householder, 'ΠΑΡΩΙΔΙΑ', *Classical Philology* 39(1) (1944), 4.

Modernist Parody. Sarah Davison, Oxford University Press. © Sarah Davison (2023).
DOI: 10.1093/oso/9780192849243.003.0002

8   MODERNIST PARODY

deluded poet who is on trial for plagiarizing once popular works and exposing them to the ridicule of inexpert imitation.[3] While Jonson's own entertaining use of deliberately bad parody in that play has the sophistication of irony, the idea that parody is derivative and abuses the original author's meaning in ways that are disreputable and, *in extremis*, dangerous enough to society to warrant legal redress proved surprisingly persistent.

By the mid-eighteenth century, the term parody in English usage was further complicated by its conflation with travesty and burlesque, which strengthened the association with ridicule and absurdity at the expense of its other more transgressive qualities. Travesty, from the Italian *travestire*, literally to put on someone else's clothes, was made known through Paul Scarron's *Le Virgile travesty en vers burlesques* (1648).[4] It has come to denote debased imitation, characterized by ludicrous or coarse treatment of a serious work. Parody, by contrast, is neither limited to manipulating serious works nor necessarily coarse in its effects. Burlesque, from the Italian *burla*, meaning 'ridicule', was imported to England in the seventeenth century. It became a generic term for comic writing, generously accommodating parody, travesty, and the mock heroic. The popularity of *Le Lutrin* (first published in its entirety in 1683), in which Nicolas Boileau used the term 'burlesque' in his prologue to distinguish his comic innovation—in which a watchmaker and his wife speak in the elevated language of Dido and Aeneas—from the more common formula, used by Scarron and others, where Virgil's protagonists speak like fishmongers, resulted in Augustan writers applying the term to mock-heroic writing.[5] In contradistinction to burlesque, parody specifically subsumes the stylistic and formal qualities of its model(s) into its imitation, which precludes it from ridiculing its model(s) in any straightforward way.

The long eighteenth century is justly celebrated as a golden age of parody in English literature, both for its satirical animus and as a *sine qua non* for the rise of the novel. In poetry, mock heroic came to be one of the period's most characteristic modes: *Mac Flecknoe* (1682), *The Rape of the Lock* (1712), and *The Dunciad* (1728–43) conflate the epic with the bathetic, misapplying the grand decorum of classical convention to emphasize the smallness of their contemporary subjects to such hilarious effect that they are among John Dryden's and Alexander Pope's most obviously entertaining and original works.[6] In an age in which poetry

---

[3] Ben Jonson, *Every Man in His Humour*, ed. Gabriele Bernhard Jackson (New Haven, CT: Yale University Press, 1975), V.v.26–7.

[4] Paul Scarron, *Le Virgile travesty en vers burlesques* (Paris: Chez Toussaint Quinet, 1648).

[5] Nicolas Boileau Despréaux, *Boileau's Lutrin a Mock-heroic Poem. In Six Canto's, Render'd into English Verse. To Which Is Prefix'd Some Account of Boileau's Writings, and This Translation*, trans. N. Rowe Esq (London: Printed for R. Burrough and J. Baker; E. Sanger and E. Curll, 1708).

[6] John Dryden, *Mac Flecknoe*, in James Kinsley, ed., *The Poems of John Dryden*, vol. I (London: Oxford University Press, 1958), 265–71; Alexander Pope, *The Rape of the Lock*, in John Butt, ed., *The Poems of Alexander Pope: A One Volume Edition of the Twickenham Text with Selected Annotations* (London: Methuen, 1963), 217–42; *The Dunciad*, in *The Poems of Alexander Pope*, 709–805.

functioned as an effective weapon in the ongoing parliamentary feud between the Whigs and Tories, parody was particularly apt for combining personal attack with political satire, for instance the thoroughgoing drubbing Dryden gave the Whig poet Thomas Shadwell in *Mac Flecknoe*. The group of Augustan satirists known as the Scriblerians habitually parodied the Whiggish hackwork of the many emulators and detractors or 'Dunces' of Grub Street who were snapping at their heels as a means to fend off the debasement of the literary standards they themselves upheld as professional writers, at least in their own estimation. Among the best-recognized examples are Pope's *The Dunciad* and Jonathan Swift's *A Tale of a Tub* (1704), which seethe with parodic allusions not only to their respective authors' rivals but also to their own critics.[7] In this respect, parody performed the function of literary criticism in an age before that discipline was formalized, save that the works are invigorated by the very texts that they subvert.

The most canonical illustration of parody's starring role in the rise of the eighteenth-century novel begins with Henry Fielding's short pamphlet *Shamela* (1741), a direct and polemical parody of Samuel Richardson's prurient yet nevertheless highly eroticized epistolary novel *Pamela* (1740–1).[8] Fielding reproved Richardson's conventionally romantic plot of female virtue rewarded by elevated marriage, insinuating instead that the eponymous heroine's show of innocence was in fact a sham calculated to ensnare her master rather than a refutation of his lascivious designs. Fielding also exposed *Pamela*'s pretensions to immediacy by rendering the conceit that characters are writing about events happening in real time ridiculous. In the more fully novelized but hastily written picaresque adventure *Joseph Andrews* (1742), Fielding further inverted the conventional premises of Richardsonian romance, so that Pamela's brother, Joseph, must defend himself against the licentious advances of Lady Booby. To the attack on Richardson in *Joseph Andrews*, Fielding added imitation of Miguel de Cervantes's *Don Quixote* (1605–15).[9] In Cervantes's work, the errant wanderings of the crazy knight Alonso Quijano, who has filled his head with so many chivalric romances that he has lost his mind, are recounted in a series of interpolated stories that are suffused with the character and sentiment of the romance genres. When the giants Quijano resolves to slay in battle are revealed to be but windmills romance collapses in on itself and the story again becomes believable. In this way, Cervantes compounded the chivalric books that formed the inner life of his hapless protagonist into a new aesthetics of prose fiction composed of parodies so self-conscious that they segued

---

[7] Jonathan Swift, *A Tale of a Tub, The Battle of the Books and other Satires* (London: J. M. Dent & Sons, 1916).

[8] Henry Fielding, *The History of the Adventures of Joseph Andrews, and of his friend Mr. Abraham Adams, and An Apology for the Life of Mrs Shamela Andrews*, ed. Douglas Brooks-Davies, rev. and intro. Thomas Keymer (Oxford: Oxford University Press, 1999).

[9] Miguel de Cervantes Saavedra, *Don Quixote De La Mancha*, trans. Charles Jarvis, ed. and intro. E. C. Riley (Oxford: Oxford University Press, 1998).

10 MODERNIST PARODY

into reflections on writing and reading. His example inspired Fielding's wider parody of romance conventions in *Joseph Andrews*, as well as the many authorial interpolations that draw attention to the narrative's self-conscious construction, for instance a digression entitled 'Of Divisions in Authors', which reflects on the manner and purpose of dividing novels into chapters.[10]

In the preface to *Joseph Andrews* Fielding took care to explain that his work was a 'comic Epic-Poem in Prose', to be distinguished from the crass genre of 'burlesque' because it exhibited real men and had the good-humoured and benevolent object of making light of affectation, which must furnish the accurate observer of life with the true and proper source of the ridiculous.[11] He justified the many outbursts of burlesque (mock-heroic) diction (for instance in battle scenes) as extra amusement for classical readers, distancing himself from impropriety by insisting he had 'carefully excluded it from . . . Sentiments and Characters'.[12] His play with multiple styles reached its parodic height in the rambunctious and distinctly unRichardsonian novel *The History of Tom Jones: A Foundling* (1749), in which high language repeatedly rubs against low reality for comic effect, even to the extent that characters are given to apostrophize in parodied dialects. The narrator pauses to reflect on his 'poetical embellishments' (the multiple styles he parodies), which are included partly to 'refresh the mind' and keep things interesting, but also function as a comment on the florid literary conventions that could be pressed into the services of his own claims to truth.[13] For instance, in Book IV, chapter I the narrator announces that the heroine Miss Sophia Western will be introduced with the 'utmost solemnity in our power with an elevation of style, and all other circumstances proper to raise the veneration of our reader'.[14] In the chapter that follows, titled 'A short hint of what we can do in the sublime, and a description of Miss Sophia Western', the narrator calls on the 'noisy Boreas' and the 'bitter-biting Eurus' winds to hush so that the sweet Zephyrus might call forth his wife Flora, the goddess of flowers, and set a suitably lush scene:

> for lo! adorned with all the charms in which nature can array her; bedecked with beauty, youth, sprightliness, innocence, modesty, and tenderness, breathing sweetness from her rosy lips, and darting brightness from her sparkling eyes, the lovely Sophia comes![15]

The narrator asks 'Reader, perhaps thou hast seen the statue of the Venus de Medici', or 'the galleries of beauties at Hampton Court', proffering these as

---

[10] Fielding, *Joseph Andrews*, 76.
[11] Fielding, *Joseph Andrews*, 3.
[12] Fielding, *Joseph Andrews*, 4.
[13] Henry Fielding, *Tom Jones*, ed. John Bender (Oxford: Oxford University Press, 1998), 131.
[14] Fielding, *Tom Jones*, 133.
[15] Fielding, *Tom Jones*, 134.

analogues for Sophia's beauty, but follows this rhetorical flight with 'Now if thou hast seen all these, be not afraid of the rude answer which Lord Rochester once gave to a man who has seen many things'.[16] The answer does not appear in Fielding's text, but readers well versed in Rochester would instantly recognize it as a rude interruption of the narrative and a shift in tone that mocks the classical sublime, and deflates any claims it might make to veracity. The reference is to Rochester's poem 'To all Curious Criticks and Admirers of Metre' (1680), which asks readers if they have seen a series of improbable or mythical things, all of which have the feel of hackneyed subjects for poetry, and concludes with the memorable line 'If you have seen all this, then kiss mine Arse'.[17]

The statement that 'truth distinguishes our writings from those idle romances which are filled with monsters, the productions, not of nature, but of distempered brains' is as close as Fielding ever got to admitting that the novel's claim to truth is underwritten by its parodic distance from the languages and sentiments of other fantastical genres.[18] This formulation is repeated in many novels through the centuries, although the object of parody changes according to the dominant mode of the age, be it sentimental, gothic, bourgeois, pastoral, or journalistic. It is borne of a profound faith in the novel's ability to apprehend the real world. For instance, much of the comedy and narrative tension of Jane Austen's novel *Northanger Abbey* (drafted in 1797–8 but published in 1818) derives from the superficial resemblance of Catherine Morland's stay at the abbey to Emily St Aubert's distressing imprisonment in a castle at the hands of Signor Montoni in Ann Radcliffe's sensational gothic novel *The Mysteries of Udolpho* (1794). Whereas Austen's mature male love interest Henry Tilney vouches for *Udolpho* as a pleasurably thrilling page-turner, commenting 'when I had once begun it, I could not lay it down again;—I remember finishing it in two days—my hair standing on end the whole time', the naive and impressionable Catherine is so absorbed in *Udolpho* that she allows it to shape her understanding, leading her to imagine all manner of gothic horrors, only to discover that the reality is much more mundane.[19] An intriguing cabinet does not contain anything so exciting as 'some awful memorials of an injured and ill-fated nun', but an 'inventory of linen' wrapped in 'a farrier's bill'.[20] Henry's father General Tilney is no Montoni. He has not murdered or imprisoned his wife, as Catherine comes to suspect, but is instead guilty of acting 'neither honourably nor

---

[16] Fielding, *Tom Jones*, 134.

[17] Lord Rochester [John Wilmot], 'To all Curious Criticks and Admirers of Metre', *The Works of the Earls of Rochester, Roscommon, Dorset, &c. In Two Volumes. Adorn'd with Cuts*, 4th edn (London: printed for E. Curll, at the Dial and Bible against St. Dunstan's Church in Fleet-Street, 1714), 33.

[18] Fielding, *Tom Jones*, 131.

[19] Jane Austen, *Northanger Abbey, Lady Susan, The Watsons, Sandition*, ed. John Davie (Oxford: Oxford University Press, 1990), 82.

[20] Austen, *Northanger Abbey*, 110, 137.

12 MODERNIST PARODY

feelingly—neither as a gentleman nor as a parent.'[21] In essence, then, *Northanger Abbey* is about reading—and not only about reading gothic novels—but also the serious difficulties faced by a young woman like Catherine who must learn to read the social world around her and interpret it accurately and independently. Austen's parody exposes the falsity of the gothic novel with its creaking machinery and improbable plots, but it does so in the service of affirming her belief in the truth-telling capacity of realist fiction. And it is for this reason that Austen addresses her readers directly, to insist that novels that aim at realistic characterization and depiction of social and domestic life such as *Cecilia, or Memoirs of an Heiress* (1782) and *Camilla, or, A Picture of Youth* (1796) by Fanny Burney and *Belinda* (1801) by Maria Edgeworth are among those 'in which the greatest powers of the mind are displayed, in which the most thorough knowledge of human nature, the happiest delineation of its varieties, the liveliest effusions of wit and humour, are conveyed to the world in the best chosen language.'[22]

But when novelistic discourse in general recognizes itself to be in some way parodic, then the novel must become suspicious of its own language and the very foundations of its construction. From this intuition proceed the riotously destabilizing comic fictions of writers such as François Rabelais and Lawrence Sterne. Rabelais's sprawling multivolume story *The Life of Gargantua and Pantagruel* (1532–64) combines parodies of discourses from all fields of literature, learning, and life. The mockery is intensified by code switching—for instance from impeccable Latin to vulgar speech—and also the relentless materiality of the human body, the most visceral reality known to humankind, which is gruesomely magnified in the giants' enormous faeces and feasts.[23] Sterne's bawdy and brilliant *Life and Opinions of Tristram Shandy* (1759–67) freely parodies and plagiarizes diverse genres of writing for comic effect, making merry with the intellectual hobbyhorses of the period, from scholarship, sermons, and legal documents to treatises on warfare, fortification, and obstetrics.[24] Its largest parody makes a comedy of the nascent conventions of the eighteenth-century novel in its repeated confrontations with the false premise that writing can refer straightforwardly to life in its rich complexity. Compelled to explain the slapstick circumstances of his conception and birth, the principle of perpetual regress leaves Tristram unborn until volume IV (of nine) and manifestly unable to keep pace with unfolding events. The expectation that first-person confessional life-writing will exhibit forward progression is thwarted as the narrative disintegrates into teasing forms that are discontinuous,

---

[21] Austen, *Northanger Abbey*, 190

[22] Austen, *Northanger Abbey*, 22.

[23] François Rabelais, *The Works of the Famous Mr. Francis Rabelais, Doctor in Physick Treating of the Lives, Heroick Deeds, and Sayings of Gargantua and His Son Pantagruel: to Which Is Newly Added the Life of the Author*, trans. Sir Thomas Urquhart (London: Printed for R.B., 1664).

[24] Laurence Sterne, *The Life and Opinions of Tristram Shandy, Gentleman*, ed. Melvyn New and Joan New (London: Penguin, 1997).

digressive, elliptical, and even non-verbal (the squiggly line, the white, black, and marbled pages).[25] As Tristram avers:

> from the beginning of this, you see, I have constructed the main work and the adventitious parts of it with such intersections, and have so complicated and involved the digressive and progressive movements, one wheel within another, that the whole machine, in general, has been kept a-going;—and, what's more, it shall be kept a-going these forty years, if it pleases the fountain of health to bless me so long with life and good spirits.[26]

The novelty of *Tristram Shandy* was not lost on the reading public, but the popular craze for Shandyism soon died down: in 1776 Samuel Johnson told James Boswell, 'Nothing odd will do long. Tristram Shandy did not last'.[27]

Yet Rabelais, Cervantes, and Sterne did find favour with later generations of writers and theorists, particularly those working in the early twentieth century. For instance, Virginia Woolf expressed a strong affinity with Sterne. She marvelled at his ability to be present in the moment and convey a vivid impression of real life even as he articulated the impossibility of doing so:

> For though the writer is always haunted by the belief that somehow it must be possible to brush aside the ceremonies and conventions of writing and to speak to the reader as directly as by word of mouth, anyone who has tried the experiment has either been struck dumb by the difficulty, or waylaid into disorder and diffusity unutterable. Sterne somehow brought off the astonishing combination. No writing seems to flow more exactly into the very folds and creases of the individual mind, to express its changing moods, to answer its lightest whim and impulse, and yet the result is perfectly precise and composed.[28]

Accordingly, her own fiction often approaches Sternean levels of self-awareness and levity in its quest to convey the texture of lived experience, making use of many of his technical devices, including dashes, fragmentary impressions, and direct addresses to readers.

In the 1920s, the Russian formalists discerned the lineaments of all literary writing in the antics of singular, self-consciously parodic texts such as *Gargantua, Don Quixote,* and *Tristram Shandy* (although their work only came to prominence in English when it began to be translated in the 1950s and 1960s).[29] Viktor Shklovsky

---

[25] Sterne, *Tristram Shandy*, 391–2, 389, 29–30, 185–6.

[26] Sterne, *Tristram Shandy*, 59.

[27] James Boswell, *The Life of Samuel Johnson*, ed. R. W. Chapman (Oxford: Oxford University Press, 2008), 696.

[28] Virginia Woolf, 'The "Sentimental Journey"', in Stuart N. Clarke, ed., *Collected Essays by Virginia Woolf*, vol. 5 (London: Hogarth Press, 2009), 402–3.

[29] For an extended discussion of Russian formalist views of parody, see Margaret A. Rose, *Parody: Ancient, Modern, and Post-Modern* (Cambridge: Cambridge University Press, 1993), 103–25.

14   MODERNIST PARODY

was among the first to recognize the destructive but creative applications of parody when he praised Sterne for giving ossified and ineffectual literary devices a new lease of life. Because it was characteristic of Sterne to 'lay bare' his technique, and comment wryly on its workings, Shklovsky could then make the counterintuitive declaration 'Tristram Shandy is the most typical novel in world literature'.[30] The idea that parody could serve an evolutionary process was also explored by Yuri Tynianov in his landmark essay 'Dostoevksy and Gogol: Towards a Theory of Parody' ([1921] 1975). It shows how Fyodor Dostoevsky parodied Nikolai Gogol's style, beliefs, and personality (as expressed in *Select Passages from Correspondences with Friends* (1847)) in his presentation of Foma Opiskin, a character who is given to speechifying and literary pronouncements in *The Village of Stepanchikovo* (1859). Dostoevsky's parody not only served to mechanize Gogol's devices, but also shifted literary values, yielding to creative advances in the presentation of complex, contradiction-ridden characters that were distinctively Dostoevskian and yet could not have been developed immanently.[31]

From the late 1920s onward, Mikhail Bakhtin began to develop some of the formalists' ideas about parody, literary evolution, and laying bare, working with a similar canon of anglophone texts. He perceived that 'Parodic stylizations of canonized genres and styles occupy an essential place in the novel', and cast the history of the European novel in these terms, arguing that it renews itself through parodies of official or dominant writings, from epic, to sermons, to romance, and scholarship, from ancient times, to medieval *parodia sacra*, to eighteenth-century comic novels.[32] Across his writings, Bakhtin developed a series of persuasive theoretical and stylistic frameworks to illuminate parody's inner workings and show its most vivid and historically profound applications in the hands of radical writers like Cervantes, Rabelais, Fielding, and Sterne, whose parodies penetrate 'the deepest levels of literary and ideological thought itself, resulting in a parody of the logical and expressive structure of any ideological discourses as such (scholarly, moral and rhetorical, poetic)'.[33]

For Bakhtin, in ancient and medieval times, 'parody was inseparably linked to a carnival sense of the world', to the ritualistic folk laughter of festivals and holidays where the highest authorities were brought low and the world was temporarily

---

[30] Victor Shklovsky, 'Sterne's *Tristram Shandy*: Stylistic Commentary', *Russian Formalist Criticism: Four Essays*, trans. Lee L. Lemon and Marion J. Reis (Lincoln, NE: University of Nebraska Press, 1965), 57.

[31] Yuri Tynianov, 'Dostoevsky and Gogol: Towards a Theory of Parody'; part I in Priscilla Meyer and Stephen Rudy, ed. and trans., *Dostoevsky and Gogol: Texts and Criticism* (Ann Arbor: Ardis, 1979), 101–17; part II in Victor Erlich, ed. and trans., *Twentieth-Century Russian Literary Criticism* (New Haven, CT: Yale University Press, 1975), 102–16; Nikolai Gogol, *Selected Passages from Correspondence with Friends*, trans. Jesse Zeldin (Nashville, Tenn.: Vanderbilt University Press, 1969); Fyodor Dostoevsky, *The Village of Stepanchikovo: and Its Inhabitants: from the Notes of an Unknown*, rev. edn, trans. and intro. Ignat Avsey (London: Penguin, 1995).

[32] 'Epic and Novel', *TDI* 6.

[33] 'Discourse in the Novel', *TDI* 308.

PARODY   15

turned inside out to become its *'decrowning double'*.[34] The fires of ridicule burn away all that is stilted and stiff, but doubleness precludes complete destruction of the core image, which is reborn and renewed in the flames. Bakhtin's more complex stylistic analyses of parody in the novel retain the doubling of perspective but focus on the laughter that arises from the play of high and low languages in mutually illuminating combination, as well as the straightforward traduction of high to low. Inevitably, the language of formulation prevents what is fundamentally a comic mode from sounding particularly funny. Parody's free and familiar investigation is structurally similar to the powers Bakhtin ascribes to laughter, which:

> has the remarkable power of making an object come up close, of drawing it into a zone of crude contact where one can finger it familiarly on all side, turn it upside down, inside out, peer at it from above and below, break open its external shell, look into its center, doubt it, take it apart, dismember it, lay it bare and expose it, examine it freely and experiment with it.[35]

Bakhtin's basic premise is that language is always 'stratified not only into linguistic dialects . . . but also . . . into languages that are socio-ideological'; 'literary language itself is only one of these heteroglot languages—and in its turn is also stratified into languages (generic, period-bound and others)'.[36] By Bakhtin's account, the novel arose to embrace the centrifugal forces that make language a live and ever-changing entity at a time when poetry was accomplishing the task of national and political centralization. The novel thrived on unofficial languages (holiday forms, familiar speech, profanation), organizing heteroglossia through parodic styliza-tion. Bakhtin defined heteroglossia, once incorporated into the novel, as *'another's speech in another's language*, serving to express authorial intentions in a refracted way'.[37] Heteroglossia therefore functions as a form of *'double-voiced discourse'* in which the 'two voices, two meanings and two expressions' are 'dialogically interre-lated . . . as if they actually hold a conservation with each other'.[38] Examples include 'comic, ironic or parodic discourse, the refracting discourse of a narrator, refract-ing discourse in the language of character and finally the discourse of a whole incorporated genre'.[39] By 'stylization' Bakhtin meant 'an artistic image of another's language'.[40]

---

[34] Mikhail Bakhtin, *Problems of Dostoevsky's Poetics*, ed. and trans. Caryl Emerson (Minnesota: University of Minneapolis Press, 1984), 127, Bakhtin's italics.

[35] 'Epic and Novel', *TDI* 23.

[36] 'Discourse in the Novel', *TDI* 271–2.

[37] *TDI* 324, Bakhtin's italics.

[38] *TDI* 324, Bakhtin's italics.

[39] *TDI* 324.

[40] *TDI* 362.

16   MODERNIST PARODY

Bakhtin was the first to develop a linguistic framework for analysing parody's special qualities, distinguishing between the language that represents (the linguistic consciousness of the author) and the one that is represented, which is stylized:

> In actual fact, in parodic discourse two styles, two 'languages' [both intra-lingual] come together and to a certain extent are crossed with each other: the language being parodied (for example, the language of the heroic poem) and the language that parodies (low prosaic language, familiar conversational language, the language of the realistic genres, 'normal' language, 'healthy' literary language as the author of the parody conceived it). This second parodying language, against whose background the parody is constructed and perceived, does not—if it is a strict parody—enter as such into the parody itself, but is invisibly present in it.[41]

From this structural analysis proceeds Bakhtin's fundamental point that 'every parody is an intentional dialogized hybrid. Within it, languages and styles actively and mutually illuminate one another.'[42] Because it is in 'the nature of every parody to transpose the values of the parodied style, to highlight certain elements while leaving others in the shade', 'parody is always biased in some direction', and this bias is felt in the 'distinctive features of the parodying language, its accentual system, its structure.'[43] It is this bias that opens up the space for formal and socio-ideological critique.

Bakhtin argued that when heteroglot language enters the novel in the form of parodic stylization, 'the intentions of the representing discourse are at odds with the intentions of the represented discourse; they fight against them, they depict a real world of objects not by using the represented language as a productive point of view, but rather by using it as an exposé to destroy the represented language.'[44] To avoid 'a gross and superficial destruction of the other's language, as happens in rhetorical parody', and to be instead 'authentic and productive, parody must be precisely a parodic *stylization*, that is, it must recreate the parodied language as an authentic whole, giving its due as a language possessing its own internal logic and one capable of revealing its own world inextricably bound up with the parodied language.'[45] So, on the one hand there is the rhetorical ridicule that cuts its represented language down to size and on the other there is the stricter form of internally consistent stylization that approaches the represented language and its world closely and is not diminished for it in literary terms.

Bakhtin is not explicit about the precise mechanisms by which the reader detects a parody, especially in those cases when the parodying language is only invisibly

---

[41] 'From the Prehistory of Novelistic Discourse', *TDI* 75.
[42] *TDI* 75.
[43] *TDI* 75.
[44] 'Discourse in the Novel', *TDI* 364.
[45] *TDI* 364, Bakhtin's italics.

present—it would be left to the Reception theorists of the 1960s and 1970s to account for the evocative role that quotation and imitation play in setting up readers' expectations and recalling pretexts even in the act of distortion.[46] But from Bakhtin's discussions of actual texts, it is clear that he considered the second kind of parodic stylization to be the creative force that 'revealed its full potential and began to play such a titanic role in the formulation of a new literary and linguistic consciousness'.[47] Rabelais, Fielding, and Sterne are representatives of what Bakhtin calls the 'Second Stylistic Line' where 'Languages cease to be merely the object of a purely polemical or autotelic parodying: without losing their parodic coloration completely, they begin to assume the function of artistic representation, of a representation with value in its own right'.[48] They make such extensive use of parodic stylization that the truth 'does not receive its *own* word—it reverberates only in the parodic and unmasking accents in which the lie is present'.[49] Their writing concedes there is no single normative language—only styles—and shuttles back and forth between different modes of parodic stylization 'so that first some, then other aspects of language are thrown into relief'.[50] In this respect, the most self-conscious writers of comic prose intuitively reached to parody to confront the terms of the eternal dilemma that Nietzsche set out with renewed urgency at the end of the nineteenth century: what is to be done when the wardrobe of the past is fully stocked but no costume fits?

Bakhtin's analysis of the forces of novelization provides a rich literary context for the historically specific conditions of Nietzsche's complaint. Throughout the nineteenth century parodic stylization remained fundamental to the English comic novel, animating the works of nineteenth-century writers such as Charles Dickens and William Makepeace Thackeray. Simultaneously, the novel's confidence in its ability to represent the world reached its apogee in the mid-nineteenth century with the rise of realism. Meanwhile, as Bakhtin observed, the remaining genres had 'to a greater or lesser extent "novelized"', that is to say their language began to renew itself through heteroglossia, becoming 'dialogized, permeated with laughter, irony, humour, elements of self-parody', admitting 'indeterminacy' and 'semantic open-endedness' (Bakhtin cited Henrik Ibsen, Gerhart Hauptmann, the whole of naturalist drama, Lord Byron's epic poems *Childe Harold* (1812) and *Don Juan* (1824), and Heinrich Heine's lyrical verse, to which might be added earlier authors such as Pope and Swift).[51] An effect of this shift—one which was clearly palpable by the time Nietzsche was writing—was that the forces of novelization ossified historical styles to the extent that any strict adherence to a

---

[46] For a discussion of Wolfgang Iser and reception theory, see Rose, *Parody*, 175–7.
[47] 'From the Prehistory of Novelistic Discourse', *TDI* 80.
[48] 'Discourse in the Novel', *TDI* 386, 409.
[49] *TDI* 309, Bakhtin's italics.
[50] *TDI* 302.
[51] 'Epic and Novel', *TDI* 5, 7.

18   MODERNIST PARODY

genre began to feel like 'a stylization, taken to the point of parody, despite the intent of the author'.[52] A further consequence—in Bakhtin's view, at least—was that the language had become so 'free and democratized' that 'the complex and multi-leveled hierarchy of discourses' on which stylistic parody thrived in the Renaissance had collapsed, so that the mode's remit became 'narrow and unproductive'.[53] He concluded: 'Parody has grown sickly, its place in modern literature is insignificant'.[54]

This book hopes to prove Bakhtin wrong in this one respect only and uses many of his insights into parody and stylization to reveal their creative agency in modernist literature. It acknowledges, however, the rising prominence of that more narrow species of rhetorical parody that Bakhtin considered sickly and insignificant. In the nineteenth century, parody acquired the status of a minor literary genre in its own right and began to be practised as popular entertainment and theorized in relation to its propriety. Graeme Stones and John Strachan's painstakingly annotated five-volume anthology *Parodies of the Romantic Age* (1999) reveals the variety and vivacity of the different registers this protean form assumed by placing diverse parodies within their polemical context. Volume I focuses on the political parodies that filled the pages of the Tory newspaper the *Anti-Jacobin* (1797–8) denouncing the radicalism of the French Revolution, which used their literary models as a snappy form for Jacobin-bashing. The remaining volumes revel in parody's more literary pleasures, collecting and selecting from miscellaneous parodies in verse and prose that target dominant authors and genres of writing, for instance: William Wordsworth's poems and poetics in John Hamilton Reynold's *Peter Bell* (1819); Percy Bysshe Shelley's *Peter Bell the Third* (1839)) and chapter 13 of Samuel Taylor Coleridge's *Biographia Literaria* (1817); Charles Lamb's mock-theological letter to Coleridge; and William Beckford's satire on sensationalist fiction *Azemia* (1797). They also featured examples of the new genre of belletristic entertainment in which contemporary authors are parodied to fit with a theme, represented by selections from James and Horace Smith's hugely successful *Rejected Addresses* (1812) and full editions of William Deacon's *Warreniana* (1824) and P. G. Patmore's popular *Rejected Articles* (1826). *Rejected Addresses* hijacked the widely publicized cash-prize competition sponsored by Whitbread's brewery for a poem to celebrate the reopening of the Drury Lane Theatre by publishing amusing submissions in the characteristic modes of the age's greatest poets on the unpromising topic of fire and rebuilding, *Warreniana* contained spoof advertisements for Warren's brand of boot blacking as if the product were endorsed by the likes of Byron, Wordsworth, and Coleridge, while *Rejected Articles* featured polished imitations of leading prose stylists (among them Lamb and William Hazlitt)

---

[52] *TDI* 6.
[53] 'From the Prehistory of Novelistic Discourse', *TDI* 71.
[54] *TDI* 71.

PARODY   19

that were supposedly turned down by leading magazines and newspapers.[55] The more literarily motivated parody of the period mediated its audience's encounter with the more pretentious, esoteric, and representationally complex aspects of romanticism, as well as its explorations of childlike language, performing the cultural work of literary criticism in the age before that discipline was formalized. But publications like *Warreniana* are also suggestive of parody's role in the effective commodification of literary style enacted by the burgeoning print and periodical culture of the 1820s. They reveal parody's affinities with modern marketing and branding, which likewise depend on the ability to mobilize a compelling and recognizable image. The popularity of parody as an entertaining genre was itself a contributing factor to the late nineteenth- and early twentieth-century sense that any given style becomes hackneyed once it has been classified.

Parody's position in periodical culture contributed to its downgraded status. As Judith Priestman notes, 'Magazines like *Blackwoods* (1817), *Fraser's* (1830), and *Tait's* (1832) often printed serious reviews with parodies accompanying them; and most parodies in the nineteenth century were first published in the columns of a magazine or newspaper.'[56] Periodicals catered to the growth and tastes of a middle-class readership, who were very prepared to be entertained by parodies that gratified their desire to feel well-read. At the most anodyne end, magazines featured a great deal of what Priestman describes as 'simple content-substitution within an original form, where the new content would be comic after the style found acceptable in middle-class drawing rooms—tales of domestic mishap, cheeky children, rude servants, sea-sickness, and so on.'[57] These word games promoted a populist understanding of parody as a crude but entertaining device that separates form from content to produce light verse. The format of the comic magazines like *Punch* (1841), the leading publisher of parody in the second half of the nineteenth

---

[55] Graeme Stones and John Strachan, eds., *Parodies of the Romantic Age*, 5 vols., I: *The Anti-Jacobin*, II: *Collected Verse Parody*, III: *Collected Prose Parody*, IV: *Warreniana*, V: *Rejected Articles* (London: Pickering & Chatto, 1999). The immediate and lasting success of *Rejected Addresses* sparked a craze for parody collections that was embraced by belletrists and serious authors alike. Further examples include: James Hogg, *Poetic Mirror, or the Living Bards of Great Britain* (London: Printed for Longman, Hurst, Rees, Orme, and Brown, 1816); Theodore Martin and William Edmonstoune Aytoun, *The Book of the Ballads* (London: W. S. Orr, 1845); Cuthbert Bede, *Medley* (London: Blackwood, 1856); W. H. Mallock, *Every Man His Own Poet* (Oxford: Shrimpton & Son, 1872); C. S. Calverley, *Verses and Translations* (Cambridge: Deighton, Bell & Co., 1861) and *Fly Leaves* (Cambridge: Deighton, Bell & Co., 1872); A. C. Swinburne, *The Heptalogia, or, the Seven against Sense: A Cap with Seven Bells* (London: Chatto & Windus, 1880); J. K. Stephen, *Lapsus Calami* (Cambridge: Macmillan & Bowes, 1891).

[56] Judith Priestman, 'The Age of Parody: Literary Parody and Some Nineteenth Century Perspectives', Diss., University of Kent, 1980, 54. Priestman's thesis remains the fullest account of nineteenth-century parody to date, exploring parody in the romantic poets and novelists, the popular sub-romantic genres of the mid-nineteenth century, the late romantics, and the aesthetes. She focuses particularly on parody's critical aspects and presents parody as a valuable source of contemporary opinion relating to the major literary movements of the period.

[57] Priestman, 'Age of Parody', 54.

20 MODERNIST PARODY

century, was favourable to parodies of bestselling and celebrated contemporaries, dashed off at top speed, with readily digestible jokes.

This is not to say that the cultural work of Victorian parody was facile or that light verse was necessarily trifling. For instance, Lewis Carroll's nonsensical parodies of religious songs, poems, and nursery rhymes in *Alice's Adventures in Wonderland* (1865) and *Through the Looking-Glass and What Alice Found There* (1872) stand out for their profound exploration of epistemological uncertainty. The White Knight's song ridicules the second half of Wordsworth's 'Resolution and Independence' (1807), a poem that had always amused Carroll 'a good deal (though it is by no means a comic poem)' for 'the absurd way in which the poet goes on questioning the poor old leech-gatherer, making him tell his history over and over again, and never attending to what he says'.[58] The Knight variously calls his song 'Haddocks' Eyes', 'The Aged, Aged man', 'Ways and Means', and 'A-sitting on a Gate', bewildering Alice, who cannot make sense of these acts of naming or penetrate his system of reference.[59] All she notes is that far from being the Knight's own invention, as he himself proudly boasts, the song is to the tune of 'I Give Thee All, I Can No More'.[60] Alice's confusion shows that Carroll's parodies do not just make play with literary texts, but question the sense-making structures of language itself, unmasking the arbitrariness of words and their socially negotiated meanings by exposing familiar authorities to the meticulous, internally coherent logic of his nonsense.[61]

Walter Hamilton's copious *Parodies of the Works of English and American Authors* (six vols., 1884–9) gathered examples of varying quality from newspapers, comic magazines, and books of the past fifty years, including a staggering eighty-six versions of Thomas Gray's *Elegy*, and twenty-five of Henry Wadsworth Longfellow's 'Excelsior'.[62] On reviewing these materials, Terry Caesar concluded that 'Victorian parody came to express ... a way of realizing the affection Victorian readers felt for the poems they parodied'.[63] The parodies that decked the pages of Victorian periodicals domesticated familiar and contemporary texts, making them part of public discourse, showing them being read and rewritten in the expectation of recognition, raising their profile through repeated exposure. In this sense,

---

[58] Lewis Carroll, *The Letters of Lewis Carroll*, ed. Morton N. Cohen, vol. I (New York: Oxford University Press, 1979), 177, Lewis's italics.

[59] Lewis Carroll, *Through the Looking Glass and What Alice Found There* (London: Macmillan, 1872), 175.

[60] Carroll, *Through the Looking Glass and What Alice Found There*, 177.

[61] For a detailed account of the White Knight's song as a parody, see U. C. Knoepflmacher, 'Revisiting Wordsworth: Lewis Carroll's "The White Knight's Song"', *Victorians Institute Journal* 14 (1986), 1–20. On nonsense verse, see Hugh Haughton, ed., *The Chatto Book of Nonsense Poetry* (London: Chatto & Windus, 1988).

[62] Walter Hamilton, ed., *Parodies of the Works of English and American Authors*, 6 vols. (London: Reeves & Turner: 1884–9).

[63] Terry Caesar, '"I Quite Forget What—Say a Daffodilly": Victorian Parody', *English Literary History* 51(4) (1984), 805.

PARODY   21

parody can be said to gesture towards canonization regardless of its polemical intent because it grants an afterlife to the material it reconstructs. As Samuel Taylor Coleridge observed: 'Parodies on new poems are read as satires; on old ones (the soliloquy of Hamlet for instance) as compliments. A man of genius may securely laugh at a mode of attack, by which his reviler in half a century or less, becomes his encomiast.'[64]

Whereas a man of genius may laugh at a parody, a lesser talent has much to fear when his reviler has the mark of true brilliance. Byron took exception to the serving Poet Laureate Robert Southey's poem *A Vision of Judgement* (1821), in which Southey falls into a dream-like trance and bears witness to the triumphant apotheosis of King George III. Not only was Byron provoked by the 'gross flattery, the dull impudence, and renegado intolerance and impious cant of the poem', which sought to 'canonize a Monarch, who . . . was neither a successful nor a patriot king', but he was also personally insulted by a passage in the preface where Southey attacked 'Men of diseased hearts and depraved imaginations' who had effectively formed a 'Satanic school' of poetry.[65] Byron replied with a suave, rebarbative satire 'The Vision of Judgment' (1822), a poem far less flattering to the dead king, whose place in heaven is a matter for debate. Southey is transported to heaven's gates to testify in George III's favour and reads from his 'Vision'. By the time Southey gets to line four, 'The angels stopp'd their ears and plied their pinions;/The devils ran howling, deafen'd, down to hell.'[66] By line five, St Peter has had enough and knocks Southey back down to Derwent water, where:

> He first sank to the bottom—like his works,
>   But soon rose to the surface—like himself;
> For all corrupted things are buoy'd, like corks,
>   By their own rottenness, light as an elf
> Or wisp that flits o'er a mass: he lurks.
>   It may be, still, like dull books on a shelf,
> In his own den, to scrawl some 'Life' or 'Vision',
>   As Welborn says—'the Devil turn'd precisian.'[67]

Amid the commotion, the dead King George III slips into heaven unnoticed and reads from the psalms in a sham display of piety. In his 'Vision', Southey

[64] Samuel Taylor Coleridge, 'Contributions to *Omniana*', in H. J. Jackson and J. R. de. J. Jackson, eds., *The Collected Works of Samuel Taylor Coleridge*, vol. 11 (Princeton, NJ: Princeton University Press, 1995), 304.
[65] Lord Byron, 'Preface', in Jerome J. McGann and Barry Weller, eds., to *The Vision of Judgment*, in *Lord Byron: The Complete Poetical Works, Volume 6, 1821–22* (Oxford: Oxford University Press, 1991), 309, 310; Robert Southey, 'Preface', in Tim Fulford and Lynda Pratt, eds., to *A Vision of Judgement*, in *Robert Southey: Later Poetical Works, 1811–1838*, vol. III, *Poems from the Laureate Period* (London: Pickering & Chatto, 2012), 543.
[66] Byron, *The Vision of Judgment* in *Lord Byron*, 344.
[67] Byron, *The Vision of Judgment*, 345.

22 MODERNIST PARODY

sought to make innovative use of hexameters by writing in lines of varying syllabic length, but this unfashionable and cumbersome form proved no match for Byron's highly entertaining and virtuosic *ottava rima*. The parody consisted not in the formal imitation of style and metre but in the inversion of Southey's sycophantic account of events. The uninhibited ridicule inflicted lasting damage on Southey's reputation.

Mocking original writing from within a derivative form can exert a powerful effect on public taste. For this reason, many of the canniest parodists present themselves as apologists for their craft. For instance, the Smiths maintained that the purpose of *Rejected Addresses* was 'to raise a harmless laugh' claiming that parody 'has never blinded us to those beauties and talents which are beyond the reach of all ridicule'.[68] However, such exculpatory protestations are seldom credible. Theodore Martin's sentimental declaration 'Let no one parody a poet unless he loves him' in defence of *The Book of the Ballads* (1845)—the collection of parodies that he co-authored with William Edmonstoune Aytoun and first published in *Fraser's* and *Tait's* under the pseudonym 'Bon Gaultier'—belies the trite and often tawdry nature of their burlesques on popular authors. There is little evidence of love in their poem 'The Lay of the Lovelorn', a travesty of Alfred Lord Tennyson's 'Locksley Hall' (1842), written with scant feeling for Tennyson's style.[69] The speaker likewise tells the story of his unrequited love for a shallow-hearted cousin Amy in rhyming couplets, but the resemblance ends there. The wistful musings of Tennyson's protagonist and his fleeting fantasy of a retreat to the Orient are replaced by the crass and offensive ruminations of one who first resolves to 'wed some savage woman—nay, I'll wed at least a dozen' and finally debases himself by penning an advertisement for a wife to be printed in a newspaper:

> WANTED—By a bard, in wedlock, some young interesting woman:
>   Looks are not so much an object, if the shiners be forthcoming!
>
> Hymen's chains the advertiser vows shall be but silken fetters;
>   Please address to A. T., Chelsea. N. B.—You must pay the letters.[70]

'The Lay of the Lovelorn' reduces 'Locksley Hall' to a crude expression of sexual frustration in a personal attack on Tennyson that displays a level of vulgarity that is starkly at odds with Martin's adage. Nevertheless, and despite all the evidence to the contrary, by the mid-nineteenth century, the parody that constituted a minor genre in its own right had been firmly conceptualized by belletrists as a good-humoured and above all harmless expression of affection and admiration,

---

[68] James Smith and Horace Smith, 'Preface', in *Rejected Addresses: Or the New Theatrum Poetarum*, 18th edn (London: John Murray, 1833), xii, xiii.

[69] Alfred Lord Tennyson, 'Locksley Hall', *Poems* (London: George Bell & Sons, 1905), 166–79.

[70] Theodore Martin and William Edmonstoune Aytoun, 'The Lay of the Lovelorn', in *The Book of the Ballads* (London: W. S. Orr, 1845), 18.

one which conceded its status as a secondary form by offering a very back-handed acknowledgement of the superior talent of primary authors.

There is one more distinctive impulse in nineteenth-century literature which is relevant for assessing the critical morass into which parody had passed before the advent of modernism. The role of literary parody in the formation and reception of aestheticism was well recognized at the time. In *The Aesthetic Movement in England* (1882), Hamilton noted that the cartoons of *Punch*'s leading society artist George du Maurier (who developed a full *dramatis personae* of aesthetes, with characters such as Cimabue Brown, Jellaby Postlethwaite, and Maudle, who went in for Art and affected artifice in their language and dress, and their opponents, the nameless 'philistines') and the accompanying captions and parodies of F. C. Burnard served up a compelling image of aesthetic life 'in a highly-spiced and dangerously exaggerated form' that introduced 'the manners and customs of a very exclusive section of society, of whose very existence only a vague and uncertain idea had previously been formed'.[71] Hamilton insisted that the joke was on *Punch*, concluding that 'Caricature, which was once a deadly weapon, is now but another means of advertising, and so ... Æsthetes have only flourished the more, and they now openly practise that which previously they felt almost bound to restrain within their own immediate circle'.[72] The mischievous question James Whistler put to du Maurier and Oscar Wilde, 'I say, which of you two invented the other, eh?', encapsulates the synergies between aestheticism and its image as reflected by its parodists, be they sympathetic or 'philistine'.[73]

In truth, aestheticism was hospitable to studied imitation, parody, and self-parody well before the movement was pummelled by *Punch*, not only in its mockery of middle-class values and naive faith in representational art, but also in its conscious self-fashionings and intensely mannered language. The career of Algernon Charles Swinburne provides a case in point. William Michael Rossetti defended Swinburne's *Poems and Ballads* (1866) from charges of sensuality, immorality, inauthenticity, and insincere copy-work by praising his gift for assimilating and reproducing so many poetic models of style and form, among them Italian canzoni, Greek tragedy, Old French, and Middle English:

> It seems quite clear that this poet could do, if he chose, an imitation, a take-off, of almost any style, so close that only the most knowing critics could detect it: but he always stops short of that extreme point, preserving his own poetic individualism and liberty, exhibiting ... 'the independence and remoulding force of an original work' ... A true critic can discern with equal clearness that Mr. Swinburne is a very different sort of writer from a Greek tragedian or a Chaucer, writing things

---

[71] Walter Hamilton, *The Aesthetic Movement in England* (London: Reeves & Turner, 1882), viii.
[72] Hamilton, *Aesthetic Movement in England*, 80–1.
[73] Leonée Ormond, *George du Maurier* (London: Routledge & Kegan Paul, 1969), 468.

24　MODERNIST PARODY

which have a very different ring, and also that his voluntary assimilation to these and other poets is both a genuine and a most singular effort of poetry.[74]

In *Specimens of Modern Poets: The Heptalogia or The Seven Against Sense* (1880), Swinburne then turned to parody to take the measure of his contemporaries and also answer his own critics' charges of obscurantism, deliberately pushing his own long-winded lyricism to abstruse extremes almost beyond sense in the final poem 'Nephelidia' [cloudlets], in which, as the ersatz ancient Greek suggests, the sensual play of language virtually clouds the content. Although *The Heptalogia* was published anonymously, its author was evidently Swinburne, who was asserting that, far from being lost in reveries and the beauty of art, caressing words without reference to concrete reality, he was at his most authentic and original when he used parody and pastiche to make sense of his relationship with his literary heritage.[75]

In *Aestheticism and Sexual Parody 1840–1940* (2001), Dennis Denisoff notes that the movement's concomitant parodists (many of whom were in basic support of its philosophy) characteristically turned to an erotically inflated rhetoric to satirize the non-conformist desires that were already latent in the writings of its leading figures. His broad argument is that parodic representations of aestheticism—from the leering creatures of W. H. Mallock's *The New Republic* (1877) and Vernon Lee's *Miss Brown* (1884), to the innuendo and camp of W. S. Gilbert's *Patience* (1881) and Robert Hichens's *The Green Carnation* (1894)— became increasingly receptive to the sexually coded language they exaggerated, unintentionally promoting and familiarizing that discourse and so creating the conditions for the public to accept and enjoy the performance of non-normative sexuality.[76] Denisoff's work makes a fine contribution to the theorization of queer identity and its relation to sexual parody and camp. His insights also provide a context that helps to explain why literary parodies of aestheticism dried up in the wake of the Oscar Wilde trials in 1895: parodies that made insinuations about sexual conduct could no longer be said to be harmless. Ada Levenson, who was sympathetic to aestheticism, wisely left off parodying Wilde after 'The Advisability of Not Being Brought up in a Handbag: A Trivial Tragedy for Wonderful People' appeared in *Punch* on the day that the Marquess of Queensberry had him arrested for libel.[77] The Wilde trials created a mainstream literary climate that was hostile to aesthetic sensibility—and by extension—the very idea of an artistic movement that enacted a serious philosophical programme through parody and parodic stylization to the extent that it was receptive to its own spoofs.

---

[74] W. M. Rossetti, *Swinburne's Poems and Ballads: A Criticism* (London: John Camden Hotten, 1866), 334.

[75] Swinburne, 'Nephelidia', *The Heptalogia*, 99–102.

[76] Dennis Denisoff, *Aestheticism and Sexual Parody 1840–1940* (Cambridge: Cambridge University Press, 2001).

[77] Ada Levenson, 'The Advisability of Not Being Brought up in a Handbag: A Trivial Tragedy for Wonderful People', *Punch* (2 March 1895), 107.

PARODY   25

By the end of the nineteenth century, parody had receded from the literary mainstream and resettled back into its status as a minor genre of derivative, ridiculing writing, but with a shift in emphasis. The supposedly affectionate tribute beloved by Victorians was re-theorized as polemical criticism that was as reactionary as it was self-assured, both by influential practitioners such as Owen Seaman, who proposed 'In its highest form . . . parody is a department of pure literary criticism', and essayists such as Christopher Stone, who argued that parody 'explodes the pompous, corrects the well-meaning eccentric, cools the fanatical, and prevents the incompetent from achieving success. Truth will prevail over it, falsehood will cower under it', thereby figuring parody as a trial by tribute or travesty.[78]

The standard view that parody is critical not creative persisted into the most productive years of high modernism and beyond. It was articulated by writers such as Aldous Huxley, who was himself highly sceptical of experimental writers' apparent preoccupation with the mode:

> Parody is one of the best forms of criticism, and a composer has every right to turn critic if he wants to. But it must be admitted, I think, that parody, at least in any quantity, does not mix well with original writing. The place of parody is in the text-book, not in the work of art. Those who have ploughed through the interminable chapters of parody in Mr. Joyce's portentous *Ulysses* will, I am sure agree with this.[79]

A notable exception to this view was Max Beerbohm, the most gifted of the aesthete parodists, who began his career in the heavily parodic 1890s and continued to ply the art with scrupulous care in the first half of the twentieth century.[80] What made his practice so special was the intimacy of his attack: he approached his victims' stylistic idiosyncrasies and characteristic preoccupations so closely, and with such panache, that he eclipsed his models and asserted the primacy of his own creations as original works of art.

Beerbohm made his scandalous debut in the first issue of the *Yellow Book* with 'A Defence of Cosmetics' (1894), which ostentatiously argued in favour of women's elaborate toilette, proceeding from the insinuating declaration that 'Artifice must

---

[78] Seaman, quoted in C. L. Graves's introduction to *Owen Seaman: A Selection* (London: Methuen, 1937), xx. (Seaman continued to promote this perspective on parody at various London guilds and clubs into the 1930s. For accounts of these lectures, see 'Sir Owen Seaman on "Parody": Lecture to English-Speaking Union', *Times* 45365 (20 November 1929), 12; 'Sir Owen Seaman on Parody: A Form of Literary Criticism', *Times* 46439 (9 May 1933), 12.) Christopher Stone, *Parody* (London: Martin Secker, 1914), 8.

[79] Aldous Huxley, 'Eclecticism' (1923), in Robert S. Baker and James Sexton, eds., *Aldous Huxley: Complete Essays—Volume 1, 1920–1925* (Chicago: Ivan R. Dee, 2000), 342.

[80] Beerbohm's sophisticated parody has received considerable critical attention, pre-eminently John Felstiner's *The Lies of Art: Max Beerbohm's Parody and Caricature* (New York: Knopf, 1972) and Lawrence Danson's *Max Beerbohm and the Act of Writing* (Oxford: Clarendon Press, 1989).

26 MODERNIST PARODY

queen it once more in the town' to insist that nature could only be perfected by rouge and perfume:[81]

> For the era of rouge is upon us, and as only in an elaborate era can man, by the tangled accrescency of his own pleasures and emotions, reach that refinement which is his highest excellence, and by making himself, so to say, independent of Nature, come nearest to God, so only in an elaborate era is woman perfect. Artifice is the strength of the world, and in that same mask of paint and powder, shadowed with vermeil tint and most trimly pencilled, is woman's strength.[82]

Beerbohm's imitation of Wilde's most Paterian art criticism is close to perfect: it tenderly caresses the fanciful expression and solemn cadence, as well as Walter Pater's special vocabulary of aesthetic appreciation, extending aesthetic arguments about the beauty of artifice (and the cultivation of an exquisite sensibility that is attuned to the experience of pleasure and sensation) to insist that nature is not only perfected by art, but by the feminine wiles of rouge and perfume. It is forecast that in this era of rouge those 'horrific pioneers of womanhood who gad hither and thither' (the bicycling New Women who trespass on men's affairs) will be supplanted by a more modern incarnation of femininity, the self-embellished beauty who recognizes her status as the 'resupinate sex' and remains in a state of perpetual repose lest her powder should fly or her enamel should crack.[83] Her body may be idly draped upon a couch but behind that superficially attractive mask her active mind can 'play without let', devising schemes to exert influence over the men who are foolish enough to admire her.[84]

Arguments for the beauty of artifice had been rehearsed many times since Charles Baudelaire initiated that decadent conversation in 'Éloge du maquillage' (1860), but never so immodestly. However, because the terrain and tone were so familiar, reviewers were primed to overlook Beerbohm's obvious ironies, silly neologisms, and swooping descents from the heights of classical exemplar to the depths of delicious daftness—entreaties that 'The white cliffs of Albion shall be ground to powder for loveliness, and perfumed by the ghost of many a little violet' and 'The fluffy eider-ducks, that are swimming round the pond, shall lose their feathers, that the powder-puff may be moonlike'—and duly condemned the parody as if it were the latest and most affected critical pronouncement yet.[85] Beerbohm courted the resulting furore with a teasing 'Letter to the Editor' that assured 'the affrighted mob that it is the victim of hoax' and expressed incredulity that critics had failed to see that an essay 'so grotesque in subject, in opinion so flippant, in

---

[81] Max Beerbohm, 'A Defence of Cosmetics', *Yellow Book: An Illustrated Quarterly* I (April 1894), 65.
[82] Beerbohm, 'Defence of Cosmetics', 68.
[83] Beerbohm, 'Defence of Cosmetics', 69, 70.
[84] Beerbohm, 'Defence of Cosmetics', 70.
[85] Beerbohm, 'Defence of Cosmetics', 82.

PARODY 27

style so wildly affected, was meant for a burlesque upon the "precious" school of writers', but concluded by taunting 'the men of Grub Street' with the very prospect they feared had come to pass with the publication of 'A Defence', stating that English literature was poised to 'fall at length into the hands of decadents' and suggesting that artifice was already at the gates.[86] In 'A Defence' Beerbohm posed as a decadent *provocateur* so that he might revel in the pleasurable excesses of that '"precious" school of writers', from which many of his own literary values and practices were derived, while simultaneously positioning himself beyond reproof. In private, Beerbohm was no defender of cosmetics, but the notion of make-up as mask provided a droll proxy for his own dissembling parody, behind which his mind could 'play without let', projecting a decadent image that foregrounded his own brilliance as an imitator and his originality as a comic.

The parodic literary portraits collected in *A Christmas Garland* (1912) inhabit the idiosyncrasies of Beerbohm's contemporaries so completely that they are widely considered to be the most accomplished parodies in the English canon.[87] They participate in the best Victorian parodic tradition of making a game of victim's mannerisms—of reading through style to the man—but are so exacting that they had the disquieting effect of making their subjects feel like *their* original work was inauthentic. 'The Mote in the Middle Distance' by 'H∗nry J∗mes' is so exquisitely Jamesian that it could only have been written by someone who derived the 'finest of all literary joy out of Henry James'.[88] It parodies the episode at the end of *The Wings of the Dove* (1902) where Merton Densher issues Kate Croy with an ultimatum: she can either accept his hand in marriage and leave the envelope they can scarcely bear to look at unopened or he will make the ill-gotten inheritance contained therein over to her and she will lose him forever.[89] Beerbohm instead presents two infants, Keith and Eva Tantalus, precociously afflicted with the adult sensibilities and passionate regard shared by Merton and Kate, discussing another moral dilemma of paramount intensity: whether or not to peer into their Christmas stockings. The tantalizing question as to whether Eva had indeed 'peered'—Beerbohm suspends the word in quotation marks, as if it were one of the vulgarisms James himself holds at arm's length—remains unresolved.[90] Beerbohm renders this small-scale Jamesian psychodrama in a luminous

---

[86] Max Beerbohm, 'A Letter to the Editor', *Yellow Book: An Illustrated Quarterly* II (July 1894), 281–4.

[87] For analysis of the level stylistic communion that made Beerbohm's parodies so different from the efforts of contemporaries such as Seaman and Chesterton, see Terry Caesar, 'Betrayal and Theft: Beerbohm, Parody, and Modernism', *Ariel* 17(3) (July 1986), 23–37.

[88] Max Beerbohm, *Letters of Max Beerbohm, 1892–1956*, ed. Rupert Hart-Davies (Oxford: Oxford University Press, 1989), 94.

[89] Henry James, *The Wings of the Dove*, vol. II (New York: Scribner's, 1902), 431–9.

[90] Beerbohm, 'The Mote in the Middle Distance', *A Christmas Garland* (London: William Heinemann, 1912), 9.

28   MODERNIST PARODY

parody of the extraordinary discretion and habitual circumlocution of James's later manner:

> It occurred to him as befitting Eva's remoteness, which was a part of Eva's mag-
> nificence, that her voice emerged somewhat muffled by the bedclothes. She was
> ever, indeed, the most telephonic of her sex. In talking to Eva you always had, as
> it were, your lips to the receiver. If you didn't try to meet her fine eyes, it was that
> you simply couldn't hope to: there were too many dark, too many buzzing and
> bewildering and all frankly not negotiable leagues in between. Snatches of other
> voices seemed often to intertrude themselves in the parley; and your loyal effort
> not to overhear these was complicated by your fear of missing what Eva might
> be twittering. 'Oh, you certainly haven't, my dear, the trick of propinquity!' was
> a thrust she had once parried by saying that, in that case, *he* hadn't—to which his
> unspoken rejoinder that she had caught her tone from the peevish young women
> at the Central seemed to him (if not perhaps in the last, certainly in the last but
> one, analysis) to lack finality. With Eva, he had found, it was always safest to 'ring
> off'. It was with a certain sense of his rashness in the matter, therefore, that he
> now, with an air of feverishly 'holding the line', said 'Oh, as to that!'[91]

James's style is brilliantly caricatured in the splendidly stretched metaphor of Eva's telephony; the ponderous, minutely qualified sentences that convey Keith's contemplation of Eva's magnificence; Eva's darkly coy and ultimately indecipherable exclamation; and the final ambiguity as to what has been said. Beerbohm has assimilated the stylistic turns of James's writing so perfectly that satirical touches like 'twittering', which belong to Beerbohm's evaluation and not James's idiom, do not detract from the fineness of the parody.

'The Mote in the Middle Distance' reiterates Beerbohm's observations about James's work in his critical writing, for instance how James's characters share 'The passion of conscience, a sort of lyrical conscience, conscience raised to the pitch of ecstasy, both in great matters and in small'.[92] As John Felstiner notes, for all its evident fondness for Jamesian affectation, the parody is far from benign: 'Keith thinks about Eva as nervously as one of James's lovers would' and 'the name Eva Tantalus clearly implies that some kind of sexual frustration lies behind James's imagining of his characters and their experiences'.[93] F. R. Leavis (who was not attuned to the sexualized undercurrent) complained that 'it is impossible to forgive [Beerbohm] for his kindly parody of poor James; a parody which did all it could to identify James with the complacently stupid preconceptions of that literary world

---

[91] Beerbohm, 'Mote in the Middle Distance', 5–6.
[92] Max Beerbohm, 'Mr. Henry James's Play', *Around Theatres* (London: Hart-Davies, 1924), 544.
[93] Felstiner, *Lies of Art*, 143.

which—to his death—denied him all intelligent recognition'.[94] James himself took a different view of *A Christmas Garland*, as recorded in a letter Beerbohm received from Edmund Gosse, dated Christmas night 1912:

> He [Henry James] called the book 'the most intelligent that has been produced in England for many a long day'. But he says you have destroyed the trade of writing. No one, now, can write without incurring the reproach of somewhat ineffectively imitating—*you!*[95]

Beerbohm approached his victims' work so closely that they could no longer write without those aspects of their manner that Beerbohm identified to be amusingly characteristic asserting themselves as inadvertent self-parody. The fate of Beerbohm's victims was to ineffectively imitate Beerbohm, whose personality—and point of view—prevails.

Parody for Beerbohm was not merely an act preparatory to writing, it was writing itself. While the preface to *A Christmas Garland* does present 'the habit of aping, now and again, quite sedulously, this or that live writer—sometimes, it must be admitted, in the hope of learning rather what to avoid' as a stage in his artistic development towards mature prose style, the polished parodies in that volume (which include heavily revised selections from seasonal supplements of the *Saturday Review* (1896, 1906) and new parodies written especially for book publication) are to be read as confirmation that his 'own style is, at length, more or less formed'.[96] In *A Christmas Garland* readers behold what Beerbohm termed 'the complete mimic': the man who retains the youthful knack for catching 'the tone of voice and tone of mind of his friends' but possesses 'a distinct individuality'—a critical point of view—that inflects his mimicry with his own personality.[97] Virginia Woolf, one of Beerbohm's many modernist admirers, understood this paradox well: 'We only know that the spirit of personality permeates every word that he writes... Never to be yourself and yet always... This art is possessed to perfection by Mr. Beerbohm'.[98] Of course, Beerbohm differed from the modernists in his sympathy with aestheticism, his distaste for extreme experimentation, and the limitation of his literary interests to the near past. He did not care to be thought of as *modern* and enjoyed the pretence that he had already passed into senescence

---

[94] F. R. Leavis, 'Mirrors up to Art', *Spectator* 6967 (5 January 1962), 13.

[95] Beerbohm, *Letters of Max Beerbohm*, 87.

[96] Beerbohm, 'Note', *Christmas Garland*, vi.

[97] Max Beerbohm, 'A Play and a Mimic', *Last Theatres, 1904–1910* (London: Hart-Davis, 1970), 67.

[98] Virginia Woolf, 'The Modern Essay', *The Common Reader*, vol. 1 (New York: Harcourt, Brace & Co., 1925), 301.

30 MODERNIST PARODY

and belonged to a bygone age. In 'Diminuendo' (1896), an essay on Pater, in parody of his style, Beerbohm, then 24, declared:

> Already I feel myself to be a trifle outmoded. I belong to the Beardsley period. Younger men, with months of activity before them, with fresher schemes and notions, with newer enthusiasm, have pressed forward since then.[99]

As later chapters will explore, the extremely close mode of parody that Beerbohm practised penetrated beyond mere mimesis to reflect upon originality and literary artifice in ways which his many modernist admirers later found productive, not least because he was able to leave his own lasting mark on the materials he transformed and reordered, asserting his own creative primacy.[100]

Beerbohm moved to Rapallo, Italy, in 1911. With his departure, the parody that presumed its status as primary authentic art in its own right seemingly withdrew from mainstream literary culture. Why the strategies used by modernist writers in their confrontations with their literary heritage have not traditionally been given the formal designation of parody is partially explained by the critical morass into which parody had fallen in the early decades of the twentieth century, after its reincarnation as a genial Victorian game and its fall from grace in the wake of aestheticism and decadence. The many minor monographs, pamphlets, and anthologies on the subject of parody that appeared in the first half of the twentieth century attempted to redeem the mode by framing it as a fundamentally conservative form of (admittedly derivative) literary criticism that subjected achievement to trial by travesty or tribute in the name of middlebrow entertainment.[101] The dominant belief, espoused in George Kitchin's *A Survey of Burlesque and Parody in English* (1931), that 'Parody is for the man of medium taste', cast a long shadow that helped to obfuscate its presence in high modernism.[102]

---

[99] Max Beerbohm, 'Diminuendo', *The Works of Max Beerbohm, with a Bibliography by John Lane* (London: John Lane/Bodley Head, 1896), 160.

[100] Several scholars have remarked that Beerbohm's use of parody is his most modernist trait, including Lawrence Danson, who observes in passing: 'we can notice that Joyce, Pound and Eliot—and Virginia Woolf—are the next great parodists after Beerbohm. For all the high seriousness of their modernist project, the parodic motive runs as deeply in their work as (to different effect it does in Beerbohm's) . . . Beerbohm's parodic art is a response to similar creative dilemmas' (Danson, *Max Beerbohm and the Act of Writing*, 22). Terry Caesar has similarly argued that 'the kind of writing which Beerbohm evolved, though it was given the formal designation of parody, is not so different from that written by Eliot, Pound or Joyce', who also faced the 'the common problem of inherited forms and "false orders"' before they could 'shape fresh forms, new and vital strategies, of literary representation', concluding that 'parody constituted one condition by which modern art made use of its own formal processes by, precisely, re-presenting them in order to explore its own origins' ('Betrayal and Theft', 23–4).

[101] See, for example, Carolyn Wells, *A Parody Anthology* (New York: Scribner's, 1904); Walter Jerrold, *A Century of Parody* (London: H. Milford/Oxford University Press, 1913); Stone, *Parody* (1914); J. C. Squire, ed., *Apes and Parrots: An Anthology of Parodies* (London: Herbert Jenkins, 1928); Mrs. Herbert Richardson, *Parody*, English Association Pamphlet 92 (London: H. Milford/Oxford University Press, 1935); Leonard Russell, ed., *Parody Party* (London: Hutchinson, 1936). Contributors to *Parody Party* included Rebecca West, Rose Macaulay, and John Betjeman.

[102] G. Kitchin, *A Survey of Burlesque and Parody in English* (London: Oliver & Boyd, 1931), 283.

PARODY   31

The writings of the Russian formalists and Bakhtin were finally brought to a wider international audience in the 1950s and 1970s respectively, and their ideas about parody as a device for laying bare artifice that is fundamentally dialogic were subsumed into discussions of two related but distinct modes—metafiction and intertextuality—neither of which are necessarily comic or exist in a transformative relation to specific pretexts. Metafiction is 'fictional writing which self-consciously and systematically draws attention to its status as an artefact in order to pose questions about the relationship between fiction and reality'.[103] It reflects on how illusions are constructed in fiction, typically to communicate higher truths about the external world. While all (novelistic) parody is to some degree metafictional, it does not follow that all metafiction is parodic since there are many other means of displaying self-reflexivity. In criticism that focuses on metafiction, parody is characterized as a meta-critique of literary language and convention that exposes the illusion that literature is verisimilar or autonomous. The term 'intertextuality' was coined by Julia Kristeva to describe the way that 'any text is constructed as a mosaic of quotations; any text is the absorption and transformation of another', with the consequence that 'poetic language is read at least double' (a theory she developed after Bakhtin, whom she credited as 'one of the first to replace the static hewing out of texts with a model where literary structure does not simply exist but is generated in relation to another structure').[104] This lineage explains why parody so easily disappears into the Kristevan model of intertextuality and post-structuralist accounts of literary language in general, even to the extent that Pierre Macherey once defined 'literary discourse as parody, as a contestation of language rather than a representation of reality', a reduplicative move that equated parody with literariness and therefore effectively reduced literature to its distinguishing feature.[105]

From the 1960s onwards, the growing fascination with the interdependence of all literary endeavour reignited critical interest in parody, which has subsequently been rediscovered and analysed in its postmodern manifestations. The emphasis on the metafictional and intertextual elements of parody helped to edge out the laughter that was, for Bakhtin, an essential consequence of its dialogic contrast of oppositional codes and focused attention instead on parody's function as a system of reference and self-reference. Parody, once characterized in this way, could then be mapped onto definitions of postmodernism that emphasized its

---

[103] Patricia Waugh, *Metafiction: The Theory and Practice of Self-Conscious Fiction* (London: Routledge, 2003), 2. For discussion of parody as metafiction, see also Robert Alter, *Partial Magic: The Novel as a Self-Conscious Genre* (Berkeley: University of California Press, 1975); Linda Hutcheon, *Narcissistic Narrative: The Metafictional Paradox* (London: Methuen, 1984); Margaret Rose, *Parody//Meta-Fiction: An Analysis of Parody as a Critical Mirror to the Writing and Reception of Fiction* (London: Croom Helm, 1979).

[104] Julia Kristeva, 'Word, Dialogue and Novel', *The Kristeva Reader*, ed. Toril Moi (Oxford: Basil Blackwell, 1986), 37, 35–6. By 'poetic' Kristeva means all literary language.

[105] Pierre Macherey, *A Theory of Literary Production*, trans. Geoffrey Wall (London: Routledge & Kegan Paul, 1978), 61.

32   MODERNIST PARODY

relativistic use of 'double-coding', for instance Charles Jencks's influential theory of postmodernist architecture, which combines elements of high modernist form with references (often eclectic) to other older historical codes and structural models.[106] In *A Theory of Parody: The Teachings of Twentieth-Century Art Forms* (1985), Linda Hutcheon was inspired by Jencks to redefine modern parody as a form of historiographic 'trans-contextualization' akin to neoclassical imitation that entails 'ironic playing with multiple conventions' and 'extended repetition with critical difference', suggesting that the ridiculing strain ended with the nineteenth century.[107] Her aim was to eliminate the trivializing associations with ridicule that have inhibited critical appreciation of parody as 'one of the major forms of modern self-reflexivity'.[108] While she is correct that the object(s) of a parody's satire need not be its model(s), her solemn prose does not fully succeed in decoupling the parody she examined from its comic effects (the words 'ironic' and 'playing' indicate some trace of humour, as do circumlocutions she employs, 'ironically thumbed nose', 'a certain teasing of the reader mixed with ironic self-mockery', 'the smirk, the knowing smile').[109] Her generalizations about parody in twentieth-century art forms obscure a definite bias towards the postmodern incarnations from which her theory descends, so that while she does refer to Beerbohm, G. K. Chesterton, Eliot, André Gide, Ernest Hemingway, Joyce, René Magritte, Thomas Mann, Pablo Picasso, Pound, and Marcel Proust, her analysis of parody as a form of double-directed irony is heavily weighted towards the historiographic play in postmodernism. This bias is clearly expressed in her subsequent work, which proceeds from the observation that 'Parody—often called ironic quotation, pastiche, appropriation, or intertextuality—is usually considered central to postmodernism, both by its detractors and its defenders'.[110] Extrapolating from postmodernism to expand the pragmatic range of parody to include all forms of transcontextualization, and then making that species of parody definitional to the extent that it is cited as 'a perfect postmodern form', inhibits appreciation of how deep the practice of the parody in modernism actually goes.[111] When Hutcheon does finally attempt to pin down significant differences in the final impact of the parody that inscribes and yet signals its distance from convention and history as manifested in modernist and postmodernist art in *The Politics of Postmodernism* (1989), she suggests that 'postmodernism's irony rejects the resolving urge of modernism toward closure', noting that complicity always attends postmodernism's critique.[112] Her comments

---

[106] See Charles Jencks, *The Language of Post-Modern Architecture* (New York: Rizzoli International, 1977).

[107] Linda Hutcheon, *A Theory of Parody: The Teachings of Twentieth-Century Art Forms* (London: Methuen, 1985), 7.

[108] Hutcheon, *Theory of Parody*, 2.

[109] Hutcheon, *Theory of Parody*, 33, 33, 61.

[110] Linda Hutcheon, *The Politics of Postmodernism*, 2nd edn (New York: Routledge, 2002), 89.

[111] Hutcheon, *Poetics of Postmodernism*, 11

[112] Hutcheon, *Politics of Postmodernism*, 95.

PARODY   33

demonstrate how the fashionable rediscovery of parody in the image of postmodernism leads to a simplified view of its role in modernism and of modernism in general.

The notion that parody is so fundamental to postmodernism that it might serve to distinguish it from modernism has further displaced productive discussion of the parody in modernism. Ihab Hassan was the first to attempt to define postmodernism in this way in 'POSTmodernISM: A Paracritical Bibliography' (1971), in which he compiled 'a curious chronology of some Postmodern criticism' that included four essays that make direct mention of parody in modernism and indicate the topic's potential and scope.[113] The first, Susan Sontag's 'Against Interpretation' (1966), proposed that 'To avoid interpretation, art may become parody' (she was thinking of abstraction's retreat from signification and the imposition of content).[114] The remaining three essays, 'The Politics of Self-Parody' (1968) and 'The Literature of Waste' (1967) by Richard Poirier and 'The Literature of Exhaustion' (1967) by John Barth, variously admired Jorge Luis Borges's 'parody of creation', the self-parody practised by Joyce and Vladimir Nabokov, the medley of voices and mimicked styles in *Ulysses* and *The Waste Land*, and Samuel Beckett, Borges, and Nabokov's use of parody to trade on the 'used-upness of certain forms or exhaustion of certain possibilities'.[115] Hassan then proceeded to quote from Poirier's book *The Performing Self* (1971) to reveal the revision of modernism taking place in postmodern literature:

> *Moby Dick, Ulysses, The Waste Land*, are written in mockery of system, written against any effort to harmonize discordant elements, against any mythic or metaphoric scheme . . . But while this form of the literary imagination is radical in its essential parodistic treatment of systems, its radicalism is in the interest of essentially conservative feelings . . . The most complicated examples of twentieth-century literature, like *Ulysses* and *The Waste Land*, the end of which seems parodied by the end of *Giles* [*Goat-Boy*], are more than contemptuous of their own formal and stylistic elaborateness.[116]

Poirer's insight emboldened Hassan to characterize the postmodern parody of modernism's essentially 'parodistic treatment of systems' as 'insane parody', which Hassan then cited as one of many qualities that distinguish postmodern cultural

---

[113] Ihab Hassan, 'POSTmodernISM: A Paracritical Bibliography', *New Literary History* 3(1) (1971), 14, Hassan's capitals.

[114] Susan Sontag, 'Against Interpretation', *Against Interpretation and Other Essays* (New York: Farrar, Straus and Giroux, 1966), 10.

[115] Richard Poirier, 'The Politics of Self-Parody', *The Performing Self: Compositions and Decompositions in the Languages of Contemporary Life* (London: Chatto & Windus, 1971), 41; Richard Poirier, 'The Literature of Waste: Eliot, Joyce and Others', *The Performing Self*, 47; John Barth, 'The Literature of Exhaustion', in Malcolm Bradbury, ed., *The Novel Today: Contemporary Writers on Modern Fiction* (Manchester: Manchester University Press, 1977), 70.

[116] Hassan, 'POSTmodernISM', 15.

34 MODERNIST PARODY

productions.[117] In Hassan's later work, the modernist legacy was forgotten and parody was again identified outright as a central postmodern aesthetic that belongs to the family of words that 'create a context, if not a definition for' postmodernism.[118] Setting aside for now the dubious notion that modernist parody is essentially conservative in character, the slippage from modernism to postmodernism (which is again said to specialize in its own particular style of parody) has the effect of tucking modernist practice away from sight.

In 'Postmodernism, or The Cultural Logic of Late Capitalism' (1984) Fredric Jameson likewise appealed to parody to identify the difference between modernism and postmodernism, but only looked at modernist parody askance. He argued that the 'high-modernist ideology of style—what is unique and unmistakable as your own fingerprints'—was dissipated under postmodernism, in which architects, artists, and writers restlessly alluded to historical styles, neutralizing the political or satirical messages they once embodied, in a form of aestheticized cultural recycling that mimicked the relentless recirculation of commodities in rapacious capitalism.[119] Under these circumstances, he claimed that parody found 'itself without a vocation; it has lived, and that strange new thing pastiche slowly comes to take its place':

> Pastiche is, like parody, the imitation of a peculiar mask, speech in a dead language: but it is a neutral practice of such mimicry, without any of parody's ulterior motives, amputated of the satiric impulse, devoid of laughter and of any conviction that alongside the abnormal tongue you have momentarily borrowed, some healthy linguistic normality still exists. Pastiche is thus blank parody, a statue with blind eyeballs.[120]

Characterizing pastiche as a species of 'blank parody' that it is inert and unseeing failed to recognize that the recollection of a style is in itself a politicized and therefore critical act. Pastiche imitates style by selecting, concentrating, and accentuating, and operates by similarity and correspondence. The classical definitional distinction in literary studies is that pastiche is a positive, admiring imitation of a writer's individuating style, whereas parody is a critical, satirical transformative mode of appropriation (although in practice the boundary is permeable, since parody still depends on perceived resemblance for its effects and pastiche always entails some degree of deformity or discrepancy, a nuance or a degree of

---

[117] Hassan, 'POSTmodernISM', 25.

[118] Ihab Hassan, 'From Postmodernism to Postmodernity: The Local/Global Context', *Philosophy and Literature* 25(1) (2001), 2. See also Ihab Hassan, *The Postmodern Turn: Essays in Postmodern Theory and Culture* (Columbus, OH: Ohio State University Press, 1987).

[119] Fredric Jameson, 'Postmodernism, or The Cultural Logic of Late Capitalism', *New Left Review* 1(146) (1984), 65.

[120] Jameson, 'Cultural Logic of Late Capitalism', 65.

self-consciousness, that separates it from reproduction).[121] The furore surrounding Jameson's negative identification of postmodernism with 'blank parody' deflected critical attention from his commentary on parody and modernism, in which Jameson used 'parody' in the highly specific sense of designating how the individuating idiosyncrasies of leading modernists—for instance the Faulkerian long sentence or Lawrentian nature imagery—'strike one as somehow "characteristic", insofar as they ostentatiously deviate from a norm which then reasserts itself, in a not necessarily unfriendly way, by a systematic mimicry of their deliberate eccentricities', which is to say that Jameson considered modernist style to be so unlike other contemporary forms of language use that it appeared parodic.[122]

Theorists with interests beyond postmodernism are less prone to separating ridiculing parody from ironic play with codes and systems of reference and then reinterpreting parody through the prism of metafiction, intertextuality, transcontextualization, or pastiche. In *Parody: Ancient, Modern and Post-Modern* (1993), a comprehensive and detailed history of how parody has been theorized through the ages, Margaret A. Rose offers '*the comic refunctioning of preformed linguistic or artistic material*' as a definition that is transhistorical and yet sufficiently precise to distinguish parody from related modes.[123] This book works with Rose's definition and recognizes parody as a mode that makes a comedy of refunctioning codes and systems of reference, irrespective of whatever other cultural work it might be performing.

Robert Phiddian posed the provocative question 'Are Parody and Deconstruction Secretly the Same Thing?' in his 1997 article of the same name. Here, he enmeshed parody with the movements of deconstruction on the basis that parody is an iterative form that undermines a given text's claims to truth through repetition with alteration, stating that 'deconstruction frames all writing as parody in the sense that it treats it as caught up in a tissue of echo, allusion, appropriation, and misprision'.[124] Phiddian noted that 'Parody did not need Derrida to tell it that mimesis is an imperfect and deeply paradoxical proposition in the complex play of presence and absence that constitutes signification' because parody is already engaged in intertextuality and 'knows that language differs from things and defers meanings into a prolonged (and potentially infinite) play of echoes and substitutions'.[125] Phiddian therefore argued that 'parody *is* a form of deconstruction' that operates from within, building up a 'very peculiar and intense intimacy'

---

[121] Gérard Genette states that 'strict parody and travesty proceed through a transformation of the text, and satirical pastiche (like every pastiche) through an imitation of style', *Palimpsests: Literature in the Second Degree*, trans. Channa Newman and Claude Dubinsky (Lincoln, NE: University of Nebraska Press, 1997), 25.

[122] Jameson, 'Cultural Logic of Late Capitalism', 65.

[123] Rose, *Parody*, 52, Rose's italics.

[124] Robert Phiddian, 'Are Parody and Deconstruction the Same Thing?', *New Literary History* 28(4) (1997), 680.

[125] Phiddian, 'Are Parody and Deconstruction the Same Thing?', 680.

36 MODERNIST PARODY

with the discourses it invades, so that the 'genesis and structure of those discourses appear "under erasure" (visible but problematized and devalued)'.[126] He did however concede that there is 'almost always a supplementary movement in parody (that seldom accompanies deconstruction)' that has already seen its way out of treating 'language as an endless and odorless play of differences' by returning 'the reader to something resembling the world' by generating critical, satirical perspectives.[127]

This model works brilliantly for a relentlessly negating parodic text such as *A Tale of a Tub* (1704), the subject of *Swift's Parody* (1995), in which Phiddian offers a meticulous account of Swift's use of parody to construct and deconstruct textual and cultural authority in late-Stuart England by 'Inscribing and subverting ... conflicting stories of origin and authority, made up of the casually collected scraps of other ridiculous books, spawning multiple allusions, confusions, and misunderstandings' and opposing orthodox writings from the field of theology, biblical exegesis, literature, politics, and science, dividing them against themselves and thereby refusing to be answerable to canons of authority.[128] Indeed, deconstruction 'provides a powerful mode for questioning authority and the ideological and structural force on which it depends', but it 'can only provide negative liberation', being 'no respecter of value', as Phiddian himself notes.[129] However, this is not necessarily the case where parody is concerned. As much as parodists may love to torment bad writing, exposing falsity where they find it, parody also frequently functions as an arbiter of value and may therefore also seek positive associations with the materials it transforms. The reduction of parody to deconstruction, but with added levity, mistakes the nature of parody's admittedly parasitical system of signification. Literary parodists rarely make a primary issue of the linguistic impasse that are no signifieds, just signifiers (with the exception of Dada at the extreme of the avant-garde), and are usually more directly concerned with questions of originality, rather than absolute origin, and the desire to communicate, rather than its impossibility. In fact, there is a sense in which, as Michelle Hannoosh argues, 'It is in the nature of parody to set the reader on a quest for the original, only to reveal, once found, that he did not really need it anyway.'[130] The shifts in register or style that alert a reader to the fact that a parody is taking place tend to be marked whether or not the reader is familiar with the material parodied. Admittedly, the least skilled parodies are widest of the mark, but the best parodic writing reconstructs its model(s) in a way that enables the reader to apprehend

---

[126] Phiddian, 'Are Parody and Deconstruction the Same Thing?', 681–2.
[127] Phiddian, 'Are Parody and Deconstruction the Same Thing?', 691.
[128] Robert Phiddian, *Swift's Parody* (Cambridge: Cambridge University Press, 1995), 195.
[129] Phiddian, 'Are Parody and Deconstruction the Same Thing?', 676.
[130] Michele Hannoosh, *Parody and Decadence: Laforgue's 'Moralités Légendaires'* (Columbus, OH: Ohio State University Press, 1989), 22.

PARODY 37

and reconstruct the salient qualities of the material under scrutiny, so that parody is both dependent and sufficient in and of itself as a primary creative act.

To say that a parody places its model(s) 'under erasure' implies that all parody is essentially deconstructive and, while the most destructive parody conforms to this description, it is more helpful to understand its latent textual transformations by broader reference to figure of the palimpsest, whereby, as per Gérard Genette's definition, 'on the same parchment, one text can become superimposed upon another, which it does not quite conceal, but allows to show through'.[131] While the idea that parody designates literature as a palimpsest has been endorsed by structuralists such as Genette, parodists themselves instinctively reach for the metaphor to figure their manipulation of source material(s) without losing sight of intended comic effects. For example, C. S. Calverley invited readers to imagine that his parodies were transcribed on the blank pages at the beginning and end of the books he spoofed in *Fly Leaves* (1872), while J. K. Stephen styled his parodies as a slip of the pen in *Lapsus Calami* (1891). Beerbohm even went so far as to actualize the metaphor, making comic textual incursions in the books he owned to turn them into their own parodies, for instance crossing through the final lines of the Henry James's short story 'The Death of the Lion' and substituting his own alternative, more essentially Jamesian ending, or amusing himself by inserting 'h's' before vowels and substituting apostrophes for initial aspirates to transpose the highfalutin speeches of Herbert Trench's classical sailor into cockney in 'Apollo and the Seaman', imposing unauthorized variant texts on volumes from genuine editions.[132]

Parody is profoundly palimpsestual in its invitation to readers to peer through its text and reconstruct the original material(s) in which it is implicated from the traces that it organizes, and then to interpret both writings alongside and against one another. In this sense, it is particularly productive to look at parody as a form that enables writers to display their innovative and originary strategies by developing writings from other writings, including their own, which is why this book takes particular account of unpublished compositional documents, including juvenilia, notes, and drafts, as well as unpublished writings. It should be remembered, though, that parody is not just backward-looking but also has an eye to its own future: parodists' construal of the original material(s) they transform gives readers a model for comic and questioning interpretation that can also be applied to the parody in question. Parody includes itself in its own criticism and

---

[131] Genette, *Palimpsests*, 398–9.

[132] Beerbohm's copy of Henry James, *Terminations* (London: Heinemann, 1895), 64, Beerbohm Collection 3.62, Merton College, Oxford; Herbert Trench, *New Poems: Apollo and the Seaman, The Queen of Gothland, Stanzas to Tolstoy, and Other Lyrics* (London: Methuen, 1907). For an account of the mischief Beerbohm made with his copy of *New Poems*, see S. N. Behrman, *Conversations with Max* (London: Hamish Hamilton, 1960), 181. For further discussion of Beerbohm's habit of Grangerizing the book in his personal library, see Sarah Davison, 'Max Beerbohm's Altered Books', *Textual Cultures* 6(1) (2011), 48–75.

38 MODERNIST PARODY

contains an indirect invitation to further parody and continued innovation. This tendency is activated in the 'insane parody' Hassan identifies in strains of postmodernism that respond to the pervasively parodic concerns of modernism with a more frenzied form of recitation.

The fashionable contemporary alignment of parody and postmodernism has occluded the parody within modernism to the extent that the topic has been substantially overlooked by literary criticism. With the notable exception of Joyce, whose use of parody is well recognized, the modernists' extensive use of the mode has so far received only cursory critical attention. Parody has long been acknowledged as a central technique in the outrages perpetuated by various European avant-garde movements—for instance the 'deliberate strategy of bluff and counter-bluff, bewilderment and parody' advocated by the Berlin Dadaists or Filippo Marinetti's Futurist commitment to the 'destruction of immortal masterworks by plagiarizing or parodying them'—but its role in the evolution of Anglo-American modernism has only been examined sporadically.[133]

Malcolm Bradbury comes the closest to describing the premises of modernist parody in the course of his essay 'An Age of Parody, Style in the Modern Arts' (1980). In Bradbury's account, it is modernism that marks the beginning of our age of parody, which persists in postmodernism:

> Certainly many of our greatest moderns in writing and painting—from Joyce and Beckett to Picasso, Duchamp, Matisse, Magritte and Escher—have not only been parodists but have inhabited some of the central paradoxes *of* parody. We can take them as great modern stylists, while acknowledging that in their concept of style there is a profound undermining, an awareness that there is no stylistic certainty, no ultimate assertion that words and forms can convey as a totality. Indeed in their work we can see parody moving towards the centre of modern forms, becoming a constitutive mode of art.[134]

According to Bradbury, in its emphasis not on 'what is written but what is in the writing' parody gave modernist writers a means to investigate the premises of a movement that 'proposed the disintegration of social substance, of first-order references, secure narrative traditions' as it 'defamiliarised, derealised, made fragments the essence, aestheticised, abstractified, conceptualised'.[135] He takes a balanced assessment of its character, viewing parody both as a deconstructing

---

[133] Malcolm Green's preface to Richard Huelsenbeck, *The Dada Almanach*, ed. and trans. Malcolm Green (London: Atlas Press, 1993), viii; F. T. Marinetti, 'The Variety Theatre' (29 September 1913), in Lawrence Rainey, Christine Poggi, and Laura Wittman, eds., *Futurism: An Anthology* (New Haven, CT: Yale University Press, 2009), 162.

[134] Malcolm Bradbury, 'An Age of Parody: Style in the Modern Arts', *Encounter* 55(1) (1980), 36–53, reprinted in Malcolm Bradbury, *No, Not Bloomsbury* (London: Deutsch, 1987), 58.

[135] Bradbury, 'Age of Parody', 57.

enterprise and 'a major form of creative play and artistic self-discovery which can give us a joyously experimental art'.[136]

The only book-length comparative study of parody as a distinctive technique of modernist literature to date in English is David Kiremidjian's *A Study of Modern Parody: James Joyce's 'Ulysses', Thomas Mann's 'Doctor Faustus'* (1985), which traces a line of influence from Joyce to Mann to insist that parody becomes a part of the basic expressive approach in modern art, but limits its focus to these two authors.[137] Of the many critics who appreciate that parody was the medium of Joyce's art, Hugh Kenner is the most influential. In *Dublin's Joyce* (1955), Kenner suggests that Joyce's parody arises from the linguistic self-consciousness particular to Dubliners, who are aware that the language they speak is not their own, and argues Joyce parodies precisely to acknowledge the distortions of language in his pursuit of a higher realism.[138] In *Joyce's Voice's* (1978), Kenner proceeds to examine how 'Joyce began *Ulysses* in naturalism and ended it in parody', a view complicated by Karen Lawrence in *The Odyssey of Style in 'Ulysses'* (1981), who recognizes that parody undermines naturalism from the novel's very beginning.[139] By contrast, in *Gestural Politics: Stereotype and Parody in Joyce* (2000), Christie L. Burns focuses on physical and verbal gestures in Joyce's work, which she argues amount to a form of parody that slides from 'more ardently reified negative types to those that playfully dissipate such aggressive portraiture', creating dynamic and unstable combinations of contrary representations of womanhood, nationalism, and homosexual desire.[140] She proceeds to explore how gestural parody acts on the very body of words themselves, rendering Joyce's language libidinal and sensual rather than formal and descriptive. Beyond Joyce, books on late nineteenth- and early twentieth-century writers for whom parody was an important aesthetic, such as Michelle Hannoosh's *Parody and Decadence: Laforgue's 'Moralités légendaires'* (1989), Michael Shallcross's *Rethinking G. K. Chesterton and Literary Modernism: Parody, Performance, and Popular Culture* (2018), or John Felstiner's *The Lies of Art: Max Beerbohm's Parody and Caricature* (1972), tend to focus on figures who have complicated relationships to high modernism.[141]

---

[136] Bradbury, 'Age of Parody', 64.

[137] David Kiremidjian, *A Study of Modern Parody: James Joyce's 'Ulysses', Thomas Mann's 'Doctor Faustus'* (New York: Garland, 1985). Andreas Höfele's study, *Parodie und literarischer Wandel: Studien zur Funktion einer Schreibweise in der englischen Literatur des ausgehenden 19. Jahrhunderts* (Heidelberg: Winter, 1986) makes the broad argument that twentieth-century literature proceeds from parodies of *fin-de-siècle* writing but focuses particularly on the works of Oscar Wilde. He takes a functionalist approach to parody, identifying it as an agent that can transcend authors' dependence on preformed literary material by bringing that dependence to the fore.

[138] Hugh Kenner, *Dublin's Joyce* (London: Chatto & Windus, 1955).

[139] Hugh Kenner, *Joyce's Voices* (Rochester, NY; London: Dalkey Archive Press, 2007), ix; Karen Lawrence, *The Odyssey of Style in 'Ulysses'* (Princeton, NJ: Princeton University Press, 1981), 45.

[140] Christie L. Burns, *Gestural Politics: Stereotype and Parody in Joyce* (Albany, NY: State University of New York Press, 2000), 7.

[141] Hannoosh, *Parody and Decadence*; Michael Shallcross, *Rethinking G. K. Chesterton and Literary Modernism: Parody, Performance, and Popular Culture* (New York: Routledge, 2018); Felstiner, *Lies of Art*. Hannoosh focuses on Laforgue, who is of course an important author for Eliot and Pound, whereas

40 MODERNIST PARODY

A number of critics have reflected on particular instances or modes of modernist parody, affirming the potential interest and scope of the topic. In *Flaubert, Joyce, Beckett: The Stoic Comedians* (1962), Kenner touches on the metafictional tendencies of modernist parody when he reflects on the effects of the eighteenth-century enlightenment culture of encyclopedism on the modern novel and the different ways in which Gustave Flaubert, Joyce, and Beckett make a comedy of writing books as books (as printed texts) by 'selecting elements from a closed set and arranging them inside a closed field'.[142] Modernist belatedness is the topic of Christopher Ames's thoughtful article 'The Modernist Canon Narrative: Woolf's *Between the Acts* and Joyce's "Oxen of the Sun"', which compares and contrasts the different ways in which Joyce and Woolf restage their literary heritage by using 'parody and narrative framing to mitigate the disabling authority of past tradition'.[143] Feminist appropriation is a standard theme in criticism of *Orlando: A Biography* (1928), another of Woolf's canon narratives, which, as Kari Lokke notes, 'revisits the history and development of English literature from the Renaissance to 1928 in the spirit of feminist parody in order to free its heroine—and by extension its author—from the burden of this largely masculine tradition'.[144] Then there is Leslie Fiedler's brisk essay 'Pound as Parodist', which commences with a quick census of instances of parody in *The Waste Land* and *Ulysses*, proceeding to the suggestion that 'travesty, parody, and burlesque have been the hallmarks of Modernism from the start'.[145] Fiedler then speeds off in another direction entirely, attributing Pound's parody to his Americanism, setting his parodies of Walt Whitman and Henry Wadsworth Longfellow and his travesties of American speech in his personal correspondence and infamous wartime propaganda broadcasts on Italian radio in the context of W. H. Auden's comment that 'The danger of the American poet' (without a standard received literary tradition or literary language) 'is not that of writing like everybody else but of crankiness and a parody of his own manner'.[146] On a different track entirely, Leonard Diepeveen's critical edition *Mock Modernism: An Anthology of Parodies, Travesties, Frauds, 1910–1930* (2014), introduces a fascinating array of ridiculing ephemera from Anglo-American newspapers, periodicals, and anthologies, revealing the culture

---

Shallcross rethinks the ambivalent relationship between the anti-modern Chesterton and modernists such as Eliot, Lewis, and Pound, proposing it to be more reciprocal than previously thought, continuing the work of moving modernism across the 'great divide' between high art and popular culture. Felstiner foregrounds the sophistication of Beerbohm's parody, its flippancy, and its modernity.

[142] Hugh Kenner, *Flaubert, Joyce and Beckett: The Stoic Comedians* (Boston: Beacon Press, 1962).

[143] Christopher Ames, 'The Modernist Canon Narrative: Woolf's *Between the Acts* and Joyce's "Oxen of the Sun"', *Twentieth Century Literature* 37(4) (1991), 395.

[144] Kari Elise Lokke, '*Orlando* and Incandescence: Virginia Woolf's Comic Sublime', *MFS Modern Fiction Studies* 38(1) (1992), 235–52.

[145] Leslie Fiedler, 'Pound as Parodist', in *Ezra Pound: The Legacy of Kulchur*, ed. Marcel Smith and William A. Ulmer (Tuscaloosa, AL: University of Alabama Press, 1988), 131.

[146] Fiedler, 'Pound as Parodist', 132.

PARODY 41

of parody in which modernist productions circulated and the level of suspicion modernism's sceptics directed at experimental works.[147] Diepeveen's most recent book *Modernist Fraud: Hoax, Parody, Deception* (2019) builds on this research, exploring the notion that modernism was ludic to the point of being insincere and investigating what the persistent suspicion that modernism was fraudulent says about the latter's place in social and cultural life and its ethical function.[148]

The central importance of parody within modernism is often acknowledged in passing in studies on separate topics as a generally accepted truth: for instance Vincent Sherry observes that 'Mockery strikes close to the heart of modernist greatness', while David Trotter notes 'A crucial term in definitions of highbrow (Modernist) fiction is parody: the locus classicus being the "Nausicaa" section of *Ulysses* which parodies sentimental Victorian fiction' in *The English Novel in History* (1993).[149] Robert Chamber's *Parody: The Art that Plays with Art* (2010) is so strident in its mission to rectify the low esteem in which the mode has often been held that a brief chapter 'Parodic Innovation and Modernism' generalizes its presence in technical breakthroughs before asserting that 'parody did not seem to fit in anywhere with the high seriousness of modernist art, so modernist-orientated criticism, naturally, never found room for it', presuming that Eliot and Joyce 'resorted to priestly displays of elitism and scholarly obfuscation to steer around the fact that their work is baldly parodic', without developing analyses of the parodic elements of *The Waste Land* or *Ulysses*.[150] The omission in scholarship on the detail of parody's vitally creative role in the genesis of individual modernist authors' styles—and the evolution of modernism more broadly—is the gap that this book hopes to fill.

As theory has become increasingly informed about kinds of postmodern reflexivity on the nature of language, it is paramount that it reflects on its own linguistic limitations. This book hopes to avoid the scientific and clinical register adopted by over-earnest critics of parody and do its best to return to parody its exuberance and humour.[151] To speak of *a theory* of parody is to assume that parody can be sufficiently articulated by a sharp and singular theoretical framework, when it is in

---

[147] Leonard Diepeveen, *Mock Modernism: An Anthology of Parodies, Travesties, Frauds, 1910–1935* (Toronto: University of Toronto Press, 2014).

[148] Leonard Diepeveen, *Modernist Fraud* (Oxford: Oxford University Press, 2019).

[149] See Vincent Sherry, *Ulysses* (Cambridge: University of Cambridge Press, 1994), 15; David Trotter, *The English Novel in History: 1895–1920* (London: Routledge, 1993), 181.

[150] Robert Chambers, *Parody: The Art that Plays with Art* (New York: Peter Lang, 2010), 181, 182. Chambers develops an alternative critical terminology of 'banging', 'blinding', and 'blending' to explain how parody sets off contrasts between different conventions.

[151] Paul Chipchase has complained 'It is hard to imagine anyone who enjoys parody enjoying' Hutcheon's *A Theory of Parody*, which is 'so earnest in tone as to be touched almost with pathos' (*Tempo* 154 (1985), 41), while Ann Jefferson similarly criticized Rose's 'rather deadly prose style' in her review of *Parody//Metafiction* in *Poetics Today* 3(3) (1982), 232.

essence rather more slippery, appearing in multiple guises, each with subtly different emphases requiring different kinds of analysis. To theorize from example, considering the particular factors at play in each individual instance, is the way to proceed. The next chapter investigates the early career of Ezra Pound, who knew by instinct what parody is and revelled in its literary pleasures.

2

Pasticherie

Ezra Pound's Apprenticeship from His College Verses to *Canzoni*

Young writers have always apprenticed themselves to their crafts by absorbing and projecting other authors' voices, and the modernists were no exception. By the time their generation was coming of age, this writerly apprenticeship had been formalized in British and American schools. Imitation formed an integral part of the classical and literary curriculum, often in the guise of the imitative practices recommended by Marcus Fabius Quintilian in *Institutio Oratoria*, who advised that it is from:

> authors worthy of our study that we must draw our stock of words, the variety of our figures and our methods of composition, while we must form our minds on the model of every excellence. For there can be no doubt that in art no small portion of our task lies in imitation, since, although invention came first and is all-important, it is expedient to imitate whatever has been invented with success.[1]

Memorization, imitation, and paraphrase encouraged pupils to assimilate the best qualities of each model and subsume them into a larger rhetorical purpose, and easily yielded to the altogether more entertaining discipline of parody. In his last year at Charterhouse, Thackeray's *alma mater*, Beerbohm wrote 'Carmen Becceriense', a 14-line Latin elegiac on the topic of an uproarious piano recital by the eccentric music master, attributed by the 'editor', 'H. M. B.', to no lesser authority than Lucretius, and accompanied by copious footnotes mocking the textual scholarship of genuine nineteenth-century classicists. The parody was so accomplished that another school master arranged an edition of twenty-five copies.[2] Eliot too received formal encouragement in this kind of educational recreation: his oldest surviving poem, 'A Lyric', in imitation of Ben Jonson's 'Song to Celia', was written aged 16 in response to a classroom exercise set by his English master, who discerned in it great promise and had it printed in *Smith Academy Record*.[3]

---

[1] Marcus Fabius Quintilian, *Institutio Oratoria*, vol. IV, trans. H. E. Butler (Cambridge, MA: Harvard University Press, 1921), 75.

[2] Max Beerbohm, 'Carmen Becceriense', in J. G. Riewald, ed., *Max Beerbohm: Collected Verse* (Hamden, CT: Archon Books, 1994), 3.

[3] T. S. Eliot, 'A Lyric', *Poems Written in Early Youth* (London: Faber & Faber, 1967), 17; Ben Jonson, 'Song to Celia', in C. H. Herford and Percy and Evelyn Simpson, eds., *Ben Jonson*, vol. 8 (Oxford: Clarendon Press, 1947), 106.

Modernist Parody. Sarah Davison, Oxford University Press. © Sarah Davison (2023).
DOI: 10.1093/oso/9780192849243.003.0003

44 MODERNIST PARODY

As Peter Ackroyd notes, Eliot's further contributions to the *Record* are 'interesting for their ironic and parodic note—the author in one case claiming merely to be the "editor".[4] Other surviving poems by Eliot written in early youth continue this apprenticeship by imitating the styles of admired authors: for instance, 'Humouresque (after J. Laforgue)', which appeared in the *Harvard Advocate* (12 January 1910).[5]

The subversive spirit of parody had obvious appeal for playful young men who wanted to test their strength as writers by aping esteemed authorities or twitting their contemporaries in school newspapers and university magazines. Pound touched on this culture of homosocial one-upmanship in his preface to the posthumous edition of *Poetical Works of Lionel Johnson* (1915), where he quoted from the best of Johnson's juvenilia, stating that it was quite natural that Johnson at 17 should have been writing Swinburniania, noting that Johnson's first submission to the *Wykehamist* (the Winchester College magazine), a graceful lyric signed 'ICH', 'was promptly parodied by someone signing himself "V"'.[6]

Schoolboys' enthusiasm for parody carried over into university newspapers such as *Granta*, the *Cambridge Review*, and the *Oxford Magazine*, which provided the perfect forum for aspiring wits to publish diverting skits on topical matters, drawing on a broad and strong foundation of Greek, Latin, and English literature. Owen Seaman, who took a first in part one of the classical tripos at Cambridge in 1883, was the exemplary product of this culture.[7] Like many students of his time, he came under the spell of the previous generation of Cambridge parodists, including Calverley and Stephen, and sought to emulate their satirical light verse.[8] The title of Seaman's second book, *Horace at Cambridge* (1895), acknowledged the two sensibilities, classical and Cantabrigian, which he fused in his parodies (in this case odes celebrating undergraduate life, first published in *Granta*).[9] Seaman graduated from the university school of humour to submit parodies to the *National Observer* and the *World*, and was invited to join the editorial staff at *Punch* on the strength of his poem 'The Rhyme of the Kipperling', a marine-themed parody of Rudyard Kipling's 'The Rhyme of the Three Sealers'.[10]

J. C. Squire was another prominent figure in British journalism whose career sprung from his talent for topical parody. A weekly column for *Granta* reporting the debates at the Cambridge Union in verse parodies of the romantics led

---

[4] Peter Ackroyd, *T. S. Eliot* (London: Hamilton, 1984), 28.

[5] Eliot, 'Humouresque (after J. Laforgue)', *Poems Written in Early Youth*, 30–1.

[6] Ezra Pound, 'Preface', in Ezra Pound, ed. Lionel Johnson, *Poetical Works of Lionel Johnson* (London: Elkin Mathews, 1915), xvii–xviii.

[7] John Adlard, *Owen Seaman: His Life and Work* (London: Eighteen Nineties Society, 1977), 38.

[8] Seaman wrote an introduction to Calverley's poetry: C. S. Calverley, *Verses and Translations by Charles Stuart Calverley. With an Introduction by Owen Seaman*, 17th edn (London: Blackie & Son, 1905).

[9] Owen Seaman, *Horace at Cambridge* (London: A. D. Innes & Co., 1895).

[10] Owen Seaman, 'The Rhyme of the Kipperling', *Punch* (13 January 1894), 13.

PASTICHERIE 45

to a post as a parliamentary reporter for the National Press Agency, a role that supplied material for a series of political parodies for the *New Age*, entitled 'Imaginary Speeches'.[11] These were succeeded in 1910 by 'The Sort of Poems Modern Poets Write', which parodied hackneyed literary modes.[12] These activities helped to establish Squire as a regular writer for the *New Age*, where his repertoire enlarged to include literary criticism and original poetry, setting him on the path towards securing the position of editor of the *London Mercury*, a post that he held from 1919 to 1934, transforming him into one of most influential literary professionals in England and one of modernism's most scornful and mocking opponents.[13] The rise of Seaman and Squire demonstrate parody's power to turn young amateurs into professional writers who could boast workmanly proficiency in different styles and registers.

The promotion of parody as a pedagogical tool made its mark on many high and late modernist writers who referred to it as the ideal model for artistic growth. W. H. Auden even designed a fantasy curriculum for his 'daydream College for Bards' where 'The library would contain no books of literary criticism, and the only critical exercise required of students would be the writing of parodies'.[14] In an otherwise even-handed review of Squire's *Tricks of the Trade: Parodies in Verse and Prose* (1917), Virginia Woolf snippily suggested that 'If we had to teach children how to write English, no doubt this would be one of our instruments of torture'.[15] Squire's satirical point was that the qualities that make individual authors' styles distinctive are repeatably formulaic and are therefore tricks that can be learned. In the first part of *Tricks of the Trade* he professed that his parodies of leading Georgians, including Hilaire Belloc, John Masefield, Chesterton, and George Bernard Shaw, showed 'How They Do It'; he then proceeded to make a comedy of anachronism by transposing the styles of canonized writers to anomalous topics and genres in a further section entitled 'How They Would Have Done It'.[16]

Although Woolf was home-educated, she was closer to the tradition of Cantabrigian parody than one might think, being the first cousin of J. K. Stephen and the

---

[11] J. C. Squire, 'Imaginary Speeches', *New Age* VI(7) (16 December 1909), 151; *New Age* VI(8) (23 December 1909), 175; *New Age* VI(9) (30 December 1909), 199; *New Age* VI(10) (6 January 1910), 222; *New Age* VI(11) (13 January 1909), 247; *New Age* VI(12) (20 January 1909), 272.

[12] J. C. Squire, 'The Sort of Poems Modern Poets Write', *New Age* VII(21) (22 September 1910), 500–1; *New Age* VII(24) (13 October 1910), 562; *New Age* VII(26) (27 October 1910), 605.

[13] J. E. Wetherwell claimed of Squire that 'no living poet has a wider influence on the literary views and tendencies of his age'. See J. E. Wetherwell, *Later English Poems: 1901–1922* (Toronto: McClelland & Stewart, 1922), 36. Under Squire's editorship the *London Mercury* had a circulation rivalling the *Times Literary Supplement*.

[14] W. H. Auden, 'The Poet and the City' (1962) in *The Dyer's Hand and Other Essays* (London: Faber & Faber, 1963), 77. Auden's skill at parody is demonstrated in *The Orators: An English Study* (London: Faber & Faber, 1932), a social satire on England, consisting of parodic odes, school speeches, and sermons.

[15] Virginia Woolf, 'Parodies', *Times Literary Supplement* 790 (8 March 1917), 112.

[16] J. C. Squire, *Tricks of the Trade* (London: Martin Secker, 1917), 3–45, 47–79.

46 MODERNIST PARODY

daughter of Leslie Stephen, a Cambridge don.[17] What Woolf did not mention in her review of *Tricks of the Trade* was that she had assiduously imposed a similar training on herself in her youth, not to expose writing as something mechanical or to mock the follies of individual writers as Squire did, but first to impress family members and then to assimilate literary enthusiasms. As a young girl she wrote 'Tragedy in a Duckpond' in journalese and a letter to impress Clive Bell in 'a pastiche of eighteenth-century epistolary manners'.[18] She began to apply herself to the task of becoming a writer in earnest in 1897 by reading avidly and writing imitatively, as she later recollected in a diary entry of 8 December 1929:

> It was the Elizabethan prose writers I loved first & most wildly, stirred by Hakluyt, which father lugged home for me—I think of it with some sentiment—father tramping over the Library with his little girl sitting at H[yde] P[ark] G[ate] in mind. He must have been 65; I 15 or 16, then . . . I used to read it & dream of those obscure adventurers, & no doubt practised their style in my copy books . . . & I also wrote a history of Women; & a history of my own family—all very longwinded & El[izabe]than in style.[19]

The young Woolf, like other female and feminist writers of her generation, was consciously seeking a place for herself and for the history of women's lives within formidably masculine traditions, preoccupations that would remain central to her work. But it was not just a question of learning 'How They Do It'. The key component in the modernists' self-education that separated juvenile imitation from mature literature was learning how to achieve fine control over the materials they admired; how to inflect stylized writing so that it was at once incisive, personally expressive, and originally creative.

Parody was a crucial element in modernist writers' self-imposed training in stylization. Proust, that most celebrated and arch *pasticheur* of the French literary tradition, advocated the desacralizing practice of parody precisely to enable the writer to grow out of intemperate admiration and turn saturation into self-determination:

> For writers intoxicated with Flaubert . . . I cannot recommend too highly the purgative, exorcizing virtue of parody; we must make an intentional pastiche in order not to spend the rest of our lives in writing in involuntary pastiches.[20]

[17] The Woolfs owned copies of Stephen's *Lapsus Calami* and Calverley's *Verses and Translations*. See Julia King and Laila Miletic-Vejzovic, *The Library of Leonard and Virginia Woolf: A Short-title Catalogue* (Pullman: Washington State University Press, 2003), 214, 36.

[18] Hermione Lee, *Virginia Woolf* (London: Vintage, 1997), 248.

[19] Virginia Woolf, *Diary of Virginia Woolf, Volume 3, 1925–1930*, ed. Annie Olivier Bell and Andrew McNeillie (London: Hogarth Press, 1980), 271.

[20] 'A propos du style de Flaubert' [On the Style of Flaubert], quoted in George D. Painter, *Marcel Proust: A Biography*, vol. 2 (London: Chatto & Windus, 1965), 99–100.

As Proust perceived, strong influence could only be overcome by a reciprocal assertion of creative primacy. In his case, as in Beerbohm's, complete self-effacement facilitated the ultimate exhibition of control: recreating the style and habitus of other authors from the inside. Proust exhibited his mastery over the luminaries of the previous generation in the literary pages of *Le Figaro* (most of which appeared in February and March 1908). Aspects of the *Lemoine Affair*—a famous fraud whereby the diamond company De Beers was briefly tricked into believing a man had discovered a way to manufacture true diamonds—were narrated in the styles of Honoré de Balzac, Jules Michelet, Edmond and Jules de Goncourt, Flaubert, and others. The scandal provided the perfect analogy for the sparkle and finish of Proust's luminous parodies, which could easily pass for the real thing. These literary gems were later published as *Pastiches et mélanges* (1919), 'pastiche' in French usage having connotations of satire and being closer to the English term 'parody'.[21]

In many ways, Proust's trajectory was typical of writers of his generation. Yet modernist parody was not just about surpassing more powerful authors, while enjoying their writing all the same, but learning how to manipulate and layer different voices and points of view to create palpably original experimental art. Alert to opportunities for self-promotion, Proust told readers to look out for a further Goncourt parody in the book he was then working on, which would become *À la recherche du temps perdu* [In Search of Lost Time] (1913–27). In the last volume, *Le Temps retrouvé* [Time Regained], Proust's alter ego, Charles Swann, a faltering writer, returns home flattened by artistic failure and reads an account of a society dinner attended by Edmond de Goncourt of the kind he himself had reported to be banal. Goncourt's journal entry is concerned with apparent superficialities such as décor and crockery design, rather than character revelation.[22] For a time, Swann doubts his own vision and approach and unsettles the entire construction of the preceding narrative by revealing how different everything might have looked from an alternative point of view.[23] Mastering that process of writing from different stylistic perspectives engendered in the modernists a wry perspective on individuating styles that extended to their own self-fashionings, and often bordered on self-parody. The apprenticeships in parodic stylization that modernist writers devised for themselves had different emphases according to their literary enthusiasms and their sense of purpose, but what united them all was that parody was not merely a developmental stage quickly discarded as a youthful folly, but one continued in full maturity. The parody modernist writers practised cultivated a highly discerning and critical attitude towards different modes of stylization and the representational and ideological values they encode; the technique was fundamental to the production of their own highly original work.

---

[21] Marcel Proust, *Pastiches et mélanges* (Paris: Gaston Gallimard, 1919).
[22] Marcel Proust, *Time Regained*, trans. Stephen Hudson (London: Chatto & Windus, 1931), 16–26.
[23] Proust, *Time Regained*, 26–34.

48 MODERNIST PARODY

Among the modernists, Pound was the most self-conscious advocate of pedagogical parody, to the extent that he transmitted it as the culminating stage in an exercise in imitation in one of the 'Further Tests' he devised for pupils of literature in *ABC of Reading* (1934):

1. Let the pupil try to write in the metre of any poem he likes.
2. Let him write words to a well-known tune.
3. Let him try to write words to the same tune in such a way that the words will not be distorted when one sings them.
4. Let the pupil write a poem in some strophe form he likes.
5. Let him parody some poem he finds ridiculous, either because of falsity in the statement, or falsity in the disposition of the writer, or for pretentiousness, of one kind or another, or for any other reason that strikes his risible faculties, his sense of irony.

The gauging pupil should be asked to recognize what author is parodied. And whether the joke is on the parodied or the parodist. Whether the parody exposes a real defect, or merely makes use of an author's mechanism to expose a more trivial content.

Note: No harm has ever yet been done a good poem by this process. FitzGerald's *Rubaiyat* has survived hundreds of parodies, that are not really parodies either of Omar or FitzGerald, but only poems written in that form of strophe.

Note: There is a tradition in Provence it was considered plagiarism to take a man's form, just as it is now considered plagiarism to take his subject matter or plot.[24]

The focus on melody reflects Pound's belief that emotion and thus meaning is latent in the music of words. The exercises therefore build up to parody by encouraging pupils to study the craft of musical composition in order to emulate signature techniques, hence the note on plagiarism. Pound retains an expansive conception of the mode. He does not limit the preserve of parody to ridiculing falsehood or preciosity but allows that it might be inspired by any other feature that strikes the reader to be comic or ironic. Nor does he assume that the butt of the parody is the author of the original, knowing only too well how parody can rebound on second-rate writing and expose the parodist as the lesser talent. And he declines to fix its effects in favour of presenting the evaluating pupils with a choice of contrasting options. The benefits Pound envisaged extended beyond the individual acquisition of technique to pupils of literature perceiving themselves to be reading and writing as part of a community and entering into dialogue with others to gain valuable externalized perspectives on their work. This is the outlook that parodists must themselves cultivate so that they can judge their composition's literary merit and,

---

[24] Ezra Pound, *ABC of Reading* (London: Faber & Faber, 1991), 68–9.

crucially, develop the aesthetic discernment to perceive the hierarchies of value that were fundamental to Pound's concept of literary history. In Pound's view, the course of literature was contoured by 'Inventors' ('Men who found a new process') and 'The masters' ('Men who combined a number of such processes, and who used them as a well as or better than the inventors') and plagued by 'The diluters', 'Good writers without salient qualities', 'Writers of belles-lettres', and 'The starters of crazes'.[25] It would be a mistake, therefore, to conclude from Pound's comments that good poems could not be the subject of accomplished parodies; on the contrary, the fact that they cannot be harmed allows that they might be augmented by the most masterful practitioners.

Parody was of paramount importance to Pound because it could make an immediate connection between the forms and languages of literature, the complexities of historical hierarchy, canon formation, contingent questions of literary value, and thus the role of art in society. By casting writing as a form of reading that is aware of its audience and likely reception, parody is not merely a pleasurable formal game that draws attention to the artifice of art, but an antidote to etiolated aestheticism and dissipated decadence because its satire directly links the production of art to social practices. Parody makes this connection through its reciprocal, socially negotiated comparative doubling of perspective and the agency of its laughter, which signals a quickened moment of recognition between writer and reader of the kind that the romantics held to be an instance of true communication. In *The Spirit of Romance* (1910), Pound reflected that the business of the literary artist is to 'relieve, refresh, revive the mind of the reader—at reasonable intervals—with some form of ecstasy, by some splendour of thought, some presentation of sheer beauty, some lightning turn of phrase—for laughter, especially laughter of the mind, is no mean ecstasy'.[26] The Blakean ideal that art should concern ecstasy is tempered by his plea for 'a greater levity, a more befitting levity, in our study of the arts', a call to readers not to be solemn before literature but to respond to what is risible (whether intentional or unintentional) with fitting mirth.[27]

Pound's recommendations for pupils had extra piquancy because he himself had started out writing derivative doggerel and over-earnest pastiche and had to learn to temper his enthusiasms through desacralizing parody before he could achieve the necessary critical distance, compression, and control to rearrange this literary heritage around his own vision. There is evidence that the young Pound instinctively put himself through precisely the kind of exercises set out in 'Further Tests' in a folder labelled 'Doggerel' in the Beinecke Rare Book and Manuscript Library, Yale University, which also includes several squibs on undergraduate life and his professorial foes, and so most likely dates from Pound's time at the University

---

[25] Pound, *ABC of Reading*, 39–40.
[26] *SR* vii.
[27] *SR* vi.

50   MODERNIST PARODY

of Pennsylvania (1905–7), where he enrolled on a master's course in Romance languages, following a BA at Hamilton College. It includes two rudimentary parodies of Kipling that were inspired by *Barrack Room Ballads* (1892), a key text for young parodists who were keen to sharpen their teeth on one of the day's strongest and most recognizable voices. The first typescript, 'Mr. K', is considerably less accomplished than Seaman's 'Rhyme of the Kipperling', but shows Pound imitating Kipling's metre and writing words to the bouncing cadence of his ballads:

> The style of Mr. Kipling
> it is ruffled it is rippling
> and it hath a wondrous adaptation
> to the purpose of vexation
> of soggy time-encrusted custom in all places .
>
>   Mr. Kipling
> whom I love honor and revere
>   as a prophet bard and seer
> But thank God his meetre isnt under patent .
>
> Ah I got the trick from Ruddy
> But I'm the damdest understudy
> That prophet of the ages eer fell heir to .
>
> Nevertheless I thought of usinm Hewlets
>   Masque of dead florentines .[28]

Here, Pound adds imitation to flattery, paying a compliment to Kipling's driving rhythms, nifty rhymes, and vernacular voice. In the final lines, Pound admits the temptation to imitate Maurice Hewlett's *A Masque of the Dead Florentines* (1895), a playscript in which the shades of famous Florentines such as Dante Alighieri, Guido Cavalcanti, and Petrarch lament their demise in affected but charmingly rhymed verses, in a gesture that indicates the strong attraction romantic medievalizing held for Pound.[29]

In a second typescript, 'Med', Pound shifts critical attention from Kipling's metre to his moral vision:

> Mr. Kipling that   there
>   aint none seen ell but the sojer
> Tin plated   , war-elated
> Shaw-despised sojer of the queen

---

[28] Ezra Pound, 'Mr. K', typescript, n. d., Ezra Pound Papers, Yale Collection of American Literature, Beinecke Rare Book and Manuscript Library, Yale University, YCAL MSS 43, box 89, folder 3809. All transcriptions of Pound's typescripts preserve his original spelling and spacing, including typographical errors.

[29] Maurice Hewlett, *A Masque of Dead Florentines* (London: J. M. Dent & Co., 1895).

> With is boots an is canteen
> an is noble undisputed noble   , conduct
>   in field ~~al~~ action
> But if ~~ee's ee~~ ee'd stop a fraction
> of a moment   Mr.Kipling
> would seen some slimy corners
> filled with nothing like chied mourners
> But with meds .
> Anticsptic   ,   ~~ee~~ stereleptic , pasturized
>   gosh dast your eyes
> padded fingered meds
> a cutting up stale heads
> an trunks and toes an femur tendons .[30]

The familiar cockneyfied brogue warmly used by Kipling to stir national feeling and depict straight-talking military men of the people is instead applied to expose the unsung and gory reality of combat and show the grimmer reality of a battlefield filled with medics treating body parts. To evoke and then displace the world of barrack-room bonhomie that held so much romance for Kipling, Pound sneers at the refrain 'The So-oldier of the Queen!' from Kipling's satirical ballad 'The Young British Soldier', in which a commander bluffly advises new recruits to drink good beer not grog, act upstandingly with sangfroid, whether they catch their wives cheating with comrades or are caught in gunfire, and to be sure to shoot themselves if they are left wounded on the battlefield.[31] 'Med' lacks the finesse of Beerbohm's parodies of Kipling: the bathos of 'pasturized' and 'gosh dast you eyes' belongs not to Kipling's poetry, but Pound's satire and youthful excess. In both these exercises, then, the joke rebounds on the parodist, but a lesson has been learned. The second poem breaks up Kipling's metre and criticizes Kipling from within, fingering what is false in his jocose treatment of military life. The technique of tilting embedded quotation parodically to summon a context that is shown in a new perspective would prove to have future promise.

Pound's earliest poems and writings provide a candid record of his battle to become a writer who could summon the vigour of past masters and energize his vision of the present, providing the raw materials for his later, incisive commentary on the role of imitation in his evolution as a writer, and thus the foundations on which his modernism was built. He described his own literary self-education impersonally in 'Prolegomena', an article for *Poetry Review* (1912), in which he stated that the poet 'should master all known forms and systems of metric' just as 'all the old masters of painting recommend to their pupils that they begin by

---

[30] Ezra Pound, 'Med', typescript, n. d., Ezra Pound Papers, Yale Collection of American Literature, Beinecke Rare Book and Manuscript Library, Yale University, YCAL MSS 43, box 89, folder 3809.

[31] Rudyard Kipling, 'The Young British Soldier', *Barrack-Room Ballads* (London: Methuen & Co., 1892), 46–9.

52 MODERNIST PARODY

copying masterwork, and proceed to their own composition.[32] How pupils might proceed once they have mastered the basics is not discussed. However, examining Pound's self-imposed apprenticeship, and his acquisition of (and gradual command over) imitative technique, it appears that he was only able to write original compositions after he had learned to evaluate derivative writing with the sensibility of a practised parodist.

As a student and erstwhile tutor, Pound spend his time at university floundering 'somewhat ineffectually through the slough of philology', reading Anglo-Saxon, Latin, Provençal, Old French, Italian, and Spanish texts, as well as more contemporary English poetry, and attempting to discover by translation, imitation, and parody, how to match the masters he exalted in his own language.[33] Pound's imitative writing before 1912 tirelessly probed the expressive potential of sincere pastiche to embody something of the power of his idols. His early copy work was focused on the medieval literature of southern Europe, mediated through the recent voices in British poetry that were still a part of living memory: Robert Browning; the Pre-Raphaelites; the aesthetes, especially Swinburne; the writers of the 1890s; and early W. B. Yeats.[34] Pound insisted on the fitness of his approach to poetic invention in the prose reflections that accompanied his poem 'To R. B.' (1907), in a typescript which has been quoted and extensively discussed by George Bornstein in *Ezra Pound among the Poets* (1985)):

> Are our riming and our essays to be confined only to such secondary things as missed the eyes of our fore-goers? Dante, Browning, and a half hundred others are not known in detail to a dozen men, and when one stumbles of a flaming blade that pierces him to extacy is he to hide it for some rabbit fear of 'copyist' 'blind follower' or alley taunt 'He hath not thought's originality'? Is it, tell me whether, is it more original to cry some great truth higher and more keen, to add a candle to the daylight that none see, or to reverse some million proverbs that the mob may laugh to see the worthies butt-end up displayed to common view?[35]

[32] Ezra Pound, 'Prolegomena', *Poetry Review* I(2) (February 1912), 73, 74. There have been several major studies of Pound's early verse and his meticulous approach to apprenticing himself to his craft to discover his own voice. N. Christopher de Nagy positions Pound as the last of the aesthetes in *The Poetry of Ezra Pound: The Pre-Imagist Stage* (Bern: Francke, 1960); Thomas H. Jackson focuses on Pound's Pre-Raphaelite medievalism in *The Early Poetry of Ezra Pound* (Cambridge, MA: Harvard University Press, 1968) and Thomas F. Grieve foregrounds his affinities with Yeats and the Celtic Twilight in *Ezra Pound's Early Poetry and Poetics* (Columbia: University of Missouri Press, 1997). The first two chapters of Mary Ellis Gibson's study *Epic Reinvented: Ezra Pound and the Victorians* (Ithaca, NY: Cornell University Press, 1995) concern the formative influence of Robert Browning and nineteenth-century historians on Pound's early writings (later chapters focus on the *Cantos*).

[33] *SR* v.

[34] 'I have enjoyed meeting Victorians and Pre-Raphaelites and the men of the nineties through their friends', Ezra Pound, 'How I Began', *T.P.'s Weekly* (6 June 1913), 707.

[35] Ezra Pound, unpublished typescript, Beinecke Rare Book and Manuscript Library, Yale University, quoted in George Bornstein, 'Pound's Parleyings with Robert Browning', in George Bornstein, ed., *Ezra Pound among the Poets: Homer, Ovid, Li Po, Dante, Whitman, Browning, Yeats, Williams, Eliot*

PASTICHERIE   53

If nothing fundamental about human experience remained to be said, Pound reasoned, the poet who confined himself to saying new things condemned himself to work of secondary importance.

Pound's 'half hundred' were largely drawn from the foreign literatures he systematically studied and so part of the challenge was to find post-romantic modes of English expression that were fit for the task of propagation. The problem was that Pound was overpowered by sincere pastiche until he discovered the critical discipline to distance himself from the styles of his immediate forebears by bringing a mocking, questioning sensibility to imitation through parody. In 'To R. B.' Pound voiced his thoughts on Browning's masterful adaptations of 'fore-goers' at one remove, speaking in the person of John Cowper, a minor poet and one of Browning's admirers and contemporaries, who, like Pound, hoped to derive strength from Cavalcanti and revive his work, just as Browning had honoured and reinvigorated Euripides in his dramatic monologue *Balaustion's Adventure* (1871):

> As the grass blade in its sheathe
> so are we like in tendency, thou Robert Browning
> and myself. And so take I no shame
> to grow from thee.[36]

'To R. B.' and the accompanying prose exposition provides an early, unembarrassed expression of the young Pound's desire to enfold himself within the traditions initiated by other poets and grow organically from them by emulating their adaptive strategies and even speaking through their voices to address the present while summoning the past.[37] Far from being burdened by a Bloomian struggle against the anxiety of influence, Pound was actively seeking communion with his strongest precursors.[38] And so he made his relations to admired forebears, the men through whom his own efforts must be read, the explicit subject of his early verse and justificatory prose.

Time and again, Pound expressed his desire to become his poetic masters in order to channel their energy, but the realm of his own invention repeatedly slipped his grasp each time he tried on, put on, took off, packed away, and above all *studied* a new piece of prehistory or the literature of a foreign country. 'Pagentry', an unpublished typescript (in two drafts) in the Beinecke Rare Book

---

(Chicago: University of Chicago Press, 1985), 109. For an extended discussion of this document, see Bornstein, 107–13.

[36] Ezra Pound, 'To R. B.', unpublished typescript, Beinecke Rare Book and Manuscript Library, Yale University, quoted in Gibson, *Epic Reinvented*, 61.

[37] On the subject of Pound's relationship to Browning's concept of the poet as ragpicker, see Gibson, *Epic Reinvented*, 39–78.

[38] See Harold Bloom, *The Anxiety of Influence: A Theory of Poetry* (New York: Oxford University Press, 1997) for his account of writers' anxious imitations of the achievements of the strong poets they feel compelled to emulate.

54 MODERNIST PARODY

and Manuscript Library, Yale University, dating from Pound's college days, is an exercise in canon composition that parades the achievements of the 'bards of eld' in such a way that Pound hoped he might himself be seen to be following in their train.[39] (He signed the second more developed typescript twice: the words 'Ezra Pound./Crawfordsville'. are typewritten at the bottom of the page, while his aesthetic *nom de plume* 'Weston Llewmys' is written in pen with a flourish.)[40] The presence of too many powerful forebears results in ahistorical antique diction that provides no leverage to pass comment on particulars:

Spenser in broidered vair
Where is thy spirit   ?   Where
Is the naked truth
That standeth in Browning's line
        'Thout ruth   ?
Dante , amid the spheres
Where in the flow of years
        Thy following   ?
Who from the   " Olde French booke   "
Can take as Chaucer took
Live folk in true romance   ?
Where are the songs for dance
        Of Provencal troubadour   ?
Where is the rumbling line
That runic lettres twine
        In Saxon minstrelsy ?
Where are the bards of eld
They that lon since beheld
Deirder and Yseult in the Erin-green   ?
What man of you hath seen
        Master Villon , whose singing
Erst set all France a-ringing
In poignant , piteous note
Who singeth to lute and rote
        The songs of your
Of the masters old   ?
Who among you is so bold
As dare to follow them
That be gone with the wind   ?[41]

---

[39] Ezra Pound, 'Pagentry', typescript, n. d., Ezra Pound Papers, Yale Collection of American Literature, Beinecke Rare Book and Manuscript Library, Yale University, YCAL MSS 43, box 88, folder 3778.
[40] Ezra Pound, 'Pagentry'.
[41] Pound, 'Pagentry'.

PASTICHERIE   55

These illustrious masters are followed by William Shakespeare, Jonson, Christopher Marlow, Thomas Carew, Lope de Vega, Cervantes, and Pedro Calderón de la Barca, but there is no sense in which Pound might be 'so bold/As dare to follow them' beyond donning their borrowed finery and lining their verses with the heraldic vair that signifies his ancestry. Indeed, the parting rhetorical question 'What one of you all , man-jack ,/Dareth as Cyriac/Of Ancona , "Go forth to raise the dead " ?' figures the poet who dares to answer that call as a scholar and antiquarian, an archaeologist of history rather than an architect of the present.[42] The typescript itself foregrounds the comic incongruity between Pound's generic historical pastiche and the modern conditions of its production: the second more developed draft is decorated with typeface *fleur-de-lys* motifs in a failed attempt to give the typescript the appearance of an old heraldic text. *Faux* archaism would not bring Pound closer to his idols. And pallid historical pageantry was no way to enter the apostolic succession.

In 'Histrion', another early poem, selected for *A Quinzaine for this Yule* (1908), Pound revisited his fundamental point that to be significant a poet must commune with the souls of his masters before him:

> Thus I am Dante for a space and am
> One Francois [*sic*] Villon, ballad-lord and thief
> Or am such holy ones I may not write,
> Lest blasphemy be writ against my name;
> This for an instant and the flame is gone.
>
> 'Tis as in midmost us there glows a sphere
> Translucent, molten gold, that is the "I"
> And into this some form projects itself:
> Christus, or John, or eke the Florentine;
> And as the clear space is not if a form's
> Imposed thereon,
> So cease we from all being for the time,
> And these, the Masters of the Soul, live on.[43]

Pound's explanation for his earnest adoption of various poetic personae amounts to a form of spirit possession: the self is luminous and yet also a clear space through which the souls of great masters pass. However, this explanation is undercut by the deprecatory title 'Histrion', which concedes a degree of bad acting or poor buffoonery. On some level Pound already knew he was falling comically short and he sensed his lack of power.

Reflecting impersonally on youthful poetry in 1913, Pound identified that the 'artist's inheritance from other artists can be little more than certain enthusiasms,

---

[42] Pound, 'Pagentry'.

[43] Ezra Pound, *A Quinzaine for this Yule: Being Selected from a Venetian Sketch-book, 'San Trovaso'* (London: Pollock & Co., 1908), 26.

56 MODERNIST PARODY

which usually spoil his first work; and a definite knowledge of the modes of expression, which knowledge contributes to perfecting his more mature performance. This is a matter of technique.'[44] And indeed the strength of Pound's admiration for the great poets of the past did spoil his early verse for a time. In another of his college verses, 'Have I Not, O Walt Whitman', Pound resolved that when he 'had something real to say', he would 'blurt it out bald as Browning/no tom foolery, no tinsel/no pre-raphaelite zithern and citoles', eschewing Pre-Raphaelite lyricism in favour of Browning's argumentative voice.[45] But rehashing Browning alone would not be enough, as Pound tacitly acknowledged in the draft letter intended for a prospective magazine editor introducing another of his college verses, 'In Praise of the Masters'.[46] Here he struck a self-consciously post-Raphaelite pose as he paid homage to Rembrandt, whose dark, earthy palette was the antithesis of the vivid colour of medieval Florentine art fetishized by Dante Gabriel Rossetti and his circle. The postscript, in which Pound explained that 'Most anyone who knows Rembrandt at all . will be able to fathom the first of these poems . Wherein he speaketh', only emphasized that Pound's reincarnation of the Dutch master spoke in the manner of Browning's most quarrelsome dramatic monologues, as Pound testily admitted:[47]

> Oh yes . i have stu,ied Browning . but one does not imitate by using a sonnet of Dantesque form .. I had been reading Shelly within the week . but so far as i know Shelly has written not poem for painting . Tho you may a find my opening line form at the beginning of "Queen Mab" .[48]

The contention that Pound was saying something unprecedented by using the examples of Browning, Shelley, and Dante in novel combination shows that he was beginning to think about methods for adapting and arranging imitation to the production of original work. But in truth, the accumulated effect of sub-Browningesque colloquialisms, neologisms, and testy expostulations, far exceeded pastiche. At the time Pound was confident he had 'hit a real thing', as he explained to his prospective editors, but the level of affectation in phrases such as 'Vain sir, God please you/is this a phiz of o large vanity/But tis truth sir . so please you tis truth sir'; 'This like Mona Lisa? Drat your Elizas', and 'no bless you/just our days toggery, and old day sir/Life's no fine fluffery, wish-waddled delicacy' suggested otherwise.[49]

---

[44] 'Troubadours—their Sorts and Conditions', *LE* 102.

[45] Ezra Pound, 'Have I Not, O Walt Whitman', unpublished college verse, most likely dating from 1906–7, Ezra Pound Papers, Yale Collection of American Literature, Beinecke Rare Book and Manuscript Library, Yale University, quoted in Gibson, *Epic Reinvented*, 70.

[46] Pound, 'In Praise of the Masters', Ezra Pound Papers, Yale Collection of American Literature, Beinecke Rare Book and Manuscript Library, Yale University, YCAL MSS 43, box 86, folder 3712.

[47] Pound, 'In Praise of the Masters'.

[48] Pound, 'In Praise of the Masters'.

[49] Pound, 'In Praise of the Masters'.

PASTICHERIE 57

The strategy of putting Browning's voice in dialogue with those of other admired masters did not produce the desired results either, as demonstrated by 'Piazza San Marco' (one of several poems in praise of Pound's masters copied in to the 'San Trovaso Notebook') where Pound tries to bring together different voices from the past.[50] The poem consists of two pseudo-sonnets in which Pound reflects on Shakespeare's achievement. Part I expresses admiration for Shakespeare's insight into human behaviour in a voice that owes much to Browning. Part II establishes Shakespeare's method to be creative theft. In part III, Pound then appropriates Shakespeare's method in an attempt to reproduce the tone and texture of Sonnet XCVIII:

> When proud-pied April leadeth in his train
> And yellow crocus quick'neth to the breath
> Of Zephyr fleeting from the sun-shot rain,
> Then seek I her whom mine heart honoureth.
> She is a woodland sprite and suzerain
> Of every power that flouteth wintry death.
>
> When proud-pied April leadeth in his train
> And freeth all the earth from cold's mort-main,
> Then with her fairness mine heart journeyeth
> Thru bourgeon wood-ways wherein tourneyeth
> Earth's might of laughter 'gainst all laughter slain
> Ere proud-pied April led in feat his train.[51]

Pound's alteration of Shakespeare's line 'When proud-pied April (dressed in all his trim)' to 'When proud-pied April leadeth in his train' betrays an over-eagerness to endow his Shakespearean pastiche with a period feel.[52] Pound's mock-Tudor English includes phoney archaisms that are equal to if not worse than Edmund Spenser's. Far from creating a poem to equal Shakespeare's sonnet, Pound's slight exercise in the imitative mode is spoilt by the '–eths', inversion, indiscriminately aureate diction, and the undesirable mockery of forced rhyme. Coming after cut-price Browning, the effects of Pound's Shakespearean pastiche were so bad as to be unintentionally comic. It reads like a composition in the 'How They Would Have Done It' vein: if Browning had introduced Spenser doing Shakespeare. And so 'Piazza San Marco' lapses into the kind of inadvertent parody identified by Jonson that arises when a bad poet inexpertly imitates superior artists, reaching the same kind of tipping point that pushed Proust to start practising 'intentional pastiche'.

---

[50] 'Piazza San Marco', *CEP* 238. See also: 'Roundel, After Joachim du Bellay', *CEP* 234; 'For a Play. (Maeterlinck)', *CEP* 241–2; 'Autumnus, To Dowson—Antistave', *CEP* 249.

[51] 'Piazza San Marco', *CEP* 238.

[52] William Shakespeare, 'Sonnet 98', in Colin Burrow, ed., *The Complete Sonnets and Poems* (Oxford: Oxford University Press, 2002), 577.

58   MODERNIST PARODY

Pound's first, self-published collection, *A Lume Spento* (1908), continued to wrestle with the question of how other poets' 'modes of expression' might profitably be used and how to follow the Victorian luminaries Browning, Rossetti, and Swinburne. After an invocation, *A Lume Spento* begins with a stiff 'Note Precedent to "La Fraisne"', which was once to be the collection's title poem, in which Pound explains that the poem retells the medieval Provençal legend of Peire Vidal in the mood of Yeats in his Celtic Twilight.[53] The resulting poem indiscriminately mixes variations on lines from *In the Seven Woods* (1903) with terminal '-eths' and fourteenth-century diction ('boles', 'syne', and 'Tho'), paying tribute to Yeats without improving on his art.[54] A contemporary reviewer of *A Lume Spento* rightly commented:

> One may tolerate such Chaucerian words in modern verse as 'swevyn' for 'dream', and 'everychone' for 'everyone'. But 'ellum' for 'elm', in a poem written not in dialect, and 'mine fashion' for 'my fashion', are merely silly.[55]

Nevertheless, the ethereal realm of Yeats's enchanted woodland in 'La Fraisne', inhabited by exhausted souls in transitional states yearning for communion with the living, replete with myths of metamorphosis, natural images of decay and renewal, and the motif of songs and dried leaves blowing on the wind, provided a unifying mood for many of the poems in *A Lume Spento* in which Pound sought to breathe new life into materials he deemed to be of enduring value.

The organization of *A Lume Spento* enacts yet another apostolic succession. Yeats, the living poet Pound most wanted to impress, is positioned at the helm, and then other admired masters are evoked in his train. First, there is a series of Browningesque dramatic monologues that attempt to convey the vitality of the literatures of medieval Europe—presenting, for instance, Cino, the womanizing exile, travelling on the open road, Bertran de Born, the troubadour, and his erotic song of unrequited love, or Villon carousing as he awaits the gallows after a brawl. They are rich with allusions and attempts to convey their command of metre and rhyme, but also riddled with archaic diction and nods to the torpid poetry of the 1890s. Later, Pound turns to answer Browning in his own voice in 'Mesmerism' and the tone suddenly changes. 'Mesmerism' is striking for the transition Pound has achieved from the poor pastiche of 'In Praise of the Masters' to what W. L. Courtney described in an unsigned review for the *Daily Telegraph* as 'a triumphant piece of parody', and merits quoting in full:[56]

---

[53] 'Note Precedent to "La Fraisne"', *CEP* 8.
[54] 'La Fraisne', *CEP* 9–10.
[55] Unsigned review, 'Heresy and Some Poetry', *Nation* V (28 August 1909), 789–91, in Eric Homberger, ed., *Ezra Pound: The Critical Heritage* (London: Routledge, 1972), 56.
[56] W. L. Courtney, '*A Lume Spento* by Ezra Pound', rev., *Daily Telegraph* (23 April 1909), 6, in Homberger, *Ezra Pound*, 45.

PASTICHERIE 59

Mesmerism

"And a cat's in the water-butt"

Robt. Browning, *"Mesmerism"*

Aye you're a man that! ye old mesmerizer
Tyin' your meanin' in seventy swadelin's,
One must of needs be a hang'd early riser
To catch you at worm turning. Holy Odd's bodykins!

"Cat's i' the water butt!" Thought's in your verse-barrel,
Tell us this thing rather, then we'll believe you,
You, Master Bob-Browning, spite your apparel
Jump to your sense and give praise as we'd lief do.

You wheeze as a head-cold long-tonsilled Calliope,
But God! what a sight you ha' got o' our innards,
Mad as a hatter but surely no Myope,
Broad as all ocean and leanin' man-kin'ards.

Heart that was big as the bowels of Vesuvius,
Words that were wing'd as her sparks in eruption,
Eagled and thundered as Jupiter Pluvius,

Sound in your wind past all signs o' corruption.
Here's to you, Old Hippety-hop o'the accents,
True to the Truth's sake and crafty dissector,
You grabbed at the gold sure; had no need to pack cents
Into your versicles.
Clear sight's elector![57]

Humphrey Carpenter rightly identified this poem to be 'the most skilful thing he [Pound] had written so far'.[58] Pound appropriates 'A cat's in the water-butt', a slight line of verse contrived to rhyme with 'shut' and 'smut' from Browning's poem of the same name, for a comic epigraph, pretending that the quotation is weighty enough to stand citation. The poem does not take after the form or style of Browning's original, it merely takes his title as an analogy for his mesmeric ability to summon an individual's shape and soul, a quality that holds Pound spellbound to the point of influence. Instead, Pound affectionately parodies the over-familiar, pithy spoken style of Browning's dramatic monologues to toast 'Old Hippety-hop o'the accents', his master in rhythm and accented speech, teasing him with audacious rhymes, while expressing a preference for his hard-talking protagonists over his slighter

---

[57] 'Mesmerism', *CEP* 17–8.
[58] Humphrey Carpenter, *A Serious Character: The Life of Ezra Pound* (London: Faber & Faber, 1988), 67.

60   MODERNIST PARODY

lyrics. 'Mesmerism' thus provides the first published instance of Pound success-fully taking on Browning's mannerisms: tricks he would finally master, complicate, and dissipate as he moved beyond the narratorial of guise of Browning's *Sordello* as he wrote and rewrote the first three *Cantos*.[59] The purgative value of the exercise is clear from the following poem, 'Fifine Answers', in which Pound offers a confident and creative reply to the question 'Why is it that, disgraced, they seem to relish life the more?', posed to a carnival dancer in Browning's 'Fifine at the Fair' (1872), with a monologue that has little in common with the theme of Browning's poem.[60] But the desacralizing gesture is not enough on its own, and Pound quickly returns to sing of speculative songs and harmonies in a mannered and archaic diction.

Now and then, through the course of *A Lume Spento*, Pound paused to answer, but by no means better, other nineteenth-century poets who were close to his heart with ripostes that lacked the satirical grip on their raw materials that he achieved in his parody of Browning. For instance, 'Donzella Beata' responds to Dante Gabriel Rossetti's most famous poem 'The Blessed Damozel', which depicts a maiden who observes her love from heaven and yearns for reunion, inspired by the situation of Dante's Beatrice.[61] In 'Donzella Beata' Pound reproduces the colour palette of Rossetti's poem and subsequent painting, but reverses the premise, so that the speaker chides his damsel for pining after him:

> Soul,
> Caught in the rose-hued mesh
> Of o'er fair earthly flesh,
> Stooped you this thing to bear
> Again for me? And be
> Rare light to me, gold-white
> In the shadowy path I tread?
>
> Surely a bolder maid art thou
> Than one in tearful, fearful longing
> That should wait
> Lily-cinctured at the gate
> Of high heaven, Star-diadem'd,
> Crying that I should come to thee.[62]

---

[59] For early cantos see Ezra Pound, *A Draft of XVI Cantos of Ezra Pound* (Paris: Three Mountains Press, 1925). For commentary on successive revisions as Pound gradually moved beyond Browning's *Sordello*, see Ronald Bush, *The Genesis of Ezra Pound's Cantos* (Princeton, NJ: Princeton University Press, 1976).

[60] 'Fifine Answers', *CEP* 18–9; Robert Browning, 'Fifine at the Fair', *Fifine at the Fair, and Other Poems* (Boston: James R. Osgood & Co., 1872), 10.

[61] 'Donzella Beata', *CEP* 26–7; Dante Gabriel Rossetti's poem 'The Blessed Damozel' was first published in the *Germ* in 1850; Rossetti's painting of the same name (1875–8) bears the first four stanzas of the text of the Tauchnitz 1873 edition of the poem on the frame. Dante Gabriel Rossetti, 'The Blessed Damozel', *Poems by Dante Gabriel Rossetti* (Leipzig: Bernhard Tauchnitz, 1873), 1–7.

[62] 'Donzella Beata', *CEP* 27.

PASTICHERIE 61

The poem pays Rossetti the compliment of imaginative engagement with his most important literary work without making any comment on his style. Instead, it expresses Pound's affection for Rossetti, and his sense of his own lineage, for it was Rossetti who mediated Pound's first contact with Villon, Dante, and Cavalcanti, whom he first read in Rossetti's translations. When Pound introduced his own versions of Cavalcanti's poetry in 1912, he acknowledged this debt, commented 'In the matter of these translations and of my knowledge of Tuscan poetry, Rossetti is my father and my mother'.[63] 'Donzella Beata' is very much the work of a derivate poet positioning himself as Rossetti's literary heir.

By contrast 'Salve O Pontifex!/To Swinburne; an hemichaunt' is intoxicated with admiration for its dedicatee.[64] The tribute takes the form of a mannered incantation to 'The High Priest of Iacchus', Iacchus being the ancient Greek deity that neophytes prayed to when they were initiated into the Eleusinian Mysteries (secret religious rites).[65] When Iacchus is presented as 'Wreathed with the glory of years of creating/Entangled music that men may not/Over readily understand', it is clear that Swinburne himself is the supreme priest to whom Pound prays 'Breathe thou upon us!' in the hope that his example might inspire his generation of poets.[66] The poem expresses Pound's fervent wish that he might be initiated into the sacred mysteries of Swinburne's art and discover the source of his imaginative power just as Swinburne himself had found in the myths of ancient Greece and the works of past masters.

At his height, Swinburne, like Rossetti and Browning, had achieved Pound's own aim, being his most characteristic in the guise of his forebears. As Pound reflected in 'How to Read' (1929), 'Swinburne's Villon is not Villon very exactly, but it is perhaps the best Swinburne we have'.[67] But in 'Swinburne versus His Biographers', a review of Edmund Gosse's *The Life of Algernon Charles Swinburne* (1917), Pound also recognized that Swinburne struggled to sustain his momentum: 'He habitually makes a fine stanzaic form, writes one or two fine strophes in it, and then continues to pour into the mould strophes of diminishing quality'.[68] As Pound perceived, Swinburne 'neglected the value of words as words, and was intent on their value as sound. His habit of choice grew mechanical, and he himself perceived it and parodied his own systematization'.[69] While Swinburne's self-parody, 'Nephelidia', deliberately overdid his characteristic style with unrestrained alliteration and prosodic intricacy to produce a splendidly amphigoric verse that teetered on the brink of meaningfulness, Pound recognized that this

---

[63] Ezra Pound, *Sonnets and Ballate of Guido Cavalcanti, with Translation of them and an Introduction by Ezra Pound* (London: Stephen Swift & Co., 1912), 6.
[64] 'Salve O Pontifex!/To Swinburne; an hemichaunt', *CEP* 40–3. For an extensive discussion of Swinburne's influence on Pound, see de Nagi, *The Poetry of Ezra Pound*, 68–80.
[65] 'Salve O Pontifex!', *CEP* 40.
[66] 'Salve O Pontifex!', *CEP* 42, 43.
[67] 'How to Read', *LE* 36.
[68] 'Swinburne versus His Biographers', *LE* 292.
[69] 'Swinburne versus His Biographers', *LE* 292.

62 MODERNIST PARODY

technique did not initiate new departures for Swinburne's art, which had become cut off from relevance just like the man himself in his later years, kept from harm under virtual house arrest by the ever-watchful Theodor Watts-Dunton. 'Salve O Pontifex' completely lacks any such critical awareness but strikes an attitude of reverence that is positively servile. Pound republished the poem several times on account of being excited by its metrical freedoms, but by 1917 he had gained sufficient critical distance from it to realize its faults and insisted that the following note be appended to 'Salve O Pontifex' in the American edition of *Lustra*: 'Balderdash but let it stay for the rhythm'.[70] Slavish expressions of admiration would not secure Pound's place in the apostolic succession, nor would mannered diction. John Quinn, lawyer and patron of the arts, sensed the particular vice of 'Salve O Pontifex!' was *faux* archaism. Pound agreed in a letter of 4 October 1917, 'you are quite right about the "thrice", I would damn also "encinctured", plus the "hasts" etc. etc'.[71] And rightly it made the mature Pound cringe: 'The "Salve Pontifex" poem is SO bad', he reflected, 'In short it is a case of reform it altogether. That ass Maurice Hewlett thought it the best poem in *Ripostes*.'[72]

Many of the poems of *A Lume Spento* ache with Pound's own longing for that moment he describes in 'Scriptor Ignotus':

> ... when
> That great sense of power is upon me
> And I see my great soul-self bending
> Sibylwise with that great forty-year epic
> That you know of, yet unwrit.[73]

But is clear that Pound's prophetic intuition of the achievement of the *Cantos* could not come to pass without first shaking off his idols or the torpor of the 1890s. Towards the end of *A Lume Spento*, Pound mocks the self-pitying expostulations of dissolute poets who are aimless and weary, yet nonetheless swear their devotion to art in 'The Decadence':

> Tarnished we! Tarnished! Wastrels all!
> And yet the art goes on, goes on.
> Broken our strength, yea as crushed reeds we fall,
> And yet the art, the *art* goes on.[74]

---

[70] See King's notes to *CEP* 297.

[71] Timothy Materer, ed., *The Selected Letters of Ezra Pound to John Quinn, 1915–1924* (Durham, NC: Duke University Press, 1991), 131.

[72] Materer, *Selected Letters of Ezra Pound to John Quinn*, 131, Pound's capitals. Hewlett was known for romanticized historical fiction and poetry such as *The Forest Lovers: A Romance* (1898) and *The Song of the Plow: Being the English Chronicle* (1916). His approval only confirmed how crassly outmoded 'Salve O Pontifex!' was.

[73] 'Scriptor Ignotus', *CEP* 24–5. Pound includes a note at the end of the poem identifying the speaker: 'Bertold Lomax, English Dante scholar and mystic, died in Ferrara 1723, with his "great epic", still a mere shadow, a nebula crossed with some few gleams of wonder light', *CEP* 26.

[74] 'The Decadence', *CEP* 44, Pound's italics.

PASTICHERIE   63

But Pound goes on in their vein all the same. For instance, 'In Tempore Senectutis (*An Anti-stave for Dowson*)' responds to Ernest Dowson's poem of the same name in Dowson's voice. It replies to Dowson's speaker's expressed wish that his love remembers him as a young man 'When I am old' with a monologue in Dowson's voice in which the speaker instead affirms the sweetness of the 'love I bear to thee when I am old'.[75]

The title *A Lume Spento* [with tapers quenched] alludes to Dante's description of the funeral rites of a heretic son of a holy Roman emperor in Canto III of *Purgatorio*, in memory of William Brooke Smith, who first introduced Pound to the English decadents, before dying of consumption. In this sense, the volume could also be seen as an attempted funerary procession for the dimming light of the 1890s and its quaint archaisms, the lure of which Pound could not quite bring himself to resist parading, even though he knew its time had passed. His quaint copy work was equivocal: not purgative, but purgatorial, a means to avoid evaluating his own writing critically. The only answer he had found to the question of where poetry must go after the heights of Browning, Rossetti, and Swinburne, if it was to avoid dead-end decadence, was parody, and that technique was not easily reconciled with ecstasy, or beauty, or permanence, or the collection's wistful motto 'Make-strong old dreams lest this our world lose heart'.[76]

Undeterred, Pound continued his exercises in quaintness in *A Quinzaine for this Yule* (1908), which he prefaced with a statement on the role of marvel and wonder in the perception of beauty, signed Weston St. Llewmys.[77] The urge to modernize remained, but the necessary technical breakthroughs had not yet come fully into focus. 'Revolt: Against the Crepuscular Spirit in Modern Poetry', first published in *Personae* (1909), augured no such revolution. Pound begins strongly, declaring 'I would shake off the lethargy of this our time', but the limp imitation of 1890s poetic diction that follows fails to convince.[78] The compulsion to clothe himself in the mantle of admired masters' styles continued unabated in *Personae* and *Exultations* (1911). Indeed, more than half of the poems in *Personae* had already appeared in *A Lume Spento*. Pound would later reflect in 'Vorticism' (1914, reprinted in *Gaudier-Brzeska: A Memoir* 1916):

I began this search for the real in a book called *Personae*, casting off, as it were, complete masks of the self in each poem. I continued in a long series of translations, which were but more elaborate masks.[79]

---

[75] Ernest Dowson, 'In Tempore Senectutis', *The Poems of Ernest Dowson, with a Memoir by Arthur Symons, Four Illustrations by Aubrey Beardsley and a Portrait by William Rothenstein* (London and New York: John Lane/Bodley Head, 1905), 50–1; 'In Tempore Senectutis (*An Anti-stave for Dowson*)', *CEP* 50.

[76] *A Lume Spento, CEP* 52. The motto that appears at the end of *A Lume Spento* also serves as an epigraph in *Personae* (1909) (*CEP* 77).

[77] Pound, *A Quinzaine for this Yule*, 6.

[78] Ezra Pound, *Personae* (London: Elkin Mathews, 1909), 53.

[79] Ezra Pound, *Gaudier-Brzeska: A Memoir* (London: John Lane/Bodley Head; New York: John Lane Company, 1916), 98.

64   MODERNIST PARODY

For a time, this search resulted in having almost no authentic voice of his own at all. One early poem that showed promise of the mature work to come was 'Sestina: Altaforte', which Eliot judged to be 'A complete success in a most difficult form' with 'no false antiquity . . . in either word or phrase'.[80] It was, however, another false start. Hoping to capitalize on the success of 'Altaforte', which had caused a stir at one of T. E. Hulme's Thursday evening sessions at the Tour Eiffel restaurant, Pound wrote another vigorous poem in the idiomatic vein, the blasphemous 'Ballad of the Goodly Fere', spoken by Simon Zealotes after the Crucifixion, which, as Carpenter pointed out, is so full of unnecessary archaism that merely reads like 'a pastiche of the Chesterton or even Newbolt-Masefield manner'.[81]

To convey the full vigour and dynamism of the literatures of his illustrious fore-bears, Pound would have to extricate himself from uncritical admiration of the Pre-Raphaelite-led cult of medieval revivalism, overblown imitations of Browning's voice, the spell of Swinburne's 'pure' art, and the melancholy languor of the decadents that he found so irresistibly attractive, and discover his own source of vitalizing imaginative power. Only then could he begin to work alongside his masters and derive energy from the spirit of their greatness by arranging what was enduring in them around his own vision. That power would be derived from evaluative parody, which gave Pound the advantages discussed in 'Further Tests for the Pupil' by showing him where his own virtue as an imitator lay. It would not be until *Canzoni* (1911), a self-conscious attempt to 'master all known forms and systems of metric', that Pound would begin to see the necessary reforms clearly, though he ultimately withdrew from publication the self-directed satire that fingered what was false. Like Pound's previous volumes of poetry, *Canzoni* is a series of exercises parading historical modes, styles, and personalities, including Cavalcanti, Dante, Pico della Mirandola, Sextus Propertius, and Joachim du Bellay. As Pound explained to Dorothy Shakespear in a letter of 16 July 1911, *Canzoni* was conceived as 'a sort of chronological table of emotions: Provence; Tuscany, the Renaissance, the XVIII, the XIX, centuries, external modernity (cut out) subjective modernity. finis' and it was arranged in such a way that the progress of poetry also signalled Pound's own progress as an imitative talent who aspired to the production of original, modern verse.[82]

As David Moody has noted, the emotion Pound 'was primarily concerned to purge and purify was of course love', which, 'in Pound's mind at least, had its origins in the rites of Persephone at Eleusis; attained an ultimate realization in the work of Dante and Cavalcanti; enjoyed a kind of afterlife in the Renaissance; and

---

[80] T. S. Eliot's draft notes for Ezra Pound, *Selected Poems*, intro. T. S. Eliot (London: Faber & Gwyer, 1928), quoted in Carpenter, *Serious Character*, 109.

[81] Carpenter, *Serious Character*, 118.

[82] Pound and Litz, eds., *Ezra Pound and Dorothy Shakespear: Their Letters 1910–1914*, 37–8; 'external modernity (cut out)' refers to Pound's decision to cut 'Redondillas, or Something of that Sort' at proof stage.

PASTICHERIE 65

lapsed into decay in the modern era.[83] The first poem in the collection, 'Canzon: The Yearly Slain (written in reply to Frederic Manning's "Korè")', stood outside this chronological design, save for its Dantean epigraph.[84] Pound considered Manning, then a close friend, to be 'seriously concerned with overhauling the metric, in testing the language and its adaptability to certain modes', and Pound's decision to answer Manning's 'Kore' indicated his intention to engage with these concerns, although interestingly it did not prevent him from replying in even more stilted language.[85]

The forward movement of *Canzoni* propelled Pound towards a new reckoning of modern style. It is structured as a record of Pound's reluctant awakening to his predicament: that exulted pastiche was inimical to modernity. When he synthesized nineteenth-century verse, Pound produced 'Her Monument, the Image Cut thereon/From the Italian of Leopardi' (which, like its title, is rife with inversion), three dreary 'Victorian Eclogues', and 'A Prologue' for a nativity play that exemplified the worst Elizabethanizing excesses of dramatic poetry as is evident from the concluding speech:[86]

Diana in Ephesus

(Lucina dolentibus:)
    "Behold the deed! Behold the act supreme!
    With mine own hands have I prepared my doom,
    Truth shall grow great eclipsing other truth,
    And men forget me in the aging years."

Explicit.[87]

This neoclassical nonsense is the very kind of verse that Nietzsche objected to and that Beerbohm parodied in his short story 'Savonarola Brown', in which he satirized the late nineteenth-/early twentieth-century fashion for fustian plays.[88] However, when Pound let go of fashionable pastiche and finally attempted to tap into the spirit of modernity, he modernized his voice in a poem called 'Aria':

    My love is a deep flame
        that hides beneath the waters.

---

[83] David Moody, *Ezra Pound: Poet; A Portrait of the Man & His Work, Volume 1: The Young Genius 1885–1920* (Oxford: Oxford University Press, 2007), 135–6.

[84] 'Canzon', *C* 1–3. Frederic Manning, 'Kore', *Poems* (London: John Murray, 1910), 38–9. 'Kore' does not have an accent in this edition.

[85] 'A Retrospect', *LE* 12.

[86] 'Her Monument', *C* 28–9; 'Victorian Eclogues', *C* 30–3, 'A Prologue', *C* 34–6.

[87] 'A Prologue', *C* 36.

[88] See Friedrich Nietzsche, *Beyond Good and Evil: Prelude to a Philosophy of the Future*, ed. and trans. Walter Kaufmann (New York: Vintage, 1989), 342, §224; Max Beerbohm, 'Savonarola Brown', *Seven Men* (London: William Heinemann, 1919), 185–215.

66 MODERNIST PARODY

> —My love is gay and kind,
> My love is hard to find
> > as the flame beneath the waters.
>
> The fingers of the wind
> > > meet hers
>
> With a frail
> > swift greeting.
>
> My love is gay
> > and kind
> > > and hard
> > > > of meeting,
>
> As the flame beneath the waters
> > hard of meeting.[89]

'Aria' might only be a slight musical lyric, but in its simplicity, and its use of fractured lines, free verse, and disjunctive correlatives for emotional complexes, it anticipates Imagist poetics.

After 'Aria' the tone of *Canzoni* changes decisively. Exultation and lyricism give way to greater informality, irony, and parody as Pound stages his attempts to reconcile his idolization of the medieval sublime with contemporary literary culture. The turn is even more marked in the text of *Canzoni* as it was conceived at proof stage, before Pound 'was affected by hyper-aesthesia or over-squeamishness and cut out the rougher poems' (that dealt with 'external modernity').[90] 'L'Art' (what was kept from 'Leviora', a longer sequence) uses the sonnet form to make the satirical point that all writing is ultimately formulaic, either a 'second stew' or a 'brew' in which ingredients ferment:

> When brightest colours seem but dull in hue
> And noblest arts are shown mechanical,
> When study serves but to heap clue on clue
> That no great line hath been or ever shall,
> But hath a savour like some second stew
> Of many pot-lots with a smack of all.
> 'Twas one man's field, another's hops the brew,
> 'Twas vagrant accident not fate's fore-call.
> Horace, that thing of thine is overhauled,
> And "Wood notes wild" weaves a concocted sonnet.
> Here aery Shelley on the text hath called,

---

[89] 'Aria', *C* 37.

[90] Ezra Pound to Elkin Mathews, 30 May 1916, Forrest Read, ed., *Pound/Joyce: The Letters of Ezra Pound to James Joyce, with Pound's Essays on Joyce* (New York: New Directions, 1967), 285.

And here Great Scott, the Murex, Keats comes on it.
And all the lot howl, "Sweet Simplicity!"
'Tis Art to hide our theft exquisitely.[91]

The punchline draws attention to the way Pound uses the very practices the poem satirizes, making a game of concocting his own verse from oblique references. Pound quotes from Milton's widely imitated and highly allusive pastoral poem *L'Allegro* (which is itself in the lyric mode of Horace), wherein Shakespeare is conceived as a poet who took inspiration from nature, warbling 'his native Wood-notes wilde'.[92] From this 'second stew' comes the work of Keats and Shelley, who are accused of rank imitation for absorbing these traditions but concealing the lineage.

'L'Art' is followed by 'Song in the Manner of Housman', a deliberately glib parody of A. E. Housman's pastoral poem 'A Shropshire Lad' (1896), which mocks his bleak ballads with Byronic pararhyme ('pleasanter'/'*etcetera*'), blasé statement, and wearily simulated sentiment:

> O WOE, woe,
> People are born and die,
> We also shall be dead pretty soon
> Therefore let us act as if we were
> > dead already.
>
> The bird sits on the hawthorn tree
> But he dies also, presently.
> Some lads get hung, and some get shot.
> Woeful is this human lot.
> > *Woe! woe, etcetera....*
>
> London is a woeful place,
> Shropshire is much pleasanter.
> Then let us smile a little space
> Upon fond nature's morbid grace.
> > *Oh, Woe, woe, woe, etcetera....*[93]

In his review of *Canzoni*, Squire complained that the 'heavy incrustations of verbiage are very tiring', but found Pound's parody much to his liking:

---

[91] 'L'Art', *C* 37.

[92] John Milton, 'L'Allegro', in Roy Flannagan, ed., *The Riverside Milton* (New York: Houghton Mifflin, 1998), 70.

[93] 'Song in the Manner of Housman', *C* 38, Pound's capitals and italics.

68 MODERNIST PARODY

> Even those of us who carry about our copies of 'A Shropshire Lad' with our pipes and bunches of keys, must confess that the following lines of Mr. Pound's get home on Mr. A. E. Housman's matter if not on his manner.[94]

Squire missed Pound's true target: the contemporary culture that overvalued emotional, smugly parochial writing. Pound's parody of Housman was to have been preceded by 'To Hulme (T. E.) and Fitzgerald (A Certain)', written as a comic complaint on Pound's lack of income from poetry for the amusement of the Poets' Club, but pulled at proof stage. The poem parodies Robert Burns's ballad 'Is There for Honest Poverty' (commonly known as 'A Man's a Man for a' That'), making laughing reference to Pound's own 'Aesthetic phrases by the yard', which ruined his earlier verse, joking 'It's but E. P. for a' that/For a' that and a' that'.[95] These parodies, though they were facile, provided a sardonic means for Pound to focus attention on what was inherently ridiculous about modern literary culture, its dominant modes of writing, and his own style and approach.

The questionable propriety of parody only added to its appeal. To cock a snook at serious work or to use it as a pretext to be plain silly showed a pleasing lack of reverence for original writing. However, Pound's last-minute decision to the pull the poems at proof stage registers a degree of anxiety about whether the effect of the parodies would be cheapening if they were placed in proximity to 'serious' poems. The publisher Elkin Mathews expressed similar concerns after he got an expanded version of Pound's *Lustra* set up in type and then 'got a panic and marked 25 poems for deletion'.[96] Mathews's unnamed reader had denounced 'Ancient Music' (a hearty satire on miserable English weather to the tune of 'Sumer is icumen in', beginning 'Winter is icummen in/Lhude sing Goddamn') as a 'Pitiful Parody of beautiful verse'.[97] And Mathews himself had also condemned 'Ancient Music' with the note, strengthened by revision, 'Blasted blasphemy & a damned parody } ~~delete~~ must be omitted'.[98] While he had stomached the gentler subversions of the 1890s, to Mathews's mind this kind of parody was irredeemably inane and potentially obscene. But while the suppression or omission of parodic material from book editions might give the impression that parody was beneath the dignity of modernism's wider experiment, spirited parody

---

[94] J. C. Squire, 'Canzoni by Ezra Pound', rev., New Age X(8) (21 December 1911), 183–4, in Homberger, Ezra Pound, 84.

[95] Ezra Pound, 'To Hulme (T. E.) and Fitzgerald (A Certain)', CEP 215; Robert Burns, 'Is There for Honest Poverty', in James Kinsley, ed., Poems and Songs of Robert Burns, vol. 2 (Oxford: Clarendon Press, 1968), 762–3.

[96] LEP 130.

[97] Ezra Pound, Lustra (New York: Knopf, 1917), 61; a postcard from Elkin Mathew's reader, in Homberger, Ezra Pound, 122.

[98] Elkin Mathews's proposed emendations and deletions for Lustra, in Homberger, Ezra Pound, 124.

would ultimately prove central to the formation and advancement of the modern movement.

Even as Pound contemplated the external conditions of modernity in *Canzoni*, he could not quite bring himself to forsake the traditions that nourished him. In the roughest excised poem 'Redondillas, or Something of that Sort', a Whitmanesque catalogue of the kinds of poetry he would sing (loosely based on *Leaves of Grass* (1855–92)), Pound set out and satirized his credo, stating his own literary preferences in an age he considered both gaudy and effete:

> They tell me to "Mirror my age,"
>> God pity the age if I do do it,
> Perhaps I myself would prefer
>> to sing of the dead and the buried.[99]

The final lines of the poem complete the peevish self-caricature of a poet who has effectively consigned himself to irrelevance, asking readers to behold in him 'London's last foible in poets', one who is 'sententious' and '*dégagé*', who loves 'all delicate sounds', 'quaint patterns interwoven', and 'passionate moods of singing'.[100]

'Translations from Heine' (from *Die Heimkehr* [The Homecoming]), which followed 'Song in the Manner of Housman' in the final text of *Canzoni*, marked a further significant departure from the foregoing medieval stew. Heine's urbane, cosmopolitan lyrics of unrequited love—noted by Bakhtin and others for their irony, humour, and elements of self-parody—stirred Pound to find a convincingly cultivated contemporary voice that combined the rhythms of laconic speech with the arch inflection of satire. When Pound slipped a pedantic Latinate word into the following precisely phrased yet casual quatrain, he communicated the lady's insouciance in the face of Heine's amorous attentions with a feeling for the wry effects that could be achieved through conscious stylization rather than mere imitation or literal translation:

> This delightful young man
> Should not lack for honourers,

---

[99] 'Redondillas, or Something of that Sort', *CEP* 218. Pound makes heavy use of first-person Whitmanian formulae such as 'I sing . . .', 'I would sing . . .', and 'I believe . . .' in 'Redondillas' but signals his distance from Whitman's Americanism with the lines such as:

> I would sing the American people,
>> God send them some civilization.

>>>>>>>>>>>>>> (*CEP*, 216)

See Walt Whitman, *Leaves of Grass* (London: G. P. Putnam's Sons; Boston: Small Maynard & Co., 1897).

[100] 'Redondillas', *CEP* 221–2.

70 MODERNIST PARODY

> He *propitiates* me with oysters,
> With Rhine wine and liqueurs.[101]

Having laughed at second-hand romanticizing, decadent despair, and his own aestheticist tendencies, eventually finding a viable contemporary voice in the guise of Heine, Pound concludes the collection with 'Und Drang', a poem in twelve parts that takes up the positions articulated in the foregoing poems and sets them in unresolved opposition.[102] He expresses his weariness with attempts to find meaning in life and his frustrations with a contemporary culture that bygone traditions no longer sustain, regretting:

> How our modernity,
> Nerve-wracked and broken, turns
> Against time's way and all the way of things
> Crying with weak and egoistic cries![103]

He lacks confidence in the 'restless will' that 'Surges amid the stars/Seeking new moods of life,/New permutations', uncertain that a celestial perspective of that kind could counter his anxiety that 'the very sense of what we know/Dodges and hides as in a sombre curtain/Bright threads leap forth, and hide, and leave no pattern'.[104] Fruitlessly seeking the face of a lady love in the 'flurry of Fifth Avenue', he turns to imagine her amid 'The House of Splendour', bathed in aureate light, in an opulent pastiche of Rossetti and his gilded Pre-Raphaelite portraits:

> And I have seen my Lady in the sun,
> Her hair was spread about, a sheaf of wings,
> And red the sunlight was, behind it all.
> And I have seen her there within her house,
> With six great sapphires hung along the wall,
> Low, panel-shaped, a-level with her knees,
> And all her robe was woven of pale gold.[105]

While Pound acknowledges 'there are powers in this/Which, played on by the virtues of her soul,/Break down the four-square walls of standing time', the

---

[101] 'Translations from Heine', *C* 41, my italics. See:

> Diesen liebenswürd'gen Jüngling
> Kann man nicht genug verehren;
> Oft traktirt er mich mit Austern,
> Und mit Rheinwein und Liquören,

Heinrich Heine, *Buch der Lieder* (Hamburg: Hoffmann und Campe, 1847), 229.

[102] 'Und Drang', *C* 43–52. The title refers to the German phrase 'Sturm und Drang' [Storm and Stress]).

[103] 'Und Drang', *C* 46.

[104] 'Und Drang', *C* 46.

[105] 'Und Drang', *C* 47.

unreality of her image is palpable.[106] The sequence ends with a comic reworking of the clichéd traditions of courtly love. A lady, irritated by the unromantic address 'O you away high there', twice quotes '"The jester walked in the garden"', the first line of Yeats's poem 'The Cap and Bells' (1894), in which a jester dies for love when he bids his heart, soul, and hat, to go to a lady.[107] The quotation is twice answered with the nonchalant response 'Did he so?'[108] Pound's speaker steps away from the idealized lady as a source of poetic inspiration, and departs from the clichéd attitude of the lovelorn poet who would woo with songs, but does so in a casual voice that lacks the verve or polish of his translation of Heine. 'Did he so?' ends the collection on an uncertain note: how could Pound's songs project modernity when he was at his most characteristic in the costume of the past?

Pound gave Ford Madox Ford (then Hueffer) a copy of *Canzoni* when holidaying in Giessen, keen to impress one whose mind had been enriched by contact with Victorian and Pre-Raphaelite men of genius and retained the effects of it.[109] Instead, Ford showed his contempt for Pound's poetry by rolling around on the floor in mock agony, in a performance that stayed with Pound for years to come:

And he felt the errors of contemporary style to the point of rolling (physically, and if you look at it as mere superficial snob, ridiculously) on the floor of his temporary quarters at Giessen when my third volume displayed me trapped, fly-papered, gummed and strapped down in a jejune provincial effort to learn, *mehercule*, the stilted language that then passed for 'good English' in the arthritic milieu that held control of the respected British critical circles, Newbolt, the backwash of Lionel Johnson, Fred Manning, the Quarterlies and the rest of 'em.[110]

Ford articulated his position more fully in the introduction to his *Collected Poems* (1916), in terms that would have held particular sway with Pound:

I have kept before me my one unflinching aim—to register my own times in terms of my own time, and still more to urge those who are better poets and better prose-writers than myself to have the same aim ... I would rather read a picture in verse of the emotions and environment of a Goodge Street anarchist than recapture what songs the sirens sang. That after all was what François Villon was doing for the life of his day, and I should feel that our day was doing its duty by posterity much more surely if it was doing something of that sort.[111]

---

[106] 'Und Drang', *C* 48.

[107] 'Und Drang', *C* 51–2; W. B. Yeats, 'The Cap and Bells', *The Wind Among the Reeds* (New York: John Lane/Bodley Head, 1899, 32).

[108] 'Und Drang', *C* 51–2.

[109] See 'How I Began', *T.P.'s Weekly* (6 June 1913), 707.

[110] Ezra Pound's obituary for Ford Madox Ford in *Nineteenth Century and After* CXXVI (August 1939), 178–81 in *Ford Madox Ford: The Critical Heritage*, ed. Frank MacShane (London and New York: Routledge, 1972), 216.

[111] Ford Madox Hueffer, *Collected Poems* (London: Max Goschen, 1916), 13–19.

72 MODERNIST PARODY

Ford was exasperated by Tennyson, William Morris, and especially the 'poets of the Nineties—Dowson, Johnson, Davidson and the rest—[who] struck us as just nuisances, writing in derivative language uninteresting matters', lamenting the second-handedness that prevented them from registering their own times in terms of their own time.[112] And he expressed the same exasperation with the copy work in *Canzoni*, in which Pound had imbibed the derivative attitude of Pre-Raphaelite and decadent verse. Ford put the case to Pound in the parodically entitled 'Canzone a la Sonata (To E. P.)', which is written in the idiom of contemporary speech. He asked Pound 'What's left behind us for a heritage/For our children?' if the poetry of the early twentieth century fails to respond to its age.[113] Time's galloping progress, Ford argued, could not be overcome by Pound's complacent recreation of bygone ages.[114] Ford was not advocating that poets should jettison their literary heritage, but that they should go beyond the acquisition of 'imitative faculties' in order to find their own contemporary voice.[115] He commended those poets who 'record their emotions at receiving the experience of the emotions of former writers. It is an attitude critical rather than imitative, and to the measure of its truth it is the truer poetic attitude.'[116] Rightly, then, Ford objected to uncritical pastiche, written without an eye to the present.

Far from exalting his masters, Pound came to realize that he had to date only mastered what he would later call the language of 'the common verse of Britain from 1890 to 1910', which consisted of 'a horrible agglomerate compost, not minted, most of it not even baked, all legato, a doughy mess of third-hand Keats, Wordsworth, heaven knows what, fourth-hand Elizabethan sonority blunted, half melted, lumpy'.[117] Ford's mockery finally convinced Pound that his poems were a mere pastiche and that the five-finger exercises he practised in *Canzoni* could only be the start of a larger campaign to respond to the past as it bears on the present. Accordingly, Pound repudiated his earliest poems and translations when he reissued them as *A Lume Spento and Other Early Poems* (1965) with the epigraph 'A collection of stale creampuffs. "Chocolate creams, who hath forgotten you?"'[118] The mock-grave quotation parodies the refrain '*Who hath forgotten you?*'

---

[112] Hueffer, *Poems*, 23. Of course, all these poets thought they were doing their best to do what Ford described. And some were quite successful. Eliot particularly admired Davidson's 'Thirty Bob a Week', where he felt that Davidson had succeeded in freeing 'himself completely from the poetic diction of English verse of his time'. See Eliot's preface to John Davidson, *John Davidson: A Selection of His Poems*, ed. Maurice Lindsay (London: Hutchinson, 1961), xi.

[113] Hueffer, *Poems*, 59.

[114] In fact, 'Ford had been hammering this point of view into me from the time I first met him (1908 or 1909)', Pound recalled, but it was only when he rolled around on the floor in mock agony that Pound finally took notice. See Harriet Monroe, *A Poet's Life: Seventy Years in a Changing World* (New York: Macmillan, 1938), 267, n. 2.

[115] Hueffer, *Poems*, 27.

[116] Hueffer, *Poems*, 27.

[117] 'Hell', *LE* 205.

[118] Ezra Pound, Foreword, *A Lume Spento, and Other Early Poems* (New York: New Directions, 1965), 7.

PASTICHERIE 73

from '*Piccadilly*', a sombre lyric from *Personae* (1909) on the rush of people going about their business in London's bustling Piccadilly Circus.[119] '*Piccadilly*' stands out because it is the last poem in *Personae* (1909) and it is set in italics throughout. The mismatch between that poem's archaic manner and its modern, urban subject is unintentionally comic. The line '*And O ye vile, ye that might have been loved*' is itself a parodic echo of '*Ô toi que j'eusse aimée, ô toi qui le savais!*' [Oh you whom I would have loved, oh you who knew it], the final line of Baudelaire's '*À une passante*' [To a Passerby], a much more skilful poem.[120] The full force of the cream-puff metaphor becomes clear in light of the critical brochure Pound commissioned Eliot to write, *Ezra Pound: His Metric and Poetry* (1917). When Eliot first encountered Pound's early poetry, he was not particularly impressed and considered it to be 'rather fancy old-fashioned romantic stuff, cloak and dagger stuff'.[121] However, he dutifully promoted Pound's evocations of the old Provençal, Spanish, and Italian traditions in *Personae* and *Exultations*, contrasting them with Tennyson's *Idylls of the King* (1859), which he dismissed as 'hardly more important than a parody' to those well acquainted with Arthurian legend.[122] Pound followed up Eliot's criticism in 'Swinburne versus His Biographers' (1918), where he accused Tennyson of writing 'verbal *patisserie*'.[123] Eliot's 1917 distinction between Tennyson's work and Pound's was kindly at best, which is why when Pound came to introduce *A Lume Spento* (1965) from the vantage point of masterful maturity he put his early poems on same footing as Tennyson's Arthurian patisserie, declaring them verbal *pasticherie*.

Earnest historical pageantry was to be replaced by orderly constellation, as Pound would explain in 'I Gather the Limbs of Osiris' (published serially in the *New Age* between November 1911 and February 1912):

> Having discovered his own virtue the artist will be more likely to discern and allow for a peculiar *virtù* in others. The erection of the microcosmos consists in discriminating these other powers and holding them in orderly arrangement about one's own.[124]

Contemporaneity was no longer to be something Pound progressed towards via solemn attempts to emulate his masters' innate greatness and follow in their train, but something he would endeavour to bring to their elemental materials,

---

[119] Pound, *Personae* (1909), 56.

[120] Pound, *Personae* (1909), 56; Charles Baudelaire, '*À une passante*', *Les fleurs du mal*, in *Œuvres complètes*, vol. 1, ed. Claude Pichois (Paris: Gallimard (Bibliothèque de la Plèia, 1975), 93.

[121] Donald Hall, interview with T. S. Eliot, 'The Art of Poetry, I: T. S. Eliot', *Paris Review* 21 (spring/summer, 1959), 52.

[122] T. S. Eliot, *Ezra Pound, His Metric and Poetry* (New York: Knopf, 1917), 9.

[123] 'Swinburne versus His Biographers', *LE* 290, Pound's italics.

[124] Ezra Pound, 'I Gather the Limbs of Osiris: VI', *New Age* X(10) (4 January 1912), 224.

74   MODERNIST PARODY

which he would assemble and transform by dint of his own virtue as a translator and prosodist who had striven to acquire techniques to convey the music of his originals—quantities, alliteration, polyphonic rhymes—as nearly as they might be reproduced in English and as an autonomous artist with the quick perceptive intelligence to seek out 'the luminous detail and present it'.[125] He introduced 'the luminous detail' with some fanfare as the new method for art: a means to designate those rare enlightening instances that say something fundamental about human psychology and metaphysics that is in tune with the spirit of its time but also enduringly relevant. The shift from pasticherie towards contemporaneity is registered in the translations Pound published within the essay. His rendition of 'The Seafarer' (1911) may contain risible schoolboy errors, but it is a remarkable exercise in melopoeia, conveying the vigour of Old English verse by finding modern English equivalents that preserve the music of the original.[126] His translations of Cavalcanti (which he selected from his soon-to-be-published book *The Sonnets and Ballate of Guido Cavalcanti* (1912)) and Arnaut Daniel are attempts to assert what is radiant and permanent in their work, but are also strategic statements of Pound's new credo. Cavalcanti's 'poetry is interesting, apart from its beauty, for his exact psychology, for an attempt to render emotion precisely': these virtues point to Pound's new commitment to accuracy of sentiment, which is necessary if poetry is to be a vital part of contemporary life rather than mere art.[127] Daniel has precision of observation and reference: his poetry is characterized as the work of 'a very real, very much alive young man who has kicked over the traces'.[128] Daniel's poetry shows 'the mediævalism of mediæval life as it was' and, accordingly, Pound's translations of four of his early poems are 'all free from' the 'Victorian mediævalism' of Morris and Rossetti, which Pound noted is very charming 'if you like it—I do more or less', but not true to life: 'Their mediævalism was that of the romances of North France, of magical ships, and the rest of it, of Avalons that were not'.[129] The new aim was to liberate emotion from florid Victorian cliché, to make art efficient and relevant to the contemporary world. Within the pages of 'Osiris' the germs of Imagism were being gathered: Pound was now looking for simplicity and directness, heightened and intensified with a dignity that separated it from everyday speech.

By his own admission, Pound only fully succeeded in sloughing off 'the crust of dead English' a few years later, the sediment present in Pound's own vocabulary, deposited by earlier authors—the language Keats made 'out of Elizabethans, Swinburne out of a larger set of Elizabethans and a mixed bag (Greeks, *und so weiter*), Rossetti out of Sheets, Kelly, and Co. plus early Italians (written and

---

[125] Ezra Pound, 'I Gather the Limbs of Osiris: II', *New Age* X(6) (7 December 1911), 130.

[126] Ezra Pound, 'I Gather the Limbs of Osiris: I. The Seafarer', *New Age* X(5) (30 November 1911), 107.

[127] Ezra Pound, 'I Gather the Limbs of Osiris: III. Five translations from "The Sonnets and Ballate of Guido Cavalcanti"', *New Age* X(7) (14 December 1911), 155.

[128] Ezra Pound, 'I Gather the Limbs of Osiris: V. Four Early Poems of Arnaut Daniel', *New Age*, X(9) (28 December 1911), 201.

[129] Ezra Pound, 'I Gather the Limbs of Osiris: V', 201.

PASTICHERIE   75

painted)'.[130] The translations of Cavalcanti that Pound selected for 'I Gather the Limbs of Osiris' from *Sonnets and Ballate* fell short because they were still 'bogged in Dante Gabriel and in Algernon'.[131] Pound would eventually realize that where he and Rossetti 'went off the rails was in taking an English sonnet as the equivalent for a sonnet in Italian', noting that the '*verbal* weight' of Italian, its natural recourse to feminine rhymes, has no unforced equivalent in English.[132] The exercises Pound set himself in 1934 to demonstrate 'What happens when you idly attempt to translate early Italian into English, unclogged by the Victorian era' show the level of control and precision he would ultimately bring to pastiche once he had disentangled historical affect from affected archaism.[133] As Pound said of Arthur Golding (1536–1605) in 'Notes on Elizabethan Classicists' (1915–16, a few years after 'Osiris'), 'his constant use of "did go", "did say", etc., is not fustian and mannerism; it was contemporary speech, though in a present day poet it is impotent affectation and definite lack of technique'.[134] In 'Cavalcanti' (1934) Pound started by taking a sonnet attributed to the thirteenth-century Italian master and playing with what he believed to be 'the simplest English equivalent', which he deemed 'very nice, but . . . hardly a translation' by lightening the sestet and the octet:[135]

> So unto Pity must I cry
> Not for safety, but to die.
> Cruel Death is now mine ease
> If that he thine envoy is.[136]

To Pound's mind this arrangement preserved 'one value of early Italian work, the cantabile', but let go of 'the fervour and intensity' of his earlier translations.[137] He proposed that:

> by taking these Italian sonnets . . . by sacrificing, or losing, or simply not feeling and understanding their cogency, their sobriety . . . by cutting away the apparently non-functioning phrases . . . you find yourself in the English *seicento* song-books.[138]

'Seicento'—Pound's transference of an Italian term into English—made larger claims for the ways in which Italian poetry was utilized in England than his exercises prove. In this instance, Pound had moved away from Victorian pastiche, only

---

[130] 'Cavalcanti', *LE* 194.
[131] *LE* 194.
[132] *LE* 199, Pound's italics.
[133] *LE* 195.
[134] 'Notes on Elizabethan Classicists', *LE* 238.
[135] 'Cavalcanti', *LE* 195, 196.
[136] *LE* 196.
[137] *LE* 196.
[138] *LE* 197.

76 MODERNIST PARODY

to arrive at an, albeit more elegant, Elizabethan variety. For his final exercise in translation Pound reached back to 'pre-Elizabethan English':[139]

> No one could ever tell all her pleasauntness
> In that every high noble vertu leaneth to herward
> So Beauty sheweth her forth as Godhede;[140]

In maturity, Pound's considered objections to presenting ancient literatures through pastiches of English historical styles were:

> the doubt as to whether one has the right to take a serious poem and turn it into a mere exercise in quaintness; the 'misrepresentation' not of the poem's antiquity, but of the proportionate feel of that antiquity, by which I mean that Guido's thirteenth-century language is to twentieth-century Italian sense much less archaic than any fourteenth-, fifteenth-, or early sixteenth-century English is for us.[141]

Pound was given to wonder if his 'bungling version of twenty years back isn't more "faithful", in the sense that it at least tried to preserve the fervour of the original', since 'in English poetry in those centuries there is no ready-made verbal pigment for its objectification'.[142] The making of an objective language for subjective emotion would be a priority for Pound in the Imagist phase of his long campaign to modernize poetry in English. The desire to reinflect fragments of past literatures through parody and pastiche in order to preserve their beauty and establish their continuity would stay with him to become a key technique of his post-Imagist career.

Learning how to temper pastiche so that it did not slip into unimportant parody or betray the 'feel' of the original was instrumental to Pound's self-education as a poet. Pastiche expressed Pound's admiration for his masters and his earnest desire to acquire the technical proficiency to achieve communion with their poetic souls and enter their worthy company. In his early poetry, it functioned as a principle of canon formation and consolidation, but it also fetishized past literatures without considering how they could be remade to intervene in contemporary life, drawing Pound towards complacent historical pageantry that was aesthetic not pragmatic. Parody and self-directed satire were the necessary correctives: they developed Pound's reflexive ability to evaluate his own copy work and disentangle himself from the languages he absorbed from recent authors; the strong voice of Browning, the romantic *pasticherie* of Rossetti and friends, or the 'fustian and

---

[139] *LE* 199.
[140] *LE* 200.
[141] *LE* 200.
[142] *LE* 200.

mannerism' that was fashionable in the 1890s. And they also provided a means to articulate the terms of the crisis the canonizing thrust of *Canzoni* precipitated when its chronological arrangement compelled him to consider the case of poetry now, enabling him to finger the follies of the age and his own faults, even if he was not then fully ready to relinquish *pasticherie* for parody, satire, and irony. Once he had fully digested Ford's criticism, Pound's modernism would be energized by interchanges with the subversive energies of parody, a ruse that would assume central importance in the development and promotion of Imagism, a movement that is often misread as an entirely earnest enterprise.

3

'An Atmosphere of Parody'

Imagism and *Blast*

Pound submitted his next volume of poetry *Ripostes of Ezra Pound: Whereto Are Appended the Complete Poetic Works of T. E. Hulme, with Prefatory Note* (1912) to the publisher in February that year: it was completed too soon after Ford's comments on *Canzoni* for Pound to have evolved a new style. Notable entries included 'The Seafarer' and 'The Return' (which Yeats considered 'the most beautiful poem that has been written in the free form').[1] But *Ripostes* did contain an appendage, in which Pound offered a foretaste of the new school he was concocting.[2] 'The Complete Poetical Works of T. E. Hulme' only consisted of five brief poems that had been published in the *New Age* that January.[3] They are refreshingly free from rhetorical ornament. The poems ground romantic tropes, pulling them back down to earth by juxtaposing them with distorted mirror images that are *faux naif*, seedy, or bathetic. Yet they also thrive on that transforming contrast, which the spare form delivers with the *éclat* of a punchline, dispensing with the unreality of cliché to communicate contempt for sham aestheticism, while giving expression to an emotion or insight that is not artificial. The moon that hangs above the docks amid the corded masts 'Is but a child's balloon, forgotten after play'; the 'fallen gentleman on a cold, bitter night' who once found 'ecstasy,/In the flash of gold heels on the hard pavement' now seeks comfort in 'The old star-eaten blanket of the sky'; the person who walks 'into the valley wood,/In the time of hyacinths' does not remain light-hearted for long, but finds its beauty as stifling as 'a scented cloth'.[4] This strain of humour was increasingly to Pound's taste because the emotion it expressed was authentically tart. As he would later explain in 'A Retrospect' (1917), his preference for 'satire, which is due to emotion, to any sham of emotion' stemmed from his classicism and his belief that poetry should 'be harder and saner . . . "nearer the bone" . . . austere, direct, free from emotional slither'.[5] Hulme's austerity and lack of slither clearly appealed to Pound, as did the satirical undercurrent, which is why he saw fit to introduce 'The Complete Poetical Works' with comic brio.

[1] W. B. Yeats, quoted in Noel Stock, *The Life of Ezra Pound* (London: Routledge & Kegan Paul, 1970), 153.
[2] *R* 58–64.
[3] T. E. Hulme, 'The Complete Poetical Works of T. E. Hulme', *New Age* X(13) (25 January 1912), 307.
[4] *R* 62–4.
[5] 'A Retrospect', *LE* 13, 12.

Modernist Parody. Sarah Davison, Oxford University Press. © Sarah Davison (2023).
DOI: 10.1093/oso/9780192849243.003.0004

'AN ATMOSPHERE OF PARODY' 79

In the facetious 'Prefatory Note', Pound presented Hulme's poems anew as the products of a fictitious school that derived from the poetry evenings at the Tour Eiffel restaurant in 1909, where Hulme had led discussions of the 'Image':

> As for the 'School of Images', which may or may not have existed, its principles were not so interesting as those of the 'inherent dynamists' or of *Les Unanimistes*, yet they were probably sounder than those of a certain French school which attempted to dispense with verbs altogether; or of the Impressionists who brought forth:
>
> 'Pink pigs blossoming upon the hillside';
>
> or of the Post-Impressionists who beseech their ladies to let down slate-blue hair over their raspberry-coloured flanks.
> *Ardoise* rimed richly—ah, richly and rarely rimed!—with *framboise*.
> As for the future, *Les Imagistes*, the descendants of the forgotten school of 1909, have that in their keeping.[6]

Hulme was acutely conscious that poetry was crying out for modernization. He was adamant that:

> Those arts like poetry, whose matter is immortal, must find a new technique each generation. Each age must have its own special form of expression, and any period that deliberately goes out of it is an age of insincerity.[7]

And so he used the meetings at the Tour Eiffel to thrash out a new language for talking about poetry and rejuvenating its techniques. Hulme derived his concept of the 'Image' from Henri Bergson's essay 'Introduction to Metaphysics' (1903), later translated by Hulme (and F. S. Flint) in 1912), which argued that the real duration of consciousness is only known intuitively, because the ceaseless flux of being is multilayered and shifting and therefore resists straightforward description, but that 'many diverse images, borrowed from very different orders of things, may, by the convergence of their action, direct consciousness to the precise point where there is a certain intuition to be seized'.[8]

Pound was a latecomer to discussions about the Image, but he was the first to get the cognate term '*Les Imagistes*' into print, using it to designate a future movement for which he had yet to devise a definite manifesto or gather practitioners.[9] His

---

[6] *R* 59.

[7] T. E. Hulme, 'A Lecture on Modern Poetry', in Karen Csengeri, ed., *The Collected Writings of T. E. Hulme* (Oxford: Clarendon Press, 1994), 51.

[8] Henri Bergson, *An Introduction to Metaphysics* (1903), trans. T. E. Hulme (Indianapolis: Bobbs-Merrill, 1949), 27–8.

[9] Pound later tried to convince readers of *Pavannes and Divisions* (1918) that Imagism was carefully planned, claiming that in 'the spring or early summer of 1912, "H. D.", Richard Aldington and myself decided that we were agreed upon the three [Imagist] principles' ('A Retrospect', *LE* 3).

80   MODERNIST PARODY

recourse to that term and its derivatives to promote his own increasingly prescriptive ideas about what modern poetry should look like rankled with other Tour Eiffel stalwarts, such as Flint, who were not given appropriate credit for the intellectual work underpinning the concepts that Pound later promulgated with great zeal. As Helen Carr has pointed out in her brilliant group biography of the Imagists, *The Verse Revolutionaries* (2009), the section of the 'Prefatory Note' quoted above must have been written when Pound revisited the proofs for *Riposte* in August 1912, because it makes reference to the avant-garde French groups that Flint first introduced to an English-speaking audience in his seminal essay in 'Contemporary French Poetry' in the special French issue of *Poetry Review* published that month, which mentioned *les unanimistes, les Whitmanistes, les paroxystes, les néo-Mallarmistes,* and *les futuristes* (Marinetti was publishing in French).[10] Because Flint reached for the Bergsonian Image to explain certain principles underlying post-Symbolist poetry, Hulme's work and that of continental schools came together in Pound's mind.[11] According to Flint, who had a wicked sense of humour, 'before August, 1912, Ezra Pound used to say that he knew no French poetry after Villon. After August 1912, he became like a cat in heat.'[12] In the 'Prefatory Note' Pound defined the 'School of Images' entirely in terms of its relation to continental trends. He mocked the lurid and sometimes ludicrous strategies that French avant-garde cliques were using to get noticed, dismissing post-Impressionist coteries with parodic *faux* quotation and comparing their precepts unfavourably to the more solid theoretical foundations of a school that did not yet exist, even as he took pains to consolidate the association by giving future adherents a frenchified name. Imagism, the movement heralded by T. S. Eliot as the '*point de repère* usually and conveniently taken, as the starting-point of modern poetry', was descended from Hulmean metaphysics, a serious philosophy that was hospitable to sardonic observations and developed out of satire on the apparent silliness of contemporary artistic schools.[13] It teetered on the precipice of parody and self-parody thereafter.

It was perhaps no coincidence that the joke that framed the coda—that 'The Complete Poetical Works of T. E. Hulme' consisted of only five short poems—came from *The Works of Max Beerbohm*, itself a conspicuously slender volume, published when Beerbohm was just 24, to which the publisher, John Lane, appended a scant bibliography purporting to represent a lifetime's achievement,

---

[10] Helen Carr, *The Verse Revolutionaries: Ezra Pound, H. D. and the Imagists* (London: Jonathan Cape, 2009), 487. For evidence that Pound was working on the second set of proofs for *Riposte*, see Ezra Pound to Harriet Monroe, <18> August 1912, *LEP* 43.

[11] 'The symbolist poet attempts to give you an intuition of the reality itself and of the forces, vague to use, behind it, by a series of images which the imagination seizes and brings together in its effort to insert itself into and express that reality', F. S. Flint, 'Contemporary French Poetry', *Poetry Review* I(8) (August 1912), 357.

[12] Le Roy C. Breunig, 'F. S. Flint, Imagism's 'Maître d'Ecole', *Comparative Literature* 4 (1952), 134.

[13] T. S. Eliot, 'American Literature and the American Language', in Iman Javadi and Ronald Schuchard, eds., *The Complete Prose of T. S. Eliot: The Critical Edition, Volume 7, A European Society, 1947–1953* (Baltimore: Johns Hopkins Press, 2018), 805.

'AN ATMOSPHERE OF PARODY' 81

introduced by a po-faced preface.[14] Now Pound played Lane to Hulme's Beer-bohm, explaining, with mock envy, that Hulme exceptionally completed his entire oeuvre at the age of 30, setting 'an enviable example to many of his contemporaries who have had less to say', to which Hulme, then 29, responded in a droll footnote: 'Mr. Pound has grossly exaggerated my age. —T. E. H.'[15]

When Pound formally introduced his new school in *Poetry: A Magazine of Verse* (1913), with Flint's help, he appeared to disavow the association with the avant-garde and instead emphasized links with his own personal canon of great writers:

> The *imagistes* admitted that they were contemporaries of the Post Impressionists and the Futurists; but they had nothing in common with these schools. They had not published a manifesto. They were not a revolutionary school; their only endeavor was to write in accordance with the best tradition, as they found it in the best writers of all time,—in Sappho, Catullus, Villon.[16]

Yet, the frequent appearance of avant-garde groups in Pound's commentary suggests that he was, in fact, highly conscious of the similarity, and that by pointing to their contemporaneity he wanted to assert an equivalent modernity while preserving a sense of separate identity.

From the very beginning, Imagism was of and against the avant-garde. Lawrence Rainey has noted that Pound's satire on continental schools alludes particularly 'to the recent developments of Futurism, and in particular to F. T. Marinetti's prescription urging the elimination of all verbs except those in the infinitive, advocated in "Technical Manifesto of Futurist Literature" (May 1912)', and has argued persuasively that Pound's creation of Imagism was, in good part, a response to the commercial success of that notorious movement, its ability to generate headlines and co-opt mass culture, and his own prospects after the death of his patron, Margaret Cravens.[17] In addition to making 'the social space of cultural production into an urgent question' for Pound—as Rainey argues—Futurism also recalibrated Pound's aesthetic sensibilities, unlocking a penchant for flippancy.[18] Certainly, Pound had no sympathy with Marinetti's incendiary calls to destroy the past, his naked contempt for museums, libraries, archaeologists, and antiquarians, or his devil-may-care attitude to anyone who would insist 'we are the summation and continuation of our ancestors'.[19] If anything, Futurism made Pound even more

---

[14] Lane, 'Preface' to 'The Bibliography of the Works of Max Beerbohm', in *Works of Max Beerbohm*, 163.

[15] *R* 58.

[16] F. S. Flint, 'Imagisme', *Poetry: A Magazine of Verse* I(6) (March 1913), 199.

[17] Lawrence Rainey, *Institutions of Modernism: Literary Elites and Public Culture* (New Haven, CT: Yale University Press, 1998), 183.

[18] Rainey, *Institutions of Modernism*, 12.

[19] 'The refined and mendacious mind tells us that we are the summation and continuation of our ancestors—maybe! Suppose it so! But what difference does it make? We don't want to listen! . . . Woe

82 MODERNIST PARODY

determined to show that the great literatures of the past were charged with vital-izing energy that could be used precisely to delineate and renovate the present. However, Pound's interest in 'the cult of ugliness'—the satirical mode he par-ticularly associated with Villon, Baudelaire, Tristan Corbière, Aubrey Beardsley, and Flaubert in 'The Serious Artist' (1913)—was not entirely out of step with proclamations such as 'Let us boldly make "the ugly" in literature, and let us everywhere murder solemnity', despite its invocation of the Symbolist masters Marinetti abjured.[20] Of course, Hulme's satirical reinflection of passé symbols such as the moon, the stars, and the flower-carpeted wood was more sober than any-thing Marinetti dreamt up (for instance the madcap caper Marinetti recounted in the second Futurist manifesto 'Let's Murder the Moonlight!', which made a comedy of a serious attack on stale aesthetics by vanquishing the most clichéd poetic symbol of all in the name of modernity, enlisting the support of the inmates of a lunatic asylum to outdazzle the moon with hundreds of light bulbs), but the fundamental point that old poetic images were thoroughly exhausted was the same.[21]

The antics of the avant-garde impacted on Pound's aesthetic priorities well in advance of his involvement in Vorticism, the movement Lewis founded in reaction against Futurism. When Pound first contacted Harriet Monroe, the Chicago-based editor of the newly founded *Poetry: A Magazine of Verse*, in August 1912, he sought to establish himself as her primary contact for 'whatever is most dynamic in artis-tic thought, either here or in Paris'.[22] He was certainly thinking along avant-garde lines when he forecast that together they would instigate an 'American Risorgi-mento' that would 'make the Italian Renaissance look like a tempest in a teapot'.[23] At first, he intimated that French tactics were *de trop*. He told Monroe, 'I don't think we need to go to the French extreme of having four prefaces to each poem and eight schools for every dozen poets', wanting to develop something more solid and permanent.[24] But the avant-garde and its strategies continued to preoccupy Pound as the new touchstone for serious artistic production. In October 1912, he sent Monroe 'some *modern* stuff by an American . . . in the laconic speech of the Imagistes . . . the sort of American stuff that I can show here and in Paris without its being ridiculed'.[25] The poem was by Hilda Doolittle, but radically refashioned by Pound, who pared it down, gave it a new enigmatic title, 'Hermes of the Ways', and scrawled 'H. D. Imagiste' at the bottom of the manuscript over tea at the British

---

to anyone who repeats those infamous words to us!', 'The Founding and Manifesto of Futurism' (20 February 1909), in Rainey, et al., *Futurism*, 53.

[20] Ezra Pound, 'The Serious Artist: I', *New Freewoman* I(9) (15 October 1913), 162; F. T. Marinetti, 'Technical Manifesto of Futurist Literature' (11 May 1912), in Rainey et al., *Futurism*, 124.

[21] F. T. Marinetti, 'Let's Murder the Moonlight' (11 April 1909), in Rainey et al., *Futurism*, 54–61.

[22] *LEP* 44.

[23] *LEP* 44.

[24] *LEP* 44.

[25] *LEP* 45.

'AN ATMOSPHERE OF PARODY'   83

Museum.[26] His next dispatch to Monroe, on 13 October 1912, contained Pound's own attempt at *modern* verse: he wondered whether America was 'ready to be diverted by the ultra-modern, ultra-effete tenuity of Contemporania', acknowledging that this first batch of poems was insubstantial, yet imagining that they would cause a stir for their amusing swerve from accepted standards.[27] Another letter to Monroe followed on 22 October 1912, reaffirming Pound's commitment to pushing the boundaries of public taste: he asked, '*If one is going to print opinions that the public already agrees with, what is the use of printing 'em at all?*'[28] To inculcate a more dynamic and discerning culture for literary appreciation, he again looked to the French example and the amused humour that post-Symbolist writers plied when they made knowing use of incongruity and surprise to arrest complacency and deflect cliché:

> The French laugh, but it's not a corrosive or hostile laughter. In fact, good art thrives in an atmosphere of parody. Parody is, I suppose, the best criticism—it sifts the durable from the apparent.[29]

Here Pound presented parody to Monroe as a valuable activity because it cast art as a social practice that cultivated discernment, making readers of writers and critics of readers, forcing them to separate works of enduring value from mere superficialities and make the productive discriminations that advance the progress of art. In effect, Pound was advocating 'an atmosphere of parody' because he recognized that the business of establishing the dominance of emergent aesthetics would be a negotiated position, one that depended on affirmations and negations that were fundamentally dialogic, of the kind that Bakhtin would later describe in his accounts of the rise of the novel. Pound's own work, increasingly of a satiric temper, was calculated to inaugurate just such 'an atmosphere of parody' in which good art could thrive.

When Pound was musing on the advantages that 'an atmosphere of parody' could confer, it is possible that he was thinking particularly of Laurent Tailhade, a post-Symbolist poet, whose *Poèmes aristophanesques* (1904, third edition 1910) Pound reviewed under the title of 'The Approach to Paris' (1913), his answer to Flint's 'Contemporary French Poetry' (which had itself appeared two months prior

---

[26] This is how H. D. recalled Pound's textual incursions: 'He slashed with a pencil. "Cut this out, shorten this line. 'Hermes of the Ways' is a good title. I'll send this to Harriet Monroe of *Poetry*. Have you a copy? Yes? Then we can send this, or I'll type it when I get back. Will this do?" And he scrawled "H. D. Imagiste" at the bottom of the page.' See H. D., *End to Torment: A Memoir of Ezra Pound, with the Poems from 'Hilda's Book' by Ezra Pound*, ed. Norman Holmes Pearson and Michael King (New York: New Directions, 1979), 18.

[27] *LEP* 45.

[28] *LEP* 47, Pound's italics.

[29] *LEP* 47.

84 MODERNIST PARODY

to Pound's letter to Monroe promising an 'American Risorgimento').[30] Pound praised Tailhade for writing in 'the "prose tradition" of poetry', using 'a practice of speech common to good prose and to good verse alike'; Tailhade presents, he does not comment, with the effect that his verses conduct a 'constatation of fact'.[31] Pound further explained that Tailhade's 'presentative method is equity':

> It is powerless to make the noble seem ignoble. It fights for a sane valuation. It cannot bring fine things into ridicule. It will not pervert a thing from its true use by trying to ascribe to it alien uses.
> It is also the scourge of fools.[32]

In support of this point, Pound quoted from Tailhade's grotesque vignette of cosmopolitan life 'Place des Victoires' and then invoked Ford's dictum for contemporary writing with a flourish, stating 'This is what is called "rendering one's own time in the terms of one's own"', before adding 'Heine wrote in this manner, and so did Catullus and so for that matter did Aristophanes'.[33] In these comments, Tailhade clearly emerges as a model for the poetry Pound now wanted to write; poetry that addressed the contemporary world directly through its satirical and unsparing depiction of modern mores.[34] But what made Tailhade capable of rendering his own time in the terms of his own was his ability to inflect words so that their specific literary and historical weight was felt.

As Pound's argument proceeds, Tailhade's 'presentative method' is revealed to be no other than parody; not the straightforward rhetorical kind, as the conversational tone of the lines from 'Place des Victoires' make clear, but the pervasively parodic stylization that Bakhtin would associate with the forces of novelization, which Pound instinctively linked to 'speech practices common to good prose and to good verse alike':

> He [Tailhade] is, one finds, full of tricks out of Rabelais and out of Villon, and of mannerisms brought from the Pléiade. He is a gourmand of great books: he is altogether unabashed and unashamed . . . When M. Tailhade parodies the antique [he] is considerably more than a parodist. He writes to his subject and the 'snatches of ancient psalmody' are but a part of the music. The cadence and

---

[30] Ezra Pound, 'The Approach to Paris: I', *New Age* XIII(19–25) (4 September–16 October 1913); Laurent Tailhade, *Poèmes aristophanesques*, 3rd edn (Paris: Mercure de France, 1910).

[31] Ezra Pound, 'The Approach to Paris: V', *New Age* XIII(23) (2 October 1913), 662.

[32] Pound, 'Approach to Paris: V', 662.

[33] Pound, 'Approach to Paris: V', 662.

[34] Scott Hamilton discusses the extent of Pound's debt to the French Romantic, 'Symbolist and post-Symbolist Traditions', in *Ezra Pound and the Symbolist Inheritance* (Princeton, NJ: Princeton University Press, 1992), showing how Pound's 'exhaustive study of modern French verse gave him poetic models and techniques that enabled him to escape his own Decadent-Symbolist inheritance and to discover the distinctively modern voice that he began to create in 1912' (viii). For an account of Tailhade's influence on Pound's *Lustra* manner, see Hamilton, *Ezra Pound*, 61–8.

the rhymes are sufficiently ridiculous, and these also are a mockery. That is to say, he is a satirist, he does not imitate a form merely for the sake of imitating. He plays with his old authors as easily as Lorenzo de Medici played with the cadences of the 'primi secoli' poets, as easily as Leopardi . . . in 'Paralipomeni'. Tailhade enjoys himself as Cervantes enjoyed himself with the 'Diana' of Montemayor. It is a pleasing and erudite irony such as should fill the creative artist with glee and might well fill the imitator with a species of apostolic terror.[35]

Tailhade is of his own moment because his poems crackle with the rhythms of present-day speech even as they are rubbed up against other parodic stylizations; the static that the contrasting textures generate measures the ironic distance between historicized modes of expression in order to constatate the facts of contemporary life. This species of parody had the hardness, sanity, and lack of sentimentality that Pound associated with classicism, as the company of authors cited suggests. Tailhade may be the scourge of fools but he is not hostile to good literature because he handles his raw materials with appreciative gusto.

It seems likely that Pound read Armand Silvestre's preface to Tailhade's *Au Pays du Mufle* (1891), which was reprinted in *Poèmes aristophanesques*.[36] Silvestre noted that Tailhade's play with the literary language he enjoys is so pervasive that his whole oeuvre is suffused with parody's insinuating perfume:

> Qui pourrait dire, en effet, jusqu'où va l'ironie de Laurent Tailhade? Peut-être quelquefois jusqu'à la parodie d'une école qui s'enorgueillit justement de ce vrai et beau poète. Pourquoi pas, puisque, dans *Virgo fellatrix*, lui-même s'est hautement raillé, imitant une de ces pièces d'inspiration catholique où se complaît souvent sa latinité dans les fumées d'encens que traverse une lumière de vitrail.
>
> [Who could say, in effect, how far Laurent Tailhade's irony goes? Maybe sometimes even up to the parody of a school that prides itself on this true and beautiful poet. Why not, since, in *Virgo fellatrix*, he highly ridiculed himself, in which his Latinity often indulged itself in the imitation of one of those Catholic inspired pieces where the smoke of incense runs through a stained-glass light.][37]

The atmosphere of parody that Silvestre described and Pound also clearly detected shuts down the prospect of straight imitation as a viable form of composition and shifts the locus of true creativity to ironic reconstellation of the languages of life and literature. It gives rise to writing that has already anticipated and welcomed

---

[35] Pound, 'Approach to Paris: V', 662. *La Pléiade* is the name given to the group of sixteenth-century French writers led by Pierre de Ronsard who aimed to ennoble the French language by imitating Greek and Roman literature.

[36] Tailhade, *Poèmes aristophanesques*, 173–6.

[37] Armand Silvestre, 'Préface pour Les Pays du Mufle' (1891), in Tailhade, *Poèmes aristophanesques*, 176.

86 MODERNIST PARODY

its own mockery. It conducts a sane evaluation of its own comparative historical weight and can therefore confidently proclaim its status as innovative, contemporary work. It is this prospect that fills the creative artist with glee because it revels in the pleasures of past literatures *and* it points the way forward: strategic parodic requisition offered a principle of genesis that is enduringly productive, consciously historicist, and yet acutely timely. This sense of the diffuse parody that goes beyond the effects of parodic stylization and advances the progress of art is implicit in the illustrative texts Pound has chosen, whereby one body of parodic writing begets another, for instance Tailhade's *Poèmes aristophanesques* or Giacomo Leopardi's *Paralipomeni della Batracomiomachia* (1842), a supplement to *The Battle of the Frogs and Mice* (itself a parody of the *Iliad*, a text that Leopardi compulsively translated).[38] And it is this atmosphere that Pound saw as congenial to the continued production of good art—the product of a highly literary intelligence that feasted on great books, and savoured fine lines and cadences, even as it made parodic play with them.

Marinetti's proximity to parody was one of the qualities that made his early manifestos so arresting, but, by contrast with French post-Symbolist tricks, the atmosphere of parody that his Futurist manifestos generated was corrosive and hostile because it aimed to destroy the institution of art. Marinetti's spasmodic proclamations were too strident to be taken in all seriousness. And his violent narrative vignettes were so ecstatic in their caress of lurid detail that they were mocked by the scorn he professed for passéism and aestheticism. The logic of inversion, contradiction, and excess shunted Marinetti's dramatic and distinctive prose beyond parodic stylization into a form of farcical self-parody that was strikingly innovative, yet also manifestly nihilistic, because its contradictions would not sustain repeated iteration. Marinetti signalled his allegiance to parody when he cited variety theatre as an ally that assisted in 'the Futurist destruction of immortal masterpieces by plagiarizing and parodying them, by making them seem commonplace in stripping them of their solemnity and presenting them as if they were just another turn or attraction.'[39] But setting out to use parody to destroy 'the Solemn, the Sacred, the Serious, the Sublime of Art with a capital A' risked robbing the past of the aura that made it worth parodying in the first place, leaving no logical choice but self-citation, which threatened to create a tradition that would become as formulaic and tired as the one it strove to replace. Futurism was fated to fall foul of its own cult of perpetual innovation, which could not ultimately be sustained by its corrosive, hostile laughter.[40]

---

[38] Giacomo Leopardi, *Paralipomeni della Batracomiomachia* (Parigi: Libreria Europa di Baudry, 1842); Matthew Hosty, *Batrachomyomachia (Battle of the Frogs and Mice): Introduction, Text, Translation, and Commentary* (Oxford: Oxford University Press, 2019).

[39] F. T. Marinetti, 'The Variety Theatre' (29 September 1913) in Rainey et al., *Futurism*, 162.

[40] Marinetti, 'Variety Theatre' in Rainey et al., *Futurism*, 162.

By contrast, for a time, Imagism thrived amid 'an atmosphere of parody' that was neither corrosive nor hostile to sustaining the production of durable literature. It was an atmosphere comparable to that initiated by the French post-Symbolist poets, one that Pound found congenial, took pains to cultivate, and which proved to be of immense benefit to its amused and often ambivalent practitioners for the work it did to deepen their impact on public consciousness. Certainly, the participants Pound co-opted first took Imagism with a pinch of salt. Flint was later to claim that 'the name . . . was adopted as a joke rather than the challenge it finally became'.[41] Richard Aldington also retained a sharp sense of what was comic about Pound's impromptu and elusive new movement, or '*mouvemong*' as he liked to call it in mockery of Pound's affected French pronunciation.[42] Recalling Pound's meeting with H. D. in the British Museum, Aldington reported 'Ezra was so much worked up by these poems of H. D.'s that he removed his pince-nez and informed us that we were Imagists./Was this the first time I had heard that Pickwickian word?'[43]

Pound wrote to Monroe on 13 October 1912 to insist that she should not print 'Contemporania' (his latest collection of poems) until she had 'used "H. D." and Aldington'.[44] It was Pound's habit to promote the work of kindred writers, but, in this instance, there was good reason to establish a body of serious and solid 'Imagiste' work before he made his own splash. Monroe had been sufficiently taken aback by Pound's poems and their truculent assault on contemporary taste to refuse publication until he had persuaded Rabindranath Tagore to champion his cause.[45] Accordingly, Aldington was the first to be introduced to readers of *Poetry* as 'one of the "Imagistes", a group of ardent Hellenists who are pursuing interesting experiments in *vers libre*; trying to attain in English certain subtleties of cadence of the kind which Mallarmé and his followers have studied in French' in November 1912, followed by H. D. whose credentials as an 'Imagiste' warranted mention on the cover of the January 1913 issue.[46]

'Contemporania' was the leading item in the April 1913 issue of *Poetry*. The Old Provençal–inspired title of the first poem, 'Tenzone', signalled that Pound's topic was literary dispute.[47] However, his quarrel was with his own former passéism and the faint-hearted (and therefore feminized) critical culture that he believed was

---

[41] J. B. Harmer, *Victory in Limbo: Imagism 1908–1917* (London: Secker & Warburg, 1975), 17.

[42] Richard Aldington, *Life for Life's Sake: A Book of Reminiscences* (New York: Viking, 1941), 133.

[43] Aldington, *Life for Life's Sake*, 135.

[44] *LEP* 46.

[45] In a letter of January 1914, Pound bragged to his mother: 'it was Tagore who poked my "Contemporania" down the Chicago gullet. Or at least read it aloud to that board of imbeciles on *Poetry* and told 'em how good the stuff was' (*LEP* 68).

[46] 'Notes and Announcements', *Poetry: A Magazine of Verse* I(2) (November 1912), 65; *Poetry: A Magazine of Verse* I(4) (January 1913).

[47] Cf. 'Tenson', from the Old Provençal *tenso*, a poem of dispute or personal abuse that takes the form of a contest in verse between rival troubadours.

88   MODERNIST PARODY

unready to embrace the wild and threatening freedoms he was now taking with poetry:

> Will people accept them?
>   (i. e. these songs).
> As a timorous wench from a centaur
>   (or a centurion),
> Already they flee, howling in terror.
> Will they be touched by the truth?
>   Their virgin stupidly is untemptable.
> I beg you, my friendly critics,
> Do not set about to procure me an audience.
>
> mate with my free kind upon the crags;
>   the hidden recesses
> Have heard the echo of my heels,
>   in the cool light,
>   in the darkness.[48]

Pound meant more by the centaur metaphor than would have been immediately apparent to readers of *Poetry*, as he would later clarify in 'The Serious Artist':

> Poetry is a centaur. The thinking word, arranging, clarifying faculty must move and leap with the energizing, sentient, musical facilities. It is precisely the difficulty of this amphibious existence that keeps down the census record of good poets.[49]

The ungainly parentheses, abbreviations, and macho swagger of 'Tenzone' conceal what small subtlety was otherwise accessible: the ambivalent symbol of a centaur (or a centurion) signalled his newly combative classicism (in distinction to pastiche romanticism), while remaining a virile conduit for primal forces, their roughness and their beauty.

The next poem, 'The Condolence', bears an epigraph from de Vega that Pound translated in *The Spirit of Romance* as:

> To my solitudes I go,
> From my solitudes return I,
> Sith for companions on the journey,
> Mine own thoughts (do well suffice me).[50]

---

[48] 'Tenzone', *Con* 1.
[49] Ezra Pound, 'The Serious Artist: III', *New Freewoman* I(10) (1 November 1913), 195.
[50] 'The Condolence', *Con* 2; *SR* 219.

In *The Spirit of Romance* these lines were used in support of his theory that the 'true poet is most easily distinguished from the false, when he trusts himself to the simplest expression, and when he writes without adjectives'.[51] In 'The Condolence' the quotation from de Vega states Pound's desire for unfussy phrasing and his sense of himself as an outlier, and is followed by feigned disgust for the 'asses' who praised his songs because they are '"virile"' but overlooked the 'delicate thoughts' they gathered.[52] In a display of self-conscious machismo, Pound insists that far from being exasperated by women, their 'ductile' nature made them pleased to serve his '"*fantastikon*"', his imaginative receptivity to impressions or images.[53]

The four poems that follow present female figures who quicken Pound's desire and poetic ambition. The first two satirize conventional scenes of courtly love, transposing them to contemporary urban life. 'The Garret' is briskly spoken to a lover in modest lodgings, enjoining her to pity those who are better off and married, or unmarried for that matter, until the speaker is taken aback by the arrival of the dawn, which 'enters with little feet/like a gilded Pavlova' and reveals to him his desire and a new contentment in 'this hour of clear coolness,/the hour of waking together'.[54] 'The Garden' depicts an unknown *flâneuse* stifled by suburban morality, whose 'boredom is exquisite and excessive', wafting past the railings of a public park, amid 'a rabble/Of the filthy, sturdy, unkillable infants of the very poor', yearning for the indiscreet contact that is in the poet's gift.[55] The second two concern the female figures who serve as muses to Pound's art. 'Ortus' lays claim to having effectively made a woman as 'beautiful as the sunlight, and as fluid' whom he has 'laboured to bring her soul into separation; /To give her a name and her being!', which Cyrena Pondron rightly reads as an address to H. D. and an assertion of his ownership of the creative identity he imposed on her.[56] Finally, 'Dance Figure' relays the fantasy of a swift-footed dancer, at one with the primal rhythms of nature, in an untouched land of simplicity and beauty, a clear symbol for Pound's desire to be a conduit for primitive forces, naked, without adornment, and as well as his freedoms with metrical feet and free verse.[57]

Having tendered examples of his own contemporary poetry, which, if it is to be cosmopolitan, must admit vital energies of sexual desire and natural rhythms and also present the mythic and neo-primitive with a delicate touch, Pound returns to his polemical theme. The first 'Salutation' addresses complacent cosmopolites

---

[51] SR 219.

[52] 'The Condolence', *Con* 2.

[53] 'The Condolence', *Con* 2, Pound's italics.

[54] 'The Garret', *Con* 3.

[55] 'The Garden', *Con* 3.

[56] 'Ortus', *Con* 4. For discussion of H. D.'s impact on Pound's poetics and Pound's reactive assertion of ownership, see Cyrena Pondron, 'H. D. and the Origins of Imagism', in Susan Stanford Friedman and Rachel Blau DuPlessis, eds., *Signets: Reading H. D.* (Madison, WI: University of Wisconsin Press, 1990), 85–109.

[57] 'Dance Figure', *Con* 4–6.

90   MODERNIST PARODY

who will be disquieted by the image the poet mediates of a more primitive society that is at one with nature, but lacking in culture:

> O generation of the thoroughly smug
> > and thoroughly uncomfortable,
> I have seen fishermen picnicking in the sun,
> I have seen them with untidy families,
> I have seen their smiles full of teeth
> > and heard ungainly laughter.
>
> And I am happier than you are,
> And they were happier than I am;
> And the fish swim in the lake
> > and do not even own clothing.[58]

The self-sufficiency, appetite, and ability to procreate will guarantee the survival of this sturdy rabble over the wan urbanites, unless they permit their emotions and intellect to be reinvigorated by Pound's virile poetry. The parting joke, an absurd observation on life forms further down the hierarchy of being, sneers at the fishermen, whom Pound positions but one rung above and at the accoutrements of civilized bourgeois life, while also taking a side swipe at post-Impressionist primitivism. 'Salutation the Second' turns to imagine the outraged response of reviewers and critics to Pound's impudent satires and indecorous verses, which are unadorned, free from archaism or quaint devices, and receptive to the image (developments that, it might be added, followed from the discovery of such qualities within H. D.'s poetry):

> Watch the reporters spit,
> Watch the anger of the professors,
> Watch how the pretty ladies revile them:
> "Is this," they say, "the nonsense
> > that we expect of poets?"
> "Where is the Picturesque?"
> > "Where is the vertigo of emotion?"
> "No! his first work was the best."
> > "Poor Dear! he has lost his illusions."[59]

Here Pound acknowledges that 'Contemporania' will appear nonsensical to stuffy readers (and admirers of his early work), but that this is frankly the point, because his vigorous challenges to received ideas about poetry, however ludicrous they

---

[58] 'Salutation', *Con* 6.
[59] 'Salutation the Second', *Con* 7.

'AN ATMOSPHERE OF PARODY' 91

might appear in their departure from established conventions, are needed to shake up the complacent (and therefore stagnant) literary culture. 'Go, little naked and impudent songs', he cries, 'Go and dance shamelessly!/Go with an impertinent frolic!', 'Greet the grave and the stodgy,/Salute them, with your thumbs at your noses', 'Go! rejuvenate things!' and 'Dance the dance of the phallus', assaulting standards of good taste through satire and self-mockery.[60]

Next, Pound turns to confront America, the scene for his intended *risorgimento*. *'Pax Saturni'* is a bitter rebuttal to those who speak of 'American virtues' and are rewarded for their oppressive dishonesty.[61] It is answered by the next poem, 'Commission', in which Pound bids his songs 'Go against, all forms of oppression', social, artistic, and sexual:[62]

> Go, my songs, to the lonely and the unsatisfied,
> Go also to the nerve-wracked, go to the enslaved-by convention,
> Bear to them my contempt for their oppressors.
> [...]
> Go to the bourgeoise who is dying of her ennuis,
> Go to the women in suburbs.
>
> Go to the hideously wedded,
> Go to them whose failed is concealed,
> Go to the unluckily mated,
> Go to the bought wife,
> Go to the woman entailed.
>
> Go to those who have delicate lust,
> Go to those whose delicate desires are thwarted.
> [...]
> Go to the adolescent who are [sic] smothered in family—
> [...]
> Go out and defy opinion
> Go against this vegetable bondage of the blood.[63]

The anaphoric catalogue is a clear parody of Whitman's universalist manner in *Leaves of Grass* and his message of sympathy with the oppressed.[64] Pound had parodied Whitman before in *The Spirit of Romance* (1910), where he expressed

---

[60] 'Salutation the Second', *Con* 7.
[61] *'Pax Saturni'*, *Con* 8.
[62] 'Commission', *Con* 11.
[63] 'Commission', *Con* 10–11.
[64] In his discussion of *Lustra* (1916)—which opens with selections from 'Contemporania'—Leslie Fiedler likewise notes that a significant number of Pound's free-verse poems are 'so close to the Whitmanian model that they seem counterfeits, impersonations, trembling on the verge of parody' ('Pound as Parodist', 136). For further commentary on the Whitmanian rhythms of Pound's addresses, see Hugh Witemeyer, *Poetry of Ezra Pound: Forms and Renewals* (Berkeley: University of California Press, 1969),

92 MODERNIST PARODY

irritation with 'all his catalogues and flounderings' and the 'horrible air of rectitude with which Whitman rejoices in being Whitman', pretending 'to be conferring a philanthropic benefit on the human race by recording his own self-complacency', when in fact his is 'the voice of one who saith':

> "Lo, behold, I eat water melons. When I eat water melons the
> world eats water melons
> > through me.
> When the world eats water melons,
> I partake of the world's water melons . . ."[65]

The parody was aimed at Whitman's egoism and his democratism, which particularly irked Pound (who believed in discernment and selection and therefore saw himself as making his primary addresses to readers with culture, or the will to acquire it). Whitman's philanthropic catalogues were indeed compromised by the intensity of his egoism and already verged on self-parody, and so they were readily subverted to communicate Pound's impatience with those who have effectively chosen oppression through ignorance, complacency, or acceptance of the status quo. But reading French poetry revealed Whitman to be the single American writer whose innovations profoundly influenced post-Symbolist experiments in *vers libre* that Pound found so attractive. As Betsy Erkkila has shown in *Walt Whitman among the French* (1980), Whitman was hailed as a prophet and master of the 'new spirit' animating avant-garde French literature, and acted as an acknowledged influence on: Jules Romains's *La Vie unanime* (1980), in which the poet ambles through urban scenes, losing himself in the collective soul of the world, marshalling the multiple impressions he receives all in their immediacy and detail; '*Le Whitmanisme*', the movement announced by Henri Ghéon in *Nouvelle Revue Française* (1912) to explain the common approach that united the diverse post-Symbolist poets collected in *Anthologie de l'effort* (1912); the *Dynamistes*, whose spokesman Henri Guilbeaux found Whitman to be essentially modern because his poetry registers the emotions of machines; and even Marinetti, who accepted Whitman as one of the five or six great precursors of Futurism.[66] And now Pound would use parody to sift through Whitman's techniques and topics to extract what was 'durable' and expose what was merely 'apparent' as he set about modernizing his own his verse.

134–8, where he discusses 'the Whitmanian envoi' (134). For an extended account of Pound's changing relations with Whitman across his career, see Hugh Witemeyer, 'Clothing the American Adam: Pound's Tailoring of Walt Whitman', in Bornstein, *Ezra Pound among the Poets*, 81–105.

[65] *SR* 163, 178, 178, 179, 179.

[66] Betsy Erkkila, *Walt Whitman among the French: Poet and Myth* (Princeton, NJ: Princeton University Press, 1980). *Anthologie de l'effort* incidentally included selections from René Arcos, Georges Duhamel, Charles Vidrac, and Jules Romains, all of whom Pound discussed in 'Approach to Paris', serialized in *New Age* XIII(19–25) (4 September–16 October 1913).

In 'What I Feel about Walt Whitman' (1909), Pound confessed 'I read him (in many parts) with acute pain, but when I write of certain things I find myself using his rhythms.'[67] He otherwise sought to assure readers that Whitman's tricks (his admixture of colloquial diction and expansive rhetoric) held no interest for him but claimed that as citizens of the same country 'The vital part of my message, taken from the sap and fibre of America, is the same as his.'[68] This was, of course, the reverse of the truth. As Fiedler has noted 'Pound in fact tended everywhere to subvert Whitman's "message", his euphoric celebration of democracy and mass society, along with his attack on the traditional High Culture of Europe', but nonetheless used 'for that purpose ... Whitman's whole bag of "tricks", particularly his metrics, that dactylic or triple falling rhythm, which is characteristic not just of Whitman but of all American as opposed to British speech and provides a viable homegrown alternative to the Old World iambs which Pound prided himself on having broken.'[69]

Having parodied Whitman's worst excesses in 'Salutation the Second' and '*Pax Saturni*', while enjoying his expansive cadences all the same, Pound had exercised what Proust called 'the purgative, exorcizing virtue of parody' and made 'an intentional pastiche' of Whitman in order to avoid 'involuntary pastiches'. Pound could now finally set out the terms of a rapprochement with Whitman in 'A Pact':

> I make a truce with you, Walt Whitman—
> I have detested you long enough.
> I come to you as a grown child
> Who has had a pig-headed father;
> I am old enough now to make friends.
> It was you that broke the new wood,
> Now is a time for carving.
> We have one sap and one root—
> Let there be commerce between us.[70]

Whitman, the 'pig-headed father ... broke the new wood' of free verse; 'Like Dante he wrote in the "vulgar tongue", in a new metric. The first great man to write in the language of his people.'[71] Now Pound, Whitman's equally defiant (self-appointed spiritual) son, will carve the Whitmanian language of his people into a thing of hard beauty, with the clean lines of sculpture, albeit with the undeclared advantage of the example of the French post-Symbolist poets whose innovations bore Whitman's influence. The result is the final poem in the suite, the luminous 'one image

---

[67] Ezra Pound, 'What I Feel about Walt Whitman', *Selected Prose: 1909–1965*, ed. William Cookson (New York: New Directions, 1973), 115.
[68] Pound, 'What I Feel about Walt Whitman', 115.
[69] Fiedler, 'Pound as Parodist', 135.
[70] 'A Pact', *Con* 11–12.
[71] 'A Pact', *Con* 12; Pound, 'What I Feel about Walt Whitman', 116.

94 MODERNIST PARODY

poem' 'In a Station of the Metro'.[72] A simple, elegant sentence has been carved into discrete forms that are placed on the page with sculptural precision:

The apparition   of these faces   in the crowd :
Petals   on a wet, black   bough .[73]

As Pound would later explain in 'Vorticism', 'In a Station of the Metro' uses 'super-position' to capture the sudden emotion he experienced on seeing 'a beautiful face, and then another and another' at the metro train at La Concorde by recording 'the precise instant when a thing outward and objective transforms itself, or darts into a thing inward and subjective'.[74] The haunting '*hokku*-like sentence' registers the vogue for Japanese poetry, while the topic and tone is indebted to Romains's *Unanimiste* apprehension of the fleeting nature of the crowd in urban space as per the preface to *L'Armée dans la Ville*, which Pound translated for readers of the *New Age* to show why they should take the French poet's work seriously:[75]

> Space belongs to no one. And no being has succeeded in appropriating a morsel of space to saturate with its unique existence. All intercrosses, coincides, cohabits. Each point serves as perch for a thousand birds. There is Paris, there is the rue Montmartre, there is an assembling, there is a man, there is a cellule on the very pavement. A thousand beings are concentric. One sees a little of some of them . . .
>   But groups! . . . Their life makes and unmakes itself, as an unstable state of matter, a condensation which does not endure. They show us that life is, at the origin, a provisory attitude, a moment of exception, an intensity between abatements, nothing continuous, nothing decisive . . . The crowd before the foreign barracks comes to life little by little as water in a kettle that sings and evaporates.[76]

'In a Station of the Metro' stills that intense moment in the unstable life of the crowd, the instant when the human murmuration is suddenly reconfigured into a new shape. And it does so with an economy, simplicity, and precision that exemplifies the commitment to 'direct treatment of the "thing"', spareness, and composition 'in the sequence of musical phrase' that Flint would later formalize (at Pound's instigation) as the three Imagist principles.[77] But it was Flint, not Pound, who was the first to see that combining the economy and elegance of the Japanese haiku with the spiritual insight of the Symbolist poets had the potential to bring English poetry up to date. Pound was simply acting on Flint's suggestion: 'To the poet who can catch and render, like these Japanese, the brief fragments of his soul's music, the future lies open. He must have the spiritual insight of the Maeterlinck of

---

[72] Pound, *Gaudier-Brzeska*, 89.
[73] 'In a Station of the Metro', *Con* 12.
[74] Pound, *Gaudier-Brzeska*, 89.
[75] Pound, *Gaudier-Brzeska*, 89.
[76] Ezra Pound, 'The Approach to Paris: III', *New Age* XIII(21) (18 September 1913), 607.
[77] Flint, 'Imagisme', 199.

'AN ATMOSPHERE OF PARODY' 95

the Trésor des Humbles, and he must write, I think, like these Japanese, in snatches of song'.[78]

Pound had sequenced the poems of *Canzoni* to narrate his predicament as a post-Victorian poet, showing how he could let his imagination run in concert with the forces of history, using pastiche and parody to locate himself within—and attempt to launch himself beyond—his literary heritage, thereby confronting the issues that made a new attitude necessary. In 'Contemporania', he used a similar diagnostic approach, working through different postures, attitudes, and influences, as he attempted to modernize himself, but succeeded in clearing the ground to deliver a luminous masterpiece that was not diminished by the 'atmosphere of parody' that surrounded it. That atmosphere was not just a function of the Whitmanian elements of 'Salutation the Second' and 'Commission'. It was also created by Pound's exaggerated swagger and satirical animus; the friction between the ludicrous and the lyric; the tolerance for internal and stylistic contradiction; the mismatch of high-hatting classical titles and weighty epigraphs with baldly descriptive headings and redacted mottos from contemporary poets; the disparity between fleet-footed free verse, musical phrase, and lumbering anaphora; and the swings from delicacy to gleeful phallicism. These mutually mocking contrasts contributed to the impression that on some level the whole performance was a grand joke that, if it was not strict parody in the conventional sense, drew energy from other models (Whitman, Romains, de Vega, H. D., the comic invective of contemporary avant-garde groups, the primitivism of post-Impressionists) to implicate them in a form of stylized self-parody that dared its critics to denounce it as 'nonsense' even as it insisted its themes and innovative techniques were entirely serious. Pound wanted his audience to laugh at his assault on solemnity, emotional frigidity, and polite conventions, but he also wanted them to appreciate the process by which he arrived at a new poetics of pared-back simplicity, exemplified by a poem that was undeniably contemporary and yet hauntingly beautiful.

Pound's shock tactics proved highly effective: the sulphurous stance of 'Contemporania' caused an outrage. Raymond Macdonald Alden condemned Pound's poems for flaunting 'occasional indecencies which are at once harmless and inexcusable, because unconnected with passion' and Wallace Rice wrote to the *Dial* in regret that '*Poetry* is being turned into a thing for laughter'.[79] Many poets responded to Pound's rallying call in the satirical and mocking vein that 'Contemporania' demanded, raising Pound's profile, and perpetuating the 'atmosphere of parody' he had cultivated. Monroe's eye was particularly drawn by two parodies by Bert Leston Taylor in his humorous column 'A Line o' Type or Two' in the *Chicago*

---

[78] F. S. Flint, 'Book of the Week: Recent Verse', *New Age* III(11) (11 July 1908), 213.

[79] Raymond Macdonald Alden, 'The New Poetry', *Nation* XCVI (17 April 1913), 386–7, in Homberger, *Ezra Pound*, 100; Wallace Rice, 'Mr. Ezra Pound and *Poetry*', *Dial* LIV (1 May 1913), 370–1, in Homberger, *Ezra Pound*, 101.

96 MODERNIST PARODY

Tribune, which she considered of sufficient importance to reprint in her biography, *A Poet's Life* (1938); one after the manner of 'Salutation', calling attention to the parallel between what Pound was attempting and Cubism, and the other after the manner of 'Tenzone'.[80]

'"Salutation"—To the New Poetry'

O degenerates in the art of writing,
    and fallen ones,
I have seen Cubists splattering their paints,
I have seen them make hideous splotches,
I have seen their riots of color
    and found nothing in them.
You are far worse than they are,
And they are much worse than nothing;
And the nude descends the staircase,
    and does not even own clothing.[81]

'Spring in State Street'

Will people accept them?
    (i.e. these bargains).
O dainty colorings and range of prices!
Gowns of charmeuse in all
    the colours of the season;
Blouse skirts of Russian cloth,
    tucked belt of softest satin,
And only at $37.50.

Get it straight. Ezra Pound is a poet, and much of his stuff contrasts refreshingly with the conventional oompa-oompa. Formal rimes and rhythms are not necessary to poetry.[82]

Taylor had got Pound's measure, signalling his appreciation for Pound's publicity exercise by recasting Pound's poem as an advertisement. The suggestion that 'Contemporania' was so degenerate as to be sub-Cubist, even worse than Duchamp's notorious *Nude Descending a Staircase* (1912) put Pound's poetry on a footing with the most radical contemporary European art. Taylor's approbation helped to reassure Monroe that she was right to print 'Contemporania' despite her reservations about Pound's mocking references to 'amateur harlots', 'disguised procurers',

---

[80] Monroe, *Poet's Life*, 310–11.
[81] Bert Leston Taylor, *Chicago Tribune* (18 April 1913), 8.
[82] Bert Leston Taylor, *Chicago Tribune* (17 April 1913), 6.

'AN ATMOSPHERE OF PARODY' 97

and 'delicate lusts', and that Pound was bringing poetry up to date with concurrent revolutions in art.[83] She answered Rice's accusations in a letter to the *Dial*, pointing out that 'Mr. Rice has edited so many anthologies—among them, *The Little Book of Brides*, *The Little Book of Kisses*, *The Little Book of Sports*—that the keen edge of his judgement as an authority on poetry is somewhat worn'.[84]

Of the many parodies 'Contemporania' inspired the most penetrating was undoubtedly Aldington's 'Penultimate Poetry', published in the second issue of the *Egoist*.[85] In addition to 'Contemporania', Aldington was also responding to sixteen further poems by Pound, which appeared in the November 1913 issue of *Poetry*, and would later be reprinted in *Lustra* (1916) with certain titles altered.[86] Pound's covering letter of October 1913 to Alice Corbin Henderson, associate editor of *Poetry*, daring her to devote an issue to his new work, indicates that he intended they would be even more outrageous than 'Contemporania':

> There'll be a *howl*. They won't like it. It's absolutely the *last* obsequies of the Victorian period...
>
> It's not futurism and it's not post-impressionism, but it's work contemporary with those schools and to my mind the most significant that I have yet brought off.
>
> BUTT [*sic*] they won't like it. They won't object as much as they did to Whitman's outrages, because the stamina of stupidity is weaker. I guarantee you *one* thing. The reader will not be *bored*. He will say ahg, ahg, ahh, ahhh, but-bu-bu-but this isn't Poetry.[87]

For good measure, Pound added '*This* series of poems is PREposterous... Still, I give you your chance to be modern, to go blindfoldedly to be modern, to produce as many green bilious attacks throughout the length and breadth of the U.S.A. as there are fungoid members of the American academy'.[88]

Aldington found Pound's shock tactics highly amusing and parodied them with aplomb. 'Penultimate Poetry', a suite of poems published in the *Egoist* in January 1914, was written at a time of heightened social and aesthetic tension between Aldington and Pound, and it shows. Pound had been instrumental in securing Aldington's position as sub-editor of the *Egoist*, but was taken aback when Aldington refused to do his bidding. And for all Aldington was grateful to Pound for supporting his career, the barrage of intrusive and unbidden editorial

---

[83] *LEP* 53, n. 1.

[84] Harriet Monroe, 'In Defense of *Poetry*', *Dial* LIV (16 May 1913), 409, in Homberger, *Ezra Pound*, 106.

[85] *PP* 36.

[86] Ezra Pound, 'Poems', *Poetry: A Magazine of Verse* III(2) (November 1913), 53–60.

[87] *LEP* 60–1, Pound's italics and capitals.

[88] *LEP* 61, Pound's italics and capitals.

98 MODERNIST PARODY

advice he received was beginning to rankle.[89] The aesthetic differences between the two men can be gauged from Aldington's essay 'Anti-Hellenism: A Note on Some Modern Art', which directly precedes 'Penultimate Poetry' in the same issue of the *Egoist*. Here, Aldington claims to have nothing but 'admiration for the artists and poets who are striving "to render their times in the terms of their times"', and cites the efforts of the 'Parnassians, Symbolists, Realists, Aesthetes, Unanimistes, Paroxystes, Imagists, etc'. as 'minor reactions' against romanticism.[90] He declares, somewhat defensively, 'I pay my shilling to go to exhibitions and I do my best to follow the latest thing in post-Whitman-splendeur-des-forces-simultaneous poetry', before acknowledging, a little grudgingly, 'the great value of, say, the sculpture of Mr. Epstein and the painting of M. Picasso and the latest poems of Mr. Pound', and then finally admitting that the qualities he observes in 'the latest reactionary art' are 'unHellenic' and 'unhealthy', yearning instead for the simplicity and beauty of the 'ordinary uninteresting things that the Greeks loved—health and beauty and youth'.[91]

Aldington's *ad hominem* parody is comprehensive in its attack. The pseudo-Greek subtitle 'Xenophilometropolitania' mocks Pound's classical posturing, and his weakness for Latin headings such as 'Lustra' and 'Xenia', while pointing to the contrast between the lost grace of ancient literatures and Pound's seedy snapshots of contemporary suburban life.[92] The mockery extends to Pound's fetish for old European forms in the first poem of the sequence, the grandiosely entitled 'Tenzone alla Gentildonna', which conflates the 'Tenzone' of 'Contemporania' with Pound's November 1913 poem 'Gentildonna', has only the single line 'Come, my songs' to its name, poking fun at one of Pound's most overused refrains.[93]

---

[89] 'Ezra had been butting in on our studies and poetic productions, with alternative encouragements and the reverse, according to his mood', Aldington, *Life for Life's Sake*, 134.

[90] Richard Aldington, 'Anti-Hellenism: A Note on Some Modern Art', *Egoist* I(2) (15 January 1914), 35.

[91] Aldington, 'Anti-Hellenism', 35–6.

[92] *PP* 36; Pound, 'Poems', 56–8; Pound, 'Poems', 58–60.

[93] *PP* 36; Pound, 'Poems', 55. Louis Untermeyer likewise targeted Pound's eclecticism, hortative style, and will to provocation in his book of parodies *And Other Poets* (New York: Holt & Co., 1916), 55–7.

> EZRA POUND
>
> Putting on a Greek Head-Dress, Provençal Slippers, and an Imagiste Air, Recites:
>
> ΠΗΑ ΠΟΥΔΙΝΓΣ [Pea Poundings]
>
> I
>
> COME, my songs, let us sing about something—
> It is time we were getting ourselves talked about.

Untermeyer proceeds to mock Pound's naked and impudent stylings, his debts to Whitman, and his tepid love songs:

> You tell me your love is platonic, and your passion
> has cooled to me,
> Like a porcelain pitcher in which hot water for shaving
> has been standing for hours.

Aldington continues to send up Pound's hortative style by repeating this line (which occurs once in 'Further Instructions', twice in 'Salvationists') six times in 'Penultimate Poetry'. In 'Cantata', Aldington takes aim at Pound the Browningesque ragpicker, who assembles miscellaneous fragments from the archive of world culture:

Cantata.

"Men pols lois puelh voys."

—Arnaut of Marvoil.

> Come my songs,
> Let us observe this person
> Who munches chicken-bones like a Chinese consul
> Mandilibating a delicate succulent Pekinese spaniel.[94]

A comically incongruous *faux* quotation from Arnaut introduces a poem which mocks Pound's newfound taste for orientalism by inviting readers to observe a person indelicately picking over the bones of chinoiserie. (Aldington's skill is evident in his choice of the word 'mandilibating', meaning 'chewing', but also evoking 'Mandarin'—a Poundian multilingual pun—in a perfect reproduction of Pound's gourmet savouring of aural effects.)

Next, 'Elevators' mocks Pound's Americanism and attitudinizing, as well as his vaunted virility and delicacy. The poet exhorts his songs to present their 'most undignified exterior' and soar with him beyond the eighteenth floor of a skyscraper to 'consider the delicate delectable monocles/Of the musical virgins of Parnassus', a description that takes its cues from Pound's knowingly preposterous invocation 'Gather about me, O Muses!/... O Muses with delicate shins,/O Muses with delectable knee-joints' in 'Ancora', while contriving to emphasize the curious lack of passion with which this supposedly virile poet renders his symbols of female inspiration, insinuating that the true muses of his art were frigid wearers of Sapphically coded eyepieces.[95] (This line of attack acquired additional resonance in relation to the complex personal circumstances that informed Pound's relationship with H. D., a muse whom he (mis)took for a protégé, also Pound's former fiancée, and Aldington's wife since 1913.) The concluding line 'Pale slaughter beneath purple skies' takes Pound's technique of superposition to absurd extremes, while also parodying the coda to Pound's 'April' ('Pale carnage beneath bright mist'), suggesting how Pound's verse is being stripped bare and slaughtered.[96]

Pound's lack of carnal appetite is again ridiculed in Aldington's 'Ancora', which appropriates Pound's title only to unmoor the fragment that follows from sense, reworking a mystifying prognostication from 'Xenia', 'Rest me with Chinese

---

[94] *PP* 36.
[95] *PP* 36; Pound, 'Poems', 53.
[96] *PP* 36; Pound, 'Poems', 55.

100 MODERNIST PARODY

colors,/For I think the glass is evil', which already has the absurd feel of a bad translation, so that it reads 'Rest me with mushrooms,/For I think the steak is evil'.[97] Then, the sterile refinement of the desired but resisted encounter in Pound's poem 'The Garden' is converted into the comic hyperbole and squalor of 'Convicted':

> Like an armful of greasy engineer's-cotton
> Flung by a typhoon against a broken crate of ducks' eggs
> She stands by the rail of the Old Bailey dock.
> Her intoxication is exquisite and excessive,
> And delicate her delicate sterility.
> Her delicacy is so delicate that she would feel affronted
> If I remarked nonchalantly, "*Saay* [*sic*], stranger, ain't you dandy."[98]

Pound's fluttering first line, 'Like a skein of loose silk blown against a wall', with its alliterative effects, is replaced by a grosser simile that combines the uncouth with the absurd.[99] The well-bred, but bored young lady of Kensington Gardens is morphed into a woman on a drunk and disorderly charge. Aldington applies Pound's poeticisms to this sad creature, transferring Pound's description of her boredom to his lady's intoxication. Pound's pet-word 'delicate', which appears eight times in in 'Penultimate Poetry' (nine if you include 'delicacy') is again petted without mercy, made ridiculous through incongruous overuse.[100]

In the fourth poem, 'Gitanjali', Aldington takes aim at Pound's rapturous praise for Tagore, whom Monroe had introduced to an American audience with great fanfare for the first time in the June 1913 number of *Poetry*.[101] Neither H. D. nor Aldington had the honour of meeting Tagore when he was in London. In his memoirs, Aldington said, 'I could always tell when Ezra had been seeing him, because was he was so infernally smug'.[102] 'We had pi-jaw stuff about Tagore for weeks', Aldington recalled, 'Yeats would read the same things over and over from *Gitanjali*, as if they had been the Book of Common Prayer'.[103]

Having expressed his irritation with the hype surrounding the discovery of Tagore, Aldington again goads Pound for his repetitive invocations, following the now customary line 'Come my songs' with the parenthesis '(For we have not "come" during three of these our delectable canzoni)'.[104] 'Altruism' then taunts Pound with the prospect that he is the smug, self-satisfied party, outing him as

---

[97] Pound, 'Poems', 59; *PP* 36.

[98] *PP* 36.

[99] 'The Garden', *Con* 3.

[100] Pound was piqued when Aldington pointed out to him that he had 'used the word delicate 947 times in "Lustra"', *Ezra Pound and Dorothy Shakespeare*, 293.

[101] *PP* 36; Rabindranath Tagore, 'Poems', *Poetry: A Magazine of Verse* II(3) (June 1913), 81–91.

[102] Aldington, *Life for Life's Sake*, 109.

[103] Aldington, *Life for Life's Sake*, 109.

[104] *PP* 36.

'AN ATMOSPHERE OF PARODY' 101

an expert self-publicist, while questioning his commitment to supporting other writers:

> Come my songs,
> Let us praise ourselves;
> I doubt if the smug will do it for us,
> The smug who possess all the rest of the universe.[105]

'Songs of Innocence' uses simple substitution to show how close Pound's attempts to emulate the laconic grace of Chinese and Japanese literature by juxtaposing fragmentary lines could bring him to naively absurd parody. Here is Pound's image of the iridescence of a field rippling in the breeze, prefiguring the harvest in 'Xenia', part IV:

> The wind moves above the wheat—
> With a silver crashing,
> A thin war of metal.[106]

In 'Songs of Innocence' Aldington renders these lines:

> The wind moves over the wheat
> With a silver crashing,
> A thin war of delicate kettles.[107]

'In a Station of the Metro' then receives the same treatment, but to different effect:

> The apparition   of these poems   in a crowd:
> White faces   in a black   dead faint.[108]

This deadpan rendition (showing a sensitivity to the original spacing that escapes many modern editions) presents an alternative image in which Pound's rebellious poems are sapped of their vital energy. Pound's luminous moment when the faces in the crowd are transformed into an image that is organic and beautiful emerges unscathed, because the parody does not identify a real defect in the original poem itself, which partakes of the grace, simplicity, and beauty he identified with Hellenism, but uses its form as a vehicle for commentary. In many respects, Pound could not have hoped for a more thorough or discriminating reader.

In 'Further Tests', Pound asked that the pupil judge 'whether the joke is on the parodied or the parodist'.[109] Aldington's parody was so close to the mark that the

---

[105] *PP* 36.
[106] *Poems* 59.
[107] *PP* 36.
[108] *PP* 36.
[109] Pound, *ABC of Reading*, 69.

102 MODERNIST PARODY

joke would have been very much on Pound, were it not for the fact that Aldington had taken Pound's bait and written poems that exaggerated the very tendencies he deemed 'unHellenic' and 'unhealthy'. The criticism that Pound's poems lacked vital energy rebounded on Aldington, who enjoyed himself so much in the role of mock provocateur that he allowed his parodies to be animated by his approximations of Pound's comically agitated style. (Aldington would later restate the case that he found Pound's fulminations wearying and false in his otherwise approving review of *Blast* (1914).)[110] That Pound was a self-publicist was beyond doubt, but Aldington's parodies only served to prove that Pound's outlandish tactics got his poetry noticed. Where Aldington did hit Pound hard was his identification of unconscious stylistic tics, eclecticism, and lack of passion. Pound shrugged off all of Aldington's criticism when he responded to his father, who was anxious that his son was becoming figure of ridicule, explaining that he had virtually overseen the parodies, gloating:

> No one whom I hadn't under my own jurisdiction could have done the job so well. They attest a definite manner and do not in the least affect one's enjoyment of the originals. I was delighted with them.[111]

That Pound had commissioned the parodies is doubtful, although he did provide indirect encouragement in the sense that 'Contemporania' is a call to parody and Aldington responded in kind.

Aldington's reception of Pound's poetry and Pound's subsequent response provides a dynamic by which the modernist attitude to parody, and indeed its defining role in the origination of literary modernism, can be understood. It is fuelled by the spirit of competition. The boldest, best work is not diminished, but energized by its parodies, and shown to be of permanent value, while the best parodies might acquire the status of original art. When modernist writers took parody or self-parody as their principle of genesis for truly new writing, they implicitly extended the same invitation to subsequent writers. They might be inspired to parody different materials to develop new modes of expression, or they might turn the parodic scrutiny back on the original work, either to expose its defects or push its avant-gardism to further extremes. Rising to meet this challenge required study and skill, as Pound explained in a letter he sent to the editor of *Poetry*, emphasizing

---

[110] 'As the uncleanness of his language increases to an almost laughable point the moral sentiment of his writing becomes more and more marked . . . It is not that one wants Mr. Pound to repeat his Provençal feats, to echo the 'nineties—he has done that too much already—it is simply the fact that Mr. Pound cannot write satire . . . I cannot help thinking that all this enormous arrogance and petulance and fierceness are a pose. And it is a wearisome pose.' Richard Aldington, 'Blast', *Egoist* I(14) (15 July 1914), 273.

[111] Mary de Rachewiltz, A. David Moody, and Joanna Moody, eds. *Ezra Pound to His Parents, Letters 1895–1929* (Oxford: Oxford University Press, 2010), 321.

'AN ATMOSPHERE OF PARODY' 103

Aldington's excellence, and criticizing the inexpert parodies of his work submitted to the journal by Leroy Titus Weeks:

> True, his parodies are unimportant as parodies, and I could, in general, advise him and the rest of the American parodists of my work to leave off until they have studied the very excellent parodies made by Mr. Richard Aldington. Mr. Aldington is himself a poet, he knows something about imagism, he has taken the art seriously and made a study of various poets and periods; whereas my American parodists have for the most part studied neither me nor anyone else.[112]

Weeks had written into *Poetry* to complain that Pound's poems were designed to be bewildering. Following his letter, he put his thoughts into verse in a poem called 'Tommy Rot', presenting a scenario where readers sense that 'None but the initiated may see the web', and so tumble over themselves to say they get it, when in fact there is no web, just 'a mighty rattling of the loom!'[113] Weeks argued that Pound's radical 'fust and ferment' was insubstantial bluster, whereas Pound pointed out the fact that even Leroy was writing in free verse as proof that the reforming Imagist programme he had instigated was having a positive influence, even in quarters where his poems were not understood: 'The effects are seen even in Mr. L. T. W.'s *vers libre*, for his words are in the normal order.'[114] By contrast, Aldington's parodies demonstrated the acuity, insight, and skill of a fellow practitioner. The merit of 'Penultimate Poetry' is that it draws on an educated sensibility and is the fruit of careful study, not only of its models but also 'various poets and periods', resulting in parody that is close to the bone and equal to measuring the true value of Pound's work, sifting the apparent (the preposterous attitudinizing) from the durable (superposition, the simplicity, and lyric elegance of spare *vers libre*).

Expert or inexpert, parody vindicates good literature and reveals the defects of the bad. When it is practised by able, educated writers, it is not merely a critical exercise, but also assumes a literary importance in its own right. And its importance is in direct relation to its excellence, which it asserts by demonstrating a mastery of its model's techniques. The jostle for primacy between Aldington and Pound, with Aldington insinuating that his 'penultimate' parodies execute a prior conception (and hence true reflection) of Pound's work and Pound attempting to reclaim authority by intimating he had all but commissioned them, is symptomatic of the distinctive dynamics of modernist parody, which seeks to deliver the shock of the new and prove its comparative modernity, and is judged by whether it succeeds in surpassing its model. In order to be *important*, to advance the cause of modernism further, parody must surpass and so eclipse its model, and

---

[112] Ezra Pound, 'A Rejoinder', *Poetry: A Magazine of Verse* VI(3) (June 1915), 158.
[113] Leroy Titus Weeks, 'Correspondence: The New Beauty', *Poetry: A Magazine of Verse* VI(1) (April 1915), 50.
[114] Weeks, 'Correspondence', 48. Pound, 'A Rejoinder', 158.

104 MODERNIST PARODY

demonstrate its unquestionable mastery of the material from which it creates new modes for art. By the same logic, Pound had to surpass Whitman and break free from convention to become truly contemporary, but he also had to be able to write material that could withstand and outshine his future parodists if he was to bring about his *risorgimento*.

'Contemporania' was only a beginning, and in many ways a wrong-footed one. As Yeats presciently observed in a lecture in Chicago in March 1914, 'Much of his [Pound's] work is experimental; his work will come slowly, he will make many an experiment before he comes into his own.'[115] Pound's next project was *Des Imagistes: An Anthology* (1914), which was designed to counter the extraordinarily success of *Georgian Poetry* (1912) and to consolidate the reputation of his new school. In an interview with the press, Pound announced that 'The Anthology does not represent the personalities of those included, nor does it represent their differences, but the line where they come together, their agreement that the cake-icing on the top of poetry—the useless adjectives and the unnecessary similes which burden verse like cumbrous ornaments—should be avoided', a comment that anticipates the patisserie charge he would later aim at *A Lume Spento* (1968).[116]

Des Imagistes collected poems by Aldington, H. D., Flint, Skipwith Cannell, Amy Lowell, William Carlos Williams, Joyce, Pound, Ford (then Hueffer), Allen Upward, and John Cournos, the majority of which had been previously published elsewhere. The frenchified title was affected, and somewhat cryptic, given the volume's eclectic mix of classical imitations and translations (H. D., Aldington, Williams, and Pound), chinoiserie (Pound and Upward), 1890s-ish nocturnes (Cannell), Joyce's poem 'I Hear an Army', admired and inspired by Yeats, and Hueffer's portrait of a statue in a German town square, 'In the Little Old Market-Place'.[117]

All in all, the collection was too baggy to be truly revolutionary. Without a preface or manifesto, the only indication of what the school stood for was the set of three parodic 'Documents' at the end of the collection, the only new compositions to feature in *Des Imagistes*.[118] The first 'document' was Pound's parody of Burns's 'Is There for Honest Poverty', 'To Hulme (T. E.) and Fitzgerald', which was pulled from *Canzoni* at proof stage, now with a note that it was written for the 'Cenacle of 1909', *vide* the Hulme poems in *Ripostes* (in a gesture to the artistic and commercial pressures that rendered aestheticism and warmed-over romanticism a dead end).[119] The two other 'documents' were the only poems specifically written for *Des Imagistes*. They called further attention to Imagism's parodic background,

[115] W. B. Yeats, quoted in Stock, *Life of Ezra Pound*, 153.

[116] M. M. B. "'The Imagists", A Talk with Mr. Ezra Pound, Their Editor', *Daily News and Leader* (18 March 1914), 14.

[117] *DI* 40, 47–50.

[118] *DI* 55–62.

[119] Pound dropped the second parenthesis from the title 'To Hulme (T. E.) and Fitzgerald (A Certain)' when he published the poem in *Des Imagistes*. *DI* 57–8.

'AN ATMOSPHERE OF PARODY' 105

its status as an in-joke among those in the know, and the in-fighting that set its contributors apart and precluded it from definitive avant-garde action. The second document, 'Vates, the Social Reformer', by Richard Aldington, parodies Ford's *High Germany* (1911), in particular 'Süssmund's Address to an Unknown God (Adapted from the High German)', intimating that Ford the (verse) reformer who insisted *ad nauseum* that writers should register their time in terms of their own time needed to re-examine his own practice.[120] Here Aldington used Ford's characteristic longwinded, conversational style to make the bitter complaint that Ford would have him forsake his 'Greek ambitions' for poetry and 'write bad novels like himself'.[121] And although Ford was Aldington's ostensible target, he was also in on the joke, because he retaliated in the next 'document', 'Fragments Addressed by Clearchus H. to Aldi', deflecting parodic attention from his own verbosity back onto *Aldi*ngton and his ardent Hellenism.[122]

Ford's composition is an amusing parody of 'Au Vieux Jardin' (one of Aldington's contributions to *Des Imagistes*), but one that has been mockingly transliterated into cod-Ancient Greek—a schoolboyish prank to insinuate that Aldington's Hellenic productions are equally jejune, inauthentic, and incongruous.[123] The subtext of Ford's 'Fragments' might be rendered thus (with genuine Greek quotations intact):

Poetry
Price fifteen cents.
p. 43

I have sat here happy in my armchair
    (Putney bus, Putney bus)[1]
Watching the still hound and the kid
With the dark hair
Which the wind of my upraised voice
Tore like a green mattered moss
    ('Ω ἄνδρες Ἀθηναῖοι)[2]
Of wet cobwebs and seaweed at twilight,
But though I greatly delighted
    (ηράμαν μεν εγω σέθεν, Ἀλδί, πάλαι πότα)[3]
In these and the Ezra whiskers
That which sets me nearest to weeping
    (ὁ δε Κλέαρχος εἶπε)[4]
Is the classical rhythm of the rare speeches
O the unspoken speeches
Hellenic.

---

[120] *DI* 59–61; Ford Madox Hueffer, *High Germany* (London: Duckworth, 1911), xxvi-xxxiii.
[121] *DI* 60, 61.
[122] *DI* 62.
[123] *DI* 11.

106 MODERNIST PARODY

Notes.

(1) A vehicle conducting passengers from Athens, the capital of Greece, to the temple of the winds, which stands in a respectable suburb.

(2) Rendered by Butler, "O God! O Montreal!"

(3) Sappho!!!!!!

(4) Xenophon's Anabasis.

F. M. H.[124]

'Poetry/Price fifteen cents' is a dig at Monroe's magazine, and its cover price, foregrounding the commercial motivations guiding the writing of new verse. The prosaic modern world of respectable suburbs, armchairs, and Putney buses is in such stark contrast to classical civilization that Ford is brought near to weeping (presumably tears of laughter) at the Hellenizing tendencies of Aldington and Pound (whose artistic self-fashionings, and Mephistophelean beard, Ford found irresistibly comic).[125] The first interjected fragment of genuine Greek might be rendered: 'O Athenian men' (which is comically misrepresented in the facetious footnotes that accompany the poem). The next is a travesty of the line that was generally considered to be 'the most memorable and beautiful of all Sappho's writing', as Ford would later explain in *The March of Literature* (1939) in which he translated the line literally as 'I loved thee, Atthis, long since, in ages past'.[126] The next fragment of Ancient Greek after that is the empty tag 'Clearchus said', from Xenophon, the great Greek historian who registered the events of his time in plain, contemporary speech, whose values align with Ford's own, hence the title 'Fragments Addressed from Clearchus H. to Aldi'. The reference is deliberately cited without substance to insist that Aldington's habit of classical quotation amounted to a superficial effect. Finally, the overexcited footnote 'Sappho!!!!!!' refers to Aldington's contribution 'To Atthis (After the Manuscript of Sappho now in Berlin)', tying the classical allusions neatly together, while mocking Aldington's eagerness to bring an attic grace to his compositions that the English language simply will not permit.[127] If the three Imagist 'documents' do anything to document the history of the school, they bear testimony to its parodic pedigree, its lack of a definite programme, its capacity to laugh at its divisions and differences, and its participants' broad commitment to generating critically incisive dialogue about the proper forms modern poetry should take.

[124] *DI* 62.

[125] According to Ford, Pound 'would wear trousers made of green billiard cloth, a pink coat, a blue shirt, a tie hand-painted by a Japanese friend, an immense sombrero, a flaming beard cut to a point, and a single, large blue earring'. See Ford Madox Ford, *Return to Yesterday* (London: Victor Gollancz, 1931), 370.

[126] Ford Madox Ford, *The March of Literature, from Confucius' Day to our Own*, intro. Alexander Theroux (Illinois: Dalkey Archive Press, 1998), 124.

[127] *DI* 19.

'AN ATMOSPHERE OF PARODY' 107

The mockery in *Des Imagistes* reflected Pound's growing reservations about the new school. Many of the contributions fell amusingly short of the directness or spareness advocated in 'Imagisme' and 'A Few Don'ts by an Imagiste', to the extent that their earnestness, which was once advertised as a strength, became ridiculous.[128] 'Imagisme' flaunted the 'formidable erudition' of the school's adherents and countered the charges of '*snobisme*' by insisting 'At least they do keep bad poets from writing!'[129] What bad writing there was in *Des Imagistes* needed to be deflated by parody and satire if the volume was to retain any integrity. Commodifying Imagism diluted its practice and weakened its force, and parody was needed to combat the resulting flabbiness, divest modern verse of Victorian habits, and hold contemporary writers to contemporary standards. After all, when Pound complained that an expression such as 'dim lands *of peace*' 'mixes an abstraction with the concrete' and so fails to recognize that 'the natural object is always the adequate symbol', he was not quoting a line by a Victorian poet, he was quoting Ford.[130]

When Lowell arranged a belated celebration of *Des Imagistes* on 17 July 1914, the ensuing farce confirmed how parodiable Imagism had become. James Wilhelm reports that Lowell called for speeches—and Ford and then Upward declared that they were not sure what the term 'Imagist' actually meant. The stage was then set for Pound:

> Ezra quietly sneaked out a side door and 'found' a tub; lugging this back into the room, he summarily dumped it onto the middle of the table, announcing that from this day on, the Imagists were dead, superseded by the Nagistes (Swimmers). This was an elaborate joke aimed at Amy's sole contribution to the anthology, 'In a Garden', which ended with the line 'Night, and the water, and you in your whiteness, bathing'. Acting as if on cue, Upward leaped up and just happened to have a parody of the poem, which he read aloud. Everyone was roaring with laughter—except Amy, who sat there grimly thinking. Later, she regained her spirits, and the evening ended with tolerably good cheer.[131]

The joke was on Lowell, at the expense of her ample form and slender contribution to *Des Imagistes*. Following the fateful party where Pound declared Imagism dead, Lowell attempted to take control of the movement by releasing a rival Imagist anthology. Pound resented Lowell's 'proposal to turn "Imagism" into a democratic beer-garden' and requested that she use a title like '*Vers Libre*' to distinguish her enterprise (which he snidely rebranded 'Amygism') from the original Imagist

---

[128] Flint, 'Imagisme', 198–9; Ezra Pound, 'A Few Don'ts by an Imagiste', *Poetry: A Magazine of Verse* I(6) (March 1913), 200–6.

[129] Flint, 'Imagisme', 200.

[130] Pound, 'A Few Don'ts', 201, Pound's italics; Ford Madox Ford, 'On a Marsh Road', in *The Face of the Night* (London: John McQueen, 1904), 69.

[131] James Wilhelm, *Ezra Pound in London and Paris, 1908–1925* (Pennsylvania: Pennsylvania State University Press, 1990), 162.

108   MODERNIST PARODY

group in a letter of 12 August 1914.[132] In defiance of Pound's wishes, Lowell brought out the first of three volumes of *Some Imagist Poets* in 1915. Pound disassociated himself from the school and applied his energies to Vorticism, a new avant-garde movement that countered earnestness with the mockery of satire, parody, and self-parody.

The first issue of Wyndham Lewis's adversarial magazine *Blast*, subtitled 'Review of the Great English Vortex', broadcast its scorn for the platitudes that passed for good taste with its shocking pink cover, boldface typography, and exclamatory editorials, to scourge the vestiges of Victorianism. The first manifesto comprised catalogues of blasts and blesses, cursing and commending fixtures in England's cultural life, after the manner of Guillaume Apollinaire's 'Distruzione' and 'Costruzione', '*Merda ai*' and '*Rose a*' catalogues in '*L'Antitradizione Futurista*', a manifesto published in the radical Futurist newspaper *Lacerba* (1913), which itself parodied the strategies and pronouncements of Futurist polemics, playing with Marinetti's ideas about *parole in libertà* by breaking with conventional syntax, punctuation, verse form, and consistent typography.[133] For all it blasted the 'years 1837–1900', along with all things retrograde, sentimental or feminine, and blessed those that embodied the modern spirit of rebellion, the avant-gardism of *Blast* was primarily aesthetic.[134] Especial disdain was reserved for the figure of the effeminate aesthete of the 1890s, out of whose etiolated shadow modernism was struggling to emerge: Lewis raged, 'CURSE WITH EXPLETIVE OF WHIRLWIND/THE BRITANNIC ÆSTHETE/CREAM OF THE SNOBBISH EARTH'.[135] For all its energy, *Blast* did not pose a serious challenge to the wider culture of post-Victorian England—its distinctive brand of English nationalism (inspired by Italian Futurism), and its emphasis on English ingenuity and industrial prowess reproduced the attitudes of British imperialism.

Lewis's first manifesto was not merely imitative, however. Vorticism was modelled on but also set in opposition to Futurism, which Lewis insisted was every bit as *passé* as the cultural formations Marinetti and his followers likewise scorned:

AUTOMOBILISM (Marinetteism) bores us. We don't want to go about making a hullo-bulloo about motor cars, anymore than about knives and forks, elephants or gas-pipes.

Elephants are VERY BIG. Motor cars go quickly.

Wilde gushed twenty years ago about the beauty of machinery. Gissing, in his romantic delight with modern lodging houses was futurist in this sense.

---

[132] *LEP* 90, 78.

[133] *B* 10–28; Guillaume Apollinaire, 'L'Antitradizione Futurista', *Lacerba* (15 September 1913), 202–3. For a reproduction of 'L'Antitradizione Futurista', see Richard Cork, *Vorticism and Abstract Art in the Machine Age, Volume 1: Origins and Development* (London: Gordon Fraser, 1976), 249.

[134] *B* 18.

[135] *B* 15, Lewis's capitals.

The futurist is a sensational and sentimental mixture of the aesthete of 1890 and the realist of 1870.[136]

Unlike Apollinaire, who threw (figurative) shit at negative influences on French culture without equivocation, Lewis mischievously muddied the waters, blasting entities that he subsequently blessed, for instance English humour, first hollering 'BLAST HUMOUR/Quack ENGLISH drug for stupidity and sleepiness', and then bellowing 'BLESS ENGLISH HUMOUR/It is the great barbarous weapon of the genius among races'.[137] 'FEAR OF RIDICULE' is cursed.[138] Lewis's second manifesto made sense of these seeming contradictions, explaining that Vorticist artists assumed a truly revolutionary stance, unleashing oppositions without subscribing to any one position, thereby freeing themselves from all allegiances to assert their own supreme selfhood:

1. Beyond Action and Reaction we would establish ourselves.
2. We start from opposite statements of a chosen world. Set up violent structure of adolescent clearness between two extremes.
3. We discharge ourselves on both sides.
4. We fight first on one side, then on the other, but always for the SAME cause, which is neither side or both sides and ours.[139]

The editorial sections of *Blast* deliberately 'set Humour at Humour's throat', including its vigorous humour in its own critique, leaving its readers helplessly caught in the ironies of the self-directed mockery that was beginning to define the modernist avant-garde project, which was being advanced by artists who were using parody to signal their contemporaneity and measure their sardonic distance from immediate predecessors.[140] Parody was the perfect form for containing opposite statements, doubly negated by discharges on both sides. No wonder Swift was blessed in the first manifesto 'for his solemn bleak wisdom of laughter'.[141]

Vorticism simply provided Pound with a new agenda and more forcefully energized rhetoric for his earlier advocacy of directness, hardness, efficiency, concentration, and precision. The Vorticist is concerned with 'the primary pigment of his art, nothing else', Pound explained in his manifesto 'VORTEX. POUND'.[142]

Every conception, every emotion presents itself to the vivid consciousness in some primary form.

---

[136] *B* 8, Lewis's capitals.
[137] *B* 17, 26, Lewis's capitals.
[138] *B* 15, Lewis's capitals.
[139] *B* 30, Lewis's capitals.
[140] *B* 31.
[141] *B* 26.
[142] *B* 153, Pound's capitals.

110 MODERNIST PARODY

It is the picture that means a hundred poems, the music that means a hundred pictures, the most highly energized statement, the statement that has not yet SPENT itself it [*sic*] expression, but which is the most capable of expressing.[143]

The revelation that 'The primary pigment of poetry is the IMAGE', still defined by Pound as 'that which presents an intellectual and emotional complex in an instant of time', and the citation of H. D.'s 'Oread' as the exemplary poem, made it clear that the technical premises of Imagism endured, even though the school itself was now spent so far as Pound was concerned.[144] But anxieties about the fate of Imagism and its swift dissipation through dispersal, inexpert imitation, and mimicry, did contour Pound's definition of the vortex as 'the point of maximum energy', the perpetual vanguard of art.[145] Within the space of a short manifesto, the primacy of primary expression is repeatedly contrasted with the dissipation of mimicry and imitation:

Elaboration, expression of second intensities, of dispersedness belong to the secondary sort of artist. Dispersed arts HAD a vortex ...

The vorticist relies not upon similarity or analogy, not upon likeness or mimicry ...

VORTICISM is art before it has spread itself into a state of flacidity [*sic*], of elaboration, of secondary applications ...

The vorticist will not allow the primary expression of any concept or emotion to drag itself out into mimicry.[146]

Vorticism in poetry, as Pound sought to define it, was not to be Amygism but Imagism undissipated, recharged to the point of maximal energy. The enemy of primacy and primary expression was secondary mimicry and imitation and a subsequent lack of self-created identity—a foe which had to be continually vanquished to prevent the radical and the really new from settling into complacency and losing its edge once it had effected changes that were felt in wider practice.

The irony was that Pound's poetic contributions to *Blast* merely continued in the dyspeptic manner of 'Contemporania', taking his assault on uncomprehending pressmen to newly rebarbative (and comically coarse) extremes:

Salutation the Third

Let us deride the smugness of " The Times ":
GUFFAW !

---

[143] *B* 153.
[144] *B* 154, Pound's capitals.
[145] *B* 153, Pound's capitals.
[146] *B* 154, Pound's capitals.

>   So much the gagged reviewers,
>   It will pay them when the worms are wriggling in their vitals;
>   These were they who objected to newness,
>   HERE are their TOMB-STONES.
>   They supported the gag and the ring:
>   A little black BOX contains them.
>   SO shall you be also,
>   You slut-bellied obstructionist,
>   You sworn foe to free speech and good letters,
>   You fungus, you continuous gangrene.[147]

In *Time and Western Man* (1927) Lewis complained (with particular reference to *Cantos* XVII–XIX):

> All Pound's comic reliefs speak the same tongue; they are all jocose and conduct their heavy german-american [*sic*] horseplay in the same personal argot of Pound . . . They are a caricature of Pound attempting to deal with real life—they are Pound at his worst.[148]

Lewis also reported that other members of the *Blast* group noted the discrepancy between Pound's stated programme for reform and his own practice:

> What struck them principally about Pound was that his fire-eating propagandist utterances were not accompanied by any very experimental efforts in his particular medium. His poetry, to the minds of the more fanatical of his group, was a series of pastiches of old french and old italian [*sic*] poetry and could lay no claim to participate in the new burst of art in progress. Its novelty consisted largely in the distance it went *back*, not forward; in archaism, not in new creation.[149]

To be fair, Pound was fully aware that his comic assays in *Blast* were merely outrages that would not form part of his durable body of material, and said as much in 'Monumentum Aere, Etc':

>   In a few years no one will remember the " buffo;"
>   No one will remember the trivial parts of me,
>   The comic detail will not be present.[150]

---

[147] *B* 45, Pound's capitals.
[148] Wyndham Lewis, *Time and Western Man* (London: Chatto & Windus, 1927), 90.
[149] Lewis, *Time and Western Man*, 55.
[150] *B* 46.

112 MODERNIST PARODY

However, Pound's deadpan renditions of the fragmentary 'Epitaphs' of the Tang dynasty poets Fu I and Li Po imply that whatever the limitations of heavy-handed satire, self-mockery is no bar to poetic immortality:

Fu I.

"Fu I loved the green hills and the white clouds,
Alas, he died of drink."

Li Po.

And Li Po also died drunk.
He tried to embrace a moon
In the yellow river.[151]

Pound was however confident in the durability of the clarity and expressive primacy of the Image, a fine example of which he delivered as the punchline to 'Come my Cantilations', which reads as if it were one of Aldington's parodies of Pound's invocations to his own songs save that it ends with the resonant line, 'We speak of burnished lakes,/And of dry air as clear as metal', fulfilling his promise to the 'gagged reviewers' who balk at his newness: 'And I will laugh at you and mock you,/And I will offer you consolations in irony,/O fools, detesters of Beauty'.[152]

The radical aesthetic of *Blast* typically met with derision. But poor reviews did not necessarily mean the magazine failed in its avant-garde ambitions. In many respects, *Blast* contrived to sear its image on public consciousness because the mocking shock tactics in its manifestos actively solicited parody. The *New Age* was one of the many organs that stood in broad opposition to Lewis's movement. Writing as 'R. C. H.', the editor A. R. Orage stated 'It is, I find, not unintelligible—as most of the reviewers will doubtless say—but not worth the understanding'.[153] Orage later complained that Rebecca West's contribution, a story entitled 'Indissoluble Matrimony', suffered 'all the vices of the "Blast" school, excessive and barbaric ornamentation, violent obscurity, degraded imagery; but unmixed with any idea' and professed that 'the movement appears to me to be the very devil' for its opposition to the 'Brilliant common sense, which we of THE NEW AGE have taken for our watchword'.[154] However, the pointed parodies of various contributions to *Blast* by Carl Erich Bechhöfer that appeared in the regular 'Pastiche' column of the *New Age* a fortnight later confirmed the relevance and interest of Vorticism to the magazine. They showed that Bechhöfer had taken careful note of specifics and presumed that readers of the column had been similarly attentive

---

[151] *B* 48.
[152] *B* 46.
[153] 'R. C. H.' [Alfred Orage], 'Reader and Writers', *New Age* XV(10) (9 July 1914), 229.
[154] 'R. C. H.', 'Readers and Writers', 253, Orage's capitals.

'AN ATMOSPHERE OF PARODY' 113

or would be prepared to accept these parodies as shorthand introductions to recent developments with which they would need to be acquainted should they fancy themselves up to date. The crosshead 'More Contemptoraries' (a play on Bechhöfer's regular banner 'More Contemporaries') introduced a parody of the *Blast* manifesto, which employs a simplified version of the Blast/Bless formula to mock Lewis's blustering contradictions, posturing, hasty editing, shouty typography and self-congratulatory tone, while echoing Orage's serious point that its rebel aesthetics posed a direct challenge to the politics of the *New Age*:

BLAST

BLAST GRAMMAR,	BLESS CLICHE [*sic*],
BLAST SPELLING,	BLESS BIG PRINT,
BLAST REASON,	BLESS BLOOD.
BLAST SENSE, SO	BLESS SELF, SO
BLAST THE NEW AGE	BLESS WYNDY LEWIS.[155]

There follows a skit on Pound's American redneck mode of abusive address, with a parody of his satirical poetry that mocks his lowbrow methods of impressing his high-brow credentials on readers with gratuitous references to Milton and Dante, and, as a final flourish, the Latin motto of Idaho, Pound's native state. Next, genuine information concerning how copies of *Blast* and subscriptions can be obtained is presented as if it were one of Pound's autonomous compositions, emphasizing how banal his smug satirical writing could be while flagging the commercial and promotional considerations that attend even the most avant-garde projects:

THIS BOOK.

Copies may be obtained from
Mr. Wyndham Lewis,
The ascetic of Great Ormond Street,
At the Rebel Art Centre,
Queen's Square, W.C.
(Hours, 11 a.m. to 1 p. m.),
And it is
2s. 6d., published quarterly;
10s. 6d yearly subscription.
Am I not a highbrow poet?
Sure thing.[156]

---

[155] C. E. Bechhöfer, 'Pastiche', *New Age* XV(13) (30 July 1914), 308. Bechhöfer's capitals.
[156] Bechhöfer, 'Pastiche', 308, Bechhöfer's capitals.

114   MODERNIST PARODY

In this respect, Bechhöfer's parody is remarkably prescient: it is only in recent decades that the conflation of art and advertising has been explored by scholars as an integral part of *Blast's* radical aesthetics.[157]

Further parodies serve to emphasize *Blast's* lack of a coherent programme. 'Indissoluble Matrimony', West's obscenely graphic account of an unhappily married couple who assault one another in a murderous rage, only for the husband to make the startling discovery that the mixed-race wife he left for dead is sleeping in the very bed he imagined for his suicide, is traduced in the ironically entitled snippet 'Joie de Vivre', which offers a much reduced account of the action, reinterpreting the husband's appalling racially motivated attack as part of a continuing cycle of slapstick violence:

Joie de Vivre
By Rebecca West

Chapter I V.—The Fourth Attempt.

"My dear Mamma, my poor black Mamma," she cried, and he held her under the water, and her lungs blew up with a giggling jerk. His eyes dilated, his bosom swelled, he went back to bed, and she was there. Next time he would cut her eyelashes off and tie her up in a sack with a cat.[158]

The difference in tone between 'Indissoluble Matrimony' and the excerpt from Ford's novel-in-progress *The Saddest Story* is then emphasized in another ironically entitled parodic snippet called 'Horrible Details', which relays a gentleman-raconteur's dreary observations on the progress of a game of cards in a drawing room, poking fun at the slow pace of Ford's narrative in which the 'details' are only 'horrible' in the sense that Bechhöfer finds them tiresome.[159]

The sequence culminates in 'The Joy of Contention', a parody of Lewis's highly experimental and anti-mimetic play-text *Enemy of the Stars*, in which two seemingly opposed characters, the effeminate aesthete Arghol (who is supremely detached from world affairs and preoccupied with his superior selfhood) and the brutish and animalistic Hanp (who is the mocking embodiment of everything Arghol despises and has sought to transcend) brawl in gory gladiatorial combat.[160] The parody of Lewis's terse and highly abstract style is near perfect telegraphic lines such as 'Man rushes out, blue asbestic. Fist falls pulverisingly on prostrate nose, blood spurts in yellow shafts, entangling icy sunlight.'[161] However, Bechhöfer misses the mark when he proposes that the characters' truncated speech derives

---

[157] For an account of the aggressive promotional strategies Lewis and others used to get *Blast* noticed and the reach of their ambitions see Mark Morrisson, *The Public Face of Modernism: Little Magazines, Audiences, and Reception 1905–1920* (Madison, WI: University of Wisconsin Press, 2000), 117–19.

[158] *B* 98–117; Bechhöfer, 'Pastiche', 308.

[159] *B* 87–96; Bechhöfer, 'Pastiche', 308.

[160] *B* 51–85.

[161] Bechhöfer, 'Pastiche', 308.

'AN ATMOSPHERE OF PARODY' 115

from the fact that one is Chinese and speaks pidgin English. The sketch ends with parody stage directions:

> THE CURTAIN FALLS.
> AUDIENCE EXITS MARVELLING.
> THE PLAY IS OVER.
> SENSATIONAL SUCCESS.[162]

They mock Lewis's already tongue-in-cheek stage directions, which are set in the signature sans serif block capitals Lewis used in his manifestos, for instance the announcement that 'THE BOX OFFICE RECEIPTS HAVE BEEN ENORMOUS' that Lewis makes as if *Enemy of the Stars* was already a popular phenomenon that would change the social practice of art, rather than a play-text that is to be staged in the circus ring of the reader's imagination.[163] For all Bechhöfer may have mocked the attention-grabbing typeface and boldly self-promoting aspects of *Blast*, he also contributed to the magazine's success. Whatever their limitations as works of literary criticism, Bechhöfer's parodies performed the cultural work of codifying certain salient elements of *Blast* even as it criticized them, making those codes accessible and giving them broader exposure than they might otherwise have received.

The success of *Blast* in penetrating public consciousness might be measured by its appearance in Evelyn Waugh's *Vile Bodies* (1930), in which Lewis's once adversarial lists are adapted to make chic party invitations that enable a society hostess to signal that she is stylish and clever.

> Perhaps it should be explained—there were at this time three sorts of formal invitation card; there was the nice sensible copybook hand sort with a name and *At Home* and a date and time and address; then there was the sort that came from Chelsea, *Noel and Audrey are having a little whoopee on Saturday evening: do please come and bring a bottle too, if you can*; and finally there was the sort that Johnny Hoop used to adapt from *Blast* and Marinetti's *Futurist Manifesto*. These had two columns of close print; in one was a list of all the things Johnny hated, and in the other all things he thought he liked. Most of the parties which Miss Mouse financed had invitations written by Johnny Hoop.[164]

It was not simply the case that early modernism would initiate its most forward advances through parody, parodic stylization, and self-mockery, but also that these strategies effectively set an unstable publicity machine in motion by eliciting further parody in response. The formal invitation a parody extends to

---

[162] Bechhöfer, 'Pastiche', 308, Bechhöfer's capitals.
[163] *B* 61, Lewis's capitals.
[164] Evelyn Waugh, *Vile Bodies* (London: Penguin, 2000), 94–5, Waugh's italics.

116　MODERNIST PARODY

readers to perform an equivalent comic transformation on the parody itself is writ largest in works that make audacious assaults on conventions of representation while including themselves in their own mockery, forcing readers to confront and codify those features which strike them as abstract or absurd while they simultaneously attempt to determine how sincerely they are meant. The upstart artists who attempted to make radical interventions in literary practice produced parodically stylized works that effectively dared their detractors to parody their very foundations. This is not to say that all self-consciously *modern* writers actively courted ridicule or that even the most grinning *arrivistes* were not serious about the need to reform the institution of art. As Gertrude Stein firmly stated: 'It's not our idea of fun to work for thirty or forty years on a medium of expression and then have ourselves ridiculed.'[165] But the mocking subversions of experimental modernism were sufficiently strange and striking for the gathering movement to attract a truly remarkable number and range of parodic responses. These, in turn, raised the public's awareness of the most innovative works, broadening and deepening their impact, thus enabling modernism to flourish in 'an atmosphere of parody' of its own cultish creation.

[165] Quoted in James R. Mellow, *Charmed Circle: Gertrude Stein & Company* (New York: Praeger, 1974), 371.

4

Mocking Modernisms

Parody in Little Magazines

The publicity value of the parodies of experimental modernism that proliferated in contemporary newspapers, magazines, and intellectual weeklies was obvious. When Aldington looked back on the early years of Imagism, he cited the way that 'Columnists parodied the poems, or reproduced them (without payment) accompanied by derisive remarks' as testament to its success at stirring up public consciousness, while Monroe told her readers in no uncertain terms that the many mocking attacks that appeared in the press were to be welcomed and cultivated:

> Even that satirical newspaper editor who turns one of our fugues upside down, or that other who gaily parodies imagism, or that graver one who points at us the finger of scorn—all these are more or less consciously our friends, for they are helping the public to WAKE UP, to observe that something, through whatever illusions and extravagances, is going on, that poetry is not a dead art but a living one, and that the poet today, like the liberator of long ago, WILL BE HEARD.[1]

The parodies continued well beyond Imagism's most active years. For instance, the May 1921 issue of the *Chapbook: A Monthly Miscellany* even featured a section parodying Imagist anthologies, called 'Pathology des Dommagistes' (*dommage* meaning 'damage' but also 'shame' or 'pity').[2] Whatever sport detractors made with emergent modernism, the unrelenting attention confirmed that there was something going on that was distinctive, unprecedented, and sufficiently radical to be *worth parodying*. While modernism's parodists and satirists performed the cultural work of assessing the value of experimental writing, they also alerted a wider audience than might otherwise have been reached to the fact that revolution was afoot.

The 'great divide' between modernism and mass culture so eloquently described by Andreas Huyssen makes it easy to imagine that general readers were unaware of the modernist revolution that was taking place in little magazines.[3] However, the work of scholars such as Karen Leick has confirmed that 'mainstream readers had

---

[1] Aldington, *Life for Life's Sake*, 138; H. M., 'Comments and Reviews: Give Him Room', *Poetry: A Magazine of Verse* VI(2) (May 1915), 83–4, Monroe's capitals.

[2] 'Pathology des Dommagistes', *Chapbook* 23 (May 1921), 21–4.

[3] Andreas Huyssen, *After the Great Divide: Modernism, Mass Culture, Postmodernism* (Bloomington, IN: Indiana University Press, 1986).

Modernist Parody. Sarah Davison, Oxford University Press. © Sarah Davison (2023).
DOI: 10.1093/oso/9780192849243.003.0005

118   MODERNIST PARODY

not only heard of these publications' but 'were familiar with many of the writers who were published there', not least because modernism 'was discussed so frequently in daily newspapers and in popular magazines', featuring in everything from editorials, literary pages, and book reviews to satirical columns, parodies, and cartoons.[4] In *Gertrude Stein and the Making of an American Celebrity* (2009), Leick examines the conditions of Stein's rise to prominence as a personality whose fame was premised on the idiosyncrasy and inaccessibility of her works, providing a superb case study of the ways in which mainstream culture mediated high modernist poetics for the appreciation and amusement of a middlebrow audience. Parodies in newspapers and smart magazines play a prominent role in Leick's history, from the early days when Stein was strongly associated with Cubism and her name appeared in connection with the copious poems that parodied the New York Armory Show (where Stein was the only non-visual artist to exhibit) to 'the repetitive "Steinese" used by critics and reviewers who parodied Stein's style throughout her career', to the appearance of 'When Helen Furr Got Gay with Harold Moos' in the October 1923 issue of *Vanity Fair* (a parody of Stein's prose poem 'Miss Furr and Miss Skeen', which had appeared in that magazine in July 1923).[5] As Leick notes, for all that parodists in popular newspapers and magazines represented Stein's writing as amusingly unintelligible, they nevertheless took the fact of her experimentation seriously.

Daniel Tracey focuses attention on the irreverent parodies of contemporary experimental, realist, and popular literatures that were a mainstay of smart magazines such as *Vanity Fair* and the *New Yorker*, which promised to keep readers abreast of all things smart, presenting what was fashionable and clever with wit and panache. Parody was the perfect match for this remit, being smart in all senses. It flattered readers' sense of their own sophistication by teaching the object parodied, while denying that they ever needed to be taught; it made readers smarter by increasing their general knowledge, their ability to identify and classify current trends, and their confidence in approaching texts and deriving pleasure from them; and its satire could certainly smart. Tracey notes that the term 'modernist' made one of its very first appearances in *Vanity Fair* in 'A Dramatic Career in Modernist Art' (August 1916), in which Max Eastman gave a parodic description of an artist who rejected mimesis for a series of avant-garde identifications from Impressionism to Futurism.[6] Tracey suggests that this sketch identifies a moment where 'modernism' and its synonyms had been codified to the extent that they began to designate a genre, setting initial terms for the revolutionary movement

---

[4] Karen Leick, 'Popular Modernism: Little Magazines and the American Daily Press', *PMLA* 123(1) (January 2008), 126.

[5] Karen Leick, *Gertrude Stein and the Making of American Celebrity* (New York: Routledge, 2009), 38, 13, 86.

[6] Daniel Tracey, 'Investing in "Modernism": Smart Magazines, Parody, and Middlebrow Professional Judgement', *Journal of Modern Periodical Studies* 1(1) (2010), 50.

that was beginning to cohere. In Tracey's account, parody emerges as a spirited display of professionalized expertise, where writers such as Dorothy Parker and Henry Thurber jockey for authority, fulfilling 'smart magazines' contract to exercise judgment over aesthetic forms, exposing any weaknesses even in the most legitimated', thereby interweaving 'the marketing and critical agendas of the magazines' by promoting different kinds of writing 'as varieties of amusement and aesthetic experience'.[7]

Leonard Diepeveen likewise proposes that modernism's parodists were so active in the 1910s and 1920s that their representations played a significant and diverse role in the critical construction of modernism at a time before its meaning was clearly understood. In *Mock Modernism: An Anthology of Parodies, Travesties, and Frauds, 1910–1935* (2014), Diepeveen collects a wealth of parodic ephemera that seek to interpret modernism's newness and strangeness, its strategies for attracting attention, and its affronts to aesthetic standards. They range from the hostile to acts of tongue-in-cheek homage, and include: 'hoaxes, doggerel, cartoons, accounts of staged trials, mock interviews, parodies in adjacent media (such as Futurist fashion shows), mock manifestos, even a special "children's" book *The Cubies ABC*, which was published in response to the New York manifestation of the Armory show'.[8] Diepeveen focuses on modernism's sceptics, who responded to the gathering movement's incipient threat by aiming to 'expose the tawdry power of elitism, of difficulty, of the opaque, of fashion, of publicity, of relevance' and by appealing to 'common-sense' standards to rein in 'too-earnest, ambitious seriousness', often through 'banal recontextualizings' or the suggestion that experimental modernism was '*easy* to produce'.[9] His incisive commentaries emphasize how sensitive modernism's early parodists were to the fact that its revolutionary aesthetics were 'accompanied by an inseparable, enabling context, made up of manipulations of publicity, performances of machismo, lightweight but portentous analogical references to science, and obfuscating theoretical justifications and explanations', showing that they possessed a contextual understanding of modernism's social aspects that has only been considered by modernist studies in the last twenty years.[10]

Although modernism was eventually canonized as aloof from mass culture, Diepeveen notes that many of the pieces collected in *Mock Modernism* assert that its 'immersion in publicity, fashion, speed, mass replication, professional organization, and culture of celebrity' compromised its claims to aesthetic excellence, creating the suspicion that it 'wasn't allied with eternity, but had sold itself to the *now*'.[11] Furthermore, modernism's parodists also undermined the

---

[7] Tracey, 'Investing in "Modernism"', 57, 53.
[8] Diepeveen, *Mock Modernism*, 6.
[9] Diepeveen, *Mock Modernism*, 13, 14, 15, 22, Diepeveen's italics.
[10] Diepeveen, *Mock Modernism*, 10.
[11] Diepeveen, *Mock Modernism*, 20, Diepeveen's italics.

120   MODERNIST PARODY

gathering movement's ambitious claims for the generalizable reach of its innovations into every area of art and culture and its insistence that its works 'were not just about themselves, but about *modernity*', making play with the broad claim that 'modernism had an aesthetic and context that was transferable' by 'extending the absurdities of one aesthetic manifestation into another medium, exposing even more starkly its obvious banalities'.[12] The cumulative effect was to deepen readers' suspicion that modernism was indeed a case of the emperor's new clothes.

Leick, Tracey, and Diepeveen broadly agree that modernism's parodists made its languages and *modus operandi* more recognizable by emphasizing what was difficult, unintelligible, nonsensical, or ludicrous about experimental works, thereby consolidating the sense that a definite movement in art was afoot, even as they questioned its legitimacy. By contrast, this book is principally concerned with the parody that is *in* modernism and contends that the mode is in fact so fundamental to avant-garde modernist experimentation that it should be considered constitutive. However, this chapter also responds to and builds on Leick, Diepeveen, and Tracey's insights into the cultural work performed by parodies *of* modernism to reveal that parodying modernist experimentation was not just the preserve of dyed-in-the-wool modernist sceptics but that hard-core parody was also an activity enjoyed by modernist writers of many stripes. Like the middlebrow parodists of smart magazines, participants in the modern movement often had recourse to parody to flaunt their professional expertise, jockey for authority, and settle scores. They turned to parody to demark their territories, intervene in internal debates about the forms emergent writing should take, and make complex interventions in theoretical debates. Beyond its capacity to entertain and amuse, parody afforded modernist writers the opportunity to try—but not fully commit—to alternative personae. It also enabled them to gauge the utility of *really new* innovations by testing them from the inside and, in the case of the most avant-garde practitioners, push their work to more experimental extremes.

Indeed, those who mocked advanced poetry by writing parodies and circulating them (or imagining the consequences of circulating them) tended to presume that the modernists were already parodists of a kind, as the Spectra hoax and Squire's short story 'The Man Who Wrote Free Verse' (1924) show. Irreverent reframings by modernism's detractors not only responded to what was controversial or eccentric about early modernist experimentation but were effectively summoned by the strategies of parody and self-parody that were already latent in the most innovative works, a circumstance that made modernist writing so amenable to that particular genre of mockery above all others.

Witter Bynner and Arthur Davison Ficke were two poets who were deeply influenced by Imagism and well connected in modernist circles. Bynner was a regular contributor to the *Little Review*, Ficke less frequent. They both wrote free

---

[12] Diepeveen, *Mock Modernism*, 20–1, Diepeveen's italics.

MOCKING MODERNISMS   121

verse that took inspiration from Japanese literature and culture but were annoyed by the cultish aspects of Imagism and the avant-garde in general. They used the 1916 lecture series Maurice Browne organized in Chicago to speak out against recent developments in Anglo-American poetry: Ficke argued that free verse was 'an instrument of narrow range, and imagism effective only in the presentation of detached details, incapable of larger completeness', while Bynner attacked the Imagists, and Pound in particular.[13] Such was their irritation with the absurdity of recent schools that they cooked up their own parodic movement, the Spectric group, designed to expose the pretensions of modernist poets and their admiring critics.

Bynner dreamt up the hoax while watching a performance of *Le Spectre de la Rose*, a ballet of the Ballets Russes. He was in conversation with friends, ridiculing the new schools of poetry and, glancing at the programme, casually asked if any of them had heard of the latest school, the Spectrists. He subsequently let Ficke in on the joke and the two men retired to a hotel, where 'from ten quarts of excellent Scotch in ten days they extracted the whole of Spectric philosophy'.[14] The result was *Spectra: A Book of Poetic Experiments* (1916) by 'Emanuel Morgan' (Bynner) and 'Anne Knish' (Ficke). A preface, ostensibly written by Knish, set out the group's resolve 'to push the possibilities of poetic expression into a new region—to attain a fresh brilliance of impression by a method not so wholly different from the methods of Futurist Painting'.[15] Whereas the Imagists advocated 'direct treatment of the object', the Spectrists claimed to render 'the overtones, adumbrations, or spectres which for the poet haunt all objects both of the seen and the unseen world—those shadowy projections, sometimes grotesque, which, hovering around the real, give to the real its full ideal significance and poetic worth'.[16] On the surface, the preface had many of the qualities of an earnest modernist critical pronouncement, proffering a new philosophy with a pseudo-scientific underpinning, promising to bring poetry up to speed with developments in continental Europe, especially in the visual arts, and claiming to supersede previous schools. On closer inspection, the theory it set forth was double-coded and intentionally parodic: while 'Spectra' pertains to the values that vary over a continuum, especially the colours of visible light, and is therefore suggestive of breadth as well as radiance, the adjective 'spectral' also suggests that Spectric poems were insubstantial phantoms. The aim was to expose the new writing that they considered to be without substance, applying modish techniques and strategies to produce mere apparitions that would ultimately show the paucity of the originals by revealing them to be on the same spectrum as their parodies. As skilled writers of free verse, Bynner and Ficke were

---

[13] As summarized in Monroe, *Poet's Life*, 406.
[14] William Jay Smith, *The Spectra Hoax* (Middletown, CT: Wesleyan University Press, 1961), 17.
[15] Emanuel Morgan and Anne Knish, *Spectra: A Book of Poetic Experiments* (New York: Mitchell Kennerley, 1916), ix.
[16] *Spectra*, x.

122   MODERNIST PARODY

able to present eccentric images and enigmatic analogies for emotional states with such control and polish that more obvious satiric touches were easy to overlook, especially given the avant-garde's tendency towards self-mockery and self-parody. As a result, poems such as Morgan's 'Opus 6', which begins 'If only I were dafter/I might be making hymns/To the liquor of your laughter/And the lacquer of your limbs', were readily accepted as genuine modernist productions.[17]

Mitchell Kennerley, a New York publisher, accepted *Spectra* 'at once for publication, apparently (as Mr. Bynner remembers it) as a bona fide manuscript; and when informed of the real identity of the authors, agreed to keep the secret'.[18] An unprepossessing volume with grey binding and a simple motif of two superimposed triangles, *Spectra* arrived on the desks of editors and reviewers of poetry in autumn 1916. The motif was a covert allusion to a parody of Erasmus Darwin's *The Loves of the Plants*, 'The Loves of the Triangles', published in the *Anti-Jacobin* in 1798.[19] Poems by Knish and Morgan were published by *Reedy's Mirror* and the *Little Review*, and Alfred Kreymborg, the editor of *Others*, was so convinced by Spectrism that he devoted the January 1917 issue to this latest school.[20] Kreymborg had published the entire contents of *Des Imagistes* in February 1914 in the fifth issue of his magazine, which was then called the *Glebe*, and earnestly believed that Spectrism was the next big thing.[21] Harriet Monroe was sufficiently impressed with Morgan's poem 'Opus 102' that she requested a further 'two pages [of Morgan's poems so that] the reader would have the chance to get it'.[22]

Although Bynner and Ficke's motives were conservative, the acceptance and dissemination of their poems in little magazines paradoxically accorded their parodies the status of *actual* modernist works. It was proof they had succeeded in displacing their model—a quality the poet Edgar Lee Masters inadvertently identified in a private letter of 1 December 1916 when he congratulated Morgan on his achievement, pronouncing Spectrism to be 'at the core of things and imagism at the surface'.[23] The Spectrists even acquired their very own parodists, the Ultra-Violets, a spoof school headed by 'Manual Organ' and 'Nanne Pish', with a suitably ridiculous manifesto:

> It will be observed that the basic principle of the new school is the association of ideas ordinarily unassociated. To the unimaginative, this savors of insanity; but the psychologist recognizes the phenomenon, while the poet goes one step farther and sees in it the highest manifestation of inspiration. One man, says the poet, sees a tomcat on a back fence and thinks of brickbats and shotguns, which

---

[17] *Spectra*, 56.
[18] Smith, *Spectra Hoax*, 19.
[19] Smith, *Spectra Hoax*, 19.
[20] *Others* III(5), The Spectric School (January 1917).
[21] *Glebe* I(5), Des Imagistes—An Anthology (February 1914).
[22] Harriet Monroe to Emanuel Morgan, 4 January 1917, quoted in Smith, *Spectra Hoax*, 11.
[23] Edgar Lee Masters to Emanuel Morgan, 1 December 1916, quoted in Smith, *Spectra Hoax*, 6. (Bynner had set up a fake postal address for Morgan.)

MOCKING MODERNISMS   123

is banality and matter-of-fact prose; another man sees the same cat and immediately associates it with false teeth and a lawn party in Chicago, which is genius
and Ultra-Violet poetry.[24]

But unlike the Ultra-Violets, whose satire was clearly signalled and unmistakable,
Bynner and Ficke were attacking modernist poetry with the very kind of parody that sustained many of its experiments, the parody that presumes parity and
does not concede secondary status as commentary without any originally creative
impulse.

Before *Poetry* had a chance to publish Spectric poems, the hoax was uncovered. Bynner could not resist hinting at the true nature of Spectrism whenever the
opportunity arose, puffing the Spectrists' achievements in reviews and lectures.
He was taken aside after a lecture at the University of Wisconsin in April 1918 and
challenged directly. Monroe declined to comment publicly on the uncovering of
the hoax, but Alice Corbin Henderson responded with hauteur in her editorial for
the June 1918 number of *Poetry*:

> And yet there is no reason why one should not have supposed Emanual [*sic*] Mor-
> gan and Anne Knish to be real persons, for the poems in *Spectra* are no worse and
> no better, and hardly any less intelligible, than much of the free verse which has
> been thrust upon us.[25]

She neglected to admit that the magazine had been temporarily taken in and
claimed, with unconscious acuity, that 'If the joke proves anything at all, it is simply
that critics are an unselective lot, particularly in the presence of the "new poetry",
or "new art", about which there is a fair amount of uncertainty', quietly admitting
that editors in the period were apt to chase the next new thing and were not always
mindful of quality.[26]

In June 1918 Jane Heap published an acid editorial in defence of the *Little
Review*, noting that only one poem of the fat bunch that Morgan submitted to the
magazine was good enough to appear in print. That poem was 'Opus 96', which
appeared in the July 1917 issue of the *Little Review*. It blended fashionable Japon-
isme with references to ancient Greece and Egypt and well-worn poetic tropes
of birdsong and seasons, mixing metaphors to say something rather vague but
suitably resonant about the beauty and permanence of love:

> You are the Japan
> Where cherries always blossom.
> With you there is no meantime.

---

[24] 'An Introduction to Ultra-Violet Poetry', *Wisconsin Literary Magazine* (January 1917), 111–12.
[25] Alice Corbin Henderson, 'Baiting the Public', *Poetry: A Magazine of Verse* XII(3) (June 1918), 170.
[26] Henderson, 'Baiting the Public', 170.

124 MODERNIST PARODY

> Your [*sic*] are the nightingale's twenty-four hours of song,
> The unbroken Parthenon,
> The everlasting purring of the sphinx.
>
> At the first footfall of an uncouth season,
> You migrate with one wing-sweep
> To beauty.[27]

Even then Margaret Anderson was sufficiently dissatisfied to print the ditty 'Banish/Anne Knish,/Set the dog on/Emanuel Morgan' as a 'Note' in the regular 'The Reader Critic' editorial column of the same issue.[28] When Morgan's true identity was revealed, Heap insisted the joke was on Bynner, arguing 'If a man changes his name and writes better stuff, why does that make the public so ridiculous?'[29] For good measure she quoted from Pound's criticism of Morgan from a letter of 10 August 1917 (written before the hoax was uncovered) to insist that Spectrism was in fact belated and second-rate:

> Morgan's 'spectric' business is a little late. People intending to be 'schools' should have 'done it first'.
> Or rather they should base their school on something having to do with their art, not on a vague aesthetic theory. His manifesto advances no proposition affecting his own medium, i.e., words, rhythm, etc., only some twaddle about ultra-violets. Jejune. There is no difference between his free verse and any other free verse . . .
> Morgan is only another Imagist imitator with a different preface from Amy's.[30]

Setting Pound's differences from Lowell aside, it is striking that Pound recognized no difference between Morgan's parodies and Lowell's free verse, which was without parodic intent but could be framed as accidentally parodic by Pound in the sense that he viewed it as trespassing on his own poetic innovations, but without the requisite understanding or skill.

Whatever the (deliberate) shortcomings of Spectrism in terms of its inability to project an autonomous identity that was completely separate from the material it parodied, the unfortunate fact was that many of the Spectrist poems were superior to any Bynner and Ficke had published under their own names. 'The disclosure would be a good joke on the public', quipped *Reedy's Mirror* of 24 May 1918, 'were it not for the fact that the burlesque poetry is more successful than the authors'

---

[27] Emanuel Morgan, 'Opus 96', *Little Review*, IV(3) (July 1917), 25.

[28] M. C. A. [Margaret Anderson], 'The Reader Critic: Note', *Little Review*, IV(3) (July 1917), 29.

[29] J. H. [Jane Heap], 'The Reader Critic: The Hoax of the "Spectrics"', *Little Review* V(2) (1 June 1918), 53.

[30] Ezra Pound, quoted in J. H., 'Reader Critic: The Hoax of the "Spectrics"', 53.

serious work'.[31] Both poets saw the truth in these accusations: Bynner found that he was unable to separate his own voice from Morgan's, so well had the mask come to fit, and Ficke confided to Bynner with 'a distinct note of grief in his voice: "Do you know, some of my best work is in *Spectra*?"'[32] The critical culture that found much to admire in works that appropriated fashionable avant-garde techniques, even if only with the intention of discrediting them, responded to the disclosure of the hoax by reprocessing parodic impostures as works that actually supported modernism's pre-eminence, maintaining that some of the poetry was aesthetically good despite its creators' intentions because it observed conventions that were now established tenets of good writing. Bynner and Ficke's mistake was to use parody as a weapon to make modern schools confess to charlatanry. The level of professional expertise that they were able to exercise over Imagist style energized their parodies, but also imperilled them, because they approached the models so closely that they were too easily mistaken for the real thing. Unable to foresee how their own parodies included themselves among the very category of writers they sought to destroy, the perpetrators of the Spectra hoax found—as conservative practitioners are apt to find—that they could not retain control of the joke.

By contrast, Squire, then one of the most vocal and influential critics of the avant-garde in England, intuitively understood that direct parodic assaults on modernist literature were unwise. His short story 'The Man Who Wrote Free Verse' rehearses the scenario of the Spectra hoax. Two young men, Reggie Twyford and Adrian Roberts, complain about the 'isms and experiments', 'absurd posing', and 'cacophonous gibberish' that passes for fashionable literature.[33] Adrian takes the view that these impenetrable productions are mere publicity stunts and that the perpetrators are charlatans peddling poetry that asserts its aesthetic value through wilful, unintelligible obscurity, arguing that 'The second-rate have discovered the trick of incomprehensibility in our own time; the trick of bogus audacity has always been known'.[34] He persuades Reggie to write his own bogus poetry and start 'a career as an advanced poet!': 'Get them all to take you seriously', Adrian exclaims, 'and then give it away'.[35] Adrian encourages Reggie to slash away everything in the way of contextual explanation in a long narrative poem to produce suitably terse and obscure verse:

> Gyrating cowls.
> Ink.
> Oh God! A Lobster![36]

---

[31] Quoted in Smith, *Spectra Hoax*, 42.
[32] Quoted in Smith, *Spectra Hoax*, 43.
[33] J. C. Squire, 'The Man Who Wrote Free Verse', *London Mercury* X(56) (June 1924), 128.
[34] Squire, 'Man Who Wrote Free Verse', 128.
[35] Squire, 'Man Who Wrote Free Verse', 129.
[36] Squire, 'Man Who Wrote Free Verse', 130.

126　MODERNIST PARODY

Emboldened by success, Reggie then runs through the gamut of modernist styles with great despatch: including 'the classical one'; 'the very simple kind which consists of leaving out everything conjunctive, running together a series of objects, and ending with an exclamation'; and 'the one which is allowed to rhyme, by way of compensation for its especially polysyllabic obscurity'.[37] The heavy-handed satirical point is, of course, that the avant-garde, far from advancing a new method, is itself formulaic.

Reggie's advanced poems are unleashed on the unsuspecting public under the pseudonym 'Sidney Twyford'. The poems receive a rapturous reception in fashionable London and draw comparisons with other advanced schools, some real, some only plausible, even though its many luminaries (who strongly resemble the Bloomsbury group) gaily confess that they do not understand them. Like Bynner and Ficke, Reggie enjoys far greater success as a parodist than he ever had as a serious poet. Twyford's popularity duly spreads to all the advanced circles of England and America, proving Adrian's original thesis that absurdity and obscurity make poetry fashionable. But before Reggie reveals the hoax, the joke rebounds on him. 'The Great Bolshevik Revolution' comes, inspired in part by Reggie's seditious poetry. The Bolsheviks discovered Twyford's true identity and appoint Reggie 'Poet of the Revolution'.[38] The man who wrote free verse is then unveiled 'to a people which had thrown off its chains' as the 'official Laureate of the British Republic'.[39] His duty is to continue writing unintelligible avant-garde poetry and he dies 'in the end, poor fellow, of boredom and intellectual starvation'.[40]

In *The Difficulties of Modernism* (2003) Diepeveen cited 'The Man Who Wrote Free Verse' as an exemplary account of the ways in which difficulty entered social discourse, producing 'a crisis in aesthetic evaluation that made inevitable discussions as to whether a given work might be a hoax'.[41] Diepeveen perceptively argued that Squire's satire addressed 'the social and textual conditions . . . central to modernism's formation' by using parody to provide a 'taxonomy of the kinds of art that modern readers as a group found difficult to understand'.[42] His specific interest in difficulty precluded further comment on what Squire's story might say about parody's social and textual role in the formation of modernism. Like Bynner and Ficke, Reggie and Adrian disliked the way that new schools broke with tradition, but what made them all suspect that the coterie of poets and reviewers who admired these new kinds of literature were kidding themselves, and worse still their audiences, was their failure to see how advanced schools could parody their own innovations and still claim their writings as original, autonomous works of art. Squire himself only made small claims for parody as light-hearted 'topical criticism' despite his

---

[37] Squire, 'Man Who Wrote Free Verse', 130.
[38] Squire, 'Man Who Wrote Free Verse', 137.
[39] Squire, 'Man Who Wrote Free Verse', 137.
[40] Squire, 'Man Who Wrote Free Verse', 137.
[41] Leonard Diepeveen, *The Difficulties of Modernism* (New York: Routledge, 2003), 35.
[42] Diepeveen, *Difficulties of Modernism*, 9, 50.

evident enjoyment of it.[43] Like Bynner and Ficke, Reggie and Adrian conspired to expose recent art movements as hoaxes, hoping to restore traditional standards of 'aesthetic evaluation', but failed to see that their method, combative parody, was responsible for destabilizing the very notions of aesthetic value they aimed to reinstate. The 'crisis in aesthetic evaluation' was only a 'crisis' for Georgian traditionalists; the modernist avant-garde wanted to antagonize the class of readers who respond to innovative works by saying 'ahg, ahg, ahh, ahhh, but-bu-bu-but this isn't Poetry'.[44] The ending of 'The Man Who Wrote Free Verse' depicts this crisis vividly. Because Reggie's compositions presume to exceed their models, as truly *modern* parody must, the avant-garde (here imagined literally as an incoming army, threatening social, national, and individual life) claims his work for its own rhetorical purpose. With greater practitioner's insight into parody than Bynner and Ficke, Squire shielded himself from Reggie's fate by conducting his hoax within a narrative frame, so that he himself was unimpeachable. Squire did print parodies of modernist literature elsewhere, but in contexts that clearly marked his parodies as criticism and not modernist imposters—for instance 'If a very new poet had written "The Lotus Eaters"', in which he satirized self-congratulatory commentary on the process of writing, and 'Piebald Unicorn', part of a series of parodies in the regular 'Editorial Notes' column of the *London Mercury*.[45] Moreover, he made his distaste for the modernists' particular kinds of parody clear by declining to include any examples of their work in *Apes and Parrots: An Anthology of Parodies Collected by J. C. Squire* (1928), and refusing even to review *Ulysses* in the *London Mercury*.[46] 'The Man Who Wrote Free Verse' functions as a cautionary tale against the kind of revolutionary art 'advanced poets' practise, but Reggie's fate, like that of the architects of the Spectra hoax, also reinforces the virtually unassailable quality of parody as an avant-garde aesthetic.

Kitchin highlighted the bind faced by parodists of modernism in his *Survey of Burlesque and Parody* (1931):

Modern poetry would seem to invite the wittiest kind of parody, because it has taken refuge in a world which is rather like the world of nonsense verse ... But for that very reason it is the harder to parody in any true sense. How is the parodist to satirise what already, on the surface, looks like luminous nonsense? And how he must perspire to give his verse the admitted delicacy of the original, nonsense or no nonsense? The truth is we are at once of those critical junctures in art, when a new philosophy of art 'puts all in doubt'.[47]

---

[43] J. C. Squire, 'Preface', *Collected Parodies* (New York: George H. Doran Company, 1921), n. p.

[44] *LEP* 61.

[45] J. C. Squire, *Tricks of the Trade* (London: Martin Secker, 1917), 65–7; J. C. Squire, 'Editorial Notes', *London Mercury* XVIII(106) (August 1928), 342.

[46] J. C. Squire, ed., *Apes and Parrots: An Anthology of Parodies* (London: Herbert Jenkins, 1928).

[47] Kitchin, *Survey of Burlesque and Parody in English*, 345.

128   MODERNIST PARODY

Here the effects generated by the parody within modernism—specifically the superficial proximity to nonsense when the reader does not understand or subscribe to the rationale for experimental techniques—are linked, albeit indirectly, to a sense that art has entered a new epoch, one in which the very institution of art is threatened by the presence of a parodic sensibility that is seemingly impervious to corrective mockery. The logic of Cyril Connolly's snarky compliment about Gertrude Stein's prose provides a good point of comparison: 'Every parody of her has failed because one cannot parody the monotonous boredom of her writing unless one has an equal amount of learning and intelligence to suppress; a smaller mind will lack the courage to be so dull'.[48]

The most innovative and avant-garde modernist writers tended to be wilier than Bynner and Ficke. Those who made elements of parody and self-parody part of their aesthetic understood the terms of the game because they themselves played it. They took care to avoid being mistaken for also-rans or writers of the second-rate by signalling their differences in ways which were sufficiently exaggerated to be explicit, using pseudonyms, or restricting the audience to initiates who would certainly get the joke. When the most experimental modernists parodied works that already used elements of parody and self-parody, they understood intuitively that parody could not function simply as criticism but took advantage of the way that parody implicated them in its criticism, either to comment on their own practice or to produce writing that was exploratory and questioning in nature, in preparation for the production of further original art.

Parodies of experimental writing proliferated in little magazines where modernist works were first published. The format of little magazines created the ideal conditions for parody to flourish, mixing new writing with critical reflection, accommodating short pieces and individual poems, generating dialogue and debate, and creating communities of educated readers prepared to enjoy in-jokes that could be sustained across several issues or indeed magazines with similar outlooks. These *jeux d'esprit* consolidated writers' sense of being part of a movement that was still in formation, where nothing save the fact of experimentation was fixed. Individual works were energetically contested, but with an urgency and exuberance that affirmed the necessity of debate and made literary culture seem vital again.

Writers who were genuinely knowledgeable about modern writing frequently settled their differences by parodying one another's work as part of their ongoing quest to separate the 'durable' from the 'apparent', as per Aldington's spat with Pound over the propriety of shock tactics and proper form Imagism should take in *Poetry* and the *Egoist*, where Aldington evidently enjoyed acting out avant-garde outrage even as he criticized it.[49] The *Egoist* was especially hospitable to debate and

---

[48] Cyril Connolly, 'Gertrude Stein', *Previous Convictions* (London: Hamish Hamilton, 1963), 283–4.
[49] In much the same spirit, Aldington attended Marinetti's lecture on Futurist clothing in a crude bright blue and orange costume of his own fashioning, in mockery of the prophesy that there would

MOCKING MODERNISMS 129

differences of opinion. The 'Correspondence' column regularly featured responses to the magazine's frequent articles on Imagism, including verse commentaries (a staple mode for responding to current affairs in the newspaper columns of the period, another circumstance that explains the proliferation of parody in printed media at this time). Although the *Egoist* was (among other things) a key Imagist organ, Allen Upward was given the space to air his grievances in a letter written in free verse in which he expressed irritation at Pound's presumptuous imposition of the Imagist label on his established work and instead let it be known that the movement was in fact started by Edward Storer and T. E. Hulme, while Horace Holley was permitted to cut the Imagists down to size in 'The Mice', a poem which used *vers libre* to satirize the timid nibbles its poets have taken from the anthologies of ancient Greek literature and the fat tomes of Chinese wisdom they encountered as they scampered in the world's store cupboard.[50] The editors could brook contraries so comfortably that the magazine could assume antithetical positions within the same issue. As a signatory to Lewis's manifestos, Aldington was obliged to review *Blast* positively, but reservations about the project were signalled by the rough-hewn cartoon by Horace Brodsky that ran on the very same page, itself a crude parody of the skilled woodcuts by Lewis, Wadsworth, and others that provided visual texts for Vorticism which bore the caption 'The Lewis–Brzeska–Pound Troupe. Blasting their own trumpets before the walls of Jericho.'[51]

The contradictions inherent in parody's form (which is, after all, unavoidably implicated in the materials it mocks) generated more significant issues for magazines that claimed to uphold to a consistent aesthetic and political programme such as the *New Age*, which concerned itself with the wider culture of modern literature and its potential to contribute to social progress. The literary pages contained editorials and articles rebutting works and essays that did not conform to the magazine's socialist vision, but also promoted modernist works that met with approval, for instance select translations by Pound, including 'The Seafarer' in 'I Gather the Limbs of Osiris', and 'The Song of the Bowmen of Shu' and 'The River Merchant's Wife: A Letter' in the regular column 'Writers and Readers'.[52]

Topical and literary parodies were a staple feature of the *New Age* even before the establishment of its regular 'Pastiche' column, which first appeared in 1912. For instance, Katherine Mansfield and Beatrice Hastings submitted a series of parodies of novels by leading male Edwardian authors on the breezy pretence that they had nothing better to do on a quiet day by the seaside:

---

be a utilitarian single garment fastened with a zip. See Norman T. Gates, ed., *Richard Aldington: An Autobiography in Letters* (Pennsylvania: Pennsylvania State University Press, 1992), 10.

[50] Allen Upward, 'Correspondence: The Discarded Imagist', *Egoist* II(6) (1 June 1915), 98; Horace Holley, 'Correspondence. Imagists', *Egoist* I(12) (15 June 1914), 236.

[51] Horace Brodsky, 'The Lewis–Brzeska–Pound Troupe', *Egoist* I(14) (15 July 1914), 272.

[52] Ezra Pound, 'I Gather the Limbs of Osiris: I. The Seafarer', *New Age* X(5) (30 November 1911), 107; R. C. H., 'Readers and Writers', *New Age* XVII(14) (5 August 1915), 332–3.

130 MODERNIST PARODY

> Sir,—Finding ourselves on Sunday in Ditchling-on-Sea, without any literature, we were driven to rely upon memories of our favourite authors. We forward our summaries for the benefit of your readers who may sometime find themselves in a similar situation. K. M. and B. H.[53]

But far from being neutral, the 'memories' they presented ridiculed the likes of Chesterton, H. G. Wells, Eden Phillpotts, Richard Le Gallienne, and Arnold Bennett for their self-important male protagonists and their inability to identify imaginatively with women, among other things. The 'summaries' were forerunners of the 'Pastiche' column, which became a regular feature of the *New Age*. It provided opportunities for young talent to sharpen their teeth and also functioned a playground where the magazine's more established voices could intervene in the reception of literary works, featuring parodies that were calculated to amuse and gratify an enlightened readership and, where necessary, to inform. Interestingly, 'The Complete Poems of T. E. Hulme' were published directly after the first 'Pastiche' column, positioned and presented in such a way as to make it unclear whether or not they were serious compositions or whether they had been placed on that page to signal that they were apt to be read as if they were also parodies.

Many of the senior contributors, like Hastings (the magazine's de facto literary editor from 1907 to 1914), submitted contributions under pseudonyms to enable them to write freely without compromise to other aspects of their careers as professional writers.[54] More substantial parodies and satires appeared in the main body of the magazine as standalone articles, alongside other polemical essays, often providing a dialogical gloss on materials published in recent weeks or in the very same issue. The activities of the modernist avant-garde provided an especially rich seam of material for contributors to parody, from the outlandish stylings of the most experimental writers to sensational manifestos, public performances, and debates, to the enthralled reviews of latest artistic and literary productions that were a mainstay of the most advanced magazines. For instance, 'Initial Manifesto of the "Fatuists" to the Public' parodied Marinetti's overwritten proclamations to produce the agenda for the (mock) movement ready to supplant him, a juvenile school that had yet to determine what it would glorify, proud to declare 'we are out for trouble and *we* simply don't care! SO THERE!!!!! . . . Our Crown is Obscurity, our Sceptre—Disdain.'[55] The parody provided a counterbalance to the more even-handed coverage that Futurism and Futurist art had previously received following the opening of a new exhibition at the Sackville Gallery.[56] 'Art and Artists', signed

---

[53] Katherine Mansfield and Beatrice Hastings, 'Letters to the Editor: A P. S. A.', *New Age* IX(4) (25 May 1911), 95.

[54] Beatrice Hastings insisted that she 'had entire charge of, and responsibility for, the literary direction of the paper' between 1907 and 1914 (Beatrice Hastings, *The Old 'New Age' Orage—and Others* (London: Blue Moon Press, 1936), 3).

[55] 'Initial Manifesto of the "Fatuists" to the Public', *New Age* X(22) (28 March 1912), 524.

[56] Huntly Carter, 'Art and Drama in Paris', *New Age* X(19) (7 March 1912), 443.

MOCKING MODERNISMS 131

Frank Rutter, damned Vorticist art with excessive praise, reviewing an (imaginary) exhibition by the 'newly arrived Twopenny Tubists at the Loopdeloupil Gallery', who, as the name implies, are cut-price Cubists, to wit, Vorticists, as references to the artists Mr. Bombast (David Bomberg) and Mr. Explain (Jacob Epstein) confirm.[57] Another squib, 'Futile-Ism. Or, All Cackle and No Osses', purported to be a transcription of discussion that took place at the lecture on 'Vital English Art' given by Marinetti and C. R. W. Nevinson at the Doré Galleries on 12 June 1914, to prepare readers to approach the actual text of Nevinson's lecture (which appeared later in that very issue) in an amused and sceptical spirit.[58] The parodies were so involved and written with such becoming gusto that at a reader might be forgiven for wondering why the *New Age* was giving considered sober attention to productions that it was also prepared to present as fatuous, futile, factional, all bark and no bite.

The issue came to a head when the *New Age* serialized 'The Approach to Paris' (1913) and at the same time printed Hastings's essay-by-essay rebuttals, signed 'T. K. L.'. Hastings systematically traduced Pound's arguments for a modernism predicated on classicism and the example of French post-Symbolist poets in a merciless series of parodies of his high-handed and hectoring expository manner that were designed to dismantle the bases of his authority.[59] Hastings began by mocking Pound the American expatriate for his presumptive statements about a poetic culture he had only recently joined, redacting his already sensational argument 'one might as well say that there never were any English poets until they began to study the French' to push it to ridiculous extremes.[60] Pound's *précieux* habit of using foreign terminology was undermined by Hastings's repeated use of trite French exclamations to reinforce her wider case that Pound's analysis was superficial, the result of a sudden passion for what was *au courant* rather than deep learning, satirizing his propensity to pick up and then drop celebrated authors without a second's further thought. She made play with Pound's copious practice of quotation, offering instead her own parodies of the writers under discussion.

[57] Frank Rutter, 'Pastiche: Art and Artists', *New Age* XV.4 (28 May 1914), 92.
[58] 'Charles Brookfarmer' [C. E. Bechhöfer], 'Futile-Ism. Or, All Cackle and No Osses', *New Age* XV(7) (18 June 1914), 154; C. R. W. Nevinson, 'Vital English Art', *New Age* XV(7) (18 June 1914), 160–2.
[59] Ezra Pound, 'The Approach to Paris: I', *New Age* XIII(19) (4 September 1913), 551–2; Ezra Pound, 'The Approach to Paris: II', *New Age* XIII(20) (11 September 1913), 577–8; 'T. K. L.' [Beatrice Hastings], 'The Way Back to America', *New Age* XIII(21) (18 September 1913), 604–5; Ezra Pound, 'The Approach to Paris: III', *New Age* XIII(21) (18 September 1913), 607–9; Ezra Pound, 'The Approach to Paris: IV', *New Age* XIII(22) (25 September 1913), 631–3; 'T. K. L.', 'Clear Tongue plus Pindarism', *New Age* XIII(22) (25 September 1913), 636–7; Ezra Pound, 'The Approach to Paris: V', *New Age* XIII(23) (2 October 1913), 662–4; 'T. K. L.', 'Humanititism and the New Form', *New Age* XIII(23) (2 October 1913), 669–70; Ezra Pound, 'The Approach to Paris: VI', *New Age* XIII(24) (9 October 1913), 694–6; 'T. K. L.', 'Aristophanes or Tailhade?' *New Age* XIII(24) (9 October 1913), 702–3; Ezra Pound, 'The Approach to Paris: VII', *New Age* XIII(25) (16 October 1913), 726–8; 'T. K. L.', 'All except Anything', *New Age* XIII(25) (16 October 1913), 733–4; 'T. K. L.', 'Ride a Cock Pegasus', *New Age* XIII(27) (30 October 1913), 794–5.
[60] Pound, 'Approach to Paris: II', 577.

132 MODERNIST PARODY

For instance, Pound waxed lyrical about Remy de Gourmont's 'Litanies de la rose' in *Le Pèlerin du Silence* (1896), from which he quoted extensively, interlineated with his own comments:

> Fleur hypocrite,
> Fleur du silence.

> he begins, setting the beat of his measure.

> Rose couleur de cuivre, plus frauduleuse que nos joies, rose couleur de cuivre, embaume-nous dam tes mensonges, fleur hypocrite, fleur du silence. [Pound quotes ten more verses . . .]

> And so it runs with ever more sweeping cadence with ever more delicate accords, and if you are not too drunk with the sheer naming over of beauty you will wake at the end of the reading and know that the procession of all woman that ever were has passed before you.[61]

Hastings retaliated by replacing the words '*rose*' and '*fleur*' with 'cow' in her 'translation' of Remy de Gourmont's 'Litanies de la rose' in *Le Pèlerin du Silence* (1896) to assert that Pound's rapturous admiration of its rhythmic structure in 'The Approach to Paris: II' was positively bovine:

> Cow hypocrite,
> Cow of pretence.
> Cow colour of fawn, more fraudulent than our nags, cow
> colour of faun, bedaubed with brush, walking lie,
> cow hypocrite, cow of pretence
> Cow erst in a pound, footsore down at St. Louis, cow
> erst in a pound, now corned and in tins at Paris,
> cow hypocrite, cow of pretence.[62]

She laid bare what she saw as the cruder commercial motivations of Pound's faddish endorsement of the French, reframing his comments on poetry as an art to insist instead that it is a trade. Her strongest objection to Pound's case was in response to his suggestion that Tailharde was Aristophanic, when in her view the Frenchman simply presented scenes from modern life without justification or condemnation, unlike the ancient satirists Pound cited, who, in her opinion, all rendered their time in terms of their time with 'an almost visibly throbbing anger'.[63] If the model for the English poet was to be drawn from the examples of

---

[61] Pound, 'Approach to Paris: II', 577–8.
[62] 'T. K. L', 'Way Back to America', 605; Pound, 'Approach to Paris: II', 577–8.
[63] 'T. K. L', 'Aristophanes or Tailhade?', 703.

MOCKING MODERNISMS   133

French poets, whose observations are without politics, then that literature could have no part in the progressive battles fought by the *New Age.*

Having dealt with Pound's manifesto for a European modernism that was impersonally objective, Hastings issued her parting shot. In 'Ride a Cock Pegasus', she presented Pound as having forsaken the French, sitting astride a new hobby horse, now hailing the writing of the long-awaited English epic. The idea that Maurice Hewlett's 'Prelude' to 'The Man on the Hill', a history of the agricultural labourer, might exceed the achievements of the English greats, Chaucer, Spenser, Shakespeare, and Milton, was ludicrous to say the least.[64] Endorsing Hewlett, the writer of historical romances, Hastings insinuates that Pound's true tastes are more retrograde than he would admit, mocking his faddishness as she questioned his radicalism. Pound evidently took the sequence in good humour, permitting serial publication to continue alongside T. K. L's rebuttals; the parodies did not end his association with the *New Age.*

Ann Ardis has drawn attention to Orage's trenchant defence of the practice of 'both featuring and quarrelling with Pound, and through him the modernist avant-garde more generally' in the 'Readers and Writers' column (signed R. C. H.), where he insisted that it was right and proper for the *New Age* to mimic Pound's essay even as it was being published:

> Was it right, I have been asked, for *The New Age* to allow 'T. K. L.' to 'mimick' Mr. Pound's articles on Parisian writers while these were still being published? My own answer is, Yes, and with more reasons than I can set down.[65]

Orage explained that the magazine had 'as serious and well-considered a "propaganda" in literature as in economics or politics'.[66] Arguing that 'the literature we despise is associated with the economics we hate as the literature we love is associated with the form of society we would assist in creating', he stated for the avoidance of all doubt that 'Mr. Pound—I say it with all respect—is an enemy of *The New Age*', adding that while Pound's criticisms of the philosophy of the *New Age* were not direct and personal, the fact that they were oblique or tacit made them more inimical.[67] Orage presented Hastings's parodies as part of the parry and thrust of robust and healthy debate:

---

[64] 'T. K. L', 'Ride a Cock Pegasus', 794; Maurice Hewlett, 'Prelude' to 'The Man on the Hill', *Westminster Gazette* (18 October 1913).

[65] Ann Ardis, *Modernism and Cultural Conflict, 1880–1922* (Cambridge: Cambridge University Press, 2002), 156. For a detailed discussion of the spat between Pound and T. K. L. in the context of the *New Age*'s mission to stage open-ended debate about the social and aesthetic values of modern writing, see Ann Ardis, 'The Dialogics of Modernism(s) in the *New Age*', *Modernism/Modernity*, 14(3) (September 2007), 407–34. 'R. C. H.' [A. R. Orage], 'Readers and Writers', *New Age* XIV(2) (13 November 1913), 51.

[66] 'R. C. H.', 'Readers and Writers', 51.

[67] 'R. C. H.', 'Readers and Writers', 51.

134 MODERNIST PARODY

For such as *read*, the duel between Mr. Pound and 'T. K. L.' was a debate of extraordinary intensity. The weapons on neither side were arguments, for the debate was on the plane of imagination, not reason; but the discussion could nevertheless be reduced to a clash of syllogisms.[68]

Not only was Orage making the case for parody as the most penetrating and persuasive literary criticism, because it was imaginatively affective in a way that plain argument was not, he was also justifying its central position in the cultural wars being fought on all sides to determine the forms, theoretical justifications, and politics that modern literature should take. Pound would not have disagreed.

When Hastings once again took up the cudgel to criticize 'Affirmations' (January 1915–February 1915), another essay of Pound's that was serially published in the *New Age*, she did so in the guise of 'Alice Morning', whose regular column 'Impressions of Paris' for a time addressed Pound's essay through a combination of *ad hominem* parody and critical commentary that made the complaint that his manifestos were cultish and his critical persona was 'florid, pedantic, obscurantist'.[69] Pound was sufficiently vexed that Hastings had suggested that rhetorical statements such as 'the Quattrocento shines out because the vortices of power coincided with the vortices of creative energy?' were a nonsense, just 'fiddling with terms' to write a letter to the editor, complaining she had mistaken his argument.[70] But he did affirm the value of her parody for pressing upon him the need for clarity:

> Mr. Aldington's priapic parody of his own most successful poem (In Via Sestina) is of considerably less value. Miss Morning at least advances the discussion by forcing me to define one of my terms more exactly.[71]

Pound had high respect for the redactive qualities of hardcore parody, as suggested by his letter to E. E. Cummings on 10 November 1926, where he commented:

> I shd. like to have you at hand to parody my editorials before they get into print; the difficulty of getting any simple fact or idea into terms simple enough for transmission even to the smallest conceivable number of subscribers . . . etc.[72]

Pound's love of novelty (which was seemingly at odds with his enthusiasm for the antiquated and the arcane), his brash and frequently hectoring manner, and his careerist instinct for publicity, made him a familiar target for parody and ridicule,

[68] 'R. C. H.', 'Readers and Writers', 51.
[69] 'Alice Morning' [Beatrice Hastings], 'Impressions of Paris', *New Age* XVI(12) (21 January 1915), 309.
[70] 'Alice Morning', 'Impressions of Paris', 308; Ezra Pound, 'Vorticism', *New Age* XVI(13) (28 January 1915), 359.
[71] Pound, 'Letters to the Editor: Vorticism', 359.
[72] *LEP* 275.

MOCKING MODERNISMS   135

which he accepted with good grace.[73] He gave as good as he got, policing the boundaries of his personal modernist canon by dashing off parodies of rival artists at high speed, a practice that provided him with an outlet for his manic energy that also suited his mimic talents and tub-thumping tendencies.

Pound once boasted to Monroe in a letter of 10 April 1915 that he had written a parody of the American poet Vachel Lindsay in just '1 minute 38 seconds', which was more than sufficient—to his mind at least—to emulate 'the élan, the free bravura, the fecundity, the felicity, the obvious rag-time of the cadence: jig jilly jig jilly jig' that he believed to be all that distinguished the work of one whose 'top ambition is obviously Kipling'.[74] Pound had previously told Monroe that Lindsay was unfit for inclusion in the *Catholic Anthology 1914–1915*. His parody of Lindsay was therefore calculated to demonstrate the gulf between Lindsay's poetics and his own, while simultaneously asserting that Lindsay's work was imitative, as Pound explained to Monroe in a letter likely dating from March 1915:

> Lindsay; he's all right, but we are not in the same movement or anything like it. I approve of his appearance in *Poetry* (so long as I am not supposed to want what he wants), but not in anything which I stand sponsor for as a healthy tendency. I don't say he copies Marinetti; but he is with him, and his work is futurist.[75]

Another of Pound's fatuous high-speed parodies of Lindsay appeared in 'The Reader Critic' column of the *Little Review* in January 1918 (which more commonly featured critical prose). The poem spanned two pages, and began:

> Whoop golly-ip Zopp, bop BIP!!
> I'm Mr. Lindsay with the new sheep-dip,
> I'm a loud-voiced yeller, I'm a prancing preacher,
> Gawd's in his heaven! I'm the *real* High Reacher . . .[76]

It was signed 'Abel Sanders' and appeared with the bragging strapline '(Time consumed in composition 4 minutes 31 seconds. "Try Sander's for celerity")', in order to further assert that Lindsay's poetry was hurried, swiftly reproducible, and artless.[77]

Pound's parodies of Lindsay were not simply for the purpose of personal artistic repudiation but were part of a wider strategy of critical evaluation whereby contributors to little magazines wrote about other individuals, groups, and schools in

---

[73] See for instance the many parodies of Pound collected in Diepeveen, *Mock Modernism*, 133–45.
[74] *LEP* 101.
[75] *LEP* 99.
[76] 'Abel Sanders' [Ezra Pound], 'The Reader Critic: Mr. Lindsay', *Little Review* IV(9) (January 1918), 54, Pound's italics and capitals.
[77] 'Abel Sanders', 'Reader Critic: Mr. Lindsay', 55.

136   MODERNIST PARODY

editorials, columns, and original compositions to establish the particular outlook of their publication and mark out its distinctive territory. In Lindsay's case, Pound's parodies insisted that home-grown American poetry had no place in a publication like the *Little Review* that positioned itself at the vanguard of European-inflected modernism. As Pound explained in a letter to Edgar Jepson of May 1918 in which he set out the case for only reprinting a condensed version of his essay on 'The Western School'—which had previously appeared in the *English Review*, repudiating the view that Lindsay, Masters, and Frost represented a new, indigenous American school—those writers were already 'dead as mutton so far as the *L.R.* reader is concerned . . . Masters we have said farewell to. Frost sinks of his own weight. Lindsay we have parodied.'[78] Pound was confident that his parody put Lindsay in his place and settled the case so decisively that further critical commentary was unnecessary.

However, Pound's early notion that parody inevitably settles aesthetic arguments one way or another (on the basis that the parody either outstrips the original or the ridicule rebounds on the parodist) gave way to reveal a more probing and creatively productive function for parody in another of his poems in the guise of 'Abel Sanders'. In 1917 Pound inadvertently brought the *Little Review* to the attention of the censors at the Post Office at a delicate time in the serial publication of *Ulysses*, having submitted a pseudonymous translation of a fake German document entitled 'Committee for the Increase of Population' in the name of Abel Sanders, giving notice that all German non-combatants must interest themselves in the happiness of married women and maidens for the sake of the fatherland by siring as many children as possible.[79] Pound defended himself in a letter of 29 December 1917 to Quinn (the magazine's generous patron), explaining that the author 'Abel Sanders is a spoof person, and I intended him for parody of puritan ass whom such matters excite.'[80] By 1918, Abel Sanders had evolved from 'a spoof person' into one of Pound's fully fledged personae, a parody that also reflected authentic parts of Pound's identity and critical outlook, but did so in the voice of a brash, subliterate American, one of the poses Pound found so congenial in his private correspondence.[81]

Abel Sanders was but one of many pseudonyms Pound adopted to distance his more risqué parodies from the major body of writing that was to establish his reputation as a serious artist. Indeed, Abel Sanders had much in common with another of Pound's *faux naïf* alter egos, Alfred Venison, who professed:

---

[78] *LEP* 194.

[79] 'Abel Sanders' [Ezra Pound], 'The Reader Critic: This Approaches Literature!', *Little Review* IV(6) (October 1917), 39.

[80] Materer, *Selected Letters of Ezra Pound to John Quinn*, 135.

[81] See for instance 'Abel Sanders' [Ezra Pound], 'Sculpshure [*sic*]', *Little Review* VII(4) (January–March 1921), 47.

MOCKING MODERNISMS   137

I don't claim to be as educated as some of your other poets; but I attend night schools and pick up a bit of the dictionary that way. It would tickle my missus to see this new bit in print.[82]

Venison's vaunted lack of literariness was a ruse to clarify that the primary target of Pound's satire in the eighteen doggerel verses he published under that name in *New English Weekly* in 1934 (and later collected in *Alfred Venison's Poems; Social Credit Themes by the Poet of Titchfield Street* (1935)) was not the poetry of Alfred Lord Tennyson, which Pound enjoyed, but the opponents of social credit. The poems of the former Poet Laureate merely provided snappy forms that energized Pound's ironic commentary on wider social and economic themes.[83]

It was in the guise of Abel Sanders that Pound used parody to intervene in the battle that Elsa von Freytag-Loringhoven was fighting against William Carlos Williams in the pages of the *Little Review*, a move that would have implications for Pound's own future writings and also the direction Eliot's modernist experimentation would take under his aegis. Freytag-Loringhoven had taken exception to Williams's 'Improvisations' (a sequence of fragmentary Dada-inspired prose poems that experimented with automatic writing that first appeared in that magazine (1917–19) and were later collected in *Kora in Hell* (1920)).[84] She responded with 'Thee I call "Hamlet of the Wedding Ring", Criticism of William Carlos Williams's "Kora in Hell" and why . . ', published in two consecutive issues of the *Little Review* (1921).[85] Pound then followed Part II of Freytag-Loringhoven's 'Thee I call "Hamlet of the Wedding Ring"' with 'The Poems of Abel Sanders', a series of three short poems (the first of which is dedicated '*To Bill Williams and Else von Johann Wolfgang Loringhoven y Fulano*'), printed on the very same page as the final lines of 'Thee I call "Hamlet of the Wedding Ring"', in which Pound played the now familiar satirical game of presenting a meagre corpus as if it were a life's work to emphasize its slender contribution.[86]

There could be no doubt in *Little Review* readers' minds that Dada manifested its avant-gardism through parody and self-parody. 'Dada Soulève Tout' [Dada Excites Everything] (1921), a manifesto distributed at an anti-Marinetti

[82] Ezra Pound, 'Alf's Second Bit', *Personæ: Collected Shorter Poems of Ezra Pound* (London: Faber & Faber, 1952), 266.

[83] For a discussion of these poems see Ira B. Nadel, 'Ezra Pound: Two Poems', *Journal of Modern Literature* 15(1) (summer, 1988), 141–5.

[84] William Carlos Williams, 'Improvisations I–III', *Little Review* IV(6) (October 1917), 19; William Carlos Williams, 'Improvisations I–IV', *Little Review* IV(9) (January 1918), 1–9; William Carlos Williams, 'Improvisations I–III', *Little Review* VI(2) (June 1919), 52–9; William Carlos Williams, *Kora in Hell: Improvisations* (Boston: Fours Seas Company, 1920).

[85] *HWR*.

[86] 'Abel Sanders' [Ezra Pound], 'The Poems of Abel Sanders', *Little Review* VIII(1) (autumn 1921), Pound's italics, 111. 'Thee I call "Hamlet of the Wedding Ring"' was published under the name of Else von Freytag-Loringhoven. (The Baroness's birth name was Else Hildegard Plötz.)

138   MODERNIST PARODY

demonstration (reprinted in the *Little Review* after Part I of Freytag-Loringhoven's poem), declared that Dada strikes the moment that perspective is flipped and what was once serious suddenly shows itself to be to be idiotic and absurd:

> Si vous avez des idées sérieuses sur la vie,
> Si vous faites des découvertes artistiques
> et si tout d'un coup votre tête se met à crépiter de rire,
> si vous trouvez toutes vos idées inutiles et ridicules, sachez que
> *C'EST DADA QUI COMMENCE A VOUS PARLER* ...

Dada est l'amertume qui ouvre son rire sur tout ce qui a <u>été</u> <u>fait</u> <u>consacré</u> oublié dans notre langage dans notre cerveau dans nos habitudes.[87]

> [If you have serious ideas about life,
> If you make artistic discoveries
> and if all of a sudden your head starts to crackle with laughter,
> and if you find all your ideas useless and ridiculous, know that
> *IT IS DADA BEGINNING TO SPEAK TO YOU* ...

Dada is the bitterness when opens its laugh on all that which has been *made consecrated forgotten* in our language in our brain in our habits.][88]

To parody Dada was to be a Dadaist. As Tzara put it, 'The true Dadaists were against Dada.'[89] Indeed, almost every manifestation of this latest, zaniest avant-garde was shot with parody at its most anarchic. Tzara's foundational document 'Dada Manifesto' (1918) combined Futurist strategies of provocation with satire and buffoonery to parody and criticize the programmatic pronouncements of avant-garde movements, making noisy calls for the destruction of logic itself and with it conventional patterns of language and syntax, with the aim of assembling a new language, reality, and social order from the ruins of the old.[90] This European phenomenon further galvanized the activities of the American avant-garde in New York, among them expatriates such as Marcel Duchamp and Francis Picabia, the former Futurist Mina Loy, and Freytag-Loringhoven, who mixed with American artists and writers such as Man Ray, Marianne Moore, Wallace Stevens, and Williams himself.[91]

Dadaism provided Williams with a set of techniques for composing his fragmentary, tangential 'Improvisations', prose poems inspired by his own life and the

---

[87] 'Dada Soulève Tout', *Little Review* VII(4) (January–March 1921), 62–3, *Little Review's* capitals.

[88] 'Dada Excites Everything' (1921), in Mary Ann Caws, ed., *Manifesto: A Century of Isms* (Lincoln: University of Nebraska Press, 2001), 290–1, *Little Review's* capitals.

[89] Tristan Tzara, 'Memoirs of Dadaism', later reprinted in an appendix to Edmund Wilson, *Axel's Castle* (New York: Scribner's, 1931), 308.

[90] Tristan Tzara, 'Dada Manifesto', in Caws, *Manifesto*, 297–304.

[91] For a definitive history of New York Dada, see Francis M. Naumann, *New York Dada, 1915–1923* (New York: Abrams, 1994).

ordinary experiences of citizens and immigrants in the melting pot that was modern America but restored to the plane of the imagination through their uncommon presentation. According to Williams, the strength of the sequence inhered not in the 'quality it borrows from a logical recital of events nor from the events themselves but solely from that attenuated power which draws perhaps many broke things into a dance giving them thus a full being'.[92] His aim, as stated in the lengthy 'Prologue' to *Kora in Hell*, was to instigate a new, truly American literature, as distinct from the European-inflected modernism of Pound and Eliot. Williams dismissed Pound's poetry as 'parodies of the middle ages, Dante and Langue D'Oc' and Eliot's 'more exquisite work' as 'rehash, repetition in another way of Verlaine, Baudelaire [sic], Maeterlinck—conscious or unconscious').[93] He characterized the pair of them as 'Men content with the connotations of their masters', that is expatriates who had mistaken imitation of continental forms for true innovation.[94]

The battle lines were drawn very clearly in the 'Prologue' where Williams quoted from a letter from Pound, who misread Williams's 'Improvisations' as un-American and a welcome function of his mixed English and Puerto-Rican ancestry, to highlight their difference of opinion:

> I was very glad to see your wholly incoherent unamerican poems in the L.R....
>
> You thank your bloomin gawd you've got enough Spanish blood to muddy up your mind, and prevent the current American ideation from going through it like a blighted collander [sic].
>
> The thing that saves your work is opacity, and don't forget it. Opacity is NOT an American quality. Fizz, swish, gabble, and verbiage, these are *echt Americanisch*.[95]

The German-American Freytag-Loringhoven responded to *Kora* by damning Williams to hell in 'Thee I call "Hamlet of the Wedding-Ring"', a withering experimental review that took the form of an extended Dadaist prose poem. Anderson advertised the poem to readers as 'one of the most intelligent pieces of criticism ever to have come to us' (a position qualified by Anderson's irritation that Freytag-Loringhoven had refused to submit to her editorial insight and accept substantial cuts calculated to overcome 'certain redundancies of thinking' that she felt 'destroyed the power and piquancy of the whole').[96] Freytag-Loringhoven's assaults on Williams—or 'W. C.' as she disparagingly calls him—are relentless.[97] Her disgust with the man and his writing is absolute: 'From rudeness of title

---

[92] Williams, *Kora in Hell*, 19.
[93] Williams, *Kora in Hell*, 28, 26.
[94] Williams, *Kora in Hell*, 26.
[95] Pound in Williams, *Kora in Hell*, 14, Pound's capitals.
[96] M. C. A. [Margaret C. Anderson], 'Discussion: William Carlos Williams' "Kora in Hell" by Else von Freytag-Loringhoven', *Little Review* VII.3 (September–December 1921), 59.
[97] *HWR* 48–55, 108–10.

140   MODERNIST PARODY

to crude triteness of content "Kora in Hell" does make me scream'.[98] She takes up the cudgel of Pound's criticism, berating Williams for his naive parochialism: 'Americans not possessing tradition—not born within truth's lofty echoing walls—born on void—background of barren nothingness' ('tradition' here being distinct from the spent writings of immediate predecessors).[99] She presents Williams as one who, having rejected the culture of Old Europe, 'Gazes into chasm of knowledge—void—frightened—dizzy—lacking architecture'.[100] He stands accused of juggling words without 'conviction—background—tradition', without 'rhythm', 'echo', or 'resonance', so that they are 'never to point' and 'carry no meaning'.[101] No bohemian, Williams is denounced as a bourgeois doctor, a 'wobbly-legged business satchel-carrying little louse', without the art even to manage a flea circus.[102] The rejection is intensely personal, for the Baroness, as Freytag-Loringhoven was known, speaks not only as an emissary for the European avant-gardes, but also as a woman spurned. She assails Williams's 'malebluster' and his attempts at projecting masculinity, needling what she saw as his Hamlet-like lack of courage to confront emotion and desire, his undeveloped sentiments, and his complete inability to carry or convey the 'intoxication of feeling' that the force of her own unrelenting pronouncements, delivered in scintillating jerks, curves, and twists, with the authority of an oracle, showed to be the true mark of a true artist.[103]

It was natural that 'Thee I call "Hamlet of the Wedding-Ring"' would pique Pound's interest. He was not only personally invested in debates about Americanism and modernism but he was at that time giving himself what Richard Sieburth has described as 'a crash course in Dada', having moved to Paris in 1920.[104] In Paris, Pound made it his business to make the acquaintance of leading French Dadaists and made contributions to magazines such as Tzara's *Dadaphone* 7 (March 1920), Breton's *Littérature* 16(1) (October 1920). As Andrew Clearfield notes in 'Pound, Paris, and Dada', there were already certain affinities between Pound's manner and Dada: his 'prose always had something of Dada about it' in his 'zest for overstatement, jocularity mingled with contempt for the average reader', his fondness for 'confronting and disorientating the reader' and tendency towards 'Fragmentation and quick "cutting" from one idea to another'.[105] 'The Poems of Abel Sanders' was written at a time when Pound was still coming to terms with this latest avant-garde movement. The first poem takes the form of a Dadaist collage that travesties both Williams's and Freytag-Loringhoven's positions in 'Kora in Hell' and 'I Call Thee "Hamlet of the Wedding Ring"', recoupling them against their wishes through

---

[98] *HWR* 55.
[99] *HWR* 49.
[100] *HWR* 110.
[101] *HWR* 50.
[102] *HWR* 110.
[103] *HWR* 48, 111.
[104] Richard Sieburth, 'Dada Pound', *South Atlantic Quarterly* 83 (winter 1984), 49.
[105] Andrew Clearfield, 'Pound, Paris, and Dada', *Paideuma* 7 (spring and fall, 1978), 131.

MOCKING MODERNISMS 141

interlingual wordplay and racist slang, making a game of substitution to collapse their differences and insist that both poets have European roots and that for Williams to pretend otherwise is a form of racial masquerade:

CODSWAY bugwash
Bill's way   backwash
FreytagElse ¾arf an'arf
Billy Sunday one harf Kaiser Bill one harf
      Elseharf Suntag, Billsharf Freitag
Brot wit thranen,   con plaisir ou con patate   pomodoro

Bill dago resisting U.SAgo, Else ditto on the verb
basis yunker, plus Kaiser Bill reading to goddarnd stupid wife
      anbrats works
      of simple
domestic piety in Bleibtreu coner of Hockhoff'sbesitzendeecke
before the bottom fell out.   Plus a little boiled Neitzsch
on the sabath.   Potsdam, potsdorf potz gek und keine ende.
Bad case, bad as fake southern gentlemen tells you
everymorn that he is gentleman, and that he is not black.
Chinesemandarinorlaundryman   takes forgranted youwillsee he is
not BookerTWashington.[106]

Pound (as Sanders) endorses Freytag-Loringhoven's position against Williams, importing her analytical framework and her linguistic tricks (inversions, compounds) and reiterating her criticisms, while undermining her personally.[107] Freytag-Loringhoven acquires the first names of Johann Wolfgang von Goethe, Germany's greatest literary writer, which would seem a compliment save for the fact that his famous lines 'Wer nie fein Brod mit Tränen as—/Wer nie die kummervollen Nächte/Auf feinem Bette weinend fas—/Der Kennt euch nicht, ihr himmlifchen Mächte' ['Who never ate his bread in tears,/Who never through

---

[106] 'Abel Sanders' [Ezra Pound], 'Poems of Abel Sanders', 111, Pound's capitals.
[107] An alternative reading of 'The Poems of Abel Sanders' is offered by Irene Gammel who is inclined to see the poem as 'covert homage' to the Baroness's style: 'Pound implicitly argued (as far as argument is possible in a Dada poem) for a truce, deflating the debate by turning it into parody and reminding both poets that Dada is, after all, playful, nonsensical, and silly'. Gammel notes that while Pound 'rejoiced in weaving the illicit love affair between the female Dadaist and the male modernist', he soon conspired to push female Dadaists like Freytag-Loringhoven out of the frame, championing 'a more, stately male dada, his own included' in later issues of the *Little Review*. (See Irene Gammel, *Baroness Elsa: Gender, Dada, and Everyday Modernity—A Cultural Biography* (Cambridge, MA: MIT Press, 2002), 273–5.) Certainly, Pound respected Freytag-Loringhoven and her avant-gardism. Whatever his misgivings about her feminism, he admired her chutzpah: 'Bless/The Baroness/yrs/E.' he wrote to Anderson in spring 1923 (Thomas L. Scott and Melvin J. Friedman, with Jackson R. Bryer, eds., *Pound/The Little Review: The Letters of Ezra Pound to Margaret Anderson: The Little Review Correspondence* (New York: New Directions, 1988), 298).

142   MODERNIST PARODY

the mournful night/Sat weeping on his bed with fears—/He knows not, heavenly powers, your might!'], which are quoted in the first instalment of 'I Call Thee "Hamlet of the Wedding Ring"', have been traduced by Pound so that 'bread in tears' is served with 'pleasure or with potatoes tomato'.[108] The gesture emphasizes the bathos of Dada at its most nonsensical, while nonetheless evoking a much-anthologized poem that Freytag-Loringhoven argues is invested with the kind of emotional authority in its simplicity and profundity that escapes Williams. While the association with Goethe would seem a high compliment, the insertion of male forenames constituted a swipe at Freytag-Loringhoven's mannish appearance and the premises of her female and feminist critique of Williams, as emphasized by the masculine Spanish tag '*y fulano*' [and so and so], whereby Pound insists that both poets are one of a kind. Freytag-Loringhoven's way, which she calls 'God's way' (which is 'selective—aristocratic' because it draws strength from 'tradition'), becomes 'Codsway', mere 'bugwash', while Bill's way, to repeat the Baroness's criticism, is 'backwash'.[109] Figured as Kaiser Bill (Wilhelm II), the beaten enemy of the First World War, Williams's vision of Americanism is presented as an ungentlemanly sham that lacks the true artist's aristocratic selection and unfailing equipoise.

Having added to the debate between Williams and Freytag-Loringhoven, Pound turned to reflect on Dadaism in 'Poem No. 2', questioning the fitness of Dada for social and political critique when it drifts towards degenerate nonsense:

Able Abel

Mounts dernier bateau:

@¼%&:¼?½ @¾) (&?;¼%@&%&&&&&

¼¼¼¼@¼%;34%3[110]

Pound may have ably exhibited his professional mastery over Dadaist writing, but whether Sanders is merely a late adopter or has only succeeded in boarding a ship that has already sailed is unclear. The degeneration into nonsensically conjoined fractions, associated earlier with Williams and Freytag-Loringhoven's proportionate contributions to the movement and to Sander's latest style, draws attention to Dada's capacity for mindless indiscipline, of a more extreme kind than Freytag-Loringhoven even exhibited in her *faux* interlingual phonic poems 'Irrender König', 'Klink—Hratzvenga (Deathwail)' and 'Nari—Tzarissamanili (He is

---

[108] Johann Wolfgang von Goethe, *Wilhelm Meisters Lehrjahre, Ein Roman* (Berlin: Bey Johann Friedrich Unger, 1795), 346; Johann Wolfgang von Goethe, 'Song of the Harper' in Margarete Münsterberg, ed. and trans., *A Harvest of German Verse* (New York: Appleton and Company, 1916), 52; 'Abel Sanders' [Ezra Pound], 'Poems of Abel Sanders', 101.

[109] *HWR* 59, 59, 59, 58.

[110] 'Abel Sanders' [Ezra Pound], 'Poems of Abel Sanders', 111.

Dead!)'[111] A further comment, printed sideways, 'dada/deada/what is deader/than dada', poses a typically Dadaesque riddle, attacking Dada with Dada by mocking its obsession with death, signalling Pound's divided attitude to a movement that erupted with creativity and presented a potential corrective to the stultification that beset much anglophone literature but also tended to gratuitous idiocy.[112]

French Dada made laughter its primary aesthetic affect, but by using Dada's strategies to write literary criticism in the form of poetry Freytag-Loringhoven and Pound were testing its capacity for calibrated aesthetic judgement. To what extent was parody an apt expression for avant-garde outrage; for the mocking of old orthodoxies; a form of buffoonery that is both sardonic and critical but non-committal in the sense that it endorses no position save its own strategies? This parodic experimentation continued in the editorial pages of the *Little Review*, for instance in the special Picabia issue (spring 1922) that Pound superintended. It contained a collaborative three-page assemblage of comments and responses purporting to address the concerns of the 'DEAR INDIGNANT AND WRITHING CITIZEN INQUIRING: "So nothing is Art any more but this modern stuff that doesn't feed our spirits or rest our minds?"' but in fact calculated to further infuriate any readers who were not behind the magazine's reincarnation as a de facto Dada organ.[113] The format of the piece is not dissimilar in form to the latter sections of the 'Aeolus' episode of *Ulysses*.[114] Glib subheadings in capitals offer tangential commentary on a ragbag of eccentric affirmations, negations, letters, nonsense, and aphorisms by jh [Jane Heap], Abel Sanders, Djuna Barnes, and others, in broad defence of the *Little Review*'s position. One snippet mocks the probable scoffing of 'POMPOUS WELLFED CLERGYMEN'.[115] Crass parodies synthesizing the manners of French Symbolists and the Western School, signed Abel Sanders, confirm how far behind the times these movements now were. A framed address to readers by Barnes praises fanatics and ambivalently enquires 'HAS IT EVER OCCURRED TO YOU THAT THE LITTLE REVIEW MEANS NO MORE TO US THAN IT SHOULD TO YOU . . . .'[116] The whole ensemble concludes with a Dada ditty, summarizing the magazine's new turn:

> Oh I would be a Dada
> And with the Dadas stand
> An idiot for my brother,
> Boobs on every hand.[117]

---

[111] Else von Freytag-Loringhoven, 'Poems': 'Irrender König'; 'Klink—Hratzvenga (Deathwail)'; 'Nari—Tzarissamanili (He Is Dead!)', *Little Review* VI(10) (March 1920), 10–12.

[112] 'Abel Sanders' [Ezra Pound], 'Poems of Abel Sanders', 111. Pound insisted that the special Dada issue of the *Little Review* feature 'no idiots' (Ezra Pound to Margaret Anderson, *c.* 22 April 1921, in Scott and Friedman, with Bryer, *Pound/The Little Review*, 268).

[113] 'Comments and Responses', *Little Review* VIII(2) (Spring 1922), 33, *Little Review*'s capitals.

[114] *U* 7.1-1075.

[115] 'Comments and Responses', 33, *Little Review*'s capitals.

[116] 'Comments and Responses', 35, *Little Review*'s capitals.

[117] 'Comments and Responses', 35.

144 MODERNIST PARODY

As Jane Heap explained in a further editorial defending the magazine's Dada mania, and the level of exposure it was giving to Freytag-Loringhoven, 'Dada has flung its crazy bridges to a new consciousness . . . Dada is making a contribution to nonsense'.[118] Whereas French Dada's leading exponents were at this time prone to produce anti-art (by treating artworks no differently from any other everyday artefact and shunting them into the realm of the absurd), breaking with sense-making structures became a way for the modernists to make a new language in which to defend the art they considered worthy, and thereby affirm the institution of art.

When Pound parodied Dada, he was not merely joining in critical debates about its applications or flexing his professional mastery, but feeling its contours, testing its capacity to conduct serious arguments, its utility in an aristocratic model of the arts, seeing where he himself might take what he had gleaned from that movement to advance the modernist experiment. The argument that the form of Pound's *Cantos* bore the influence of Dada was first advanced by Clearfield and Sieburth, who both cite Pound's parody of the Dada manner in 'Kongo Roux'—a poem written in French, signed 'Ezra Pound', that appeared in a special nonsense issue of Picabia's avant-garde little magazine *391*, entitled *Le Pilhaou-Thibaou* (10 July 1921)—as evidence that Pound was on the way to doing more with Dada than its French exponents had done.[119] Clearfield described the poem as 'a pastiche of historical references, contemporary events, Pound's own bizarre theorizing about the Jews and international finance, and typical Dada *jeux d'esprit*', gesturing towards the ways in which 'Kongo Roux' departed from Dada's mainstream.[120] Sieburth observed that the piece is 'as close to the real Dada thing' as Pound would ever get, commenting:

> the piece is a deliberately incoherent farrago of slogans and ramblings whose zany truculence and typographical high jinks combine Vorticist polemic with Picabian put-on. The title pun (Kangaroo/Red Congo) refers to the name of a Utopian 'denationalist' city which Pound suggests should be founded on the demilitarized banks of the Rhine,—a city 'sans armée, sans aucune importance militaire, sans aucun gouvernement sauf pour balayer les rues'—in a box to the right of the page, Pound declares 'On appellera ça KONGO, ou Venusberg ou la nouvelle Athènes selon'. Kongo, in short, is the Dada version of that ideal city or New Jerusalem which haunts the *Cantos*: 'To build the city of Dioce whose terraces are the colour of the stars'.[121]

---

[118] 'jh' [Jane Heap], 'Dada—', *Little Review* VIII(2) (spring 1922), 46.
[119] Ezra Pound, 'Kongo Roux', *391*, No. 16 (*Le Pilhaou-Thibaou*), 10 July 1921, 10, reprinted in Clearfield, 'Pound, Paris, and Dada', appendix II, 135.
[120] Clearfield, 'Pound, Paris, and Dada', 119–20.
[121] Sieburth, 'Dada Pound', 60, Pound's capitals.

MOCKING MODERNISMS   145

The pedantic references to historical events, including the Spanish and Portuguese inquisitions ('SOUVENIR/Dernier auto-da-fé, /Espagne a. d. 1759' and 'Inquisition retablie Portugal a. d. 1824') and international finance ('des contrats/Injuste d'usure. 1320–1921') were not in the least Dadaesque, nor the commentary on usurious financiers, nor the reference to Jules Laforgue, nor the explicitly political reflections on the role the artist might play in the regeneration of post-war Europe via the creation of an ideal city.[122] Vincent Sherry has further suggested that while the poem does not solve the problem of how a new political order might be wrought by a singular artist, it does 'suggest how the energies of verbal deconstruction could flow into civil reconstruction; the interlingual punning catches up the theme of Kongo Roux as international city'.[123] As a parody, 'Kongo Roux' feels like it could be a practical joke, but in light of Pound's view that 'Humanity is malleable mud, and the arts set the mould it is later cast into' (expressed in a letter to Felix E. Shelling of 9 July 1922), Sherry perceived that the prose poem was also a forum for exploring how the poet might begin to exercise the special aesthetic sensibility necessary to participate in the 'utopian motives of Dada' and thereby prescribe the ideal social formation as a function of his conscious craft.[124] In this respect, when Pound parodied Dada in 'Kongo Roux' he stretched Dada's remit and bent it to new political purpose.

It appears that it was the deconstructive/reconstructive paradigm that Pound found most attractive about Dada. In his October 1921 'Paris Letter' for the *Dial* Pound expressed his admiration for 'the nettoyage, the clearing' achieved by Picabia's 'hyper-Socratic destructivity'.[125] Picabia's montage techniques, his parodic recontextualizations of verbal and graphic *objets trouvés*, provided one model for Pound in his reorganization of the diverse sources on which his poetry increasingly relied. As Sieburth has suggested:

> the semiotics of Dada may throw light on some of the deepest contradictions in *The Cantos*, that is, Pound's paradoxical deployment of essentially deconstructive techniques (scrambled syntagms, predicates without subjects, signifiers disrupted from their signifieds, arcane referentialities) in a public, didactic 'tale of the tribe' whose avowed aim is the construction of a new paradigm, a new paideuma, a new culture.[126]

In this light, the parody of Dada in 'Kongo Roux' functions both as a destructive clearing and gesture towards reassemblage of the kind that Pound would find

---

[122] Pound, 'Kongo Roux', 10, Pound's capitals.
[123] Vincent Sherry, *Ezra Pound, Wyndham Lewis, and Radical Modernism* (New York: Oxford University Press, 1993), 154.
[124] *LEP* 249; Sherry, *Ezra Pound, Wyndham Lewis, and Radical Modernism*, 155.
[125] Ezra Pound, 'Paris Letter', *Dial* 71(4) (October 1921), 457.
[126] Sieburth, 'Dada Pound', 56–7.

146   MODERNIST PARODY

productive as he made headway with the Malatesta Cantos (1922–3), and as he advised Eliot on editing *The Waste Land*.[127]

In addition to providing a rich case study for the ways in which parody was used in little magazines to conduct debates 'of extraordinary intensity . . . on the plane of imagination', both Freytag-Loringhoven's and Pound's adventures in Dada, and their self-conscious play with national identity, fit with wider patterns in the writing of modernist literature, attesting to the creativity that sprung from mimicry and appropriation. The parodies by modernists that were most penetrating in their criticism took a questioning and experimental approach to cultural developments to transgress established genres and modes of writing, opening up new techniques and expressive possibilities that later manifested in more nuanced and complex forms in major works. The next two chapters explore the ways in which the writers who successfully positioned themselves in the modernist mainstream made use of reassemblage and parodic recontextualization to create the distinctive stylistic textures and ceaseless shifts in voice and tone that defined their mature experiments, focusing particularly on *The Waste Land* and *Ulysses*.

[127] For a detailed account of the writing of the *Cantos*, see Bush, *Genesis of Ezra Pound's Cantos*.

5

'A *Moqueur* to the Marrow'

T. S. Eliot, Parody, and the Writing of *The Waste Land*

The modernists who successfully positioned their work in the movement's main-stream embraced parody as its distinctive and defining aesthetic. Their parody had many precedents: the fashionable medievalizing pastiche that could only be redeemed through the ironic awareness realized by parody and self-parody; the wry tone achieved by French Symbolist and post-Symbolist poets who made use of parodic stylization; the zany parody and self-mockery of successive European avant-gardes and their Anglo-American counterparts; the amused assumption of different personae and the creative and transgressive potential of non-standard Englishes; the deflationary pleasures of the mock epic and mock heroic; and, of course, the novelistic tradition itself as defined by writers in Bakhtin's 'Second Stylistic Line' such as Cervantes, Rabelais, Swift, and Sterne.

In their different ways, the mature works of Pound, Eliot, and Joyce extract literary capital from localized parody that takes the form of ironic injection of semi-quotations or parodic stylizations into a larger whole. An important context for this strain of parodic play in Pound and Eliot's poetry was the example of Jules Laforgue, whose scrupulously correct manner Arthur Symons described in his influential overview *The Symbolist Movement in Literature* (1899) as 'a kind of travesty, making subtle use of colloquialism, slang, neologism, technical terms for their allusive, their factitious, their reflected meanings, with which one can play, very seriously'.[1] This chapter begins by exploring Pound's critical reflections on the Laforguean aspects of his own writing, which provide a technical explanation of how this particularly slippery and equivocal mode of parody can operate that is not only suggestive for Pound's work but Eliot's too. It then opens out to consider Eliot's early comic writings, such as 'Effie the Waif', his 'Brilliants', and the King Bolo verses, which attest to his love of parody, his talent for mimicking different voices, and his affinity for popular cultural forms such as music hall and black-face minstrelsy. These discussions provide a context for thinking about the ways in which Pound and Eliot's ideas about parody, imitation, mimicry, and historical sensibility shaped the composition of *The Waste Land*, which in its draft stages featured long narrative sections and Popean couplets that were ultimately judged

---

[1] Arthur Symons, *The Symbolist Movement in Literature*, 2nd edn (London: Archibald Constable & Co. Ltd., 1908), 102.

Modernist Parody. Sarah Davison, Oxford University Press. © Sarah Davison (2023).
DOI: 10.1093/oso/9780192849243.003.0006

148   MODERNIST PARODY

to be too derivative but in its final form made creative and original use of Dryde-nesque parody and Dadaesque assemblage. The chapter concludes by examining how the parody within *The Waste Land* conditioned contemporary responses to the poem and exploring the various ways in which the technique remained central to Eliot's private and public writings.

In 1917, Pound acclaimed Laforgue 'an incomparable artist' in 'Irony, Laforgue, and Some Satire':

> He is, nine-tenths of him, critic—dealing for the most part with literary poses and *clichés*, taking them as his subject matter; and—and this is the important thing when we think of him as a poet—he makes them a vehicle for the expression of his own very personal emotions, of his own unperturbed sincerity.[2]

That same year Pound finished his 'Homage to Sextus Propertius' (only published in 1919), a loose translation of the second and third extant books of the Roman elegist Sextus Aurelius Propertius concerning the trials he endures at the hands of his capricious mistress, Cynthia. Pound marshalled literary poses and clichés with Laforguean detachment, having detected, as he explained to Felix Schelling in a letter of 8 July 1922, that 'S[extus].P[ropertius]. is tying blue ribbon in the tails of Virgil and Horace' and 'that sometime after his first "book" S.P. ceased to be the dupe of magniloquence and began to touch words somewhat as Laforgue did'.[3] Accordingly, Pound took literary poses and clichés as his subject matter in his homage:

> A new-fangled chariot follows the flower-hung horses;
> A young Muse with young loves clustered about her
>   ascends with me into the æther ...
> And there is no high-road to the Muses.[4]

Mount Parnassus cannot be reached by the high road. Unreflexive poeticisms alone will not elevate the poet; they are fit only for irony.

While working on 'Homage to Sextus Propertius', Pound developed the the-ory that there are three kinds of poetry, the last of which is extremely productive for thinking about the parodic strain in high modernism that for all its apparent seriousness finds its piquancy in mocking echo:

> (1.) melopoeia, to wit, poetry which moves by its music ... (2.) imagism, or poetry wherein the feelings of painting and sculpture are predominant ... and there is, thirdly, logopoeia or poetry that is akin to nothing but language, which is a dance of the intelligence among words and ideas and modification of ideas and

---

[2] 'Irony, Laforgue, and Some Satire', *LE* 282, Pound's italics.
[3] *LEP* 246.
[4] Ezra Pound, 'Homage to Sextus Propertius', *Quia Pauper Amavi* (London: The Egoist, 1919), 32, Pound's ellipsis.

characters. Pope and the eighteenth-century writers had in this medium a certain limited range. The intelligence of Laforgue ran through the whole gamut of his time. T. S. Eliot has gone on with it.[5]

Pound would later expand on his definition of logopoeia as 'the dance of the intellect among words', explaining 'that is to say, it employs words not only for their direct meaning, but it takes count in a special way of habits of usage, of the context we *expect* to find with the word, its usual concomitants, of its known acceptances, and of ironical play'.[6] To Pound's mind, logopoeia was 'the latest come, and perhaps most tricky and undependable mode'.[7] Of course, it simply consisted in the knowing use of nuance, whereby incongruous registers are brushed up against one another so as to receive an ironic charge, an effect that has always been used by the best writers, including several of Pound's idols from previous generations as well as new talents such as Mina Loy and Marianne Moore, whose contributions to *Others (1917)* were the occasion for this review (in which Pound, perhaps baselessly, linked their 'arid clarity' to the influence of that masterful practitioner Laforgue).[8]

Logopoeia has a parodic colouring that is deconstructive in its impulse yet also simultaneously an invitation to productive comparison. It treats language as 'nothing but language', deferring meaning into a self-conscious play of echoes and substitutions, but it is accompanied by a supplementary movement of the kind that Phiddian argues distinguishes deconstruction from parody. While allowing for the fact that meaning cannot be still or fixed, logopoeia nonetheless contrives to inflect modified echoes satirically, so that they receive a new ironic intonation by virtue of their introduction into a foreign context, generating equivocal critical perspectives that are available to the readers who ponder the distance from established usage and puzzle over the possible significances of the terms of the contrast as they endeavour to keep pace with the dance. Logopoeia thus contains the double impulse to deconstruction and inflected reassemblage that conditions modernism's dialectic and dependent relationship to the past that it perpetually seeks to reinvent and renew. It is often created by the play between conventional literariness, signalled by direct quotation, modified echo or cliché, and inappropriate context, or conversely pedestrian context and inappropriate literary language, and is therefore culturally specific, as Pound would later explain:

> *Logopœia* does not translate; though the attitude of mind it expresses may pass through a paraphrase. Or one might say, you can *not* translate it 'locally', but having determined the original author's state of mind, you may or may not be able to find a derivative or an equivalent.[9]

[5] Ezra Pound, 'A List of Books: "Others"', *Little Review* IV(11) (March 1918), 57.
[6] 'How to Read', *LE* 25, Pound's italics.
[7] *LE* 25.
[8] Pound, 'List of Books', 58.
[9] *LE* 25, Pound's italics. 'Logopoeia' is not spelled or italicized consistently in Pound's writings.

150 MODERNIST PARODY

When Pound made unrepentant anachronistic reference to the 'frigidaire patent' in a late addition to the passage from 'Homage to Sextus Propertius' in which Propertius soliloquizes on his wine cellar, which 'does not date from Numa Pompilius', and supposes the companions of the Muses to be weary of 'historical data', Pound was seeking to find equivalently wry modes of expression that would support his interpretation of Propertius as a sarcastic raconteur and a fellow rebel artist who was 'really up against things very much as one is now'.[10] In Pound's earliest translations he strove to become his subjects' contemporary. In 'Homage to Sextus Propertius', Propertius is made Pound's contemporary, a man whose psychological presentation belongs to Pound's living world.

Pound received a lot of stick from classicists, who misunderstood what he was trying to achieve and misinterpreted his pointed use of logopoeia in 'Homage to Sextus Propertius'. Carpenter reports that Pound 'remarked to his father that the Victorian classicist J. W. Mackail, whose *Latin Literature* he had often used, had been "a complete ASS, seen no irony in Propertius, read him entirely through Burne-Jones, Vita Nuova, Victorian slosh and Xtn sentimentality"'.[11] Monroe would only agree to print 'Homage to Sextus Propertius' in bowdlerized form and so only four of the poems appeared in the March 1919 number of *Poetry*, presenting what Pound felt to be 'a very mutilated piece', as he complained in a letter to Moore of 1 February 1919.[12] The classical scholar Professor William Gardner Hale of the University of Chicago sent Monroe a strongly worded letter of complaint, bewailing Pound's flippancies, perversions, and countless, possibly intentional, certainly insouciant, howlers:

> If Mr. Pound were a professor of Latin, there would be nothing left for him but suicide. I do not counsel this. But I beg him to lay aside the mask of erudition. And, if he must deal with Latin, I suggest that he paraphrase some accurate translation, and then employ some respectable student of the language to save him from blunders which might still be possible.[13]

In highest dudgeon, Pound drafted an unprintable reply, addressed to the editor of *Poetry*: 'Cat-piss and porcupines!! The thing is no more a translation than my "Altaforte" is a translation'.[14] He hammered this point home in forceful

---

[10] Ezra Pound, 'Homage to Sextus Propertius', *Personæ: Collected Shorter Poems of Ezra Pound*, 219, 218, 219; Ezra Pound, quoted in Carpenter, *Serious Character*, 325.

[11] Carpenter, *Serious Character*, 325.

[12] *LEP* 210; Ezra Pound, 'Poems from the Propertius Series: I–IV', *Poetry: A Magazine of Verse* XIII(6) (March 1919), 291–9.

[13] W. G. Hale, 'Correspondence: Pegasus Impounded', *Poetry* XIV(1) (April 1919), 55. The play on Pound's name in the title 'Pegasus Impounded' suggests that his 'Homage to Sextus Propertius' has stopped Hippocrene, the fountain of the Muses, from bubbling forth by impounding Pegasus, the winged horse who made the waters flow by stamping his hoof.

[14] Quoted in Ellen Williams, *Harriet Monroe and the Poetry Renaissance: The First Ten Years of Poetry, 1912–22* (Urbana: University of Illinois Press, 1977), 254.

letters to Orage, Monroe, and also Schelling to whom he wrote, still fuming, on 8 July 1922:

> That fool in Chicago took the *Homage* for a translation, despite the mention of Wordsworth and the parodied line from Yeats. (As if, had one wanted to pretend to more Latin than one knew, it wdn't have been perfectly easy to correct one's divergencies from a Bohn crib. Price 5 shillings.)[15]

Lewis publicly rallied to Pound's defence, perhaps at his request, commenting, 'the parody of Yeats ... and the mention of Wordsworth ... would have indicated to a sensitive or less biased critic that Mr. Pound in his "Homage to Sextus Propertius", had some other aim than that of providing a crib for schoolboys or undergraduates'.[16] To be fair to Hale, the sections of 'Homage to Sextus Propertius' that adapted Yeats and Wordsworth were not published in *Poetry*. However, Pound and Lewis evidently felt that the parody of Yeats was a feature that distinguished 'Homage to Sextus Propertius' as an autonomous creation, rather than blundering translation or limited imitation.

As for that 'line from Yeats', it necessitates further consideration of the effects that Pound and Lewis identified to be parodic. 'Sadness hung over the house, and the desolated female attendants/Were desolated because she had told them her dreams' echoes the refrain from Yeats's mystical poem 'The Withering of the Boughs', communicating the poet's impact on his environment, which is withered by comparison to his visions of the mythological *Tuatha Dé Danan*; 'No boughs have withered because of the wintry wind,/The boughs have withered because I have told them my dreams'.[17] It is not parody of the hilarious, ribald kind, but it is pointedly ironic logopoeic play. Here Pound adapted only a fragmentary refrain, displaying it wryly, but ambivalently, making it speak in a different register and context to describe the imagined performance of a calculating mistress whose reported tears are so profuse that her mood is said to have a profound effect on those around her and whose powers of attraction are likened to witchcraft. The contrast is clear, but how that contrast is to be evaluated is far from clear-cut.

'Propertius' was first printed in its entirety in *Quia Pauper Amavi* (1919), alongside 'Langue d'Oc' (translations of five Provençal troubadour lyrics expressing amusement at adulterous trysts), 'Moeurs Contemporaines' (sharp Jamesian character sketches), and 'Three Cantos', for reasons Pound explained to Schelling:

---

[15] *LEP* 245.

[16] Wyndham Lewis, 'Mr. Ezra Pound', *Observer* (18 January 1920), 5, reprinted in Homberger, *Ezra Pound*, 168.

[17] Pound, 'Homage to Sextus Propertius', *Quia Pauper Amavi*, 38; W. B. Yeats, 'The Withering of the Boughs', *In the Seven Woods: Being Poems Chiefly of the Irish Heroic Age* (New York and London: Macmillan, 1903), 21.

152   MODERNIST PARODY

In the *Quia Pauper Amavi* vol. and Liveright's *Poems* 1921: The point of the archaic language in the Prov. trans. is that the Latin is really 'modern'. We are just getting back to a Roman state of civilization, or in reach of it; whereas the Provençal feeling is archaic, we are ages away from it. (Whether I have managed to convey this or not I can't say; but it is the reason for the archaic dialect.)[18]

Pound intended that the old-fangled diction (such as the obsolete 'plasmatour', meaning 'A creator, a shaper; *spec.* God') and wilful artificiality of 'Langue d'Oc' ('galzeardy', for instance, has no precedent in the *Oxford English Dictionary*) would throw the comparative modernity of 'Homage to Sextus Propertius' into relief.[19] *Quia Pauper Amavi* as a collection thus registers a logopoeic awareness of language and its concomitant ironies, where Pound rehabilitates the pastiche of historical styles through the refined parody of logopoeia. It is this finely calibrated, comparative historical sensibility that differentiates modernist logopoeia and the ironic juxtaposition of diverse echoes drawn from multiple registers from the nonsensical parody of Dada; it is the same sensibility that differentiates 'Kongo Roux' from Picabia's spirited play.

Whereas Pound spent many faltering years practising earnest medievalizing pastiche, eventually finding redemption in parody, self-parody, and parodic logopoeia, Eliot discovered Laforgue and French Symbolism early in his career. Eliot was able to move swiftly beyond the imitative practices fostered by his schoolmasters at Smith Academy because he selected more up-to-date models by which he might develop his obvious talent. In 'What Dante Means to Me' (a talk given in 1950), Eliot reflected on 'early influences, the influences which, so to speak, first introduce one to oneself' and cited Laforgue as 'the first to teach me how to speak, to teach me the poetic possibilities of my own idiom of speech'.[20] As F. O. Matthiessen commented, '"Prufrock", in the movement of its verse, its repetitions, and echoes, and even in its choice of theme, seems of all Eliot's poems to have been written most immediately under Laforgue's stimulus (though brought to a finished perfection of form which Laforgue's more impromptu verse scarcely attained).'[21] Eliot's logopoeic facility greatly impressed Pound, who, on reading 'The Love Song of J. Alfred Prufrock', expressed his excitement to Monroe in a letter of 30 September 1914 that here was a poet who 'has actually trained himself *and* modernized himself *on his own*.'[22]

---

[18] *LEP* 246–7.

[19] Ezra Pound, 'Langue D'Oc', *Quia Pauper Amavi*, 7, 11, 13; John Simpson and Edward Weiner, eds., *Oxford English Dictionary*, 2nd edn (Oxford: Oxford University Press, 1989), <u>plasmatour.</u>

[20] T. S. Eliot, 'What Dante Means to Me', in *The Complete Prose of T. S. Eliot: The Critical Edition, Volume 7, A European Society, 1947–1953*, 482.

[21] F. O. Matthiessen, *The Achievement of T. S. Eliot: An Essay on the Nature of Poetry* (New York: Oxford University Press, 1958), 17.

[22] *LEP* 80, Pound's italics.

'A MOQUEUR TO THE MARROW' 153

In addition to the refined parody of logopoeia, Eliot also savoured low comedy and parody of the unsubtle, mocking kind. When he was a student at Merton College, Oxford, he became a habitué of the music halls, an enthusiasm that he shared with many of his modernist contemporaries, for instance Lewis, who bestowed blessings on music-hall entertainers George Robey, George Mozart, and Harry Weldon in the first issue of *Blast*.[23] Eliot had great admiration for Marie Lloyd, the most famous music-hall singer and comedienne. In an article for the *Criterion* celebrating her life's achievements, he also praised Nellie Wallace and Little Tich, 'the most remarkable of the survivors of the music-hall stage', describing their grotesque acts as an 'orgy of parody of the human race'.[24] As Conrad Aiken, a friend of Eliot's from Harvard, fondly recalled 'There was something of the actor in Tom, and some of the clown too. For all his liturgical appearance . . . he was capable of real buffoonery', while Wyndham Lewis described Eliot as a '*moqueur* to the marrow, bashfully ironic, blushfully *tacquineur*'.[25] A gifted impersonator, when in Oxford, Eliot cultivated an accent more English than the English. Clive Bell found Eliot's 'studied primness and manner of speech . . . deliciously comic'.[26]

Eliot's appetite for low comedy and parody was formed during his time at Harvard where, as Herbert Howarth notes, 'spoofing rhymes were in the air'.[27] Aiken and Eliot bonded over popular comic strips such as George Herriman's *Krazy Kat* (1913–44), a charmingly drawn but also experimental cult cartoon starring a cat of ambiguous gender and sexuality who is hopelessly in love with a mouse, who inevitably rejected the cat's advances by throwing a brick at the cat's head, typically resulting in arrest by a bulldog chief of police. The formula barely varied, but Herriman came up with ingenious ways of keeping the scenario fresh, including play with different dialects and spelling, and even racially prejudiced slang, which the young poets found particularly entertaining:

> It was the first 'great' era of the comic strip, of Krazy Kat, and Mutt and Jeff, and Rube Goldberg's elaborate lunacies: it was also perhaps the most creative period in American slang, and in both these departments of invention he took enormous pleasure. How delighted we were with the word 'dinge' for negro![28]

---

[23] *B* 28. For an extended discussion of Eliot and the music halls, see Ron Schuchard, *Eliot's Dark Angel: Intersections of Life and Art* (Oxford: Oxford University Press, 1999), 102–18.

[24] T. S. Eliot, 'In Memoriam: Marie Lloyd', *Criterion* I(2) (January 1923), 193.

[25] Conrad Aiken, quoted in Lyndall Gordon, *T. S. Eliot: An Imperfect Life* (London: Vintage, 1998), 45; Lewis, *Blasting and Bombardiering*, 283.

[26] Clive Bell, *Old Friends, Personal Recollections* (London: Chatto & Windus, 1956), 120.

[27] Herbert Howarth, *Notes on Some Figures Behind T. S. Eliot* (London: Chatto & Windus, 1965), 123.

[28] Conrad Aiken, 'King Bolo and Others', in Richard March and Tambimuttu, eds., *T. S. Eliot: A Symposium from Conrad Aiken and Others* (London: Frank & Cass Co., 1948), 21.

154   MODERNIST PARODY

While the deplorable delight in racist slurs cannot be explained away as part of Eliot's modernist rebellion against respectability, Eliot's relationship to blackness was much more complicated than Aiken's comments suggest.

In *Since Cézanne* (1921) Bell proposed that Eliot's artistic labours were 'eased somewhat by the comfortable ministrations of a black and grinning muse', under whose aegis he 'twisted and ragged' language to the extent that he might be considered 'as much a product of the Jazz movement as so good an artist can be of any'.[29] Bell suggested 'it is only by adopting a demurely irreverent attitude, by being primly insolent' in his play with the words of writers such as Shakespeare and Milton that Eliot is able to 'deliver himself of one of those complicated and remarkable imaginings of his', thereby connecting Eliot's brilliance as a poet to a mode of ventriloquy that Bell specifically linked with blackness.[30] Michael North explores this phenomenon in full in his ground-breaking book *The Dialect of Modernism*, in which he examines white modernist writers' 'rebellion through racial ventriloquism' and the aesthetic possibilities opened by such a transgression to suggest that 'linguistic mimicry and racial masquerade were not just shallow fads but strategies without which modernism could not have arisen'.[31] As North argues, Eliot's rebellion consisted in turning his back on formal scholarship to become a 'blackface comedian', a role to which Pound gave the name 'de Possum'.[32] In their letters to one another Eliot and Pound's frequent reprisals of a distorted version of black dialect popularized by Joel Chandler Harris's Uncle Remus tales functioned as a private language, 'a violation of Standard English' and a 'sign of [their] collaboration against the London literary establishment and the literature it produced', affirming their ironic and anxious status as American 'savages' in Europe.[33] But if Eliot's 'black and grinning muse' were to be made manifest in any one single form it would be as the star of a black minstrel show.

Black minstrelsy—a typically American form of popular musical theatre that flourished in Eliot's hometown of St Louis—was intended as a comic entertainment. A troupe of actors would 'black up' to perform a series of songs, dances, skits, and impersonations, using exaggerated mimicry and mockery to perpetuate a range of racist stereotypes about African Americans. The minstrel show 'was an art of mélange, of star turns, mock oratory, sentimental songs, melodrama, ragtime, and slapstick comedy' that often incorporated 'bits and pieces of conventional white culture' such as 'American speeches, parts of operas, or scenes from Shakespeare', and, as North notes, its formal conventions provided a prototype for the 'famous techniques of quotation and juxtaposition' that Eliot perfected

---

[29] Clive Bell, *Since Cézanne* (New York: Harcourt Brace, 1922), 222–3.

[30] Bell, *Since Cézanne*, 222.

[31] Michael North, *The Dialect of Modernism: Race, Language and Twentieth-Century Literature* (New York: Oxford University Press, 1994), 9.

[32] North, *Dialect of Modernism*, 9.

[33] North, *Dialect of Modernism*, 77.

in *The Waste Land*.[34] The specific influence of blackface can be seen in the three letters Eliot sent to his cousin Eleanor Hinkley in October and November 1914 and January 1915, in which he treated her to an outline of his 'great ten-reel cinema drama, EFFIE THE WAIF', a fantasy production that parodied stock tropes of popular melodramas, documenting the trials and tribulations facing a motherless foundling.[35] The protagonists in the first instalment included 'SPIKE CASSIDY', a gambler who is 'reformed by the sweet insidious influence of the child' he takes in, 'SEEDY SAM, the blackmailer', and 'Lady Chomleyumley', who mourns the loss of her infant daughter.[36] Next Eliot imagines 'all the comic and villainous characters who fall in love with EFFIE, and all the villainous and comic characters who fall in love with WILFRED', who is to be the hero of the piece.[37] The second instalment introduces stock characters drawn from racial (and racist) stereotypes including 'DANCING BEAR the chief of the Pottawottobottommies' and 'Traihi Sheik, the maharaja of Chowwaannugger', while the third provides details of the three heroines 'who are particularly dead gone on our Wilfred', 'PAPRIKA', a 'Mexican dancer', 'EARLY BIRD', an 'Indian maiden', and 'PEGOON', an 'Irish lass'.[38] Part of the fun for Hinkley was that Eliot envisaged the cast would be drawn from various family members, friends, acquaintances, and figures from public life, with the result that many of the cast would play their parts as racial impersonators, as the references to the blackface character 'REV. HAMMOND AIGS comic negro minister, of the "come breddern" type', makes clear.[39] His role is not elaborated beyond 'a tendency to gin, chicken-stealing and prayer', but the joke was that he would be played by Eliot's respectable cousin Frederic, who graduated from Harvard Divinity School and became associate minister of the First Parish in Cambridge in 1915.[40] The whole piece was conceived as a kind of blackface minstrel variety performance that subsumed a series of mocking –and degrading– racial impersonations into its wider parody of melodrama.

There is little in the way of the kinds of dialogue that would be displayed on inter-titles in Eliot's outline of 'Effie the Waif', although what is there suggests the characters would be given to histrionics and speaking in clichés:

SHALL EARLY BIRD, DAUGHTER OF OOPALOOMPAH, CHIEF OF THE BOOZAWAYS DO OBEISANCE TO THE GREAT WHITE FATHER OF THE PALEFACES? NOT WHILE THE BISON STAMPS UPON THE PLAINS OF MY FOREFATHERS.[41]

---

[34] North, *Dialect of Modernism*, 85.
[35] *LTSE* 67, Eliot's capitals.
[36] *LTSE* 67–9, Eliot's capitals.
[37] *LTSE* 77, Eliot's capitals.
[38] *LTSE* 77, 83–4, Eliot's capitals.
[39] *LTSE* 84, Eliot's capitals.
[40] *LTSE* 84; see also *LTSE* 84, fn. 2.
[41] *LTSE* 83, Eliot's capitals.

156 MODERNIST PARODY

The inclusion of a line destined for 'Effie' in what Eliot would call his 'BRIL-LIANTS', a series of deft little character sketches in which Eliot curated snippets from conversations with the different people he met on his travels for Hinkley's amusement, shows how adept he was at playing with different dialects and registers for comic effect:[42]

> Well I never should have said you came from St. Louis . . . Is Harvard going to be your college . . . How did you enjoy your visit to America? . . . Well it 'eaves my stomach'orrible . . . My but you do have *grand* thoughts! . . . why aren't **you** dancing? . . . Very pleased to meet you . . . My name's Calkins, Michigan 1914 . . . Aw I wish I'd known what was good for me and staid in Detroit Michigan, it's a long swim to the Irish coast . . . If I ever get to Liverpool I'm going to join the church . . . Ah no sir they don't make no trouble for me, they just lays where I put 'em and honly wants to be left quiet . . . Try the tripe and onions, its just lovely . . . Yes this genlmn knows I'm speakin gospel truth (pointing at me) he's connected with the building trades hisself, he knows how business is now, its Wilson and Bryan's made all the trouble . . . &, &, &.[43]

The minstrel trick of turning mimicry into mockery is evident here, as Eliot sets what passes for polite chit-chat against instances of unlettered and non-standard speech, so that the idiosyncrasies of each utterance are thrown into sharper relief, showing his early talent for doing voices and combining them in ways that were primly comic.

One of Eliot's most characteristic blackface projects was his obscene verse on the seafaring adventures of Columbo, the King and Queen of Spain, and their encounters with two native Cubans (later Filipinos and finally Bolovians), King Bolo and his Big Black Queen, a mock-epic poem that parodied histories of the legendary colonial explorer Christopher Columbus.[44] It was written in instalments (the majority of which appeared between 1910 and 1916) and became 'part of an elaborated joke, nurtured through years' (with new material appearing in 1927 and 1928, and possibly also 1932, and variants even as late as 1963 to 1964).[45] Stanzas of Bolovian verse were shared with select (and with the exception of Vivien) male correspondents whom Eliot judged would be amused by the

---

[42] *LTSE* 79, Eliot's capitals.

[43] *LTSE* 43–4, Eliot's ellipses, italics, and bolds.

[44] For an editorial composite, see 'The Columbiad', *The Poems of T. S. Eliot: Volume II, Practical Cats & Further Verses*, ed. Christopher Ricks and Jim McCue (London, Faber & Faber, 2015), 269–85. For an overview of the poems that compose Eliot's 'Bolovian Epic', see Loretta Johnson, 'Feeling the Elephant: T. S. Eliot's Bolovian Epic', *Journal of Modern Literature* 37(4) (summer 2014), 109–29, which 'interprets the whole project and its contexts as grounded in his appreciation for the primitive and a critical disdain for the so-called civilized' (109).

[45] Bonamy Dobrée, 'T. S. Eliot: A Personal Reminiscence', in Allen Tate, ed., *T. S. Eliot: The Man and His Work* (New York: Dell, 1966), 73. For dating of the verses, and compositional history, see Ricks and McCue, *Poems of T. S. Eliot: Volume II*, 250–71, and Jayme Stayer, 'The Short and Surprisingly Private Life of King Bolo: Eliot's Bawdy Poems and Their Audiences', in John Morgenstern, ed., *The T. S. Eliot Studies Annual* (Clemson: Clemson University Press, 2017), 3–30, which quotes Valerie Eliot: 'Almost all [the Bolo verses] were written during his Harvard days and none later than 1916' (10).

'A MOQUEUR TO THE MARROW' 157

cheerfully lewd, scatological, racist, and misogynist jokes, and impressed by the conversational ease and seemingly effortless finesse he could achieve by fitting vernacular speech, slang, and indecent end rhymes to tight metrical forms. Recipients included Aiken, Pound, Lewis, Joyce, Bonamy Dobrée, and in later years Eliot's circle at Faber. To Aiken these ribald verses were 'hilariously naughty parerga'; to Pound '*chançons ithyphallique*'.[46] When viewed together as an editorial composite, *The Columbiad* is an orgy of sexual conquest, full of over-endowed men, lecherous mariners, whore-ish queens, and multiple acts of violence, buggery, and rape. So far as Eliot was concerned, humour was the redeeming factor. As he wrote in *After Strange Gods*, 'the only disinfectant which makes either blasphemy or obscenity sufferable is the sense of humour: the indecent that is funny may be the legitimate source of innocent merriment, while the absence of humour reveals it as purely disgusting'.[47]

One early instalment of Bolo sent to Aiken in a letter of 19 July 1914 featured a summary of mock-scholarly commentary written as if the stanza was a great rediscovered literary work that had been expertly recovered and glossed by German textual critics:

> Now while Colombo and his men
> Were drinking ice cream soda
> In burst King Bolo's big black queen
> That famous old breech l(oader).
> Just then they rang the bell for lunch
> And served up—Fried Hyenas;
> And Columbo said 'Will you take tail?
> Or just a bit of p(enis)?'

The bracketed portions we owe to the restorations of the editor, Prof. Dr. Hasenpfeffer (Halle), with the assistance of his two inseparable friends, Dr. Hans Frigger (the celebrated poet) and Herr Schitzel (aus Wien). How much we owe to the hardwon intuition of this truly great scholar! The editor also justly observes: 'There seems to be a *double entendre* about the last two lines, but the fine flavour of the jest has not survived the centuries'.—Yet we hope that such genius as his may penetrate even this enigma. Was it really the custom to drink ice-cream soda just before lunch? Prof. Dr. Hasenpfeffer insists that it was. Prof. Dr. Krapp (Jena) believes that the phrase is euphemistic, and that they were really drinking SEIDLIDZ POWDER. See Krapp: STREITSCHRIFT GEGEN HASENPFEFFER.[1] 1.xvii §367, also Hasenpfeffer: POLEMISCHES GEGEN KRAPP[2] I.II. 368ff. 490ff.[48]

---

[46] Aiken, 'King Bolo and Others', 22; Pound's soubriquet was written on the back of an envelope postmarked 11 January 1915 (see *Poems of T. S. Eliot: Volume II*, 269).

[47] T. S. Eliot, *After Strange Gods: A Primer of Modern Heresy* (New York: Harcourt Brace, 1934), 55–6.

[48] *LTSE* 46–7, Eliot's capitals.

158 MODERNIST PARODY

The letter also features caricatures of a bespectacled, bearded professor and King Bolo himself, who is drawn in the image of a stereotyped blackface minstrel, one who has acquired the accoutrements of the New World—a cigar, hat, monocle, and bowtie—but looks every inch the grinning buffoon.[49] Like his counterparts in minstrel shows, Bolo's repeated attempts at playing the gentleman in supposedly civilized company inevitably result in embarrassment on all sides, but the insatiably lusty Columbo hardly comes off better, in this instance graciously offering the queen something exceedingly impolite. For all the crass racial slurs in the Bolo poems, the humour is not exclusively directed at the supposedly primitive king and his highly sexed, decidedly masculine queen, but also arises from the apparent clash of cultures on contact with the superficially civilized colonials and the base instincts that unite all the characters but are repressed by the whole apparatus of Western scholarship, which is itself mercilessly parodied. In this example, comedy arises from the misapplication of highbrow scholarly annotation; the mask of erudition is worn with a grinning and insinuating insolence worthy of a performer in blackface minstrelsy or music hall. What first appears to be homosocial doggerel is also concerned with cultural divides; the gap between what is primal and bodily (eating, a penis, taking a penis into the mouth) and the finely calibrated discriminations of textual scholarship and literary appreciation (which are penetrating in a different sense entirely). The Bolo poems and accompanying pseudo-editorial paraphernalia show Columbus, King Bolo, and his Big Black Queen 'discovering' one another again and again, restaging the encounter between the Old World and the New, Europe and America, the (seemingly) civilized and the primitive, high scholarship and lowbrow amusement. While they may seem irredeemably fatuous, these improper verses use parody and mimicry to explore the very same binaries that lie at the heart of Eliot's more respectable literary and critical works.

The letter to Aiken itself begins with a separate parody of Lewis's catalogue of blasts and blesses, blessing Bolo, Columbo, and the chaplain (that 'shy old whorehouse rascal'), and blasting, among others, the bosun, King Bolo's cousin Hugh (who 'had no genitalia'), the careless cook, and Prof. Dr Krapp:[50]

BLESS

COLUMBO

BOLO   BLUBUNG   CUDJO

THE CHAPLAIN   BRUTUS   SQUIRTY PANSY

BLAST

---

[49] *LTSE* 47. For a full discussion of Eliot's play with blackface minstrelsy in the Bolo poems, see Jonathan Gill, 'Protective Colouring: Modernism and Blackface Minstrelsy in the Bolo poems', in John Xiros Cooper ed., *T. S. Eliot's Orchestra: Critical Essays on Poetry and Music* (New York: Garland, 2000), 65–84.

[50] 'The Columbiad', *Poems of T. S. Eliot: Volume II*, 280, 284.

THE BOSUN   COUSIN HUGH   THE COOK
PROF. DR. KRAPP[51]

It asserts Eliot's sense of affinity with the mockery and outrage of *Blast*, aligning his Bolovian epic with the extreme English avant-garde, signalling that he thought it was every bit as transgressive and therefore *modern* as Lewis's manifesto. It provides an early indication that the strategy of embedding parodic stylizations within wider parodies of other genres of writing served an evolutionary process for Eliot, as it did for novelists (and poets) in Bakhtin's 'Second Stylistic Line', leading Eliot to write works that were highly original, in voices that were unmistakably his own.

Eliot was keen to participate in the general commotion stirred up by Lewis and others, and indeed he sent several Columbo and Bolo stanzas to Lewis, together with 'The Triumph of Bullshit' and 'Ballade pour la grosse Lulu', as a letter from Lewis to Pound of January 1915 attests. Lewis told Pound that 'They are excellent bits of scholarly ribaldry. I am longing to print them in *Blast*; but stick to my naif [*sic*] determination to have no "Words ending in -Uck, -Unt and -Ugger".'[52] Of course, Eliot had not used those expletives and, besides, Pound, Lewis, and Eliot knew that the poems were so obscene as to be unprintable, but that was beside the point. The poems established Eliot's capacity for vulgarity and provocation. In a letter of 2 February 1915, Eliot grumbled 'I have corresponded with Lewis, but his puritanical principles seem to bar my way to Publicity. I fear that King Bolo and his Big Black Kween will never burst into print.'[53] For all that Eliot enjoyed imagining the stir that the Bolo poems would create if published, he was wise enough to confine them to circulating privately.

Sharing pieces of bathetic writing consolidated Eliot's intimacy with Pound, who reciprocated in kind. In a letter of 24 December 1921 Pound commemorated his role in the production of *The Waste Land* with the bawdy squib 'Sage Homme', which presented him not only as the editor who assisted the birth, but also—continuing the obstetric metaphor—as the poem's sire, the phallic impresario who impregnated a feminized Eliot through anal intercourse.[54] Pound did not directly encourage publication, himself taking care to publish parodic doggerel pseudonymously, developing semiliterate personae to establish separate spheres of cultural production such as 'Abel Sanders' and 'Alfred Venison'. Pound's first instinct regarding 'Sage Homme' was to tell Eliot 'My squibs are now a bloody impertinence ... don't use 'em with *Waste Land*.'[55] He then conceded Eliot could 'tack 'em onto a collected edtn, or use 'em somewhere where they would be

---

[51] *LTSE* 44.

[52] Timothy Materer, ed., *Pound/Lewis: The Letters of Ezra Pound and Wyndham Lewis* (New York: New Directions, 1985), 8.

[53] *LTSE* 93.

[54] *LEP* 234–5. For an account of 'Sage Homme', see Wayne Koestenbaum, *Double Talk: The Erotics of Male Literary Collaboration* (New York: Routledge, 1989), 120–5.

[55] *LEP* 234.

160 MODERNIST PARODY

decently hidden and swamped by the bulk of accompanying matter'.[56] Although Eliot persisted for a while in his 'Wish to use Caesarean Operation in italics in front', as indicated in a letter to Pound of January 1922, *The Waste Land* ultimately appeared without such bathetic adornment, suggesting that Eliot ultimately saw the sense in keeping serious work separate from cheapening, highly personal, comic entertainments.[57]

In a letter of January 1922, Pound recommended to Eliot that Joyce was to be 'saved the shock' of the Bolo verses, lest it unhinge his 'somewhat sabbatarian mind'.[58] Although Eliot did not know Joyce very well, when he returned copies of the 'Eumaeus', 'Circe', and 'Oxen of the Sun' episodes of *Ulysses* by registered post with a letter dated 21 May 1921, he nonetheless offered him a taste of own shocking productions by reply, once again using Bolo to signal his capacity for vulgar provocation. Eliot alluded to the Bolo poems in a way that suggested Joyce may already have been familiar with that particular opus. Eliot also expressed the wish but also foreclosed the possibility that Joyce's publisher, Sylvia Beach, 'would bring out a limited edition of my epic ballad on the life of Christopher Columbus and his friend King Bolo' but noted that:

> Bolo's big black bastard queen
> Was *so* obscene
> She shocked the folk of Golder's Green'[59]

As much as Eliot enjoyed circulating the Bolo poems in private, and imagining the shock that publication would deliver, he was very much aware of the need to disassociate his lowest work from the poetic corpus on which his reputation was being built to avoid being seen to approach too closely the vulgar, popular modes that vitalized his art.

Anxieties about the kinds of parody and mimicry that were proper for serious art contoured the eventual shape of *The Waste Land*, which Pound hailed as 'the justification of the "movement", of our modern experiment, since 1900'.[60] By the time Eliot was drafting *The Waste Land*, his repertoire included Laforguean logopoeia, the buffoonery of music hall and blackface minstrelsy, and comic poems modelled on the wry quatrains of Théophile Gautier, such as 'Burbank with a Baedecker: Bleistein with a Cigar', 'Sweeney Erect', and 'A Cooking Egg'.[61] Eliot was also adept at skilled pastiches of historical styles that were nonetheless sufficiently distanced

---

[56] *LEP* 234.
[57] *LEP* 236.
[58] *LEP* 237.
[59] *LTSE* 562, Eliot's italics.
[60] *LEP* 248.
[61] For 'Burbank with a Baedecker: Bleistein with a Cigar', 'Sweeney Erect', 'A Cooking Egg', see T. S. Eliot, *Poems* (New York: Knopf, 1920), 17–23.

from their models in their self-conscious display of artifice and their wry presentation of a contemporary subject to acquire the sardonic inflection of parody. For instance, in 'Sweeney Erect' Eliot pastiched Jacobean revenge drama to provide a comparative perspective on the sordid modern drama of Sweeney's menacing shaving ritual and the hysteria it induces in the woman he has lovelessly bedded. The epigraph is a direct quotation from Francis Beaumont and John Fletcher's *The Maid's Tragedy* (1610) in which Aspatia instructs her lady-in-waiting to re-sew the tapestry depicting the story of Ariadne (who is left utterly bereft after being abandoned by her husband Theseus), but this time convey the true misery of the scene by taking broken-hearted Aspatia as her model:

> *And the trees about me,*
> *Let them be dry and leafless; let the rocks*
> *Groan with continual surges; and behind me*
> *Make all a desolation. Look, look, wenches!*[62]

There follow two further stanzas in the same declamatory style, supplying further details of the windswept scene:

> Paint me a cavernous waste shore
>   Cast in the unstilled Cyclades,
> Paint me the bold anfractuous rocks
>   Faced by the snarled and yelping seas.
>
> Display me Aeolus above
>   Reviewing the insurgent gales
> Which tangle Ariadne's hair
>   And swell with haste the perjured sails.[63]

The image of despairing Ariadne abandoned by her lover Theseus, set against the 'perjured sails' of Theseus's ship that gave the wrong signal to his father the king who then threw himself to his death, presents an ominous parallel to the seedy scenario that is then played out between Sweeney and the unnamed woman in a boarding house. They are introduced in the next quatrain, which is no longer in the voice of beseeching Aspatia, but in the glib voice of a detached observer who sets up lofty expectations that are swiftly undone for comic effect:

> Morning stirs the feet and hands
>   (Nausicaa and Polypheme).

---

[62] Francis Beaumont and John Fletcher, *The Maid's Tragedy*, ed. T. W. Craik, (Manchester: University of Manchester Press, 1988), 102 (II.ii.74–7); Eliot, 'Sweeney Erect', *Poems*, 19, Eliot's italics.
[63] Eliot, 'Sweeney Erect', *Poems*, 19.

162 MODERNIST PARODY

> Gesture of orang-outang
> Rises from the sheets in steam.[64]

The shift in tone comes as a shock and suddenly makes the foregoing Jacobean pastiche seem highly mannered and artificial.

The woman between the steaming sheets is no virginal princess Nausicaa, but Sweeney is surely as brutish as the cyclops Polyphemus. Like the murderous orang-outang in Edgar Allen Poe's short story 'The Murders in the Rue Morgue' (1841), Sweeney is subhuman, a level below on the evolutionary scale, and every bit as dangerous with a razor in his hand.[65] Poe's orang-outang learns the civilized act of shaving by watching his master, but then acts out the violence that supposedly civilized cultures seek to suppress. Eliot's Sweeney is a throwback to *Homo erectus*, to primitive man, but he is also erect in the sense that he is sexually aroused. The act of shaving removes the hair that is a sign of the primitive, but its civilizing effects are superficial because Sweeney is inherently violent. His body and its movements are described using terms to do with cutting ('slitted', 'gashed', 'jack-nifes', 'sickle motion') and his name links him to the murderous barber Sweeney Todd.[66] When he 'Tests the razor on his leg/Waiting until the shriek subsides', the gesture is a calculated one.[67] Sweeney 'Knows the female temperament' and so must be aware that testing the razor will frighten the woman, who might well imagine herself to be next.[68] It is unclear whether the 'epileptic on the bed' has had a fit or an attack of hysteria in response, but as a description of the woman the phrase is far from sympathetic.[69] The only commentary comes from Mrs Turner, the owner of the boarding house, who tartly observes that 'hysteria/Might be easily misunderstood' and that such behaviour 'does the house no sort of good'.[70] Sweeney's reaction goes unrecorded: he effectively abandons any responsibility for the woman, whose predicament is less dignified than that of Ariadne and Aspatia, but no less wretched. Artful segues such as these, from quotation and near quotation via inflected pastiche and parodic stylization to sardonic descriptions of parallel yet debased contemporary scenes, contribute to the uneasy admixture of grim humour and pathos seen in *The Waste Land*.

When Pound gave Eliot editorial counsel on the drafts of the poem that would eventually become *The Waste Land*, he directed Eliot away from vulgar caricatural vignettes and comic voices towards the more experimental and accomplished logopoeic use of parody and pastiche that thrived on the ironic equipoise of the

---

[64] Eliot, 'Sweeney Erect', *Poems*, 19.
[65] Edgar Allan Poe, 'The Murders in the Rue Morgue', in Patrick F. Quinn and G. R. Thompson, eds., *Edgar Allan Poe: Poetry, Tales, & Selected Essays* (New York: Library of America, 1996), 397–431.
[66] Eliot, 'Sweeney Erect', *Poems*, 19–20.
[67] Eliot, 'Sweeney Erect', *Poems*, 20.
[68] Eliot, 'Sweeney Erect', *Poems*, 20.
[69] Eliot, 'Sweeney Erect', *Poems*, 20.
[70] Eliot, 'Sweeney Erect', *Poems*, 20.

sublime with the banal and the dance of Eliot's intellect among words and their allusive meanings. The poem as first drafted by Eliot is quite different from *The Waste Land* as we know it today, as Valerie Eliot's edition *The Waste Land: A Facsimile & Transcript of the Original Drafts including the Annotations of Ezra Pound* (1971) attests. The provisional title 'He do the Police in Different Voices' (which appears only on working documents for Parts I and II of the poem) reflected the emphasis on low mimicry of the kind that might be found in a music-hall skit.[71] Borrowed from chapter 16 of Charles Dicken's satirical novel *Our Mutual Friend* (1865), the phrase is spoken by 'old Betty Higden, a poor widow', who approvingly describes the performance practices of Sloppy, the foundling she has adopted, who reads her newspaper out loud: '"I do love a newspaper" she says. "You mightn't think it, but Sloppy is a beautiful reader of a newspaper. He do the Police in different voices."'[72] The quotation evokes common speech and popular genres, which feature prominently in sections of the poem that were later cut, and figures impersonation and cross-society masquerade as a mode of storytelling that is gratifyingly dramatic and surprising.

At a relatively developed stage in the poem's evolution (albeit a point when 'He do the Police in Different Voices' was still the favoured title), Part I, 'The Burial of the Dead', began with a long narrative section in which a rakish raconteur reports on the comic sequence of events during a drunken night out in Boston, recreating conversations with various of his associates as he goes in the manner of a music-hall turn.[73] Part II of 'He do the Police in Different Voices', which bears the revised title 'A Game of Chess' (previously 'In the Cage'), was already approaching something close to its final form, beginning with the parody of Shakespeare's description of the royal barge in *Anthony and Cleopatra*.[74] Part III, 'The Fire Sermon', was once introduced by a lengthy satirical passage recounting the pastimes of the wealthy socialite Fresca in Popeian couplets after the manner of *The Rape of the Lock*.[75] In draft form, Part IV, 'Death by Water', began with a bawdy narrative description containing rhyming quatrains fit for the music-hall stage, comparing the figure of the sailor to 'the drunken ruffian':

> Even the drunken ruffian who descends
> Illicit backstreet stairs, to reappear,
> For the derision of his sober friends,
> Staggering, or limping with a comic gonorrhea.[76]

---

[71] *TWLFT* 5.
[72] Quoted in 'Editorial Notes', *TWLFT* 125.
[73] *TWLFT* 5.
[74] *TWLFT* 11.
[75] *TWLFT* 23.
[76] *TWLFT* 55.

164 MODERNIST PARODY

This squib provided a comic introduction to a lengthy section inspired by the Ulysses Canto of Dante's *Inferno*, taking the form of a 'well told seaman's yarn' (to use Eliot's phrase from his 1929 essay 'Dante') set off the New England coast, recounted in the demotic voice of a modern-day cod fisherman, whose vessel drifts towards an iceberg and inevitable doom.[77] Part IV then concluded with the now familiar vision of 'Phlebas the Phoenician, a fortnight dead'.[78] The text of Part V, which was untitled in the first draft and typescript, is much as it appears in the final form, without any parodic material by way of introduction.[79]

Recent accounts of *The Waste Land*, such as those by Lawrence Rainey and David Chinitz, have revised the critical tendency to read Eliot as an impersonal neoclassicist as per 'Tradition and the Individual Talent' (1919)—albeit one who recognized that the advent of 'the new (the really new) work of art' could readjust 'the relations, proportions, values of each work of art' towards the entire canon— by focusing on his links to popular culture.[80] In *Revisiting 'The Waste Land'* Rainey notes that other essays written by Eliot at the time show him to be 'responsive to caricature and music hall, modes of cultural production which thrive on wild exaggeration, hyperbolic repetitions which pivot on the play of likeness and illusion' and links this preoccupation with the histrionic and the grotesque to 'surprise', a key word in Eliot's critical vocabulary circa 1921.[81] This move enables Rainey to draw a line from Eliot's praise for Dryden's mock-heroic poem *Mac Flecknoe*, which offers 'the most fun . . . the most sustained display of surprise after surprise of wit from line to line' by using a method that is 'something very near to parody', to Eliot's admiration for the ferocious and quick wit of music-hall artists such as Lloyd and Wallace.[82] Rainey concludes with the insight: 'Ferocity, intensity, violence, companions to the strange, the surprising, the fantastic, something very near to parody: here is the core of Eliot's aesthetics while he was writing *The Waste Land*'.[83]

The proportions of that 'something very near to parody', the method Eliot admired in Dryden and would make his own in *The Waste Land*, were adjusted in dialogue with Pound.[84] Pound's ideas about the proper forms that parody should

---

[77] *TWLFT* 63, 65, 67, 69; T. S. Eliot, 'Dante', *Selected Essays, 1917–1932* (New York: Harcourt Brace, 1932), 211.

[78] *TWLFT* 69.

[79] *TWLFT* 70–89.

[80] David Chinitz, *T. S. Eliot and the Cultural Divide* (Chicago: University of Chicago Press, 2003); Lawrence Rainey, *Revisiting 'The Waste Land'* (New Haven, CT: Yale University Press, 2005); T. S. Eliot, 'Tradition and the Individual Talent', *The Sacred Wood* (London: Methuen & Co., 1920), 44–5.

[81] Rainey, *Revisiting 'The Waste Land'*, 51.

[82] Rainey, *Revisiting 'The Waste Land'*, 50–1. For Eliot on *Mac Flecknoe*, see T. S. Eliot, 'John Dryden', in Anthony Cuda and Ronald Schuchard, eds., *The Complete Prose of T. S. Eliot: The Critical Edition, Volume 2, The Perfect Critic, 1919–1926* (Baltimore: Johns Hopkins Press, 2014), 350–61.

[83] Rainey, *Revisiting 'The Waste Land'*, 51.

[84] Eliot, 'John Dryden', *Complete Prose* II, 352.

take to propel experimentation and produce important work (developed in relation to his early pasticherie, his understanding of the European avant-gardes, including French post-Symbolist poetry, and his involvement in Imagism and Vorticism) provided the implicit criteria for his sifting the 'durable' parts of *The Waste Land* from the 'apparent'. But while Pound's editorial input would be critical in determining the eventual shape of *The Waste Land*, his insistence that imitative and parodic writing must improve on its model(s) if it was to count as more than jejune mimicry did not conflict with principles Eliot had already articulated independently regarding derivative writing and originality.

Eliot would reflect at length on the interactions between tradition and the individual talent in the years leading up to the writing of *The Waste Land*, not only in his celebrated essay of that name of 1919, but also in his critical reviews of the work of other contemporary writers. In 'Reflections on Contemporary Poetry', published in the July 1919 issue of the *Egoist*, Eliot began his review of Herbert Read's *Naked Warriors* (1919), Conrad Aiken's *The Charnel Rose* (1919), and an unnamed 'Collection Dada' edition of Tzara's poetry (evidently *Vingt-cinq poèmes* (1918)), with a candid statement of the role of imitation in the development of the writer who realizes through kinship that a degree of individual autonomy has been achieved:

> Admiration leads most often to imitation; we can seldom remain long unconscious of our imitating another, and the awareness of our debt naturally leads us to hatred of the object imitated. If we stand toward a writer in this other relation of which I speak we do not imitate him, and though we are quite as likely to be accused of it, we are quite unperturbed by the charge. This relation is a feeling of profound kinship, or rather of a peculiar personal intimacy, with another, probably a dead author. It may overcome us suddenly, on first or after long acquaintance; it is certainly a crisis; and when a young writer is seized with his first passion of this sort he may be changed, metamorphosed almost, within a few weeks even, from a bundle of second-hand sentiments into a person. The imperative intimacy arouses for the first time a real, an unshakeable confidence . . . It is a cause of development, like personal relations in life. Like personal intimacies in life, it may and probably will pass, but it will be ineffaceable.[85]

The notion that 'We do not imitate, we are changed; and our work is the work of the changed man; we have not borrowed, we have been quickened, and we become bearers of a tradition' is obviously applicable to the transformation of fragments from established literatures and other texts that Eliot would ultimately achieve in *The Waste Land*.[86] In this review, however, Eliot regrets that 'traces of this sort

---

[85] T. S. Eliot, 'Reflections on Contemporary Poetry', *Egoist* VI(3) (July 1919), 39.
[86] Eliot, 'Reflections on Contemporary Poetry', 39.

166 MODERNIST PARODY

of experience are conspicuously lacking from contemporary poetry', noting that even though Read's book of war poetry is the best he can remember having seen, 'no dead voices speak through the living voice' and there is not 'even the *saturation* which sometimes combusts spontaneously into originality'.[87] Evidently, it was that spark of originality that comes by way of saturation that Eliot intended should quicken his own verse.

When Eliot turned to evaluate Tzara's poetry, he commented:

This one opens rather pleasantly:

> froid tourbillon zigzag de sang
> je suis sans âme cascade sans
> amis et sans talents seigneur
> Je ne reçois pas régulièrement les
> lettres de ma mère
> qui doivent passer par la russie
> par la norvège et par l'angleterre. . . .

But at times he becomes difficult to follow:

> Bonjour sans cigarette tzantzanza
> ganga
> bouzdouc zdouc nfounfa mbaah. . . .

The only way to take this sort of thing is very seriously, and I have got the impression that M. Tzara is rather clever. At least it is a symptom of 'experiment', and ought not to be put in the hands of the young. M. Tzara's work does not appear to have very deep roots in the literature of any nation.[88]

This observation that would prove to be a leading comment in the light of the hysterical Dadaesque assemblage that concludes Part V of the text of the first edition of *The Waste Land*, a passage that provides a case in point for considering Eliot's understanding of the originality of saturation, his multilayered practices of

[87] Eliot, 'Reflections on Contemporary Poetry', 39, Eliot's italics.
[88] Eliot, 'Reflections on Contemporary Poetry', 39; Tzara, *Vingt-cinq Poèmes*, illustrated by Jean Arp (Zurich: Collection Dada, 1918), 13, 6. The first set of lines that Eliot quotes might be translated thus:
> cold whirlpool zigzag of blood
> I am without soul waterfall without
> friends and without talents lord
> I don't regularly receive
> the letters from my mother
> which must pass through Russia
> through Norway and England. . . .

The second set of lines begins 'Hello without cigarette' before descending into nonsense.

emulation (which are palimpsestual in their evocation of the texts he adapts and transforms) and his perspective on Dada's parody of sense-making structures.

The power of the final section of 'What the Thunder Said' derives in part from its swift changes in mood and tone. It intercuts the sacred instructions 'Datta', 'Dayadhvam', 'Damyata' from the *Upanishads* with a series of cogent mediations on 'the awful daring of a moment's surrender' (that rare instance when one feels truly alive), hopeless imprisonment (evoking the case of Ugolino della Gherardesca in Dante's *Inferno*, who was imprisoned in a tower and left to starve to death with his sons and grandsons), and a missed opportunity to connect when sailing on calm seas. The sequence precipitates a crucial question that is then answered by a hysterical assemblage of fragmentary quotations, followed by the calm of a Sanskrit prayer:[89]

> Ganga was sunken, and the limp leaves
> Waited for rain, while the black clouds
> Gathered far distant, over Himavant.
> The jungle crouched, humped in silence.
> Then spoke the thunder
> D A
> *Datta* : what have we given?
> My friend, blood shaking my heart
> The awful daring of a moment's surrender
> Which an age of prudence can never retract
> By this, and this only, we have existed
> Which is not to be found in our obituaries
> Or in the memories draped by the beneficent spider
> Or under seals broken by the lean solicitor
> In our empty rooms
> D A
> *Dayadhvam* : I have heard the key
> Turn in the door one and turn once only
> We think of the key, each in his prison
> Thinking of the key, each confirms a prison
> Only at nightfall, aetherial rumours
> Revive for a moment a broken Coriolanus
> D A
> *Damyata* : The boat responded
> Gaily, to the hand expert with sail and oar

---

[89] For details on literary sources see Eliot's 'Notes' to *The Waste Land*, *TWLFT* 149 and B. C. Southam, *A Student's Guide to the Selected Poems of T. S. Eliot*, 5th edn (London: Faber & Faber, 1991), 141–5.

168 MODERNIST PARODY

The sea was calm, your heart would have responded
Gaily, when invited, beating obedient
To controlling hands

I sat upon the shore
Fishing, with the arid plain behind me
Shall I at least set my lands in order?

London Bridge is falling down falling down falling down

Poi s'ascose nel foco che gli affina
Quando fiam ceu chelidon—O swallow swallow
Le Prince d'Aquitaine à la tour abolie
These fragments I have shored against my ruins
Why then Ile fit you. Hieronymo's mad againe.
Datta. Dayadhvam. Damyata.

Shantih shantih shantih[90]

The crucial question 'Shall I at least set my lands in order?' refers to the fertility myth of the fisher king, whose land is laid waste until a stranger arrives and poses or answers certain ritual questions. It is answered by a series of seemingly disconnected fragments suggestive of the breakdown of a mind on a descent into madness that are deeply rooted in the literatures of many nations. The sequence runs together lines from a famous nursery rhyme, Dante's *Purgatorio, Pervigilium Veneris* [The Vigil of Venus], Tennyson's *The Princess*, Gérard de Nerval's sonnet 'El Desdichado' [The Disinherited], Thomas Kyd's *The Spanish Tragedy*, before finally settling on the words 'Shantih shantih shantih' (which Eliot explained in his 'Notes' to the first book edition of the poem as 'a formal ending to an Upanishad', roughly translating as 'The Peace which passeth understanding').[91] The fragmentary quotations have the appearance of verging on meaninglessness, but they pick up on themes that run throughout *The Waste Land*, including: the decay of civilization ('London Bridge'); the pain of the lustful in the cleansing fires of purgatory (Dante); references to swallows (*Pervigilium Veneris*, Tennyson), recalling the rape of Philomena, who was turned into a swallow in Ovid's *Metamorphoses* and is mentioned in Parts II and III of the poem; disinheritance and lost tradition (de Nerval); violence and revenge (Kyd).[92]

There is a certain sympathy with Tzara's oeuvre here and his nonsensical habits of assemblage, which is not imitation but is certainly original; a resonance that perhaps also reflects Eliot's own fragile mental health and the fact that Part V of *The Waste Land* was written during a six-week stay at a sanatorium in Lausanne, Switzerland, in proximity to Zurich, the home of Dada. The lines are endowed with

[90] *TWLFT* 145–6.
[91] *TWLFT* 149.
[92] For a fuller exposition, see Eliot's 'Notes' to the poem, 149, and Southam, *Student's Guide*, 141–5.

'A MOQUEUR TO THE MARROW' 169

the same sense of *'tic-tac débile'* that Eliot discerned in Tzara (itself a phrase that Eliot took from the Belgian Symbolist Emile Verhaeren's poem 'Fleur Fatale' [Fatal Flower] (from *Les Soirs* [The Evenings] (1887)), where it refers to the feeble tick of the clock that is the ominous background noise to the descent into madness).[93] In the context of 'Reflections on Contemporary Poetry', the fragments Eliot has shored against the madness induced by civilization laid waste might be framed as a riposte to the strategies of composition and assemblage that Eliot deemed too light and too gratuitous in *Vingt-cinq poèmes*. Eliot gives these techniques a new gravity and heft through his determination to affirm 'the very deep roots of the literature of nations' and shows the present by the light of the past. The distinctly Dadaesque accumulation of disjunctive lines that concludes 'What the Thunder Said' repudiates Tzara's extreme ideation of desacralization and destruction as a response to the wreckage of civilization during the First World War. The sequence 'D A/*Datta*', 'D A/*Dayadhvam*', 'D A/*Damyata*' evokes and yet also contains the word Dada within a philosophical framework that enshrines the humanistic values that Eliot translated in his 'Notes' as 'Give, sympathize, control'.[94] Eliot emulates Tzara's mixing of Indic and European elements, but rather than using the Hindi word 'Ganga' as a nonsense word as Tzara did in the section of 'le géant blanc lépreux du paysage' quoted in 'Reflections on Contemporary Poetry', Eliot restores it to meaning as the name of the sacred river.[95] As Eliot intercuts the divine voice of the Thunder and its multiple injunctions beginning 'D A' with moments of insight, and then segues into that final accumulation of fragments that conclude the poem, he succeeds in parodying the disjunctive assemblages and programmatic statements of Dada without being derivatively Dadaesque, achieving 'the *saturation*' that 'combusts spontaneously into originality'. The sequence has a similarly repetitive structure to parts of Tzara's 'Dada Manifesto', for instance the list that includes the words 'DADA; Abolition of memory; DADA; Abolition of archaeology: DADA; abolition of the prophets'.[96] As Eliot makes use of Dada's strategies, he simultaneously asserts the need for a literary sensibility that is rooted in memory, that links the past to the present, and has not only its own archaeology and history, but also powers of future prophesy, thus enabling his Dada-inspired assemblage to achieve a greatness all of its own.

---

[93] Eliot, 'Reflections on Contemporary Poetry', 39; Emile Verhaeren, 'Fleur Fatale', *Poems*, trans. and intro. Will Stone, pref. Patrick McGuinness (Todmorden: Arc Publishing, 2014), 45–6.

> L'inconscience gaie et le tic-tac débile
> De la tranquille mort des fous, je l'entends bien!
>
> [Joyful unconsciousness and the deranged ticking
> Of the madman's quiet death, I can hear it well!]

[94] *TWLFT* 145–6; 'Notes', *TWLFT* 148.
[95] *TWLFT* 145–6.
[96] *TWLFT* 145; Tzara, 'Dada Manifesto' (1918), in Caws, *Manifesto*, 304.

170 MODERNIST PARODY

Pound—who had himself flirted with Dada but was likewise keen to discern how its methods might be made to conduct meaningful arguments about history and the rootedness of literature—let Part V of *The Waste Land* stand virtually intact. He did, however, encourage Eliot to remove the bathetic parodic narrative introductions to Parts III and IV of the poem. Having first made some small incursions into the text with a view to tidying up individual lines, Pound slashed through the Fresca episode and the detailed exposition of the sailor's voyage and shipwreck. The Boston section in Part I was untouched by Pound, Eliot having himself cancelled it in pencil. Given the closeness of the collaboration it is not unreasonable to suppose, as Donald Gallup does, that 'Eliot would at least have discussed it with him, and that Pound endorsed its deletion', especially since its suppression conformed to Pound's general efforts to shift the focus of the poem from narrative exposition to montage, to counter flaccidity, and to remove 'the remaining superfluities' (the three closing lyrics—'Elegy', 'Dirge', and, 'Exequy'—that Eliot thought to print as separate works at the end of the poem) with a view to making the poem more forceful, experimental, and thematically coherent.[97] Pound's visionary editing was also concerned with suppressing material that appeared obviously imitative or cheap, for instance attacking a line reminiscent of William Blake with the words 'Blake./Too ~~old~~/often used', chiding Eliot with the note 'Penelope/J. J'. when lines put him in mind of *Ulysses*, striking through the word 'yes!' because it was too evocative of the 'Penelope' episode of *Ulysses*, and pruning the tragic-comic tryst between the typist and the 'young man carbuncular'.[98]

Eliot had ample opportunity to read episodes of *Ulysses* while he was drafting *The Waste Land*, not only as it was being serially published in the *Little Review* and the *Egoist* but also, in the case of some episodes, in manuscript form. On 23 April 1921, Joyce had written to Harriet Shaw Weaver, urging her to pass her copies of 'Circe' and 'Eumaeus' to Eliot, as well as the typescript of 'Oxen of the Sun'.[99] By 21 May 1921, Eliot had read all three episodes, and returned them to Joyce with his compliments. His comments struck a very personal note—'I have nothing but admiration; in fact, I wish, for my own sake, that I had not read it'—not least because he was at that time actively engaged in revising and expanding the poem that would become *The Waste Land*.[100] As Eliot explained in a letter to Sydney Schiff of 3 April 1921, 'My poem has still so much revision to undergo that I do not want to let anyone see it yet, and also I want to get more of it done—it should be much the longest I have ever written. I hope that by June in will be in something like final form'.[101]

---

[97] See Donald Gallup, *T. S. Eliot & Ezra Pound, Collaborators in Letters* (New Haven, CT: Wenning/Stonehill, 1970), 19; *LEP* 233.
[98] *TWLFT* 9, 13, 33.
[99] *LJJ* III 41.
[100] *LTSE* 562.
[101] *LTSE* 549.

'A MOQUEUR TO THE MARROW' 171

While logopoeic pastiche on the cusp of parody of the kind seen in 'Sweeney Erect' was already an established part of Eliot's poetic repertoire, advance notice of Joyce's extraordinary experiments with parody and style in *Ulysses*, particularly in 'Oxen of the Sun', affected Eliot deeply. In Joyce, Eliot evidently saw a model for a writer who had achieved saturation and was resolutely autonomous yet profoundly literary, as he explained to Robert McAlmon in a letter of 2 May 1921:

> Joyce I admire as a person who seems to be independent of outside stimulus, and who therefore is likely to go on producing first-rate work until he dies . . . But Joyce has form—immensely careful. And as for literary—one of the last things he sent me contains a marvellous parody of nearly every style in English prose from 1600 to the *Daily Mail*.[102]

The Waste Land's extensive use of multiple, parodic styles and voices from phases of human culture, extending from the distant past to the near present—a feature that is particularly marked in Eliot's drafts—also reflect his immersion in Joyce's work and admiration for his techniques.

The excised narrative introductions to Parts I and VI of the poem show Eliot attempting to get past Joyce's achievement through imitation, reworking aspects of Joyce's method and plot to initiate passages that though they were false starts in and of themselves nonetheless provided direction for later patently *original* sections that would be integral to *The Waste Land* in its final form. Pound's first instinct was to try and salvage the narrative sections of Part IV. Against the ribald quatrains on the behaviour of seamen when ashore that introduced 'Death by Water' in manuscript form Pound wrote 'Bad–but/cant [*sic*] attack/until I get/typescript'.[103] The 'well told seaman's yarn' had many precedents, not only Homer's *Odyssey*, and Dante's retelling of Ulysses's voyage, but also Tennyson's 'Ulysses', the structural use of Homer's *Odyssey* in Joyce's novel, the characterization of the garrulous sailor D. B. Murphy, who accosts Bloom and Stephen in the 'Eumaeus' episode of *Ulysses* with tales of his travels (and has been to North America and seen 'icebergs plenty, growlers'), Pound's Joyce-inspired Odyssean frame for *Hugh Selwyn Mauberley*, and Pound's conflation of Andreas Divus's Odysseus with Dante's Ulysses in Canto I.[104] While the slow exposition was clearly an issue for Pound, the fact that Eliot's East Coast update (in which a mariner and his moaning crew of cod fishermen are blown off course and have an imaginary encounter with siren-like women who foretell their doom) reworked material to such little effect did not stand in the passage's favour. Far from the climax of Dante's Canto XXVI, where Ulysses recounts his joy at seeing land and then expresses the general lamentation when

[102] *LTSE* 563–4.
[103] *TWLFT* 55.
[104] 'Editorial Notes', *TWLFT* 128–9; *U* 16.461.

172 MODERNIST PARODY

a dramatic storm raises waters that close over the ship, Eliot's trivial version culminates in a weakly ironic joke, where, on seeing polar bears on the impending iceberg, the speaker assesses their chances, thinks of 'Home and mother', and then quips 'Wheres a cocktail shaker, Ben, heres plenty of cracked ice [sic]'.[105] Despite attempts to rework these lines into a less regular, more idiomatic and compressed form, Pound eventually enclosed them in double brackets, designating them for deletion. He persevered, making extensive cuts to speed the action up until he got to line 51, whereupon he started slashing in earnest and marked the remainder for deletion, leaving only a couplet and the Phlebas the Phoenician material intact.[106] By contrast, Pound immediately recognized the importance of the 'Phlebas' section of 'Death by Water', which he described in his letter to Eliot of January 1922 as 'an integral part of the poem; the card pack introduces him, the drowned phoen. sailor. And he is needed ABSOlootly where he is'.[107]

The Boston sequence in Part I likewise qualified for excision on all counts, being discursive in length, vulgar in subject, and derivative, this time for its obvious similarity to Joyce's 'Circe'. As William B. Worthen has noted, one of the drunken revellers gathered at 'Tom's place' is asked to sing 'I'm proud of all the Irish blood that's in me', but as the night progresses the group loses 'Steve', who, like his namesake Stephen Dedalus, wanders away from the group and ends up in a brothel.[108] Not unfairly, Helen Gardner has described the passage as 'a mild version of a visit to Night-town'.[109] Eliot's emendations as he drafted the excised passage indicate a desire to play up the vulgarity of the voices he projects and an uncertainty as to how far to take his caricatures. He strikes through the lyrics 'Meet me in the shadow of the/watermelon Vine/Eva Iva Uva Emmaline' adapted from *By the Watermelon Vine* (1904, words and music by Thomas S. Allen) and *My Evaline* (1901, Mae Anwerda Sloane) and substitutes 'Tease, Squeeze lovin & wooin/Say Kid what're y' doin' from [sic]' adapted from *The Cubanola Glide* (1909, words by Vincent Bryan, music by Harry von Tilzer).[110] He also introduces further grammatical infelicities (substituting 'she says' for 'Sergeant, I said', and 'we' for 'us'), but cannot decide how to phrase the awkward line 'Myrtle was always a good sport'). treated me white. real/good (?) good laugh'.[111]

Pound's substantial cuts to the passage detailing the typist's tryst with the young man carbuncular indicate why Eliot might have had reason to be wary of vulgarity. Against 'Knowing the manner of these crawling bugs' (sexually predatory

---

[105] *TWLFT* 69.

[106] *TWLFT* 63, 65, 67, 69.

[107] *TWLFT* 69; *LEP* 237.

[108] William B. Worthen, 'Eliot's *Ulysses*', *Twentieth Century Literature* 27(2) (summer 1981), 167–8; *TWLFT* 5.

[109] Helen Gardner, *The Art of T. S. Eliot* (London: Cresset Press, 1949), 79.

[110] *TWLFT* 5; see also 'Editorial Notes', *TWLFT* 125. For commentary on Eliot's use of popular music by black artists see North, *Dialect of Modernism*, 88, and Chinitz, *T. S. Eliot and the Great Divide*, 43.

[111] *TWLFT* 5; see also 'Editorial Notes', *TWLFT* 125.

men) Pound wrote 'Too/easy' and struck the line through.[112] The observation that the acne-ridden youth gropes his way down the stairs 'And at the corner where the stable is,/Delays only to urinate, and spit' Pound deemed 'Probaly [*sic*] over the mark'.[113] He also steered Eliot away from cheap caricatural grotesques towards real-life scenarios with genuine pathos, as evinced by the appreciative marginal comments 'photography' and 'photo' that Pound inserted against the realistic, nervously agitated female voice in 'A Game of Chess'.[114] The parodic introduction to Part II of the poem was the only one of the four opening sections to remain in the final text and provides the evidence for drawing a distinction between the kinds of low parodic material that were deemed unsuitable and the parody that was crucial to the affective poetic force of *The Waste Land* and its ability to 'surprise' readers by swerving sharply away from the familiar with mordant wit. It opens with a diminished echo of Enobarbus's description of Cleopatra on her ceremonial barge in Shakespeare's *Anthony and Cleopatra*, which modulates into a pastiche of Elizabethan blank verse. Compare:

> The barge she sat in, like a burnished throne
> Burned on the water; the poop was beaten gold,
> Purple the sails, and so perfumed that
> The winds were lovesick with them; the oars were silver,
> Which to the tune of flutes kept stroke, and made
> The water which they beat to follow faster,
> As amorous of their strokes. For her own person,
> It beggared all description: she did lie
> In her pavilion—cloth-of-gold of tissue
> O'er-picturing that Venus where we see
> The fancy out-work nature; on each side her
> Stood pretty, dimpled boys, like smiling Cupids,
> With divers-coloured fans, whose wind did seem
> To glow the delicate cheeks which they did cool,
> And what they did undid.[115]

> THE Chair she sat in, like a burnished throne,
> Glowed on the marble, where the glass
> Held up by standards wrought with fruited vines
> From which a golden Cupidon peeped out
> (Another hid his eyes behind his wing)
> Doubled the flames of sevenbranched candelabra

---

[112] *TWLFT* 45.
[113] *TWLFT* 47.
[114] *TWLFT* 11, 13.
[115] *The Tragedy of Antony and Cleopatra*, ed. Michael O'Neill (Oxford: Oxford University Press, 1994), 191–2 (II.li.190–204).

174 MODERNIST PARODY

> Reflecting light upon the table as
> The glitter of her jewels rose to meet it,
> From satin cases poured in rich profusion;
> In vials of ivory and coloured glass
> Unstoppered, lurked her strange synthetic perfumes,
> Unguent, powdered, or liquid—troubled, confused
> And drowned the sense in odours;[116]

Eliot applies vocabulary and images that arouse epic associations of grandeur to describe a modern lady at her dressing table. He uses degraded echo (from 'barge' to 'Chair') to manipulate an ironic parallel between the regal splendour of Cleopatra as she voyages towards her great love Anthony and Eliot's unnamed subject, whose relationship has broken down. The scene Shakespeare depicts is suffused with love: not only does Cleopatra's beauty exceed that of Venus, the goddess of love, as she is depicted in art, but the perfume that issues from the sails of Cleopatra's barge is so heady that the winds are lovesick, and even the water is amorous of the silver oar's strokes. By contrast, the modern woman's dressing table is decked with 'strange synthetic perfumes' that 'drowned the sense in odours', described using motifs that Eliot reinflects logopoeically to undercut the Shakespearean parallel with sham artifice and vulgar tat.

Eliot's technique in the initial lines of 'A Game of Chess' is indeed 'very near to parody', as he transforms Shakespeare's verse, bending it to another comically incongruous subject while achieving a tonal fidelity that is also consistent with pastiche. Eliot's commentary on Dryden's method in *Mac Flecknoe* in an essay first published in the *Times Literary Supplement* of 9 June 1921 (and likely written at some point during crucial months for the drafting and editing of *The Waste Land*) shows Eliot giving careful thought to this very technique where what first appears to be extremely close parody suddenly swerves in an unforeseen direction:

> The piece of Dryden's which is the most fun, which is the most sustained display of surprise after surprise of wit from line to line, is *MacFlecknoe* [*sic*]. Dryden's method here is something very near to parody; he applies vocabulary, images, and ceremony which arouse epic associations of grandeur, to make an enemy helplessly ridiculous. But the effect, though disastrous for the enemy, is very different from that of the humour which merely belittles, such as the satire of Mark Twain. Dryden continually enhances: he makes his object great, in a way contrary to expectation; and the total effect is due to the transformation of the ridiculous into poetry. As an example may be taken a fine passage plagiarized from Cowley,

---

[116] *TWLFT* 137; Eliot's 'Notes' refer readers to 'Shakespeare, *Anthony and Cleopatra*, II. Ii. 190' (*TWLFT* 147).

'A MOQUEUR TO THE MARROW' 175

from lines which Dryden must have marked well, for he quotes them directly in one of his prefaces. Here is Cowley:

> Where their vast courts the mother-waters keep,
> And undisturbed by moons in silence sleep. . . .
> Beneath the dens where unfledged tempests lie,
> And infant winds their tender voices try.

In *MacFlecknoe* [*sic*] this becomes:

> Where their vast courts the mother-strumpets keep,
> And undisturbed by watch, in silence sleep.
> Near these, a nursery erects its head,
> Where queens are formed, and future heroes bred;
> Where unfledged actors learn to laugh and cry,
> Where infant punks their tender voices try,
> And little Maximins the gods defy.[117]

As is so often the case in Eliot's critical commentary on other authors—and particularly with essays contemporary with the composition of *The Waste Land*—Eliot has identified techniques in Dryden that are his own. Of course, *The Waste Land* is locally parodic, but in its many parodic patches it is mock heroic in its recurrent movement from high to low. It too thrives on bathos, applying 'vocabulary, images and ceremony which arouse epic notions of grandeur' to debased modern subjects, but the effect is more subtle than ridicule because within the context of the wider poem it transforms the elements into something greater, something that leans on the grandeur of the original and yet contrives to be more poetic still.

This movement from grandeur to bathos that is no less poetic for the craftsmanship and wit with which models have been transformed is also evident in the section of 'The Fire Sermon' set on the banks of a rat-infested canal side. It ruminates on death, contains the first reference to the fisher king, and concludes with a grimly comic section where Eliot runs together parodied lines from Andrew Marvell's 'To His Coy Mistress' (1621–78), John Day's *The Parliament of Bees* (1641), a bawdy Australian ballad, and the final line from Paul Verlaine's *Parsifal* in quick succession (all of which are identified in the 'Notes to *The Waste Land*' which Eliot appended to the first book edition of the poem):

> But at my back from time to time I hear
> The sounds of horns and motors, which shall bring
> Sweeney to Mrs. Porter in the spring.

---

[117] Eliot, 'John Dryden', *Complete Prose of T. S. Eliot: Volume 2*, 352.

176   MODERNIST PARODY

> O the moon shone bright on Mrs. Porter
> And on her daughter
> They wash their feet in soda water
> *Et, O ces voix d'enfants, chantant dans la coupole!*[118]

Substituting the offhand phrase 'from time to time' for Marvell's 'always', Eliot mocks the high with the colloquial. '[H]ear' provides a pivot around which Eliot turns the verse into a low parody of Day's neoclassical 'you shall hear/A sound of horns and hunting, which shall bring/Actaeon to Diana in the spring', which is reworked bathetically for the modern age of motor cars and men, while simultaneously incorporating a reference to Igor Stravinsky's *The Rite of Spring*.[119] The horn belongs not to Actaeon but to Sweeney, the brothel-going protagonist of 'Sweeney Erect' and 'Sweeney among the Nightingales', who draws near to Mrs Porter, like Actaeon approaching Diana.[120] But unlike Diana, Mrs Porter, who douches with soda water, is no goddess of chastity. And Sweeney is no Parsifal, the grail knight who resisted lust and desire and ultimately healed the wounded king. In Verlaine's version of the legend Parsifal's triumph is celebrated by the pure voices of children singing in a cupola.[121] Here, Verlaine's line receives a sharp satiric inflection in its new role as a counterpoint to the degraded music of the tawdry modern age where subjects quickly yield to lust. Pound rewarded this stanza with approving marginal comments 'O.K.' and 'STET' on the typescript and '(Echt)' on the carbon copy, content not only with the depiction of the dingy scene and subsequent vision (the introduction of the fisher king motif), but also the downward sequence of allusions to Marvell, Day, the bawdy ballad, and the Sweeney poems where each fragment receives a new inflection from the line that follows.[122] This comic turn, worthy of a music-hall artist, is not only amusing in its clever rewiring of parodied lines, but nonetheless succeeds in linking the vision of blighted lands and death arising from the fisher king's wound to the sickness pervading modern sexual relations. Rather than ridiculing or belittling his models, Eliot expresses his admiration for their literary qualities through a combination of inflected pastiche and quotation, 'continually enhancing' them in a way 'contrary to expectation' by transplanting them into new contexts, arousing associations of grandeur for satirical effect while nonetheless making his object great in a way contrary to expectation, transforming the ridiculous into poetry.

---

[118] *TWLFT* 140.

[119] For Day and Marvell see Eliot's 'Notes', *TWLFT* 147; Eliot felt that Stravinsky's music succeeding in transforming 'the rhythm of the steppes into the scream of the motor horn, the rattle of machinery, the grind of wheels, the beating of iron and steel, the roar of the underground railway, and the other barbaric cries of modern life; and to transform these despairing noises into music'. See T. S. Eliot, 'London Letter', *Dial*, LXXI(4) (October 1921), 453.

[120] Eliot, 'Sweeney Erect', *Poems*, 19–21; 'Sweeney among the Nightingales', *Poems*, 35–6.

[121] For Verlaine see Eliot's 'Notes', *TWLFT* 147.

[122] *TWLFT* 27, 41.

'Much of Dryden's unique merit', Eliot wrote, 'consists in his ability to make the small into the great, the prosaic into the poetic, the trivial into the magnificent'.[123] Eliot likewise makes the prosaic into the poetic in the final texts of *The Waste Land* (which appeared in 1922 in the *Criterion*, the *Dial*, and in a book edition by Boni and Liveright). The tragicomic story of Lil with her need for dentures and her absent husband Albert is transformed from commonplace pub chatter to *poetry* by the 'Splendid last lines', where the voices modulate into Ophelia's crazed farewell to the ladies of the royal court in *Hamlet*:[124]

> Goonight Bill. Goonight Lou. Goonight May. Goonight.
> Ta ta. Goonight. Goonight.
> Good night, ladies, good night, sweet ladies, good night, good
>   night, good night.[125]

While Lil's plight is dignified by the comparative perspective of Ophelia's own sorrows, the shared sexual maltreatment ties both scenarios into the wider pattern of abject human relationships sustained across the poem, rendering Lil a latter-day Ophelia. Parodic echo in *The Waste Land* can thus be seen as an extreme case of what Eliot himself stated 'happens when a new work of art is created' and 'existing monuments form an ideal order among themselves, which is modified by the introduction of the new (the really new) work of art among them' in 'Tradition and the Individual Talent'.[126] The invitation to compare the present echo and the parodied original adjusts both texts, revealing them in a new light. Eliot 'continually enhances' borrowed material, and the cumulative effect is to endow the figures in *The Waste Land* with pathos through the beauty that he can wring from fragmented desolation.

The Waste Land: A Facsimile and Transcript (and related correspondence) reveals that Pound repeatedly steered Eliot to achieve the Drydenesque enhancement of parodic material by discouraging 'humour which merely belittles' throughout their collaboration on *The Waste Land*, a practice shown clearly by his decision to strike through the Fresca episode for its failure to enhance. Eliot had originally intended the couplets as a satire on *salonnières* and their literary habits. In 'Reflections on *Vers Libre*', an article for the *New Statesman* of 3 March 1917, he had written that 'We only need the coming of a Satirist—no man of genius is rarer—to prove that the heroic couplet has lost none of its edge since Dryden and Pope laid it down'.[127] But that satirist was not to be Eliot. His couplets on the

---

[123] Eliot, 'John Dryden', *Complete Prose of T. S. Eliot: Volume 2*, 354.

[124] Vivien Eliot's annotation, *TWLFT* 15.

[125] *TWLFT* 139; see *TWLFT* 15 for these lines as they appear on the typescript.

[126] T. S. Eliot, 'Tradition and the Individual Talent', *Sacred Wood*, 44.

[127] T. S. Eliot, 'Reflections on *Vers Libre*', in Jewel Spears Brooker and Ronald Schuchard, eds., *The Complete Prose of T. S. Eliot: The Critical Edition, Volume 1, Apprentice Years, 1905–1918* (Baltimore: Johns Hopkins Press, 2014), 516.

178 MODERNIST PARODY

lassitude of 'white-armed Fresca', who is 'Aroused from dreams of love and pleasant rapes', lack the finesse and concentration of *The Rape of the Lock*.[128] Pound's marginal comments on first reading the Fresca episode were: 'Too loose', 'rhyme drags it/out to/diffuseness' and 'trick of Pope etc/not to let/couple[t] diffuse 'em'.[129] His complaint was not that Eliot had attempted to reproduce Pope's style but that the reproduction was slack, as Fresca's gossipy letter demonstrates:

> "My dear, how are you? I'm unwell today,
> And have been, since I saw you at the play.
> I hope that nothing mars your gaity,
> And things go better with you, than with me.
> I went last night—more out of dull despair—
> To Lady Kleinwurm's party—who was there?
> Oh, Lady Kleinwurm's monde—no one that mattered—
> Somebody sang, and Lady Kleinwurm chattered.
> What are you reading? anything that's new?
> I have a clever book by Giraudoux...."[130]

Eliot recalled Pound's decision to slash through the 44-line Fresca section in its entirety (leaving only the first line untouched) in his introduction to *Ezra Pound: Selected Poems* (1928):

> Pound induced me to destroy what I thought an excellent set of couplets; for, said he, 'Pope has done this so well that you cannot do it better; and if you mean this as a burlesque, you had better suppress it, for you cannot parody Pope unless you can write better verse than Pope—and you can't.'[131]

This is Pound's clearest statement of the kind of parody equal to modernism: the truly modern parodist who dares to use the mode to undertake serious work with monumental ambitions must be able to enhance his original source while undercutting it. It identifies the difference between Beerbohm and *Punch*, Aldington and Weeks, the mature Pound and his young self, *The Waste Land* and its off-cuts. It seems that Eliot came round to the same way of thinking. Not only did he expunge the Popeian couplets, but he conceded in a letter to James Smith of 21 June 1926:

---

[128] *TWLFT* 39.
[129] *TWLFT* 39.
[130] *TWLFT* 39.
[131] *TWLFT* 23; T. S. Eliot's introduction to Ezra Pound, *Ezra Pound: Selected Poems*, ed. T. S. Eliot (London: Faber & Gwyer, 1928), xxi.

'A MOQUEUR TO THE MARROW' 179

You cannot improve on Pope, nor can you get anywhere by burlesquing him or ragging him because there is just sufficient element of burlesque in Pope himself to render him immune. So there you are.[132]

Three years later, in an essay entitled 'Dante', published in 1929, a year after Eliot recorded this anecdote in *Selected Poems*, he cautioned 'if you follow Shakespeare or Pope without talent, you will make an utter fool of yourself'.[133]

Pound may have induced Eliot to expunge the Popeian couplets from *The Waste Land*, but he did not however succeed in getting them destroyed for a version of the Fresca verses appears in 'Letters of the Moment—II' in the April 1924 number of the *Criterion*, which Eliot edited. The letter is signed 'F. M.' [Fanny Marlow] one of Vivien Eliot's pseudonyms. The letter begins in the manner of a seventeenth-century epistle, with apostrophes to 'my dear Volumnia', and reports on the recent revivals of 'tawdry bawdry Caroline renovations', including 'what the cultivated call The Play'.[134] Musing on 'the passing Movement', that is the fashionableness of 'seventeenth-century revivalism' of the kind practised by the Phoenix Society, a London subscription-based theatre club devoted to the performance of rarely staged early modern and restoration plays in their original form that the Eliots themselves supported, 'F. M.' offers 'for its obsequies these few poor verses', beginning:

> When sniffing Chloe, with the toast and tea,
> Drags back the curtains to disclose the day,
> The amorous Fresca stretches, yawns and gapes,
> Aroused from dreams of love in curious shapes.
> The quill lies ready at her finger tips;
> She drinks, and pens a letter while she sips:
> 'I'm very well, my dear, and how are you?
> I have another book by Giraudoux.
> My dear, I missed you last night at the Play;
> Were you not there? Or did you slip away?
> Or were you in the seats of cheaper price?
> Dorilant sat with me, and I looked nice. . . .'[135]

For all the pleasing lightness of tone, the chatter about 'the Play' is as vapid as in the drafted material in *The Waste Land: A Facsimile and Transcript*, which has been

---

[132] *The Letters of T. S. Eliot: Volume 3, 1926–1929*, ed. Valerie Eliot and John Haffenden (New Haven, CT: Yale University Press, 2012), 190.

[133] Eliot, 'Dante', *Selected Essays*, 213.

[134] 'F. M.' [Vivien Eliot], 'Letters of the Moment—II', *The Criterion* II(7) (April 1924), 360. For a detailed discussion of the textual history of these verses, and Eliot's continued interest in them, see Jim McCue, 'Vivien Eliot in the Words of TSE', *Review of English Studies* 68(283) (February 2017), 123–64.

[135] 'F. M.', 'Letters of the Moment—II', 360–1.

180 MODERNIST PARODY

expanded to match the subject of 'F. M.'s letter. Of course, the effect is deliberate, and, in many ways, Vivien's letter provides a better home for the material, which has been reworked to satirize the pretensions of wealthy theatre goers, but in no way do these 'few poor verses' overcome Pound's original objection that the parody fails to surpass Pope.

Peter Ackroyd's analysis that Pound 'removed most of the elements of stylistic reproduction—he considered the sequence in the manner of Pope to be simply parodic—and curbed the tendency of the poem towards dramatic and fictional exposition' is just wide of the mark.[136] Pound did not excise elements of stylistic reproduction purely because they were parodic. He struck them through where they failed to equal or enhance their model. Pound simply helped Eliot to refine his parodic practices in line with the kinds of parody that were actively shaping modernism and conditioning its reception, in accordance with Eliot's own theories about imitation, saturation, and originality. Ackroyd's suggestion that the four introductory sections, as first drafted, were 'as close to parody as he [Eliot] got: the music-hall monologue of a rake, the stiffened replica of Elizabethan narrative which remains as the opening of Part II, a piece of misogynistic satire in the manner of Pope, and the seaman's yarn which began "Death by Water"' is based on a narrower concept of parody as something sustained by a passage in its integrity and overlooks the many fragmentary parodic echoes dispersed throughout *The Waste Land* and the rapidly fluctuating logopoeic play with multiple texts and jarring registers.[137] Parodic logopoeia of this kind is a sustained technique throughout the text of the first edition of *The Waste Land*, which, in its integrity, can be considered a 'clever *gâchis*' of allusion and distorted quotation (much like 'The Train Journey' by 'Henry King' (John Middleton Murray), praised by Eliot in a letter to Sydney Schiff of 24 September 1919 as a 'clever *gâchis* [hash] of Laforgue, the Elizabethans, several contemporaries, sentiment and selfconsciousness').[138] It is this technique that produces the poem's surprising and disorientating effects, imbuing even the most fraught episodes with an awareness that is rueful but wry, the desolate laughter that comes of an awareness that everything has gone to hell.

Contemporary reviewers were highly attuned to what was parodic about *The Waste Land*, but failed to see how subtle and nuanced it was, and missed the point of what Eliot was doing with parody. By contrast, critics today are much more confident in their assessment of what Eliot was doing but are less apt to link it explicitly with parody. In fact, parody was one of the qualities that struck contemporary readers most forcibly, so much so that it contoured the initial reception of *The Waste Land* in the press and confirmed the impression that the most experimental modern writing was insincere to such an extreme that it had to be a joke.

[136] Ackroyd, *T. S. Eliot*, 119.
[137] Ackroyd, *T. S. Eliot*, 117.
[138] *LTSE* 398.

'A MOQUEUR TO THE MARROW' 181

Early reviewers were thrown off-balance by the disjointed, hallucinatory scenes and unnervingly abrupt shifts in voice, cadence, and tone, the contrast between the sordid and dejected subject matter, the grandeur of the literary allusions, and the astringent wit generated by the sudden bathetic redirection of parodied lines, unable to let their sense of beauty be quickened by poetry that felt so strange and forbidding.

Edmund Wilson, Conrad Aiken, Burton Rascoe, Harold Monroe, John Crowe Ransom, Edgell Rickword, Allen Tate, and F. L. Lucas all discussed Eliot's use of parody in their reviews. But the pathos, grandeur, and wit of Eliot's Drydenesque parodic method was lost on the majority of contemporary critics. For instance, Ransom complained about 'a certain novelty of Mr. Eliot's which is not fundamentally different from parody':

> To parody is to borrow a phrase whose meaning lies on one plane of intelligence and to insert it into the context of a lower plane; an attempt to compound two incommensurable imaginative creations. Mr. Eliot inserts beautiful quotations into ugly contexts.

For example:

> When lovely woman stoops to folly and
> Paces about her room again, alone,
> She smoothes her hair with automatic hand,
> And puts a record on the gramophone.

A considerable affront against aesthetic sensibilities. Using these lovely borrowed lines for his own peculiar purposes, Mr. Eliot debases them every time; there is not, I believe, a single occasion where his context is as mature as the quotation which he inserts into it; he does not invent such phrases for himself, nor, evidently, does his understanding quite appreciate them, for they require an organization of experience which is yet beyond him.[139]

As declared in the 'Notes' to *The Waste Land*, Eliot borrowed these lovely lines from Olivia's exquisitely pathetic song in Goldsmith's *The Vicar of Wakefield* (1766):

> When lovely woman stoops to folly,
>   And finds too late that men betray,
> What charm can sooth her melancholy,
>   What art can wash her guilt away?

---

[139] John Crowe Ransom, 'Waste Lands', *New York Evening Post Literary Review* 3 (14 July 1923), 825–6, in Jewel Spears Brooker, ed., *T. S. Eliot: The Contemporary Reviews* (Cambridge: Cambridge University Press, 2004), 107. For the passage Ransom quotes see *TWLFT* 141.

182   MODERNIST PARODY

> The only art her guilt to cover,
>   To hide her shame from every eye,
> To give repentance to her lover,
>   And wring his bosom—is to die.[140]

Eliot's parody of Goldsmith's poem was consistently singled out as a disgraceful abuse of fine literature. Rickword commented 'Here is a poet capable of a style more refined than that of any of his generation parodying without taste or skill—and of this the example from Goldsmith is not the most astonishing.'[141] (The lines Rickword judged the most culpable run from 'London Bridge is falling down' to '*Le Prince d'Aquitaine à la tour abolie*'.)[142] Rickword conceded that he had admired the method elsewhere in earlier poems, where Eliot had 'employed it discreetly with delicious effect', for instance when wearing the 'disillusioned smile he had in common with Laforgue', but in *The Waste Land* he judged the parody too bold.[143]

For all that the parodic echoes in *The Waste Land* were widely accused of being in poor taste, Eliot's skill was unquestionable. Eliot changed Goldsmith's simple iambic tetrameter ('when lovely woman stoops to folly') to a limping iambic pentameter ('When lovely woman stoops to folly and/paces about her room again alone'), where there is a definite glitch over the uneasily elided last foot of the first line and reverse foot of the second. The lineage is established, the element of surprise is introduced, and then the satiric point is sharply made as the quotation is rerouted to reveal the modern fallen woman's final bathetic reduction to an automaton. Ransom and Rickword failed to see that Eliot did not borrow lines from Goldsmith in order to criticize the literary original after the manner of Georgian parodists like Squire, but to use logopoeic wit to draw critical attention to the rift between the cultural sensibility of that original and of the present.

Reviewing *The Waste Land* for the *Chapbook*, Harold Monro quoted a friend who denounced Eliot's exploitation of Goldsmith 'an outrage, and a joke worthier of "Punch" than of a serious poet'.[144] Monro also reflected that *The Waste Land* seems 'calculated more to annoy Mr. Gosse, or Mr. Squire', and he was absolutely right.[145] In his 1923 review of *The Waste Land* Squire condemned the poem to be 'scarcely worthy of the Hogarth Press'.[146] He complained that 'Passages might easily be extracted from it [*The Waste Land*] which would make it look like one of those wantonly affected productions which are written by persons whose one

---

[140] See Eliot's 'Notes', *TWLFT* 148; Oliver Goldsmith, *The Vicar of Wakefield* (London: George Routledge & Sons, 1886), 222.

[141] Edgell Rickword, 'A Fragmentary Poem', *Times Literary Supplement* 1131 (20 September 1923), 616.

[142] Rickword, 'Fragmentary Poem', 616.

[143] Rickword, 'Fragmentary Poem', 616.

[144] Harold Monro, 'Notes for a Study of *The Waste Land*: An Imaginary Dialogue with T. S. Eliot', *Chapbook* 34 (February 1923), 20–4, in Brooker, *T. S. Eliot*, 98.

[145] Monro, 'Notes for a Study of *The Waste Land*', in Brooker, *T. S. Eliot*, 98.

[146] J. C. Squire, 'Poetry', *London Mercury* 8 (October 1923), 655–6, in Brooker, *T. S. Eliot*, 115.

'A MOQUEUR TO THE MARROW' 183

hope of imposing on the credulous lies in the cultivation of a deliberate singularity', accusing Eliot of exactly the kind of charlatanry he would later lampoon in 'The Man Who Wrote Free Verse'.[147] Squire could see that *The Waste Land* was 'interspersed with memories of literature, lines from old poets, and disconnected ejaculations' but confessed he could not 'make head nor tail of it', and pitied Eliot for caring so little whether anyone understood his writing.[148] The parodic aesthetic of *The Waste Land*, disjunctive, fragmentary, despairing, and wryly equivocal, was incomprehensible to Squire because it was so different from the critically acute but thoroughly smug ridicule he practised.

The concentration of parodic material that remained in *The Waste Land* raised suspicion that the opacity of the poem was a superficial effect calculated to impress and mock credulous readers. As a consequence, parody has become a mainstay of readers' responses to the poem, as many readers have found themselves unable to resist the implicit invitation that parody extends to further parody.[149] Examples range from ephemera such as Samuel Hoffenstein's 'The Moist Land—A Parody of Eliot's Poem' (1923) and Christopher Ward, 'The Dry Land' in *The Triumph or the Nut, and Other Parodies* (1923), which is replete with parodic 'Notes', to the attempts of serious poets to come to terms with and manoeuvre beyond Eliot's masterpiece by adapting his practices for their own use such as Louis Zukovsky's *Poem Beginning 'The'* (1928), which parodied many texts including *The Waste Land* and was sent to Pound to convince him of Zukovsky's talent, and E. E. Cumming's untitled typescript in five parts, which J. Alison Rosenblitt has convincingly presented as a parody of *The Waste Land*.[150]

Even Joyce could not resist parodying Eliot's poem. In a letter of 15 August 1925, he dashed off a quick parody of *The Waste Land* for Weaver's amusement on the subject of the miserably wet weather that had ruined the holiday he was then taking in France as he rested between eye operations. It begins '*Rouen is the rainiest place*' and concludes with the ironic speculation that '*we shall have great times,/When we return to Clinic, that waste land,/O Esculapios! (Shan't we? Shan't we? Shan't we?)*', adapting several of Eliot's most memorable lines as it goes.[151] Eliot's earnest invocation of the Sanskrit prayer 'Shantih shantih shantih' at the end of *The Waste Land* evidently tickled Joyce. He had further fun at its

[147] Squire, 'Poetry', in Brooker, *T. S. Eliot*, 115.

[148] Squire, 'Poetry', in Brooker, *T. S. Eliot*, 115.

[149] For discussion of the difficulty of modernist writing and the ever-present suspicion that it was fraudulent see Diepeveen, *Difficulties of Modernism*, 35–9 and his recent book *Modernist Fraud*.

[150] Samuel Hoffenstein's 'The Moist Land—A Parody of Eliot's Poem', *New York Tribune* (28 January 1923), 24; Christopher Ward, 'The Dry Land', in *The Triumph or the Nut, and Other Parodies* (New York: Henry Holt & Co., 1923), 170–8; Louis Zukovsky, 'Poem Beginning "The"', *Exile* 3 (spring 1928), 7–27; J. Alison Rosenblitt, *E. E. Cummings' Modernism and the Classics: Each Imperishable Stanza* (Oxford: Oxford University Press, 2016), 215–22.

[151] *LJJ* I 231, Joyce's italics. '*O Esculapios*' is an invocation to the ancient Greco-Roman god of medicine.

184 MODERNIST PARODY

expense in *Finnegans Wake*, in which he sporadically mocked Eliot for his practices of semi-quotation. Eliot (or 'ildiot', as Joyce insultingly calls him) is said to
have repeated 'in his secondmouth language as many of the bigtimer's [Joyce's]
verbaten words which he could balbly call to memory'.[152] Accordingly, Joyce keeps
on seizing Eliot's secondmouthings back for his own purposes by recasting lines
from *The Waste Land* in the language of the *Wake*, reascribing Eliot's borrowings
from the archive of literary culture to his own invention. Examples include such
phrases as 'washes his fleet in annacrwatter', 'when lovely wooman stoops to conk
him', 'my shemblable! My freer!', 'ebbing wasteward, leaves to the soul of light its
fading silence (allah-lah lahlah lah!), a turquewashed sky. Then:/ —Xanthos! Xanthos! Xanthos!', 'slanty scanty shanty!!!', 'Shaunti and shaunti and shaunti again!',
'Shunt us! shunt us! shunt us!', and 'Sandhyas! Sandhyas! Sandhyas!'[153] By such
means, *Finnegans Wake* recasts *The Waste Land* as 'a Fastland payrodicule', mocking those aspects of Eliot's masterpiece that already verge on parody by showing
them in a ridiculous light.[154]

It is possible that the many parodies *The Waste Land* attracted had an impact on
the interventions that Eliot sought to make in its reception as time passed, particularly on the way he accounted for the 'Notes' to the poem. For instance, Herbert
Palmer's *Cinder Thursday* (1931) is a comparatively late volume of parodies of high
modernist writers (Eliot in particular) that attests to the enduring impact of Eliot's
poem despite its criticism of his techniques. It included the following statement
about *The Waste Land* in the circumlocutionary language of Eliot's meditative
poem *Four Quartets* (1943):

> I refuse to be taken in by *The Waste Land*,
> I refuse to pretend that I am not taken in.
> I refuse to praise what I think I freely understand,

---

[152] *FW* 37.14, 37.15–6.

[153] *FW* 135.6 (cf. 'They wash their feet in soda water' (*TWTFT* 140)); *FW* 170.14 (cf. 'When lovely
woman stoops to folly' (*TWLFT* 141)); *FW* 489.28 (cf. '—mon semblable,—mon frère!' (*TWLFT* 137));
FW 235.6–9 (cf. 'Looking into the heart of light, the silence' (*TWLFT* 136), 'Weialala leia/Wallala
leialala' (*TWLFT* 142), and 'Shantih shantih shantih' (*TWLFT* 146)); *FW* 305.24, 408.33–4, 454.33,
593.1 (cf. 'Shantih shantih shantih' (*TWLFT* 146)).

[154] *FW* 70.6. For further examples of Joyce's occasional parodies either in his correspondence or
as standalone compositions, typically on topics related to his own personal circumstances, see Joyce's
Christmas greeting to Pound in 1920, which included a parody of Burns's battle-cry poem 'Scots, Wha
Hae' (1793), entitled 'Bis Dat Qui Cito Dat' [He gives twice who gives quickly], about the struggle
to find a publisher for *Ulysses* in America after the seizure and indictment of the July–August 1920
number of the *Little Review* (*LJJ* III 34); the parodies of 'Little Jim', Gertrude Stein, Ezra Pound, Robert
McAlmon, and *The Waste Land*, in letters to Harriet Shaw Weaver dating from April–August 1925 (*LJJ*
I 227, 228, 231); 'A Portrait of the Artist as an Ancient Mariner' in James Joyce, *Poems and Shorter
Writings*, ed. Richard Ellmann, A. Walton Litz, and John Whittier-Ferguson (London: Faber & Faber,
1991), 143; 'As I was going to Joyce Saint James', in *Poems and Shorter Writings*, 161; and 'Up to rheumy
Zurich came an Irishman one day' quoted in Frank Budgen, *James Joyce and the Making of 'Ulysses',
and Other Writings* (London: Oxford University Press, 1972), 205.

A hoax,
The most stupendous literary hoax since Adam . . .'[155]

It expressed reservations that Eliot himself later made play with when he gave credence to suspicious readings of *The Waste Land* when he repudiated his 'Notes to *The Waste Land*' in the Gideon Seymour Lecture, which he delivered at the University of Minnesota (1956). Eliot explained that the 'Notes' were added 'with a view to spiking the guns of critics of my earlier poems who had accused me of plagiarism' and also to appease Horace Liveright, the publisher of the first book edition of the poem, who was concerned that the text of *The Waste Land* was too short to make a satisfying volume.'[156] Eliot proceeded to confess that the 'Notes' were a 'remarkable exposition of bogus scholarship', a phrase that calls to mind the sort of textual apparatus produced by the likes of Prof. Dr Hasenpfeffer and Prof. Dr Krapp.[157] The admission was a double-edged joke, because many notes do usefully guide readers to the origins of Eliot's thefts, while others raise the suspicion that they might be paper fillers. Consider, for instance, Eliot's detailed commentary on line 357 of *The Waste Land* (and note also the scatological pun implicit in the name of the bird):

> This is *Turdus aonalaschkae pallasii*, the hermit-thrush which I have heard in Quebec County. Chapman says (*Handbook of Birds of Eastern North America*) 'it is most at home in secluded woodland and thickety retreats. . . . Its notes are not remarkable for variety or volume, but in purity and sweetness of tone and exquisite modulation they are unequalled'. Its 'water-dripping song' is justly celebrated.[158]

The notion that the notes were bogus served only to amplify the poem's parodic elements and gave further encouragement to readers to appreciate its primly comic aspects.

On the whole, Pound's editorial interventions in *The Waste Land* had the effect of encouraging Eliot to become more circumspect in his public use of parody. Eliot continued to work Drydenesque parodic echoes into his published poems but in the main reserved the low but playful parody that amused him best for private, unpublished literary recreations.[159] For instance, Eliot entertained his colleagues at Faber & Faber with a series of parodies of publishers' blurbs for books that he pretended were subsequently withdrawn from the Faber catalogue, which

---

[155] Herbert Palmer, *Cinder Thursday* (London: Ernest Benn, 1931), 17.
[156] T. S. Eliot, 'The Frontiers of Criticism', *On Poetry and Poets* (London: Faber & Faber, 1957), 110.
[157] Eliot, 'Frontiers of Criticism', 110; *LTSE* 46–7.
[158] Eliot's 'Notes', *TWLFT* 148, Eliot's ellipses.
[159] A notable exception is the parody of 'Here We Go Round the Mulberry Bush', in 'The Hollow Men' (1925), in Christopher Ricks and Jim McCue, eds., *The Poems of T. S. Eliot: Volume I, Collected and Uncollected Poems* (London: Faber & Faber, 2015), 83.

186   MODERNIST PARODY

were preserved for posterity by his friend John Hayward, who collected the type-scripts in a bound volume, 'Parodies of Publisher's "Blurbs" Composed by T. S. Eliot for the Firm of Faber & Faber' (1937).[160] Assuming the familiar register of the publisher's sales pitch, Eliot touted such unpromising material as 'Shall we Join the Ladies? A Manual of Ladies' All-in Wrestling by Helen Brook. With an Introduction by Janka Petrajwicic, Champion of Central Europe. With many illustrations':

> The sport of ladies' all-in wrestling, which has languished for many centuries, is again to the fore. Its renascence began in Poland, which still produces its most eminent exponents; but its popularity has spread within the last five years like wildfire, from Tokyo to Los Angeles, and round the other way from Vladivostok to Aberystwyth. Here we have a complete history, and a full explanation of the modern methods, so that the veriest tyro after reading this book will be able to follow a championship match with understanding appreciation. There are 36 fascinating photographs of noteworthy contests, and numerous diagrams and sketches; and the author has a simple and straightforward style such as to make the mysteries of the art intelligible to the least instructed amateur.
>
> 12s. 6d.[161]

It is an agile demonstration of the blurb writer's art. The polite title endows the sport of 'ladies' all-in wrestling' with a pleasing feminine formality. The book's comprehensive coverage of the sport is repeatedly highlighted, while its potential defects are advertised as strengths: the champion's 'simple and straightforward style' has euphemistic undertones, suggesting a lumbering lack of grace. At 12s. 6d, 'Shall we Join the Ladies?' was to retail at almost twice the average cost (7s. 6d) of the genuine books advertised in that year's *Faber & Faber Spring Book Announcements* (1937)—an expense presumably justified by the 'fascinating photographs'.[162] This parody is accompanied by four further similarly poker-faced puffs, touching on other of Eliot's perennial amusements. 'Poems 1925–1937 by Collie Cahoon', 'the chief of the modern negro poets of America . . . a modern Shelley inspired by swing rhythm', unfairly lampoons black American literary culture, while 'Tally-Ho and Nitchevo!: A Book of Fox-Hunting in the U.S.S.R' (possibly a satire on Siegfried Sassoon's *Memoirs of a Fox-Hunting Man* (1928), one of Faber's best-sellers) and 'The Trinity Beagles: A Centenary Volume' twit the English upper class.[163] The blurb for the detective novel 'Bordighera Budgerigar Murders' sends

---

[160] T. S. Eliot, 'Parodies of Publisher's "Blurbs" Composed by T. S. Eliot for the Firm of Faber & Faber', typescript (1937), Papers of the Hayward Bequest of T. S. Eliot Material HB/P9, King's College, Cambridge.

[161] Eliot, 'Parodies of Publisher's "Blurbs".'

[162] Eliot, 'Parodies of Publisher's "Blurbs".'

[163] Eliot, 'Parodies of Publisher's "Blurbs"'; Siegfried Sassoon, *Memoirs of a Fox-Hunting Man* (London: Faber & Gwyer, 1928).

'A MOQUEUR TO THE MARROW' 187

up the passion for Sherlock Holmes that Eliot shared with Geoffrey Faber, Frank Morley, and John Hayward.[164] Morley's nostalgic portrait of the Faber offices in 'T. S. Eliot as a Publisher' suggests that Eliot's parody blurbs and readers' reports were part of a wider culture of practical joking in the company, including 'OK Sauce ... which was very far from OK, the coffee which foamed over, the cigarettes which somehow produced snow-storms' and a dangerous prank that involved setting off 'giant' firecrackers under the table to liven up the Wednesday committee meeting nearest the Fourth of July.[165]

Further evidence of Eliot's continued pleasure in low parody can be found in the unpublished material Hayward had bound together with the *Old Possum's Book of Practical Cats* (1939), the typescript of which Hayward combined with early drafts of two poems and other unpublished material, including six 'Parodies of Readers' Reports Ascribed to the Members of the Firm of Faber & Faber Ltd.'[166] The pretence maintained by Eliot was that *Practical Cats* had been rejected by Faber & Faber. The parodied 'readers' reports' offered explanation as to why. 'A. P.' [Allan Pringle] found the poems 'pretentious, and cannot recommend publication' and limply suggested that they be forwarded to Mr Morley.[167] 'R. de la M.' [Richard de la Mare] had not had the time to read them.[168] Another unnamed reader consulted Mrs Crawley for her opinion, surely Mr W. J. Crawley, the Sales Manager. Having researched the market, Eliot has Crawley, ever solicitous in his role of sales manager, conclude that 'everybody agrees that the market for Cats is pretty dead', but that 'If we could get the author to do a book on Herrings, I believe I could interest the trade in Hull, Grimsby and Lossiemouth.'[169] Eliot's ironic anticipation of criticisms of *Practical Cats* continued the playful distancing of Eliot the literary statesman and leading critic from his comic work which issued directly from the Eliot that is Old Possum.

Eliot continued to pen parodic *jeux d'esprit* as tokens of bonhomie. Hermione Lee notes that after his separation from Vivien (1933), his letters to Woolf became 'freer and more playful' and included many 'funny rhyming thank-yous, satires on America, literary pastiches.'[170] He also continued to exchange parodic verses with male literary associates in the spirit of competition. The homosocial aspects of Eliot's private practice of parody are well illustrated by *Noctes Binanianae: Certain Voluntary and Satyrical Verses and Compliments as Were Lately Exchang'd between*

---

[164] Eliot, 'Parodies of Publisher's "Blurbs".'

[165] F. V. Morley, 'T. S. Eliot as a Publisher', *T. S. Eliot: A Symposium from Conrad Aiken and Others*, 69–70.

[166] T. S. Eliot, 'Old Possum's Book of Practical Cats &c. Typescript by the Author [T. S. Eliot] with Early Drafts of Two Poems, & Unpublished Material. Including His Old Possum's Letter to the Publishers and Parodies of Readers' Reports Ascribed to Members of the Firm of Faber & Faber Ltd.', typescript, n. d., The Papers of the Hayward Bequest of T. S. Eliot Material HB/V9, King's College, Cambridge.

[167] Eliot, 'Old Possum's Book of Practical Cats &c.'

[168] Eliot, 'Old Possum's Book of Practical Cats &c.'

[169] Eliot, 'Old Possum's Book of Practical Cats &c.

[170] Lee, *Virginia Woolf*, 450.

188   MODERNIST PARODY

Some of the Choicest Wits of the Age: Collected with the Greatest Care and Now Printed without Castration after the Most Correct Copies (1939).[171] The 'Choicest Wits' were O'Possum, or the Elephant (Eliot), the Coot (Faber), the Tarantula (Hayward), and the Whale (Morley), and the book was privately printed in a limited edition of twenty-five copies. Their exchanges were conducted in a number of different styles and languages, as indicated by the *faux* eighteenth-century subtitle, including rhyming couplets of a sub-Fresca standard, each writer rebutting the previous, and attempting to outdo them in wit. Gordon is acute in her analysis:

> The mannered repartee between these characters has now dated. Their jokes had the after-dinner jollity of men who evade expressiveness. Their verbal play was a feeble emulation of the poetic star, Eliot, who was, at this low point, parodying himself.[172]

Only within the private context of long-standing friendship did Eliot feel able to let his guard down and indulge his taste for low parody in the manner of *Punch*.

The fascination with reworking remained a constant in Eliot's work, private and public, though its tones changed. In *Ash Wednesday* (1930), Eliot pastiched the anaphoric style of Lancelot Andrewes's Ash Wednesday Sermons, subsuming many other echoes of literary and biblical texts.[173] The dominant styles of *The Rock* (1934) are biblical and bucolic, with literary grace notes.[174] The footfalls of Eliot's literary forebears echo in *Four Quartets* (1935–42), where the voices of admired authors fuse intermittently with Eliot's own in a medley of pastiche styles. The concord Eliot seeks with literary tradition culminates in the encounter with the 'familiar compound ghost' in 'Little Gidding', the last quartet, which is introduced by a pastiche of Canto XV of the *Inferno*—the episode in which Dante meets his old master—rendered in a modernized approximation of Dante's *terza rima*.[175]

Eliot's concern with resonant echo in *Four Quartets* extended to his own voice. According to Hayward, Eliot's 'chief fear' when writing 'Little Gidding', 'was that he was simply repeating himself and so running into the risk of producing an elegant

---

[171] T. S. Eliot et al., *Noctes Binanianae: Certain Voluntary and Satyrical Verses and Compliments as Were Lately Exchang'd between Some of the Choicest Wits of the Age: Collected with the Greatest Care and Now Printed without Castration after the Most Correct Copies* (London: Lund Humphries & Co., 1939). The title refers to John Hayward's address: Bina Gardens.

[172] Gordon, *T. S. Eliot*, 258.

[173] T. S. Eliot, *Ash Wednesday*, in *Poems of T. S. Eliot: Volume I*, 87–97; see Ricks and McCue, 'Commentary: Ash Wednesday', in *Poems of T. S. Eliot: Volume I*, 727–37.

[174] T. S. Eliot, 'Choruses from *The Rock*', in *Poems of T. S. Eliot: Volume I*, 153–6; John Xiros Cooper has noted a several examples stylistic imitation in *The Rock* in which Eliot's 'literary borrowings work mechanically, and are essentially inert, like prosthetic limbs' (John Xiros Cooper, *T. S. Eliot and the Ideology of 'Four Quartets'* (Cambridge: Cambridge University Press, 2008), 71).

[175] T. S. Eliot, 'Little Gidding', *Four Quartets*, in *Poems of T. S. Eliot: Volume I, Collected and Uncollected Poems*, 204; for Eliot's own commentary on his use of Dante in 'Little Gidding' see T. S. Eliot, *To Criticize the Critic* (London: Faber & Faber, 1965), 128.

'A MOQUEUR TO THE MARROW' 189

parody of the earlier poems in the group'.[176] Going through the second typescript of 'Little Gidding', Hayward kept a vigilant eye out for such effects, warning him that the lines 'At any time, the day time or the dark time,/Or at any season, the dead time or the may time' carried 'just a faint suggestion here, I think, of your parodying yourself'.[177] Eliot responded by striking 'through the two half lines in his working copy'.[178] Indeed, as early as the drafting of the first two sections of 'East Coker', the second quartet, Eliot expressed concern to Hayward that his labour 'may be quite worthless, because most of it looks to me like an imitation of myself'.[179] When Eliot gave the first Yeats memorial lecture at the Abbey Theatre, Dublin, in June 1940, he reflected on poets' later years and proclaimed:

> Most men either cling to the experiences of youth, so that their writing becomes an insincere mimicry of their earlier work, or they leave their passion behind, and write only from the head, with a hollow and wasted virtuosity.[180]

The 'scribbled part of the draft of "Little Gidding" on the reverse side of his Dublin lecture' suggests that these reflections were tellingly personal, for in addition to his concerns about self-parody, Eliot also expressed concern that 'Little Gidding' was written 'too much from the head'.[181] The challenge Pound faced as a young man was to avoid inadvertent pastiche of his admired masters. The challenge faced by Eliot in full maturity was to avoid sounding like a parody of himself.

---

[176] John Hayward to Frank Morley, July 1942, quoted in Helen Gardner, *The Composition of 'Four Quartets'* (London: Faber & Faber, 1978), 25.

[177] Hayward to Eliot, 1 August 1941, quoted in Gardner, *Composition of 'Four Quartets'*, 164, 165. For the textual history of these lines and their place in the compositional history of 'Little Gidding' see Ricks and McCue, *Poems of T. S. Eliot: Volume II*, 518.

[178] Gardner, *Composition of 'Four Quartets'*, 165.

[179] Eliot to Morley, February 1940, quoted in Gardner, *Composition of 'Four Quartets'*, 16–17. For fuller quotation from this letter in context see Ricks and McCue, 'Commentary: Four Quartets', in *Poems of T. S. Eliot: Volume I*, 884.

[180] T. S. Eliot, 'Yeats', *On Poetry and Poets*, 257.

[181] Ronald Bush, *T. S. Eliot: A Study in Character and Style* (Oxford: Oxford University Press, 1983), 35–6; see also Eliot to Hayward, 14 July 1941, quoted in *Poems of T. S. Eliot: Volume I*, 888.

6

A 'Bawd of Parodies'

James Joyce's Practices as a Parodist from His Early Writings to *Ulysses*

Joyce suffered none of Eliot's inhibition. By the time Joyce was working on the middle chapters of *Ulysses* he had fully embraced parody as a primary mode of literary origination that could counter naive mimesis through the comedy of stylistic excess. Joyce used parody to reveal that literature is historicized language in unstable play before it is representation. He undermined the reliability of any single point of view through parody's irreconcilable doubling of perspective, while simultaneously contriving to satirize the texts he reworked and the world he refracted through parody's all-including satire. Joyce too travelled that well-trodden path from involuntary pastiche to creative parody, but his journey was accelerated by his early decision to specialize in fiction rather than poetry, the novel being the genre born of parodic stylization.

Kenner was the first to detect the parodic doubleness of the language spoken and thought by Dubliners in Joyce's works. In *Dublin's Joyce* (1955), Kenner drew attention to conversations where the 'speakers are manipulating clichés, but they are speaking deliberately with a sense of discovering new provinces of thought', and yet 'they can speak only in quotations, and despite the consciousness of effort their thought runs in grooves'.[1] Citing Little Chandler imagining the book he might write and the notice it might get in terms of the jargon reviewers used to describe the Celtic school in 'A Little Cloud', Kenner noted 'Every Dublin phrase has a double focus: the past meaning it locks away, the present vagueness it shapes'; 'No Dubliner acts from his nature, no Dubliner knows what his nature is; he acts on the promptings of *idées reçues* and talks in words that have for too long been respoken'.[2] Kenner proceeded to argue that 'Joyce's Dublin was in fact an eighteenth-century parody', by which he meant that the city was a shadow of its former self and, by extension, that Joyce's practices align with Augustan satire:

> The technique he developed, the technique which underlies everything from the first pages of *Dubliners* to the end of *Finnegans Wake*, came out of the subject: parody; double-writing. The music-halls parodied the heroic dramas; Joyce parodied

[1] Kenner, *Dublin's Joyce*, 8.
[2] Kenner, *Dublin's Joyce*, 9, 10.

Modernist Parody. Sarah Davison, Oxford University Press. © Sarah Davison (2023).
DOI: 10.1093/oso/9780192849243.003.0007

the music-halls. Journalism parodied heroic elegance: Joyce parodied journalism. He focused, that is to say, on what was actually there, and strove so to set it down that it would reveal itself as what it was, in its double nature: a distortion, but a distortion of something real.[3]

Kenner insisted that the language of Dublin *is* Joyce's subject and that what is distinctive but simultaneously false about Dublin is comprehended in the citizens' awareness of their cultural heritage as they pick their words, refracting the world through what Stephen in *A Portrait of the Artist as a Young Man* terms 'the prism of language many coloured and richly storied'.[4] Kenner summarized Joyce's central technique as 'parody of the once vital to enact a null apprehension of the null', a view of parody that this chapter seeks to counterbalance by shifting the emphasis away from 'Dublin's dead style' to focus instead on the other side of the equation: parody's creative power as a prodigious principle of genesis that drives the progress of Joyce's art.[5] As parody proliferates throughout Joyce's oeuvre, a selective approach is necessary. Consequently, this chapter moves from a brief overview of Joyce's early career in imitation and mimesis, and the inevitable tipping via irony into parody and self-parody, to a detailed discussion of Joyce's narrative experiments with parody in the 'Cyclops' and 'Nausicaa' episodes of *Ulysses* (1922), before focusing at length on the 'Oxen of the Sun' episode, which is narrated through parodies of historical literary styles from the origins of English prose to the present day.

Like many of his modernist peers, Joyce's earliest work imitated the achievements of the previous generation. In his last years at Belvedere College, Joyce began to collect his poems in two stiff-covered exercise books entitled 'Moods' and 'Shine and Dark'.[6] The title 'Moods' suggests a debt to the decadents.[7] The tone of 'The Twilight Turns from Amethyst', the one surviving poem from 'Shine and Dark', suggests that the mood of the 1890s continued in this collection, whose title, as his brother Stanislaus noted, derived from Whitman's melodious line, 'Earth of shine and dark mottling the tide of the river'.[8] This decadent colouring persisted in the poems of *Chamber Music* (1907), which were written between 1901 and 1904. Reviewers detected a 'formality and device throughout, though well disguised, and a courtliness that reminds one of Herrick or Lovelace' and complained that 'where it does not reflect the vaporous mysticism of the early Yeats, Æ, and the other Irish

---

[3] Kenner, *Dublin's Joyce*, 11.

[4] James Joyce, *A Portrait of the Artist as a Young Man*, ed. Jeri Johnson (Oxford: Oxford University Press, 2008), 140.

[5] Kenner, *Dublin's Joyce*, 19, 21.

[6] Stanislaus Joyce, *My Brother's Keeper: James Joyce's Early Years*, 1st edn (New York: Viking Press, 1958), 100.

[7] 'Moore read some of them [Joyce's poems] languidly and then handed them back to Russell with one weary word of criticism.—Symons!' (*My Brother's Keeper*, 246).

[8] Joyce, *My Brother's Keeper*, 100.

192   MODERNIST PARODY

revivalists, it is a patent imitation of the Elizabethan song-books'.[9] Pound, who similarly apprenticed himself to a lively early modern, popular tradition, also discerned that the 'wording is Elizabethan, the metre at times suggesting Herrick', but defended *Chamber Music* stating that 'in no case have I been able to find a poem which is not in some way Joyce's own, even though he would seem, and that most markedly, to shun apparent originality'.[10]

At first Joyce took pride in the poems that were to be published as *Chamber Music*, carrying them 'in a large packet, each written up in his best hand in the middle of a large piece of parchment', but by 1906 he viewed *Chamber Music* with contempt, dismissing the volume as 'a young man's book' and wishing he could find another title which would 'repudiate the book, without altogether disparaging it'.[11] He nearly cancelled publication in 1907, complaining 'All that kind of thing is false', and remained sufficiently disenchanted with the poems to allow Stanislaus to determine their order.[12] This reticence was perhaps not so dramatic a change of attitude because the falsehood was already signalled by the collection's punning title, which refers to the songs of courtly gallants but also the occasion when Oliver St John Gogarty brought Joyce to visit a widow who interrupted a reading of the poems when she retreated behind a screen to use a chamber pot.

Joyce's recourse to parody and self-parody was in opposition to his earliest instincts about the moral responsibilities of writers of fiction and represented a reaction to the practical impossibility of writing fiction that was not in some way false. His rapid disillusionment with the artificiality of *Chamber Music* was in line with his early formulations of a fiction-writing credo whereby falsity was to be avoided at all costs. Stanislaus reported:

> He [Joyce] had no doubt that most artists, even the greatest, belied the life they knew, and offered the world a make-believe. Literature, he said, was a parody of life. He declared bitterly that he believed in only two things, a woman's love of her child and a man's love of lies, of lies of all possible kinds; and he was determined that his spiritual experience should not be a make-believe.[13]

In order not to produce a 'parody of life' ('parody' here, in that loosest and most non-literary sense of the word, meaning comically feeble or fantastical imitation) and falsify his 'spiritual experience', Joyce committed himself to unsentimental realism, guided by his enthusiasm for Ibsen, who taught him how 'out of the dreary

---

[9] 'M.A.', rev. *Chamber Music* by James Joyce, *New Republic* XVIII (8 March 1919), 191, reprinted in Robert Deming, ed., *James Joyce: The Critical Heritage: Volume 1: 1907–27* (London: Routledge & Kegan Paul, 1970), 44; Morton Zabel, 'The Lyrics of James Joyce', *Poetry* XXXVI (July 1930), 206–13, reprinted in Deming, *James Joyce*, 46.

[10] Ezra Pound, 'Joyce' in *LE* 413.

[11] Richard Ellmann, *James Joyce*, rev. edn (Oxford: Oxford University Press, 1982), 154, 232.

[12] Joyce, *Poems and Shorter Writings*, 7.

[13] Joyce quoted in Stanislaus Joyce, *My Brother's Keeper*, 105.

A 'BAWD OF PARODIES'   193

sameness of existence, a measure of dramatic life may be drawn'.[14] Joyce applied this lesson to the stories of *Dubliners*, which he advertised to Grant Richards in a letter of 5 May 1906 as 'a chapter in the moral history of my country', written 'for the most part in a style of scrupulous meanness and with the conviction that he is a very bold man who dares to alter in the presentment, still more to deform, what he has seen and heard'.[15] Here, Joyce equated facticity and truth with spare but unsparing presentation, even though he had previously expressed the anxiety to Stanislaus in a letter of 19 July 1905 that although the 'stories in Dubliners seem to be indisputably well done' they were perhaps more caricatural than he otherwise admitted:

> The Dublin papers will object to my stories as to a caricature of Dublin life. Do you think there is any truth in this? At times the spirit directing my pen seems to me so plainly mischievous that I am almost prepared to let the Dublin critics have their way. All these pros and cons I must for the nonce lock up in my bosom. Of course do not think that I consider contemporary Irish writing anything but ill-written, morally obtuse formless caricature.[16]

In this letter, Joyce figured formless caricature as the failure of realism and a kind of mocking deformation of the truth, yet simultaneously admitted that his art was caricatural, albeit in a different way. In a later letter to Richards of 20 May 1906, Joyce represented his practice as qualitatively different to caricature in the popular press, sending him a copy of 'the leading satirical paper of the Celtic nations, corresponding to *Punch* or *Pasquino*' (most likely an issue of *The Leader*, which featured many literary parodies and satirical sketches on contemporary Ireland):

> I send it to you that you may see how witty the Irish are as all the world knows. The style of the caricaturist will show you how artistic they are: and you will see for yourself that the Irish are the most spiritual race on the face of the earth. Perhaps this may reconcile you to *Dubliners*. It is not my fault that the odour of ashpits and old weeds and offal hangs round my stories. I seriously believe that you will retard the course of civilisation in Ireland by preventing the Irish people from having one good look at themselves in my nicely polished looking-glass.[17]

The comparison Joyce invited here provides a further example of the aesthetic rift between the magazine tradition of caricature and satire sustained by *Punch* on the one hand and high modernist practice on the other. Joyce described popular

---

[14] James Joyce, 'Drama and Life', in Kevin Barry, ed., and Conor Deane, trans., *Occasional, Critical, and Political Writing* (Oxford: Oxford University Press, 2008), 28.

[15] *LJJ* II 134.

[16] *LJJ* II 99.

[17] *LJJ* I 63–4.

194   MODERNIST PARODY

Dublin caricature—as in the *Pasquino*-style paper—as 'witty', 'spiritual', and 'artistic' with a heavily ironic inflexion. Joyce's stories are not caricatural in the popular
conception of the term, but accurate images of reality, and its sordidness, that are
artistic and spiritual in precisely the way that these pasquinades are not. And yet
they are animated by a mischievous spirit that holds up the rhythms of Dubliners'
speech and patterns of behaviour to ironic scrutiny.

Karen Lawrence is one of several critics to link the technique of free indirect
discourse (employed in the majority of the *Dubliners* stories, where the apparent
objective truth of third-person narration is opened up to the ironies of unreliable
narration) to 'a form of stylistic parody', albeit localized, where 'style becomes [a]
mask' and 'the author becomes a mimic, speaking in someone else's voice'.[18] (As
Bakhtin noted, 'stylizing discourse by attributing it to a person often becomes
parodic, although not crudely parodic'.[19]) This double aspect to Joyce's use of
voice, which manifests as a subtle effect in *Dubliners*, is exaggerated in subsequent fiction, eventually to the point that the deformations of parody obscure
the realist base. Joyce's thoughts on caricature registered his dawning realization that the moral authority of realist fiction could only hold true and avoid
being 'a parody of life' if the style in which it was written simultaneously exposed
the falsity of all literary conventions and, beyond that, all non-literary forms of
discourse.

A Portrait of the Artist as a Young Man holds the 'nicely polished looking-glass'
up to Joyce's own face to reveal Stephen's youthful image. In conversation with
Stanislaus, Joyce described *Portrait* as 'a lying autobiography and a raking satire'.[20]
The lie is of course Stephen's deceiving self-image, the conceit that repeatedly lifts
him skywards before his next crash down to earth.[21] *Portrait* does therefore conde-
scend in its depiction of Stephen, but that condescension is self-directed, because
Joyce, the mature artist and author of the book, betrays the young Stephen's pretensions, which were once his own. Pastiche is embraced as the mode of the naive
artist in *Portrait* (as befitted Joyce's own experience) and self-parody provides
a means of indicating the limits of immature, imitative, decadent aesthetics. In
episodes VI and V, Stephen's lyrical and spiritual aspirations are ironically undercut via a free indirect style that takes on the colouring of parody, after the manner
discussed by Lawrence (and separately theorized by Bakhtin), with increasing frequency. For instance, Stephen's ecstatic awakening in episode V of *Portrait* shows

---

[18] Karen Lawrence, *The Odyssey of Style in 'Ulysses'* (Princeton, NJ: Princeton University Press,
1981), 23.

[19] 'Discourse in the Novel', *TDI*, 348.

[20] Stanislaus Joyce, *The Dublin Diary of Stanislaus Joyce*, ed. George. H. Healey (London: Faber &
Faber, 1962), 25.

[21] Each section of *Portrait* ends with a triumphant ascent only for Stephen to be brought crash-
ing down to earth in the following section. Stephen's attempts at flight and subsequent falls, serially
repeated throughout the novel, re-enact the fate of Icarus, son of Daedalus, who fell into the sea when
he dared to fly too close to the sun.

how far the patternings of his thought have been shaped by the cadences of Pater's impressionistic prose that aspires to the condition of music:

> Towards dawn he awoke. O what sweet music! His soul was all dewy wet. Over his limbs in sleep pale cool waves of light had passed. He lay still, as if his soul lay amid cool waters, conscious of faint sweet music. His mind was waking slowly to a tremulous morning knowledge, a morning inspiration. A spirit filled him, pure as the purest water, sweet as dew, moving as music.[22]

The lyrical excess mocks Stephen who, in a state of fervent inspiration, produces not great art but a slight villanelle, which is in fact one of Joyce's early poems, 'Villanelle of the Temptress', written in 1900 when he was 18.[23] Joyce's youthful composition is used as a token of Stephen's impressionable immaturity. He remains in thrall to *fin-de-siècle* notions of fine writing and is still obedient to the emotional expression of other artists. Joyce's ironic handling of the villanelle episode in *Portrait* measures how far he himself had come as an artist since 1900.

Ulysses takes up the themes of *A Portrait*, rejoining Stephen barely two years later. It begins with Buck Mulligan mockingly performing a parody mass, signalling, among other things, the novel's broader interest in parodying the narratives by which humankind understands itself and its place in the universe. The grand parody of Homer's *Odyssey* implied by the riddling title *Ulysses* provided a structuring principle from the beginning. Setting the more pedestrian wanderings of Bloom and Stephen in a classical perspective authorized the universality and human depth of the characters while signalling Joyce's own heroic narrative feats as the Irish author who would set his productions on a par with Homer. While the *Odyssey* provides the scaffolding for Joyce's novel, the details of the correspondence are not deployed in any rigorously consistent way: while the relations are often ironic, as in the adulterous but ultimately loyal Molly Bloom who contrasts with chaste Penelope, adventures are evoked out of sequence, and in 'Wandering Rocks' the theme is taken from the obstacles that Odysseus was determined to avoid. The relationship of *Ulysses* to its namesake is loose and within it parody plays an intermittent, ambivalent, and by no means exclusive, part. Joyce does not direct literary criticism at the *Odyssey* itself. The grand parody pertains to the plot and is sufficiently diffused throughout the lengthy text of *Ulysses* to inhibit detailed commentary on Homer's form or style. The perspective it offers on the actions of the characters who populate Dublin is mock heroic, but not without pathos. Bloom and Stephen are mock-heroic figures, only diminished in comparison to Homer's heroes in martial terms but dignified by the heroic value conferred on the palpably unheroic minutiae of their lives.

---

[22] Joyce, *A Portrait of the Artist as a Young Man*, 182.
[23] Joyce, *A Portrait of the Artist as a Young Man*, 188; Joyce, *Poems and Shorter Writings*, 72.

196   MODERNIST PARODY

The Stephen that readers encounter in *Ulysses* is still immature and his unsound youth is played off against the fatherly Leopold Bloom's maturity, just as his education is played off against Bloom's autodidactism, and his aesthetic temperament against Bloom's pragmatism. This interplay between perspectives affects the style and form of the novel. In the first three episodes Stephen's interior monologue dominates, in the next three Bloom's, and then the course of the narrative becomes progressively disrupted by techniques that admit viewpoints other than the conscious thoughts of the primary characters, only to reprise interior monologue (this time female) at the very end. The first nine episodes up to and including 'Scylla and Charybdis', as they appeared when serialized in the *Little Review* (March 1918– April 1919), were written in what Joyce called the book's 'initial style' in a letter to Harriet Shaw Weaver of 6 August 1919, a variable combination of third-person narration, free indirect discourse, and interior monologue, with little in the way of disruption.[24] The disorientating subheads that confronted readers of 'Aeolus' as it ultimately appeared in book form were absent, as were the welter of references to elements related to aspects of Homer's *Odyssey* (such as flowers in 'Lotus Eaters', the heart in 'Hades', and wind in 'Aeolus'). Instead, these early episodes were concerned with scrupulous verisimilitude in their presentation of Dublin life and the parallels to events in the *Odyssey* while present were not explicitly foregrounded. Only the appearance of musical notation, free verse, and dramatic dialogue in the fair copy of 'Scylla and Charybdis', which was finished on New Year's Eve 1918, signalled Joyce's readiness to experiment with other techniques.[25]

As Michael Groden revealed in his pioneering study of Joyce's working practices, '*Ulysses' in Progress* (1977), the later proliferation of (often esoteric) Homeric references arose from a change in intention and technique that occurred between 1918 and 1919 and that marked the effective end of the first half of the book. Groden's investigations into the making of *Ulysses* uncovered three distinct stage in its composition:

> In the first stage ('Telemachus'—'Scylla and Charybdis') he developed an interior monologue technique to tell his story. In the middle stage ('Wandering Rocks'— 'Oxen of the Sun') he experimented with the monologue and then abandoned it for a series of parody styles that act as 'translations' of the story. He balanced his growing attraction to stylistic surface with a continued interest in the human story. Finally, in the last stage ('Circe'—'Penelope') he created several new styles and revised the earlier episodes. He only partly reworked the episodes, however, as if to present *Ulysses* as a palimpsest involving all three stages.[26]

[24] *LJJ* I 129.

[25] On the last page of the fair copy of 'Scylla and Charybdis' Joyce wrote 'End of First Part of "Ulysses" and the date 'New Year's Eve 1918'. See Michael Groden, '*Ulysses' in Progress* (Princeton, NJ: University Press, 1977), 17.

[26] Groden, '*Ulysses' in Progress*, 4.

As Joyce entered the middle stage, the styling of *Ulysses* would no longer conform to the scrupulous mimesis that once seemed a moral necessity. Without giving up the realist material basis of his fiction, Joyce would enlarge the scope of third-person narration, direct speech, free indirect discourse, and interior monologue by pursuing techniques for stylizing his fiction that were suggested by the symbolic associations of his subject matter, including aspects of Homer's *Odyssey*. These experiments showed up the constructed nature of all forms of omniscient narration and radically questioned the validity of any singular point of view. As Joyce explained to Weaver in a letter of 24 June 1921, the result was a text that was narrated from 'eighteen different points of view and in as many different styles'.[27]

A key statement of Joyce's thinking regarding the middle stage of composition is found in a letter to Carlo Linati of 21 September 1921, which was accompanied by a schema outlining the Homeric correspondences. It was sent shortly after Joyce had written 'Oxen of the Sun', at a time when the drama of style assumed even greater importance than the quotidian drama of Stephen and Bloom:

> It is an epic of two races (Israelite—Irish) and at the same time the cycle of the human body as well as a little story of a day (life) ... It is also sort of encyclopedia. My intention is to transpose the myth [of Homer's *Odyssey*] *sub specie temporis nostri* [in the light of our own times]. Each adventure (that is, every hour, every organ, every art being interconnected and interrelated in the structural scheme of the whole) should not only condition but even create its own technique.[28]

This conditioning was based on Joyce's subjective and often whimsical interpretation of those salient aspects of the original narrative (as filtered through modern translations) that were most suggestive for his own purposes: a method that ultimately led Joyce to parody, in which style becomes its own subject.

The play of parody in *Ulysses* is at its most extensive in the final three episodes of Groden's middle stage, 'Cyclops', 'Nausicaa', and 'Oxen of the Sun', where it works on a number of levels. 'Cyclops' is narrated by an unnamed debt collector, whose naturalistic account is distended by thirty-three anarchic interruptions that make use of parodic stylization to expand aspects of the narrative to gigantic proportions. The technique (according to the schema Joyce shared with Stuart Gilbert) is 'gigantism', which serves as a unifying theme for the episode.[29] Joyce's various methods are suggested by different facets of the Cyclops's characterization in the *Odyssey*: his single eye; his monstrous proportions; and his name, Polyphemus, meaning 'much spoken of'. There is the singular perspective of the blathering 'I' narrator, who is an eyewitness to events in Barney's Kiernan's pub, and then there

---

[27] *LJJ* I 167.
[28] *LJJ* I 146–7.
[29] Stuart Gilbert, *James Joyce's 'Ulysses': A Study*, rev. edn (New York: Vintage, 1955), 258.

198   MODERNIST PARODY

is the monocular religious and political ideology of the burly citizen, a Fenian who speaks with 'colossal vituperativeness' and plays Cyclops to Bloom's Odysseus.[30] These viewpoints are played off against the inflated prose of the stylized passages, which include: a parody of a legal document; multiple parodies of nineteenth-century retellings of Irish legends, such as the account of the abundant fertility of the land after James Clarence Mangan's translation of 'Aldfrid's Itinerary'; a parody of the jargon of medical science; a parody reporting on the execution of Robert Emmet in the overblown and romantic, sensational and sentimental style of front-page news; a parody of parliamentary proceedings; a report of a boxing match in a parody of a sporting column; a parody society column in which all the fashionable wedding guests have names linked to trees; and even a parody of the Apostles' Creed.[31] These parodies are internally divided against themselves and also provide a doubling but dissociated perspective on the main action, the bare lineaments of which appear mock heroic in relation to Homer. Bloom's narrow escape from the pub after the citizen attacks his naive but good-natured attempts to define nationhood is figured as a burlesque on Odysseus's audacious flight from Polyphemus's cave; Bloom's 'knockmedown cigar' is a manifestation of the red-hot wooden stake with which Odysseus blinds the one-eyed giant; and the Jacob's biscuit tin the citizen hurls at Bloom in his getaway car is a comic diminution of the mighty rocks that the Cyclops throws at Odysseus's ship.[32] The episode culminates with Bloom's apotheosis in the guise of Elijah ascending heavenwards.

To complicate matters further, the unnamed narrator, a 'no-man' (to use the pseudonym Odysseus adopts), also reports that he narrowly missed an eye injury when 'a bloody sweep came along and he near drove his gear into my eye.'[33] The narrator is openly anti-Semitic, but he neither sides with the thuggish citizen nor Bloom, whom he characterizes as socially awkward, dull, tight-fisted, and hypocritical (for cadging a cigar yet speaking in support of the antitreating league).[34] He says of Bloom 'It'd be an act of God to take a hold of a fellow the like of that and throw him in the bloody sea.'[35] Parody in 'Cyclops' is neither simply digressive nor reductively mock heroic in its play with perspective and relative proportion; the many different stylized elements contrast with one another in unstable interplay.

The strong resemblance of Ulysses in general and 'Cyclops' in particular to Rabelais's The Life of Gargantua and Pantagruel was immediately noticed by Joyce's circle of initiates. Valery Larbaud wrote to Joyce to tell him he was 'raving mad' about Ulysses, which he hailed as 'great and comprehensive and human

---

[30] LJJ I 126.
[31] U 12.33–51; 12.68–86; 12.468–78; 12.525–675; 12.860–79; 12.960–87; 12.1266–95; 12.1354–9.
[32] U 12.502.
[33] U 12.2–3.
[34] U 12.682–4.
[35] U 12.1661–2.

as Rabelais'.[36] Pound too raved about Joyce's parodies in 'Cyclops' in a letter to Quinn of 25 October 1919, which in his view exceeded Rabelais:

> Last ms. chapter of Joyce [Cyclops] perhaps the best thing he has done.... Parody of styles, a trick borrowed from Rabelais, but never done better, even in Rab.[37]

But while Pound raved about the altogether more serious applications of parody in the 'Cyclops' episode of *Ulysses* and remained hugely supportive of Joyce's project overall, his opinions on Joyce's methods wavered. First, he was concerned about Joyce's language in *Ulysses*, fearing suppression. Then he lost patience with Joyce's rendering of musical form in 'Sirens' and requested that Joyce shift the focus from Bloom back to Stephen. Finally, Pound lost interest in the finished novel's parodic elaboration of Homeric elements, declaring: 'These correspondences are part of Joyce's mediaevalism and are chiefly his own affair, a scaffold, a means of construction, justified by the result, and justifiable by it only. The result is a triumph in form, in balance, a main schema, with continuous inweaving and arabesque.'[38]

In 'James Joyce et Pécuchet', an essay printed in *Mercure de France* (1 June 1922), Pound again compared Joyce's all-including parody favourably to Rabelais:

> Cervantes ne parodiait qu'une seule folie littéraire, la folie chevaleresque. Seuls Rabelais et Flaubert attaquent tout un siècle, s'opposent à toute une encyclopédie imbécile,—sous la forme de fiction.
>
> [Cervantes only parodied a single literary madness, the chivalric folly. Only Rabelais and Flaubert attacked an entire century, opposing a whole imbecilic encyclopaedia in the form of fiction.][39]

Pound praised Joyce for presenting 'Cyclops' in ordinary words, and putting alongside it the grandiloquence that is parody and measure of the difference between realism and the romanticism of the braggart ['Joyce présente l'épisode du Cyclope avec les paroles ordinaires, mais à côté il pose la grandiloquence, parodie et mesure de la différence entre le réalisme et un romantisme de fanfaron'], whereby mundane events in Barney Kiernan's pub are satirized in relation to the inappropriately grand style, which is in turn mocked by the naturalistic description.[40]

Rabelais collected popular traditions and breathed new life into ancient legends, parodying the languages (and mocking the attitudes) of official culture with the mirthful laughter that is proper to understanding the true predicament of man.

---

[36] Quoted by Joyce in a letter to Weaver of 1 March 1921 (*LJJ* III 40).

[37] Read, *Pound/Joyce*, 161.

[38] Pound, '*Ulysses*', in *LE* 406.

[39] Ezra Pound, 'James Joyce et Pécuchet', *Mercure de France*, Paris CLVI 575 (1 June 1922), 307–20, in Read, *Pound/Joyce*, 208.

[40] Pound, 'James Joyce et Pécuchet', in Read, *Pound/Joyce*, 207.

200 MODERNIST PARODY

Homer is prominent among that company: adventures in the *Odyssey* and the *Iliad* are intermittently invoked by way of comparison to Rabelais's own tales. Rabelais is directly present in *Ulysses* in Molly's interior monologue, a circumstance that suggests Joyce's claim to have never read the French master should be taken with a pinch of salt.[41] In 'Penelope', Molly expresses irritation with her husband for bringing her volumes of 'the works of Master François Somebody supposed to be a priest about a child born out of her [r]ear because her bumgut fell out a nice word for any priest to write and her a—e as if any fool wouldnt know what that meant', picking up on the language of the grotesque description of the giant Gargamelle giving birth to Gargantua after having eaten excessive quantities of tripe, with the result that the midwives grope below and confuse the coming of the child with extreme diarrhoea.[42] The allusion in 'Penelope' is pointed and specific, but it also links thematically to Molly as mother and Earth mother, an earthy woman whose being is bodily, and a Gea-Tellus who is endowed with the proportions of a giantess in symbolic terms.

Joyce's wider epic of 'the cycle of the human body' also presents a parallel to Rabelais's phantasmagorical portrayals of the human body in all its gross, material, corporeality in *The Life of Gargantua and Pantagruel*. As Bakhtin has argued so compellingly, Rabelais's precise anatomies of the giants' monstrous bodily functions are drawn into the living dynamics of the action (so that cycles of eating, drinking, digesting, copulating, defecating, and urinating are shown to be essential parts of feasting, fighting, breeding, living, and dying) and therefore come to embody all aspects of human life and culture.[43] The inseparability of the human comedy of the body, its processes, and life as it is lived is also clearly thematized in Joyce's works, which partake of a similarly visceral bodily economy. But in 'Cyclops'—the episode of *Ulysses* Pound thought most Rabelaisian—the influence of the great French writer on Joyce's play with the theme of gigantism is pervasive, if diffuse, manifesting most obviously in parodic stylization of multiple genres and exuberant levels of descriptive excess.

---

[41] Joyce denied the influence of Rabelais on *Work in Progress* in a letter to Weaver of 31 May 1927, claiming 'I never read Rabelais either though nobody will believe this', having merely read 'a few chapters of a book called *La langue de Rabelais*' (*LJJ* I 255). It is doubtful whether this claim should be taken seriously. Joyce owned at least two copies of Rabelais's work, as inventories of his libraries attest: *Les Cinq livres*, 2 vols. (Paris: Flammarion, n. d.), which he left behind him on moving from Trieste to Paris in 1920 (see Richard Ellmann, *The Consciousness of Joyce* (London: Faber & Faber, 1977), 124, and the English translation of the five books of *Gargantua and Pantagruel* in *The Works of Rabelais*, trans. Sir Thomas Urquhart, illust. Gustave Doré (Nottingham, n. d.), which remained in Joyce's personal collection (see Thomas E. Connolly, *The Personal Library of James Joyce: A Descriptive Bibliography*, 2nd edn (Buffalo, NY: University of Buffalo Press, 1957), 32).

[42] *U* 18.488–90. The word 'bum-gut' appears three times in Urquhart's translation of the relevant passages of Book I, chs. IV and VI of *Gargantua and Pantagruel* in *The Works of the Famous Mr. Francis Rabelais* (1664), 22, 31.

[43] Bakhtin's most concise account of Rabelais's novel as a comic work aligned with folklore (rather than official culture) and his thoughts on the politics of Rabelais's ribald presentation of the human body can be found in *TDI*, 167–205. See also Bakhtin's extended study *Rabelais and His World*, trans. Hélène Iswolsky (Bloomington, IN: Indiana University Press, 1984).

In 'Cyclops' the citizen roughhousing his dog Garryowen and very nearly throttling him is the trigger for a parodic flight of fancy in which his appearance is anatomized in a hyperbolic blazon that inflates the citizen's bulk to gigantic size, endowing him with (mock-)heroic proportions.[44] While the description of the figure seated on a large boulder is indebted to Homer, the overstatement of his imposing physique also owes much to Rabelais's enumerations of his giants' monstrous bodies, which are rendered grotesque by reference to that which they are not, as well as Rabelais's abundant encyclopaedism and predilection for excessive lists. The citizen is seemingly transformed into 'a broadshouldered deepchested stronglimbed frankeyed redhaired freelyfreckled shaggybearded widemouthed largenosed longheaded deepvoiced barekneed brawnyhanded hairylegged ruddyfaced sinewyarmed hero'.[45] He has 'rocklike mountainous knees' that are covered with 'a strong growth of tawny prickly hair in hue and toughness similar to the mountain gorse (*Ulex Europeus*)'.[46] His 'widewinged nostrils, from which bristles of the same tawny hue projected, were of such capaciousness that within their cavernous obscurity the fieldlark might easily have lodged her nest'.[47] His eyes are 'of the dimensions of a goodsized cauliflower'.[48] The sequence is downward, from the epic proportions of classical heroism, to the lofty realm of mountain and rock, to ground-covering furze, to a humble brassica evaluated in the language of the marketplace. From his girdle hang 'a row of seastones which jangled at every movement of his portentous frame and on these were graven with rude yet striking art the tribal images of many Irish heroes and heroines of antiquity'.[49] The list, totalling eighty-six names, begins with genuine Irish heroes, from the legendary 'Cuchulin [*sic*]', defender of the realm, to various ancient Kings of Ireland, other important Irish historical figures through the ages, and men who rebelled against or defended Ireland against the English, before degenerating into farce.[50] Irish heritage is attributed to the likes of 'Dante Alighieri', 'Christopher Columbus', 'Benjamin Franklin', 'Napoleon Bonaparte', 'Cleopatra', 'Julius Caesar', 'Patrick W. Shakespeare', and 'the Queen of Sheba', as well as characters inspired by popular genres such as 'The Woman Who Didn't' (after the novel *The Woman Who Did*), 'the Man for Galway' (from a Charles James Lever song), and 'the Man that Broke the Bank at Monte Carlo' (from a music-hall number), and characters with tenuous links to the episode's Homeric theme, including 'Goliath', 'Jack the Giantkiller', and 'Captain Nemo' ('nemo' being Latin for 'no-man', the pseudonym

---

[44] *U* 12.151–205.
[45] *U* 12.152–5.
[46] *U* 12.156, 12.157–8.
[47] *U* 12.159–61.
[48] *U* 12.162–3.
[49] *U* 12.173–6.
[50] *U* 12.176. For detailed notes on the various personages engraved on the seastones, see Don Gifford, ed., *Ulysses Annotated: Notes for James Joyce's Ulysses*, 2nd rev. edn (Berkeley: University of California Press, 2008), 320–6.

202 MODERNIST PARODY

Odysseus takes). These comic figures are intermixed with references to other fictional characters and historical personages who do have some relevance to Ireland's political history, geography, and cultural identity, from 'Dark Rosaleen' (the female personification of Ireland in the anonymous sixteenth-century Irish poem famously translated by James Clarence Mangan), to 'Theobald Wolfe Tone' (the Irish revolutionary and one of the founders of United Irishmen), to 'John L. Sullivan' (an Irish-American heavyweight boxing champion), to punning personifications of Dublin's geography such as 'Dolly Mount', 'Sidney Parade', and 'Ben Howth'.[51] The passage is irreducibly double, casting doubt on the very category of 'Irishness' on which it relies, mocking the citizen's veneration for Irish heroes, his status as a champion of the nationalist cause, and his categorical black-or-white thinking. And yet, later on in the episode, when the citizen scoffs at the notion of Sassenach civilization with the retort 'Their syphilisation, you mean' and comments 'Any civilisation they have they stole from us', drawing attention to the ancient Celtic culture that has nourished European traditions, suddenly the notion of an Irish Dante or an Irish Shakespeare does not seem quite so far-fetched and the perspective is subtly adjusted.[52] After all, 'S. Fursa', the Irish visionary whose name also appears on that list, is cited by Joyce in his essay 'The Mirage of the Fisherman of Aran' (1912) as 'a precursor to Dante Alighieri' for his vivid depiction of the voyage from heaven to hell.[53]

By comparison, in the text of 'Cyclops' as it appeared in the *Little Review* in November 1919, the graven images on the talismanic seastones only featured a short series of genuine Irish figures from legendary warrior-kings and leaders:

> Cuchulin [*sic*], Conn of hundred battles, Niall of nine hostages, Brian of Kincara, the Ardri Malachi, Art Mac Murragh, Shane O'Neill, Father John Murphy, Owen Roe, Patick [*sic*] Sarsfield, Red Hugh O'Donnell, Don Philip O'Sullivan Beare.[54]

The encyclopaedic expansion of the list to include incongruous references to people from world history alongside fatuous references to made-up characters who only exist as jokes derived from various kinds of discourse came later. In no small part, the moral complexity of 'Cyclops' can be attributed to a shift in Joyce's practice of parody from straightforwardly mock-heroic recontextualization to more exuberant play with a greater variety of parodic styles, and an accompanying urge towards elaboration, expansion, and encyclopaedism.

As Groden notes, Joyce 'apparently began ["Cyclops"] with the parodies and then worked on the incidents in the pub and the first-person narrator', a move

---

[51] *U* 12.181–99.
[52] *U* 12.1197, 12.1200.
[53] *U* 12.183; James Joyce, 'The Mirage of the Fisherman of Aran', in Barry and Deane, *Occasional, Critical, and Political Writing*, 203.
[54] James Joyce, '*Ulysses*: Episode 12: part I', *Little Review* VI(7) (November 1919), 42.

that would indicate the foundational role parody would henceforth play in his writing.[55] The first few scenes in the Joyce's first draft (copybook V.A.8) include early versions of mock-heroic parody passages, including 'In Inisfail the fair there lies a land, the land of holy Michan' and 'When, lo, there came about them all a great brightness.'[56] However, as Groden explains, Joyce only 'developed a sophisticated conception' of the parodic passages and 'their possible uses after he had worked on the episode for several months.'[57] As his sense of the chapter developed, Joyce seized on 'opportunities to increase the number of parody passages' and swell their proportions to fit with the theme of gigantism.[58] He also largely eliminated parodic passages that served as a means of narration so that in the final version the majority of the parodies 'halt the narration . . . and exist out of time.'[59] In the final text of 'Cyclops', mock-heroic parodies of renditions of Irish legend and myth dominate the episode at the beginning but yield to parodies of more diverse discourses, suggested by incidental details from other episodes. This technique reaches its apotheosis in the 'Black Liz' interpolation, which comes in response to the observation 'Gob, he'd have a soft hand under hen.'[60] Amid the 'Ga Ga Gara. Klook Klook Klook' of a chicken, a childish voice describes 'Black Liz . . . our hen' and reports that 'good uncle Leo . . . puts his hand under Black Liz and takes her fresh egg.'[61] The hen is very possibly one of the 'chookchooks' who is said to frighten Bloom's pussens in 'Calypso'.[62] Black Liz then reappears in one of Bloom's hallucinations in 'Circe' with the line 'Gara. Klock. Klock. Klock' before 'she sidles from her newlaid egg and waddles off' in an uncanny echo of 'Cyclops' that gestures to the constructed nature of the whole narrative, as Bloom himself could not have known the content of the parodic interpolations.[63]

Putting multiple parodies in apposition and making them bristle with internal inconsistencies, be they stylistic or indeed factual, proved a radical and provocative technique for resisting dogmatic, monocular interpretations and insisting on the knotty, historically determined complexity of present-day ideologies. It offered an active demonstration of the ways in which, in the broadest terms, literature functions as a form of parody that conditions and constructs how the real world is perceived. In this light, Joyce is the inheritor of Bakhtin's 'Second Stylistic Line', for whom the truth 'does not receive its own word—it reverberates only in the parodic and unmasking accents in which the lie is present.'[64]

---

[55] Groden, 'Ulysses' in Progress, 44.
[56] U 12.68, 12.1910; Groden, 'Ulysses' in Progress, 117–18.
[57] Groden, 'Ulysses' in Progress, 152.
[58] Groden, 'Ulysses' in Progress, 128.
[59] Groden, 'Ulysses' in Progress, 129.
[60] U 12.845.
[61] U 12.846–9, 4.31.
[62] U 4.31.
[63] U 15.3710–11, Joyce's italics.
[64] 'Discourse in the Novel', TDI 309.

204 MODERNIST PARODY

The interplay of multiple parodic perspectives in 'Cyclops' is intricate and unbalancing, refusing straightforward interpretation or easy moral truths. The citizen half-throttling his dog is not only presented as a contemporary 'Cyclops', but he is also a parodic version of Cuchulain, who was also known as the Hound of Cullan after he accidentally killed a watchdog and took its place until another could be trained. Like Finn McCool, the gigantic hunter-warrior of Irish mythology whose feats are detailed in the Fenian cycle and who was often flanked by his loyal hounds Bran and Sceolang, the citizen sits with Garryowen, a 'bloody mangy, mongrel', but appears a shabby parody by comparison.[65] Finally, the citizen as he appears in the narrator's account, is a savage caricature of the ageing Michael Cusack, a Celtophile with an aggressive temperament who was in the habit of referring to himself as 'citizen Cusack' and was often seen about Dublin drunk with a large dog by his side.[66] Cusack was an outspoken supporter of Arthur Griffith, the founder of Sinn Féin and a member of the Irish Republican Brotherhood. In his heyday, Cusack founded the Gaelic Athletic Association, but his strong personality made him a controversial figure. When he was removed from the position of secretary, he founded his own weekly paper, the short-lived *Celtic Times*, which defined itself as 'A Weekly Newspaper for the Preservation and Cultivation of the Language, Literature, Music, and Pastimes of the Celtic Race' (1887–8).[67] Cusack's obsessive Irishness is magnified and mocked by the concurrent parodies, which are gigantic in proportion and number and extend into all areas of cultural life as the ironic run of 'Irish' heroes makes abundantly clear.

As Andrew Gibson argues in *Joyce's Revenge* (2002), the mock-bardic passages of 'Cyclops' are specifically concerned with Anglo-Irish revivalist historiography, poetry, and translation, and their dependence on the kinds of heroic forms and exaggeration that were instrumental to creating a 'national historical imagination capable of returning a people to its own mythology'.[68] Gibson cites the myth-making approach of Standish James O'Grady, the author of the two-volume *History of Ireland: The Heroic Period* (1878–81), *Early Bardic Literature of Ireland* (1879) and *The Coming of Cúchulainn* (1894), who believed that 'The gigantic conceptions of heroism and strength with which the fore-front of Irish history is thronged, prove the great future of this race and land', as a prime example of the gigantism practised by Irish revivalists, who inflated the heroic qualities of their

---

[65] *U* 12.119–20.

[66] The name 'Citizen Cusack' appears in the compositional documents for 'Cyclops'. See Groden, *'Ulysses' in Progress*, 132–4.

[67] Clare Local Studies Project, *The Celtic Times: Michael Cusack's Gaelic Games Newspaper*, foreword. Micheál Ó Muircheartaigh, pref. Breandán Mac Lua, intro. Marcus De Búrca (Ennis, Co. Clare: CLASP, 2003).

[68] Andrew Gibson, *Joyce's Revenge: History, Politics, and Aesthetics in 'Ulysses'* (Oxford: Oxford University Press, 2002), 110.

tales by purging legends of their 'sordid, vulgar, and even obscene elements'.[69] By reply, Joyce presents a gigantism that is concerned with the unheroic, the trivial, and the vulgar, which, as Gibson notes, uses 'a Rabelaisian "gigantism"—a medieval and Catholic one—to criticize, modify, and indeed transform its revivalist equivalent'.[70] Gibson's key point is that the parodies of modes of Irish writing in 'Cyclops' expose the culture that produced the citizen:

> Joyce understands the citizen (historically), rather than judging him, and invites a certain understanding of him by placing him in a particular discursive context ... Joyce recognizes how far, like Griffith's, the citizen's view of history as articulated in 'Cyclops' is an extension of and conditioned by the [gigantic, revivalist] view of history so frequently adumbrated in the 'parodies'.[71]

Even the parodies that celebrate Ireland's sporting prowess point to a revivalist culture of overly exaggerated Irish excellence. In the parody of the minutes of a meeting as written up as an advertorial for an unspecified social/political organization for the columns of a newspaper, an eloquent appeal is made for the 'resuscitation of the ancient Gaelic sports and pastimes, practiced morning and evening by Finn MacCool, as calculated to revive the best traditions of manly strength and power handed down to us from ancient ages'.[72]

If Joyce's parody specifically targets the exaggerated discourses of the Anglo-Irish revival and genteel attempts to revive Ireland's ancient culture in English, it does not follow that it repudiates the Irish nationalist cause itself. Emer Nolan has rightly taken issue with the English critical tradition that automatically supposes Joyce sides with Bloom's pacifism over the citizen's militant Irish nationalism, noting the resemblance between Joyce's early political essays and the citizen's anti-colonial arguments to suggest that there are respects in which Joyce's views and the citizen's may indeed coincide.[73] The citizen is hardly ignorant of Irish history, nor incorrect in his assessment of English barbarity. When Bloom makes his understated, universal appeal to 'Love' as a remedy with which to counter 'Force, hatred, history, all that' (a neat summary of the citizen's position), Bloom's benevolent but perhaps naively sentimental appeal for toleration is mocked by the trite and gushy interpolation 'Love loves to love love . . . And this person loves that other person because everybody loves somebody but God loves everybody'.[74] The parodic stylization is triggered by the citizen's snide assessment 'Beggar my neighbour is

---

[69] Standish James O'Grady, *History of Ireland: Critical and Philosophical*, vol. I (London: Sampson Low & Co., 1881), 57, quoted in Gibson, *Joyce's Revenge*, 108; Gibson, *Joyce's Revenge*, 111.

[70] Gibson, *Joyce's Revenge*, 118.

[71] Gibson, *Joyce's Revenge*, 124.

[72] *U* 12.909–12.

[73] See Emer Nolan, *James Joyce and Nationalism* (London: Routledge, 1995), 85–119.

[74] *U* 12.1485, 12.1481, 12.1493–501.

206 MODERNIST PARODY

his [Bloom's] motto. Love, moya! He's a nice pattern of Romeo and Juliet.'[75] But whatever the limitations of the citizen's perspective on Bloom, his grasp on the brute reality of colonial occupation is firm. As Nolan notes, the chilling counterexample the citizen provides takes account of unequal power relations in a way Bloom does not: 'What about sanctimonious Cromwell and his ironsides that put the women and children of Drogheda to the sword with the bible text *God is love* pasted round the mouth of his cannon?'[76] Against such force, and the perversion of what love means, direct action may indeed have some place, which is why Nolan argues that the episode can be interpreted as '*radicalizing*' political themes.[77] She points out 'the specific parallels the drinkers draw between the position of Ireland and the plight of other colonised countries' and their identification 'with the black subjects of British imperialism' in their response to the skit in the *United Irishman* about the Zulu chief visiting England, noting 'Irish nationalism has by no means always been comfortable with this association, as the racist repudiation of it by Arthur Griffith makes plain.'[78] Nolan's reading shows how Joyce precisely historicizes nationalist attitudes, registering the historical complexities of the current political situation while also making use of parodic stylization to transcend the limited perspective of any singular viewpoint in order to provoke robust debate. It is in 'Cyclops', therefore, that Joyce makes his first sustained appearance as a 'parodist of world history', as defined by Nietzsche. In 'Cyclops' the first-person naturalistic description of the scene in Barney Kiernan's pub is repeatedly interrupted, and profoundly unsettled, as modes of historicized writing are successively 'tried on, put on, taken off, packed away, and above all *studied*' as 'costumes' that express 'moralities, articles of faith, tastes in the arts and religions'.[79] Joyce parades these costumes 'in a carnival of the grand style', embracing parody as a realm of his invention that can laugh at false historicizing while simultaneously anatomizing its effects on cultural life. The act of unpicking historical contingencies represents the first step towards imagining a future beyond their terms.

The ways in which different discourses construct what is in effect 'a parody of life' is further interrogated in 'Nausicaa', which appears to stage a return to a combination of free indirect style and interior monologue. The episode begins in the third person, in an exaggerated and obviously parodic slushy, sentimental register, and proceeds as a form of free indirect discourse, with a lexicon appropriate to 'three girl friends' who enjoy 'a cosy chat beside the sparkling waves and discuss matters feminine'.[80] It then yields to the indirect interior monologue of Gerty MacDowell, drawing on exactly the kinds of language a young woman might use

---

[75] *U* 12.1491–2.
[76] *U* 12.1507–9.
[77] Nolan, *James Joyce and Nationalism*, 87, Nolan's italics.
[78] Nolan, *James Joyce and Nationalism*, 103.
[79] Nietzsche, *Beyond Good and Evil*, 340, §223, Nietzsche's italics.
[80] *U* 13.9, 13.11–12.

under the influence of the advice columns of 'Madame Vera Verity, directress of the Woman Beautiful page of the Princess Novelette', 'the *Lady's Pictorial*', '*The Lamplighter* by Miss Cummins, author of *Mabel Vaughan* and other tales', 'the litany of Our Lady of Loreto', sentimental poetry that was 'so sad in its transient loveliness', and 'Walker's pronouncing dictionary'.[81] As Joyce explained in a letter to Frank Budgen of 3 January 1920:

> *Nausikaa* is written in a namby-pamby jammy marmalady drawsery (alto là) style with effects of incense, mariolatry, masturbation, stewed cockles, painter's palette, chit chat, circumlocution, etc., etc.[82]

The first part of the episode, as least, is every bit as sickly sweet as the overwritten 'Love loves to love love' passage in 'Cyclops', in which we first learn that 'Gerty MacDowell loves the boy that has the bicycle'.[83] Gerty, who is seated and lost in reverie, yearns for the unattainable Reggie Wylie, the boy with the bicycle whom Gerty would watch from her window as he turned his freewheel in a street where a lamplighter would do his rounds. The reference to the lamplighter puts her in mind of Cummins' lachrymose novel about a foundling who shares Gerty's first name. Gerty MacDowell then consoles herself by imagining the man she would marry, before returning the gaze of a gentleman seated at a distance with the looks of a 'matinée idol'.[84] Appearances prove deceiving in more ways than one, because the gentleman in question is later revealed to be none other than Bloom, whose greasy complexion and uneven eyes are mocked in 'Sirens' and 'Cyclops'.[85] Indeed, in 'Nausicaa' Bloom is sufficiently self-conscious about his appearance to avoid letting Gerty see him in profile.[86] He evidently has reason to be ashamed of himself, as Gerty gives him 'a pathetic little glance of piteous protest, of shy reproach under which he coloured like a girl'.[87] At the moment of revelation, Gerty is clearly no longer the sole focalizing consciousness, and readers get a sense of Bloom's indirect monologue coming through her own:

> Leopold Bloom (for it is he) stands silent, with bowed head before those young guileless eyes. What a brute he had been! At it again? A fair unsullied soul had called to him and, wretch that he was, how had he answered? An utter cad he had been! He of all men! But there was an infinite store of mercy in those eyes, for

---

[81] *U* 13.109–10, 13.151, 13.633, 13.287–8, 13.648, 13.342–3.
[82] *LJJ* I 135.
[83] *U* 12 1493–1591; 12.1494.
[84] *U* 13.417.
[85] See *U* 11.169–180; 12.841.
[86] *U* 13.836.
[87] *U* 13.742–3.

208　MODERNIST PARODY

him too a word of pardon even though he had erred and sinned and wandered. Should a girl tell? No, a thousand times no.[88]

When Gerty gets up and Bloom realizes she is lame, readers return with a thud to 'the initial style' and are once again established in Bloom's dejected and deflated interior monologue, now and then interrupted by cursory third-person commentary. Bloom reflects on what he knows about women, focusing on the very same details that seemed to define Gerty, for instance an obsession with *lingerie* ('As for undies they were Gerty's chief care').[89] When Arthur Power asked Joyce to explain what happened between Gerty and Bloom on the beach, Joyce confided 'Nothing happened between them. It all took place in Bloom's imagination.'[90] Viewed from this perspective, the use of free indirect discourse that is stylized to the point of parody in the first part of 'Nausicaa' reflects the workings of Bloom's mind as he attempts to imagine Gerty, so that his own interior monologue proceeds as if he were composing a story along the lines of '*The Mystery Man on the Beach*, the prize titbit story by Mr Leopold Bloom' that he imagined himself submitting to a magazine earlier in the day.[91]

The obvious lesson of the parody in 'Nausicaa' is that perspective is relative and fickle. The syrupy modes of expression conditioned by the kinds of popular works that contour the emotional sensibility and fashion sense of young female readers like Gerty are no more trustworthy than sentimental Anglo-Irish revivalist mythologizing. The parodically stylized discourses that compose Gerty vie and clash. The delicacy of the ladylike, pious thoughts and feelings that are attributed to Gerty sit uneasily with expressions of irritation (with Cissy Caffrey, 'a forward piece', Edy Boardman, 'the confounded little cat', the 'squalling baby', and 'the little brats of twins'), and undermine any claims she might have had for being 'as fair a specimen of winsome Irish girlhood as one could wish to see'.[92] The Gerty of *The Lamplighter* is a foundling who finds a safe, secure, loving, male guardian and is eventually rewarded for her piety and goodness of heart by marriage, but Joyce's composite parody of many different discourses of and for female betterment shows that these ideals are unattainable for a young, lame, Irish woman of Gerty Mac-Dowell's class and social standing. The observation 'Had her father only avoided the clutches of the demon drink, by taking the pledge or those powders the drink habit cured in Pearson's Weekly, she might now be rolling in her carriage second to none', acknowledges that her father's alcoholism has damaged her prospects,

---

[88] *U* 13.744–50.

[89] *U* 13.796; 13.171.

[90] Arthur Power, *Conversations with James Joyce*, ed. Clive Hart (Chicago: University of Chicago Press, 1982), 32.

[91] *U* 13.1060.

[92] *U* 13.481, 13.581, 13.404, 13.405–6, 13.80–1.

A 'BAWD OF PARODIES' 209

while nevertheless foregrounding a touchingly misplaced faith in discourses of advertising and their empty promises of transformation.[93]

For all its tricks with perspective, and its serious criticism of the many different kinds of discourse that give the lie to the idea of a woman that could be 'so flawless, so beautifully moulded' that she is 'one an artist might have dreamed of', Joyce's deliberately purple prose is also very funny.[94] His finely calibrated parodies of popular genres expose the various discourses for what they are while simultaneously flaunting their obvious attractions. Having done 'bad' Victorian novels and other popular genres of writing aimed at a female readership in 'Nausicaa', Joyce proceeded to show that he could encapsulate and thereby surpass the whole androcentric literary English tradition in 'Oxen of the Sun'.

'Oxen of the Sun' corresponds to the adventure in Homer's *Odyssey* where Odysseus's men slaughter cattle that are sacred to the sun-god Helios, giver of life. 'Oxen' takes place in the Holles Street maternity hospital, where Mina Purefoy has been in labour for three days with her ninth child. Bloom drops in out of curiosity and concern for Mina and a desire to avoid going home to Molly. He is invited in by Dr Dixon and encounters Stephen drinking with the medical students and other hangers on in the doctors' mess. The rowdy behaviour, bawdy songs, and outrageous talk of national fertilizing farms, the taking of virginities, birth control, infant mortality, and monstrous births troubles Bloom not only because it reminds him of the painful loss of his son, Rudy, but also because their callous conversation is disrespectful to Mina and the miracle of life. Joyce set out his design for the episode in a letter to Budgen of March 1920 that is worth quoting in full:

Am working hard at *Oxen of the Sun*, the idea being the crime committed against fecundity by sterilizing the act of coition. Scene: Lying-in hospital. Technique: a ninepart episode without divisions introduced by a Sallustian-Tacitean prelude (the unfertilized ovum), then by way of earliest English alliterative and monosyllabic and Anglo-Saxon ('Before born the babe had bliss. Within the womb he won worship'. 'Bloom dull dreamy heard: in held hat stony staring') then by way of Mandeville ('there came forth a scholar of medicine that men clepen etc') then Malory's *Morte d'Arthur* ('but that franklin Lenehan was prompt ever to pour them so that at the least way mirth should not lack'), then a passage solemn, as of Milton, Taylor, Hooker, followed by a choppy Latin-gossipy bit, style of Burton/Browne, then a passage Bunyanesque ('the reason was that in the way he fell in with a certain whore whose name she says is Bird-in-the-hand'). After a diary-style bit Pepys-Evelyn ('Bloom sitting snug with a party of wags, among them Dixon jun., Lynch, Doc. Madden and Stephen D. for a languor he had before and

---

[93] *U* 13.290–2.
[94] *U* 13.582–4.

210　MODERNIST PARODY

was now having dreamed a strange fancy and Mistress Purefoy there to be delivered, poor body, two days past her time and the midwives hard put to it, God send
her quick issue') and so on through Defoe-Swift and Steele-Addison-Sterne and
Landor-Pater-Newman until it ends in a frightful jumble of pidgin English, [. . .
black] English, Cockney, Irish, Bowery slang and broken doggerel. This procession is also linked back at each part subtly with some foregoing episode of the day
and, besides this, with the natural stages of development in the embryo and the
periods of faunal evolution in general. The double-thudding Anglo-Saxon motive
recurs from time to time ('Loth to move from Horne's house') to give the sense of
the hoofs of oxen. Bloom is the spermatozoon, the hospital the womb, the nurse
the ovum, Stephen the embryo.
　　How's that for High?[95]

This celebrated statement contains quotations that are slightly more developed
than those in the second extant draft of 'Oxen' and is best read as a statement of
Joyce's work-in-progress, rather than a summary of the episode as it appears in its
final form.[96] It announces that 'Oxen' will perform different phases in the historical
development of English prose style and links this forward movement to the stages
in human gestation and the processes of evolution at large, as well as the symbolic
meeting between the immature Stephen and the fatherly Bloom in the suggestive
environs of the maternity hospital.
　　The elaborate gestational parallels Joyce set out in the letter to Budgen linking
the stylistic evolution of the episode's ostensible subject (Mina Purefoy's labour
and the meeting of the young Stephen with the fatherly Bloom) to the 'natural stages of development in the embryo and the periods of faunal evolution in
general' had a basis in the cutting-edge scientific thinking of the day. Following Charles Darwin's theories of evolution, Ernst Haeckel formulated the now
discredited biogenetic law that ontogeny (the embryological development of the
individual organism) recapitulates phylogeny (the evolutionary history of the
species), a theory that was also extended to comprehend the origin and development of human language.[97] Applying this insight to 'Oxen', the notion that the
individual's development from embryo to adult passes through successive stages
in the evolutionary development of the species strongly implies that Joyce achieves
a mature style representative of a new stage in the evolutionary process by reca-
pitulating the styles of the past. Using parody to parade the apostolic succession of

---

[95] *LJJ* I 139–40. A racist term has been omitted and glossed. For discussion of the date of this letter
and its bearing on the dating of the many compositional documents of 'Oxen', see Ronan Crowley,
'Earmarking "Oxen of the Sun": On the Dates of the Copybook Drafts', *Genetic Joyce Studies* 18 (2018).
　[96] See James Joyce, *Ulysses 'Oxen of the Sun' & 'Circe': A Facsimile of Drafts, Manuscripts, and Typescripts for Episodes 14 & 15 (Part I)*, ed. Michael Groden, James Joyce Archive, vol. XVI (New York:
Garland, 1977), ix.
　[97] Ernst Haeckel, *The Riddle of the Universe at the Close of the Nineteenth Century*, trans. Joseph
McCabe (New York: Harper, 1900).

A 'BAWD OF PARODIES' 211

the male prose stylists through whose hands the progress of English language and culture has passed, Joyce asserts himself as the effective progenitor of all who went before him, and thus (by the logic of Stephen's theory in 'Scylla and Charybdis') 'the father of all his race', the writer who delivered the Irish national epic, and the supreme artist working in English.[98] The framing theory of apostolic succession, combined with the elaborate superstructure articulated in the letter to Budgen, conspire to propose that parody is the principle of textual genesis that drives the ongoing progress of literature itself.

Joyce himself referred to 'Oxen' as 'the most difficult episode in an odyssey, I think, both to interpret and to execute' in a letter to Weaver of 25 February 1920.[99] It is not surprising therefore that first-time readers are exasperated by the level of parodic stylization and the way it obfuscates the realist base (which is nevertheless painstakingly observed and consistent with previous episodes). Editors and scholars have tended to address this difficulty by dividing 'Oxen' into a series of clearly differentiated passages in the voice of individual authors or historical styles, drawing on the work of critics such as Don Gifford, who presents the episode as 'a series of imitations of prose styles presented in chronological sequence' in 'Ulysses' Annotated: Notes for James Joyce's 'Ulysses' (2008), or Robert Janusko, who used Joyce's working documents to determine a number of his literary sources and thereby compile 'A Working Outline of the "Oxen"', in which each paragraph is attributed to a named author and a month of human gestation in The Sources and Structures of James Joyce's 'Oxen' (1983).[100] Although there are local disagreements concerning where parodies begin and end the broad consensus is that 'Oxen' traces the historical 'progression' of English prose, author by author and style by style.

However, closer investigation into the genesis of 'Oxen' and its long gestation reveals that although the episode imparts the strong impression that it presents a historically consecutive progression that evokes the styles of various canonical authors in sequence, Joyce's parodic stylizations are considerably more heterogeneous than once thought, an insight that has far-reaching consequences for understanding the episode's play with literary history. Many of Joyce's compositional documents for 'Oxen' survive, including the twenty sides of preparatory notes that are among the Joyce papers deposited at the British Museum. These notesheets contain nearly 2,000 examples of historical diction, with the remaining 1,000 or so entries pertaining to embryology, the history of the English

---

[98] U 9.868–9.

[99] LJJ I 137.

[100] Gifford, 'Ulysses' Annotated, 408, n. 1; Robert Janusko, The Sources and Structures of James Joyce's 'Oxen' (Epping: Bowker 1983), 79–82. Jeri Johnson draws on Janusko and Gifford, identifying thirty-four different styles in the notes to her superb edition of the 1922 text (James Joyce, Ulysses: The 1922 Text, ed. Jeri Johnson (Oxford: Oxford University Press, 1993), 904–20). More recently, Terence Killeen has simplified Gifford's annotations in his lucid reader's guide, presenting the episode as a series of thirty-one distinct parodies (Terence Killeen, 'Ulysses' Unbound: A Reader's Companion to James Joyce's 'Ulysses' (Bray, Co. Wicklow: Wordwell, National Library of Ireland, 2005), 164–6).

212   MODERNIST PARODY

language and detail from previous episodes. They were painstakingly transcribed by Phillip F. Herring in *James Joyce's Notesheets in the British Museum* (1972).[101] 'Each notesheet is unique in appearance', as Herring notes, 'but Joyce's note-taking process is much the same on every page':

> He would start at the top left (hardly surprising) and continue on down the page. If entries were brief phrases or words, he found extra room at the right and would start a new column on that side. If the entries were long, he filled in the available space at the right and then continued on to the margins, frequently writing in every space, even if it meant making notes upside down or vertically on the page.[102]

Joyce consulted multiple authorities on the historical development of the English language and also its literatures as he prepared to write 'Oxen', taking note of quirky words and phrases that might prove useful as he prepared his parodic recitation of the historical progress of English prose. Because Joyce jotted down examples in roughly the order in which he found them and made very few changes as he went (making only occasional minor changes to match his own orthographical preferences and/or the needs of what was to be a third-person narrative), clusters of entries on the 'Oxen' notesheets provide snippets of genetic code that are unique to individual works. This practice makes it possible to identify Joyce's precise sources for particular words and phrases as they appear on the notesheets. Indeed, it is sometimes even possible to pinpoint the exact edition Joyce used, either because the volume in question is catalogued as an item in one of Joyce's personal libraries or because the precise wording points to a particular set of textual variants.

The notesheets have proved a treasure trove for 'Oxen' scholars, who have managed to find the sources for some 1,200 dictional notes to date.[103] This work

---

[101] *N* 162–264.

[102] *N* 77–8.

[103] *N* 162–264; Robert Janusko, 'The Sources and Structures of the "Oxen of the Sun" Episode of James Joyce's *Ulysses*', diss., Kent State University, 1967; J. S. Atherton, 'The Peacock in the Oxen', *Wake Newslitter* 7 (1970), 77–8; Phillip F. Herring, 'More Peacock in the Oxen', *Wake Newslitter* 9 (1971), 51–3; J. S. Atherton, 'Still More Peacock in the Oxen', *Wake Newslitter* 8 (1971), 53; Robert Janusko, *Sources and Structures of James Joyce's 'Oxen'*; Robert Janusko, 'Yet Another Anthology for "Oxen": Murison's Selections', *James Joyce Annual* 1 (1990), 117–31; Robert Janusko, 'Grave Beauty: Newman in "Oxen"', *James Joyce Quarterly* 28(3) (spring 1991), 617–21; Robert Janusko, 'Further Oxcavations: Joyce's "Oxen": Notes from Swift, Steele, Goldsmith, Landor and De Quincey', *Genetic Joyce Studies* 2 (2002), www.geneticjoycestudies.org/; Gregory Downing, 'Joyce's "Oxen of the Sun" Notesheets: A Transcription and Sourcing of the Stylistic Entries, A Compilation of the Existing Transcriptions and Sourcings, Supplemented by New Sourcing Work: first installment: notesheet 1 and the left-hand column of entries on notesheet 2', *Genetic Joyce Studies* 2 (2002), www.geneticjoycestudies.org/; Sarah Davison, 'Joyce's Incorporation of Literary Sources in "Oxen of the Sun"', *Genetic Joyce Studies* 9 (2009), www.geneticjoycestudies.org/; Harald Beck, 'Edward FitzGerald at Sea: Oxen Notesheet 17', *James Joyce Online Notes* (2013), www.jjon.org/; Sarah Davison, 'Oxtail Soup: Dialects of English in the Tailpiece of the "Oxen of the Sun" Episode of *Ulysses*', *Genetic Joyce Studies* (2014), www.geneticjoycestudies.org/; Chrissie Van Mierlo, '"Oxen of the Sun" Notesheet 17: Annotations and Commentary with a New

A 'BAWD OF PARODIES' 213

is exciting because Joyce consulted his notes with great frequency in the process of writing 'Oxen', with the result that his literary and linguistic sources can be pinpointed with forensic precision. (He typically struck through individual entries once he had incorporated them into his writing, so he could see keep an eye on the materials he had yet to use.) Although a considerable proportion of uncommon historical diction in 'Oxen' does not come by way of the extant notesheets, locating where dictional entries on the 'Oxen' notesheets have been incorporated in the 'final' text (which for these purposes is the Gabler edition) provides very privileged information about the genesis of the episode and its granular texture.

Evidence from the notesheets reveals that Joyce had a marked preference for reference works over primary editions of literary texts, as they provided readily accessible overviews of developments in the history of the English language. Studies Joyce consulted in the writing of 'Oxen' attested by the notesheets include George Saintsbury's *A History of English Prose Rhythm* (1912), an authoritative technical study of the development of English prose style from its very beginnings in Latin and Greek, via Old English, Middle English, all the way to the beginning of the nineteenth century, with excerpts from representative, canonized authors, and Richard Chenevix Trench's popular introduction to philology, *On the Study of Words* (first published in 1851, and extensively expanded and revised subsequently), which returned common words to their etymological roots.[104] Anthologies had the advantage that they introduced excerpts from the most representative and admired authors in historical sequence, presenting their own apostolic successions as manifestations of the excellence of English character and culture. For instance, Joyce made extensive use of Annie Barnett and Lucy Dale's *An Anthology of English Prose (1332–1740)* (1912), which contained excerpts that were intended 'to be companions to histories of literature', and William Peacock's anthology *English Prose from Mandeville to Ruskin* (first published in 1903), in

---

List of Sources, and Transcriptions, or Oxtail Soup: The Ingredients', *Genetic Joyce Studies* 14 (2014), www.geneticjoycestudies.org/; Sarah Davison, 'Trenchant Criticism: Joyce's Use of Richard Chenevix Trench's Philological Studies in "Oxen of the Sun"', *Joyce Studies Annual* (2014), 164–95; Sarah Davison, '"The True-Born Englishman" and the Irish Bull: Daniel Defoe in the "Oxen of the Sun" Episode of *Ulysses*', *New Quotatoes: European Joyce Studies* 25 (2016), 111–40; Chrissie Van Mierlo, 'Joyce and Malory: A Language in Transition', *New Quotatoes: European Joyce Studies* 25 (2016), 88–110.

[104] George Saintsbury, *A History of English Prose Rhythm* (London: Macmillan, 1912); Richard Chenevix Trench, *On the Study of Words*, 21st edn, rev. and ed. A. L. Mayhew (London: Kegan Paul, Trench & Trübner, 1890). Joyce's brother Stanislaus told Richard Ellmann that Joyce studied Saintsbury as he prepared 'Oxen'. Pursuing the hint, Janusko was able to identify almost 800 notesheet entries from Saintsbury. See Janusko, *Sources and Structures of James Joyce's 'Oxen'*. *On the Study of Words* was first published in 1851 but revised and enlarged many times. Evidence from the notesheets indicates that the copy Joyce used dated from between 1882 and 1892. See Davison, 'Trenchant Criticism' for detailed commentary on Joyce's use of Trench. It is highly likely that Joyce consulted further works by Trench mediating ideas about the development of the English language to a general interest audience, making direct use of Trench's insights and word lists in editions such as Richard Chenevix Trench, *English, Past and Present*, 14th edn, rev. and ed. A. L. Mayhew (London: Kegan Paul, Trench & Co., 1889).

214   MODERNIST PARODY

which Peacock announced that 'The object of the present volume of selections is to illustrate the development of English prose'.[105] Joyce also raided A. T. Martin's *Selections from Malory's Le Morte d'Arthur, edited, with introduction, notes, and glossary* (1896) and A. F. Murison's *Selections from the Best English Authors (Beowulf to the Present Time)* (1901), as well as Austin Dobson's *Eighteenth Century Studies* (1914), a source that appears on the working document known as 'Oxen of the Sun' notesheet 16.[106] Dobson (1840–1921) was a poet, biographer, and literary critic with exquisite sympathy for the eighteenth century, an age that he cherished and wrote about extensively, recreating its atmosphere through essays and character sketches of admired authors and their associates that contained beautifully stylized pastiches suffused with the spirit of the age. The fact that Joyce consulted Dobson's book of essays is therefore of especial interest because it foregrounds the ways in which Joyce's parody of literary history is squarely focused on late nineteenth- and early twentieth-century ideas about the literature of the past. Joyce's notes on Dobson serve here as a case study to provide insight into Joyce's note-taking practices and the implications for interpreting Joyce's play with historical styles.

'Oxen of the Sun' notesheet 16 is typical of the early working documents for the episode containing examples of historical words and phrases.[107] The notes include memoranda concerning key characters and details from previous chapters, as well as gatherings of words and fragmentary phrases inspired by excerpts from texts quoted in reference works (in this instance, Saintsbury) and primary editions. They are loosely organized into two columns, which fork into further columns where space allows, with the odd note squeezed in here or there. The left-hand column of notesheet 16 includes a run of fifty words/fragmentary phrases lifted or adapted from *Letters of Junius* (1772), a collection of pseudonymous, polemical attacks on the government of King George III, later identified to be the work of the Irish-born British politician Sir Philip Francis, together with the various

---

[105] Annie Barnett and Lucy Dale, *An Anthology of English Prose (1332–1740)*, pref. Andrew Lang (London: Longmans, Green & Co., 1912), iv; William Peacock, *English Prose from Mandeville to Ruskin* (London: Grant Richards, 1903), v.

[106] Thomas Malory, *Selections from Malory's 'Le Morte d'Arthur', edited, with introduction, notes, and glossary*, ed. A. T. Martin (London: Macmillan & Co.,1896); A. F. Murison, *Selections from the Best English Authors (Beowulf to the Present Time)* (London: W. & R. Chambers, 1901); *ECS*. For specific commentary on Joyce's use of individual anthologies, see Van Mierlo, 'Joyce and Malory'; Robert Janusko, 'Yet Another Anthology for "Oxen": Murison's Selections', *James Joyce Annual* 1 (1990), 117–31; Janusko, 'Another Anthology for "Oxen": Barnett and Dale'; Atherton, 'Peacock in the Oxen', 7; Atherton, 'Still More Peacock in the Oxen', 8; Herring, 'More Peacock in the Oxen'. Andrew Gibson has further proposed H. A. Treble, *English Prose: Narration, Descriptive and Dramatic* (London: Oxford University Press, 1917) and John Dover Wilson, *Life in Shakespeare's England: A Book of Elizabethan Prose* (Cambridge: Cambridge University Press, 1911) as sources of inspiration for the episode (see Gibson, *Joyce's Revenge*, 173).

[107] For a facsimile of the document Herring named 'Oxen of the Sun' notesheet 16, see *JJA* XII 34. For a transcription of 'Oxen of the Sun' notesheet 16, see *N* 242–5. For convenience, Herring's numbering for entries on the 'Oxen of the Sun' notesheets is supplied, which corresponds to the colour reproductions index in *JJA* XII 127.

A 'BAWD OF PARODIES'   215

responses they elicited.[108] Nestled nearby is a clutch of notes inspired by Edward Gibbon, another parliamentarian who served during the reign of George III. The phrases 'be affected with some pleasantry', 'conqueror who had never', and 'eloquent historian of nature' were all taken from the excepts of Gibbon's *The History of the Decline and Fall of the Roman Empire* (1776–88) and 'Memoirs' as presented for discussion by George Saintsbury in the chapter of *A History of English Prose Rhythm* on Augustan prose stylists.[109] A further set of brief notes 'all at once', 'we are arrived at', and 'heaven ... earth ... secret rivers' were adapted from Saintsbury's excerpts from De Quincey's 'Levana, or our Ladies of Sorrow', the chapter of *Suspiria de Profundis* (1845) on the Roman Goddess of childbirth and the three morbid companions he imagines for her.[110] 'Levana' would seem a promising source given the thematic considerations of 'Oxen', save for the fact that none of the snippets Joyce noted down here from De Quincey were actually incorporated in the final text.

The largest part of the remainder of fragmentary entries on notesheet 16 come from the various sketches and vignettes collected in Dobson's *Eighteenth Century Studies*, a copy of which was among the 600 or so volumes in the personal library Joyce left behind in Trieste when he moved to Paris in 1920.[111] The notes inspired by Dobson appear in the middle of notesheet 16 at the bottom and continue down the right-hand column. Whereas the De Quincey entries drawn from Saintsbury are all taken from two consecutive pages, the thirty-one snippets inspired by Dobson's essays were not entered onto the notesheets in the order of their appearance in *Eighteenth Century Studies*, suggesting that in this case Joyce flicked through the pages, turning them back and forth, and jotting down any words, phrases and grammatical constructions that caught his fancy, without being overly concerned as to where they came from or how they signified within their original context.

The notes Joyce made on Dobson are as follows: 'quidnuncs';[112] 'milksop';[113] 'Walpole French';[114] 'fond of travelling';[115] 'time was';[116] 'I played, I am, I—';[117]

---

[108] See Janusko, *Sources and Structures*, 147–51.

[109] *N* 16.42–3, 16.44, 16.45; see Janusko, *Sources and Structures*, 99.

[110] *N* 16.54, 16.55, 16.56; see Saintsbury, *History of English Prose Rhythm*, 313, 313, 316.

[111] For the catalogue of books in Joyce's Trieste library, see Ellmann, *Consciousness of Joyce*, 107.

[112] *N* 16.47; the word appears three times in Dobson: 'Lady Mary Coke', *ECS*, 61; 'The Covent Garden Journal', *ECS*, 158; 'The Story of the Spectator', *ECS*, 179; and is worked into the text of 'Oxen' in the guise of 'sir Milksop Quidnunc' (*U* 14.662–3), who Mulligan cites as an example of a character who is devoted to idle pleasures.

[113] *N* 16.48; 'Covent Garden Journal', *ECS*, 155; *U* 14.663.

[114] *N* 16.49; see 'But the terrible object lesson of the French Revolution proved as disturbing to Mason as to Walpole' in 'Gray's Biographer', *ECS*, 294.

[115] *N* 16.50; see 'fond of stimulating' in 'Boswell's Predecessors and Editors', *ECS*, 137.

[116] *N* 16.58; 'The Journal to Stella', *ECS*, 13; *U* 14.118.

[117] *N* 16.62; see 'I play'd at Quadrille with Madame de Viry, &c .... At cards I am superstitious, & as it is only at play 'tis pardonable' in 'Lady Mary Coke', *ECS*, 70.

216 MODERNIST PARODY

'pumproom';[118] 'cut bob';[119] 'place of worship';[120] 'John Dory';[121] 'deserted village';[122] 'pad';[123] 'abigail';[124] 'Mr Commissioner Smollett';[125] 'fuddled';[126] 'rasp';[127] 'plaguily';[128] 'gentleman's gentleman';[129] 'perennial';[130] 'a footman (virtuous) who';[131] 'circumspect';[132] 'shed a pint of tears';[133] 'progress various & doubtful';[134] 'retrospect';[135] '?Whose are ?not of Elia';[136] 'quit';[137] 'coxcomb'.[138] Details of the essays that inspired these entries, together with details of the six entries that were scattered across the 'final' text of 'Oxen' can be found below in the footnotes. These fragmentary words and phrases look strikingly unpromising in their raw form, as indeed do all of the lists of 'period' diction on the 'Oxen' notesheets. Eighteenth-century-ish words such as 'coxcomb', 'quidnuncs', and 'milksop' have been torn from their contexts without regard to their origins, save for their broad historical savour, and mixed with snippets derived either from Dobson's own attempts at eighteenth-century pastiche or the primary material he briefly quoted.

Early compositional documents such as notesheet 16 suggest that Joyce was moving beyond the initial outline of the chapter he showed off to Budgen even at

---

[118] *N* 16.64; 'Pump-room' appears seven times in *ECS*, of which five instances appear in 'The Topography of "Humphry Clinker"', 37–9.

[119] *N* 16.65; 'Humphry Clinker', *ECS*, 39, 41; *U* 14.497.

[120] *N* 16.66 (Herring transcribes this notesheet entry as 'John ?Darcy'); see 'places of worship' in 'Humphry Clinker', *ECS*, 46.

[121] *N* 16.67; see 'his (and Fielding's) favourite John Dory' in 'Humphry Clinker', *ECS*, 40.

[122] *N* 16.68; see 'But Cradock was only twelve years junior to the author of the "Deserted Village"' in 'Mr. Cradock of Gumley', in *ECS*, 218.

[123] *N* 16.69; see 'she must likewise have fine clothes, her chaise, or pad, with country lodgings' in 'Humphry Clinker', *ECS*, 42.

[124] *N* 16.69; see 'an antiquated Abigail, dressed in her lady's cast-clothes' in 'Humphry Clinker', *ECS*, 39.

[125] *N* 16.70; 'Mr. Commissioner Smollett's' appears in 'Humphry Clinker', *ECS*, 49.

[126] *N* 16.71; 'Journal to Stella', *ECS*, 10.

[127] *N* 16.71; 'Journal to Stella', *ECS*, 11.

[128] *N* 16.72; 'Journal to Stella', *ECS*, 12; *U* 14.672.

[129] *N* 16.73; 'Journal to Stella', *ECS*, 12; 'gentleman's gentleman' is used to describe Mulligan (*U* 14.495).

[130] *N* 16.75; 'Story of the Spectator', *ECS*, 187.

[131] *N* 16.76; 'Richardson at Home', *ECS*, 22; inspires the phrase 'a linkboy (virtuous)' (*U* 14.895).

[132] *N* 16.77; 'circumspect' appears three times in *ECS*, of which the most likely source is 'the little figure of Richardson, shuffling along, circumspect and timorous shed a pint of tears' ('Richardson at Home', 28) because it is closest to the snippet positioned directly above on notesheet 16.

[133] *N* 16.78; 'Richardson at Home', *ECS*, 28 and 31; 'shed a pint of tears' is used to describe Lenehan's father's habitual reaction to seeing his son in straitened circumstances (*U* 14.565).

[134] *N* 16.79; see 'As they progress, they record more than one of the various attempts at advancement with which their writer, egged on by his ambition and his embarrassments, is perpetually pre-occupied' in 'The Latest Life of Steele', *ECS*, 120.

[135] *N* 16.85; 'Journal to Stella', *ECS*, 16.

[136] *N* 16.86; see 'In Lamb's day, Shaftesbury was classed with Sir William Temple as a model in the "genteel" way in writing; but as "Elia" himself employs the same epithet for Watteau' ("Graceful as Raphael, as Watteau genteel"), it is manifest that the word must then have borne a significance different from the ignoble one which it is now held to suggest' in 'Titled Authors', *ECS*, 171. 'Elia' was the pseudonym of Charles Lamb.

[137] *N* 16.87; 'Humphry Clincker', *ECS*, 37.

[138] *N* 16.89; see 'coxcombry' in 'Covent Garden Journal', *ECS*, 158.

A 'BAWD OF PARODIES'   217

an early notetaking stage in the writing process. They reveal that Joyce was treating the sources he consulted at the notetaking stage in the composition of 'Oxen' as lexicons rather than literary texts: in the main, he gathered words and fragmentary phrases that were somehow evocative of particular phases in the historical development of English prose, rather than searching for quotations that could be deployed as specific allusions that would direct readers to particular passage for comparative analysis.

The only notesheet with a clear, consistent, conceptual framework that contains examples of historical diction that are sufficiently orderly to facilitate the recapitulation of precise phases in the embryological development of English literature as initiated by particular authors set out in the letter to Budgen is 'Oxen of the Sun' notesheet 1.[139] This notesheet contains examples of vocabulary drawn from Defoe and Swift that were systematically culled from excerpts from Defoe, in Barnett and Dale, and then Peacock, a primary edition of Defoe's *Colonel Jack*, and then a primary edition of Swift's *Tale of a Tub, The Battle of the Books and other Satires*.[140] What makes notesheet 1 unique is that the columns of literary notes are arranged around nine concentric rings that represent months in the growth of the human embryo, the sixth of which being distinguished by a star at its apex. It is possible that the star marks Defoe-Swift's place in the guiding embryological design, Defoe being the father of English realism and Swift the Irish satirist and skilled parodist who wrote *A Tale of a Tub*, two authors whose work defined opposing tendencies in a golden age of English letters.

However, diction inspired by Defoe and Swift is not confined to notesheet 1.[141] 'Oxen of the Sun' notesheet 2 contains further overspill entries from *Colonel Jack* and then a long string of entries culled from various late seventeenth- and early eighteenth-century authors anthologized in Peacock's *English Prose from Mandeville to Ruskin* (Jeremy Taylor, Richard Baxter, Abraham Cowley, John Evelyn, John Bunyan, George Savile, John Dryden, and Samuel Pepys) and some fifty discrete entries from Martin's *Selections from Malory's 'Le Morte d'Arthur'*.[142] Further entries inspired by Defoe, this time *Moll Flanders*, appear on notesheet 6.[143] Notes on Swift's *Tale of A Tub* spill on to the mixed bag that is 'Oxen of the Sun' notesheet 3, which also contains overlapping sequences of notes harvested from the excerpts from: Swift, in Barnett and Dale; Swift's *Polite Conversation*; Raphael Holinshed in Peacock; Trench's *On The Study of Words*; Lord Berners in Peacock, Barnet and Dale and Saintsbury; Sir Thomas Elyot in Peacock and Barnet and Dale; Sir Philip Sidney in Peacock and Barnett and Dale; Sir Walter Raleigh in Peacock and Barnet

---

[139] N 162–5 (*JJA* XII 23).

[140] For full transcription, sourcing, and commentary see Downing, 'Joyce's "Oxen of the Sun" Notesheets'.

[141] See Downing, 'Joyce's "Oxen of the Sun" Notesheets'.

[142] See Downing, 'Joyce's "Oxen of the Sun" Notesheets'; Van Mierlo, 'Joyce and Malory'.

[143] See Davison, '"The True-Born Englishman" and the Irish Bull', 120–1.

218   MODERNIST PARODY

and Dale; John Florio in Peacock; Fulke Greville, in Barnett and Dale; Richard Hakluyt in Peacock and Barnet and Dale; Saint John Fisher in Saintsbury; Sir Thomas More in Peacock; and Sir Thomas North in Peacock.[144] The sheer proliferation of fragmentary notes would have made it impossible to keep track of the origins of every word or phrase, even for a man with Joyce's prodigious powers of memory.[145] Clearly, Joyce's notetaking practices were much more suited to recreating generic period styles as contoured by the tastes and opinions of late nineteenth- and early twentieth-century literary anthologists, philologists, grammarians, and historians, than they were to constructing *ad hominem* parodies. Even at the notetaking stage in the writing process, Joyce was no longer thinking in terms of executing a pedantically correct author-by-author recapitulation of the apostolic succession of English prose stylists but slaying the sacred cows of the English literary tradition, wherein imperialist historical narratives were presented as universally accepted truths.

The mixed nature of the notesheets is reflected in the final texture of the parodic stylizations in 'Oxen', which busily reverberate with snippets drawn from diverse sources. For instance, previous critics agree that lines depicting Bloom's arrival at the maternity hospital are written after the manner of Sir John Mandeville.[146] The first paragraph deemed to be in the style of Mandeville certainly has a fine Middle English flavour. It depicts the moment when Bloom recognizes Dixon in the doctors' mess from the time that he attended the hospital to receive treatment for a bee sting, and Dixon invites him to join them in their merriment, but it reimagines the scenario with mock-heroic brio. Bloom becomes a travelling knight, the hospital is transformed into a castle, and an old injury caused by a bee sting is figured as a wound inflicted by the spear of a dragon. While all motifs that could be said to be Mandevillean, they are of course also staple tropes of chivalric literature more broadly. The granular breakdown of words and phrases gleaned from various sources (as attested by evidence from 'Oxen of the Sun' notesheets 2 and 7, which were primary compositional documents for this passage) goes some way towards explaining how Joyce stylized his prose. In the quotation below, words and phrases that have a precedent in the notesheets are italicized, with name of the author(s) who inspired them given in bold. Specific details of the notes Joyce made and his original sources can be found in the footnotes. Words discussed by Trench in his various works are also flagged because it is clear from the frequency with which Joyce deploys examples of vocabulary that Trench found historically telling

---

[144] For a detailed list of literary sources for the entries on notesheet 3, see Davison, 'Joyce's Incorporation of Literary Sources in "Oxen of the Sun"'. Further clusters of notes deriving from Swift have also been found on notesheets 8, 14, and 15.

[145] According to Sylvia Beach, Joyce possessed 'a memory that retained everything he had ever heard', Sylvia Beach and James Laughlin, *Shakespeare and Company*, 2nd edn (Lincoln, NE: University of Nebraska Press, 1991), 71.

[146] *U* 14.123–66.

A 'BAWD OF PARODIES'   219

that Joyce had Trench's philological studies to hand and consulted them repeatedly while he was writing 'Oxen'. In this respect, Joyce was much like the Stephen of *Stephen Hero*, who scoured the works of Trench's successor, the great Anglo-Saxon and Middle English philologist William Walter Skeat, and read 'Skeat's *Etymological Dictionary* by the hour'.[147]

And whiles they spake the door of the *castle* [**Mandeville, Trench**][148] was opened and there *nighed* [**Malory**][149] them a mickle noise as of many that sat there at *meat* [**Trench**][150]. And there came against the place as they stood a young learningknight *yclept* [**Mandeville, Trench**][151] Dixon. And the traveller Leopold was *couth* [**Trench**][152] to him sithen *it had happed* [**Malory**][153] that they had *had ado* each *with* other [**Malory**][154] in the house of *misericord* [**Trench**][155] where this learningknight lay by cause the traveller Leopold came there to be healed for he was sore wounded in his breast by *a spear wherewith a horrible and dreadful dragon was smitten him* [**Malory**][156] for which *he did do make* [**Malory**][157] a salve of volatile salt and chrism as much as he might suffice. And he said now that he should go in to that castle *for to* [**Mandeville**][158] make merry with them that were there. And the traveller Leopold said that he should go otherwhither for he was a

[147] James Joyce, *Stephen Hero*, ed. J. Slocum and Herbert Cahoon (New York: New Directions, 1955), 26. Over 120 words that were of signal interest to Trench as instructive landmarks in the historical development of the English language appear in 'Oxen' in some form, of which more than fifty appear in the notesheets, suggesting Joyce was actively looking for the archaic words Trench glossed in the literary sources that he canvassed. For commentary on the proliferation of Trench in 'Oxen of the Sun', see Davison, 'Trenchant Criticism'.

[148] See 'a full fair castle and a strong' (*N* 7.104 and Sir John Mandeville, in Peacock, *English Prose from Mandeville to Ruskin*, 3) and 'clept the castle of Sparrowhawk' (Mandeville, in Peacock, *English Prose*, 4). Castle is a Norman word, dating from the eleventh-century invasion of England by the French, discussed by Trench, *On the Study of Words*, 129.

[149] See 'he nighed it so nigh' (*N* 2.57). This exact phrase appears in Martin's discussion of verbs in *Selections from Malory's Morte D'Arthur* (London: Macmillan, 1896), 192.

[150] According to Trench, 'all food was once called "meat"' (Trench, *English, Past and Present*, 311).

[151] See 'clept' (*N* 7.102) and 'clept the castle of Sparrowhawk' (Mandeville, in Peacock, *English Prose*, 4). See also 'yclept' in *English, Past and Present*, 251.

[152] Trench noted that 'the negative [uncouth] survives while the affirmative is gone' in *English, Past and Present*, 211–12.

[153] See 'it happed me' (*N* 7.36). The exact phrase appears in Sir Thomas Malory in Peacock, *English Prose*, 10.

[154] See 'had ado with' (*N* 7.48) and 'hath ado with' and 'have ado with' in Malory, in Barnett and Dale, *An Anthology of English Prose*, 7.

[155] Trench notes that Chaucer uses French words such as 'misericorde' in *English Past and Present*, 100.

[156] See 'a spear wherewith he was smitten him' (*N* 2.66). The exact phrase appears in *Selections from Malory's Morte D'Arthur*, 82. Martin comments on the syntax of this phrase in his discussion of verbs on 191–2.

[157] See 'he did do make' (*N* 2.58). The exact phrase appears in *Selections from Malory's Morte D'Arthur*, 16. And, again, the syntax is noteworthy enough for Martin to comment on this phrase in his discussion of verbs on 191.

[158] See 'Say them, for to be slain' (*N* 7.97) and 'say to them . . . for to be slain', which appears in editions of the Cotton text of *The Travels of John Mandeville* in modern spelling, for instance (London: Macmillan, 1905), 184.

220   MODERNIST PARODY

man of cautels and a subtile.[159] Also the lady was of his *avis* [**Mandeville**][160] and *repreved*[161] the learningknight though *she trowed well that the traveller had said* [**Mandeville**][162] *thing that was false* [**Chaucer**][163] for his subtility. But the learningknight would not hear say nay nor do her *mandement* [**Wycliffe?**][164] ne have him in aught *contrarious to his list* [**Mandeville**][165] and he said how it was a marvellous castle. And the traveller Leopold went into the castle *for to* [**Mandeville**][166] rest him for a space being *sore of limb* [**Malory**][167] *after many marches environing* [**Mandeville**][168] in divers lands and sometime venery.[169]

While a good deal of the diction can be traced back to Mandeville, the paragraph is enlivened by words that can be traced back to other near contemporary voices, as well as a number of words that Trench deemed historically telling. If the parodic stylization proceeds 'by way of Mandeville' and his *Travels* then it passes by many other authors *en route*.

While our knowledge of Joyce's sources for the literary and linguistic entries on the notesheets is not yet complete, no single paragraph in 'Oxen' could be described as univocal. All draw on diverse sources even if they might give the impression that there is one singular author's voice that is particularly foregrounded. Nor is there an especial effort to preserve any semblance of chronological order in terms of the diction Joyce harvested from different periods. For instance, fragments derived from works by Swift are incorporated in the text of 'Oxen' as early as the phrase 'covey of wags, likely brangling fellows' to describe the men Bloom sits with (Dixon, Lynch, Madden, Lenehan, and Stephen) and as late as 'Doctor Diet and Doctor Quiet' in the paragraph in which the medical students head off to Burke's pub and Bloom stays behind to talk to Nurse Callaghan, whom he realizes is pregnant.[170] Indeed, this section, which imparts the general

---

[159] See 'he was full of cautels and subtle deceits', in Mandeville in Peacock, *English Prose*, 4, for which there is no precedent in the 'Oxen' notesheets.

[160] See 'avis' (*N* 7.123) and 'avys' in Mandeville, in Barnett and Dale, *An Anthology*, 2.

[161] See 'repreved' (*N* 7.145).

[162] See 'and he trowed that they had said sooth' (*N* 7.110) and 'And he trowed that they had said sooth' in Mandeville, *Travels of John Mandeville*, 95.

[163] See 'thing that was false' (*N* 7.117) and 'thyng that is fals' in Geoffrey Chaucer, in Barnett and Dale, *An Anthology*, 5.

[164] 'Mandement' does not appear on the notesheets, but it does appear in a passage from Saintsbury's selections from John Wycliffe's *Sermons* that provides inspiration for six notesheet entries. See Saintsbury, *History of English Prose Rhythm*, 62.

[165] See 'contrarious to his list' (*N* 7.96). The exact phrase appears in Mandeville, *Travels of John Mandeville*, 184.

[166] See n. 158 above.

[167] See 'sore of limb' (*N* 7.29), possibly inspired by 'bruised sore' in Malory in Peacock, *English Prose*, 9, since adjacent notesheet entries were also inspired by Peacock's selections from Malory.

[168] See 'unto his own marches environing' (*N* 7.109) and 'that he was come again environing, that is to say, going about, unto his own marches' in Mandeville, *Travels of John Mandeville*, 123.

[169] *U* 14.123–40.

[170] See 'a covey of' (*N* 15.64) with 'the votaries not flying in coveys, but sorted in couples', in Jonathan Swift, 'The Mechanical Operation of the Spirit', in Jonathan Swift, *A Tale of a Tub, The Battle of the Books*

A 'BAWD OF PARODIES' 221

impression that it is styled after the manner of nineteenth-century prose, provides another instructive example of how Joyce combines words and phrases from different authors to assert his freedom to draw on any stage in the history of English, in this case Shelley, Thomas Carlyle, John Ruskin, Swift, Heinrich Baumann, and John Gibson Lockhart:

The door! *It is open?* [**Shelley**][171] Ha! They are out, *tumultuously* [**Carlyle**][172], off for *a minute's race* [**Ruskin**][173], all bravely legging it, Burke's of Denzille and Holles *their ulterior goal* [**Carlyle**][174]. Dixon follows *giving them sharp language* [**Carlyle**][175] but raps out an oath, he too, and on. Bloom stays with nurse a thought to send a kind word to happy mother and nurseling up there. Doctor Diet and Doctor Quiet [**Swift**][176]. Looks she too not other now? Ward of watching in Horne's house has told its tale in that *washedout* [**Baumann**][177] pallor. Then *all being gone* [**Carlyle**][178], *a glance of motherwit* [**Lockhart**][179] helping, he whispers close in going: Madam, when comes the storkbird for thee?[180]

Of course, Joyce's hint in the letter to Budgen that 'The double-thudding Anglo-Saxon motive recurs from time to time' and his liberal use of hyphens suggests that he was already thinking in terms of blending and fusing different voices at a local level, even if hybrids such as 'Defoe-Swift' and 'Pepys-Evelyn' by no means reveal the enmeshed richness of the final text of 'Oxen'.

---

and other Satires (London: J. M. Dent & Sons, 1916), 185; *U* 14.505; see 'Doctor Diet' (*N* 3.8) and '—Quiet' (*N* 3.9) with 'And the best doctors in the world are Doctor Diet, Doctor Quiet, and Doctor Merryman', in Jonathan Swift, 'A Complete Collection of Genteel and Ingenious Conversation—In Three Dialogues', in *Tale of a Tub*, 307; *U* 14.1402.

[171] See 'it is open?' (*N* 19.91) with 'It is open to the blue sky?' in Percy Bysshe Shelley, in Peacock, *English Prose from Mandeville to Ruskin*, 317.

[172] See 'tumultuously eddy' (*N* 19.92) with 'would the eddying vapour gather, and there tumultuously eddy, and flow down like a mad witch's hair', from Thomas Carlyle quoted in Saintsbury, *History of English Prose Rhythm*, 365, and discussed by Saintsbury as an example of 'poetic inversion', 367.

[173] See 'within a minute's race' (*N* 20.64) with 'within three minutes' race' from John Ruskin quoted in Saintsbury, *History of English Prose Rhythm*, 399.

[174] See 'their ulterior goal' (*N* 20.54) with 'their ulterior business', in Carlyle, in Murison, *Selections from the Best English Authors*, 391.

[175] See 'giving him sharp languages' (*N* 20.52) with 'giving him and others very sharp language', in Carlyle, in Murison, *Selections from the Best English Authors*, 391.

[176] See n. 170 above.

[177] See 'seedy & washed out' (*N* 17.57). The phrase appears in Heinrich Baumann, *Londinismen (Slang und Cant): Wörterbuch der Londoner Volkssprache sowie der Üblichsten Gauner-, Matrosen-, Sport- und Zunftausdrücke; mit Einleitung und Musterstücken; ein Supplement zu allen Englisch-Deutschen Wörterbuchern* (Berlin-Schoneberg: Langenscheidtsche Verlagsbuchhandlug, n. d. (c. 1902)), xxii.

[178] See 'All being gone out' (*N* 20.56). The exact phrase appears in Carlyle, in Murison, *Selections from the Best English Authors*, 391.

[179] See 'glances of motherwit' (*N* 19.98) with 'glances of mother-wit', in John Gibson Lockhart, in Peacock, *English Prose from Mandeville to Ruskin*, 324.

[180] *U* 14.1398–1406. Italics indicate words and phrases for which secure sources have been identified via evidence from the notesheets. Original authors are given in parentheses in bold.

222   MODERNIST PARODY

Indeed, 'Oxen' is studded with many hints that miscellany and misattribution guide the exploitation of English prose style. Bloom's sad reverie is introduced by the words 'The voices blend and fuse', suggestive of the fusion of literary voices in the episode.[181] The narrative pauses to reflect that 'The high hall of Horne's house had never beheld an assembly so representative and so varied nor had the old rafters of that establishment ever listened to a language so encyclopedic'.[182] And the whole episode declares itself to be a 'chaffering allincluding most farraginous chronicle', a contradiction in terms, 'chronicle' designating a detailed and continuous register of events in order of time, a historical record, especially one in which the facts are narrated without philosophical treatment or any attempt at literary style, and 'farraginous' conceding it to be a mixture nonetheless, specifically the mixture of grains in cattle feed.[183]

Groden has suggested that Joyce's 'notesheets, drafts, and revisions on the typescripts and proofs reveal a man always searching for a well-defined controlling order, but the episodes after "Oxen of the Sun" often refused to remain within the ordering design he planned for them'.[184] Exploring the genesis of 'Oxen' reveals that it was in fact deliberately executed in violation of its initial design, a circumstance that poses serious challenges to conventional readings of the episode which are premised on the integrity of the pedantic parallels between history, language, human gestation, and birth. In his 1907 essay entitled 'James Clarence Mangan', Joyce wrote that 'Poetry takes little account of many of the idols of the marketplace, the succession of the ages, the spirit of the age, the mission of the race', arguing that the 'essential effort of the poet is to liberate himself from the unpropitious influences of such idols which corrupt him from the inside and out'.[185] Borrowing freely from the full sweep of literary history liberates 'Oxen' from false idols like 'the succession of the ages' and the 'spirit of the age', gesturing both to the past and the future, militating against the idea of a straightforward teleological progression by delaying if not derailing the forward historical movement of the episode. 'Oxen' takes for granted that the achievements of great male writers are imprinted on the genetic code that makes up literature in English. But far from passing through successive stages in the evolutionary development of the species as it matured, even at the note-taking stage 'Oxen' evolved beyond recapitulation towards recombination, freely reworking the evolutionary stages through which English prose has passed, refusing to capitulate to the nightmare that is history or the notion of apostolic succession as enshrined by the early twentieth-century anthologists who promoted imperialist accounts of England's narrative heritage. The episode is thus very much a product of its own moment: at no other stage

[181] *U* 14.1078.
[182] *U* 14.1201–3.
[183] *U* 14.1412.
[184] Groden, *'Ulysses' in Progress*, 52.
[185] James Joyce, 'James Clarence Mangan (1907)', in *Occasional, Critical, and Political Writing*, 135.

in history could a writer clothe himself in the costumes of the past so effectively, imitating the styles that were now readily accessible in an age where the richness of the archive of literary history had been made newly available through critical editions, scholarly commentaries, and anthologies.

Despite the level of heteroglossia that is present at a local level, one of the great paradoxes of 'Oxen' is that readers are nonetheless apt to feel that paragraphs are written under the aegis of particular writers (Mandeville and Carlyle respectively in the passages quoted above). In *A Portrait* Stephen asks himself 'Did he then love the rhythmic rise and fall of words better than their associations of legend and colour?'[186] Although Stephen is undecided, it seems that Joyce was no less fervent than Saintsbury in his belief that prose rhythm and auditive effects are decisive factors in style, which is not simply a matter of content, vocabulary, or isolated turns of phrase. When readers respond to Joyce's parodic stylizations without knowledge of the notesheets or Joyce's source materials, they respond not only to literary evocations of characteristic topics or modes but also Joyce's wonderfully inventive syntax. It is testament to Joyce's supreme talent as a mimic and his exceptional ear for the distinctive cadences of celebrated stylists that, for all its granular anachronisms, miscellaneous micro-quotations, and echoes, 'Oxen of the Sun' nonetheless imparts the unshakeable impression that it does indeed mime the broad historical progression of English prose style and that amid Joyce's bravura performance the voices of great English authors can be discerned.

Joyce does not defer to his sources, nor do his parodic stylizations pass satirical judgement on the literary qualities of authors' works. Instead, they foreground Joyce's masterful primacy over his materials, presenting parody as the arena in which Joyce's original creativity has a future that will dictate the progress of English literature beyond imperial narratives of history. This is the future that is projected in the final paragraphs of the episode, where the language of the present day is figured through dialects of English. Joyce's performance as a parodist of history in 'Oxen' culminates in the development of an English that is open to creative deformation and an influx of racial and regional dialects and loan words from across the globe. When Joyce informed Budgen that the high-spirited stampede through the historical styles of English prose would be succeeded by 'a frightful jumble of pidgin English, [... black] English, Cockney, Irish, Bowery slang and broken doggerel' he was as good as his word in at least one respect, because the last paragraphs of 'Oxen' are frightfully jumbled to the extent that heavy glossing is required to render the underlying action intelligible.[187] When the historical pageant of English prose crashes into the present day and the drunken young men assembled in the doctor's mess spill out on to the street and head for Burke's, the narrative switches codes in such quick succession that the effect is positively vertiginous. Again, evidence

---

[186] Joyce, *A Portrait of the Artist as a Young Man*, 140.
[187] *U* 14.1440–591.

224 MODERNIST PARODY

from the notesheets regarding Joyce's sources for the episode is richly revealing for understanding how he conceived of this section of 'Oxen'.

Many of the examples of the extraordinary variety of regional dialect, pidgin English, and slang that were destined for the tail end of 'Oxen' were entered on to 'Oxen of the Sun' notesheet 17 (which also contains some notes on birth control methods in Italian).[188] Attested sources include: Heinrich Baumann, *Londinismen (Slang und Cant)* (1902), a guide to London dialect, cant and slang for German speakers; Thomas Burke, *Limehouse Nights: Tales of Chinatown* (1917), a set of stories set in the Chinatown district that occupied Limehouse in London's East End; Joseph Crosby Lincoln, *Cap'n Eri: A Story of the Coast* (1904), a popular novel by an American writer whose numerous stories in a fictionalized Cape Cod, which provided some salty examples of New England nautical dialect and terminology; Edward FitzGerald, 'Sea Words and Phrases from the Suffolk Coast' in *East Anglian, or, Notes and Queries on Subjects Connected with the Countries of Suffolk, Cambridge, Essex, and Norfolk* (1869); John Oswald Francis, *Change: A Glamorgan Play in Four Acts* (1910), concerning the social, economic and religious changes that are afoot in a South Wales coalmining town; Bret Harte, *Tales of the West* (1902), a set of nine sensational stories set on American's central frontier, as well as a series of his parodic 'Condensed Novels'.[189] While this gathering of sources looks eclectic, the logic behind their selection can assist in interpreting the most challenging passages of the most difficult episode of *Ulysses*.

The rationale underlying Joyce's selection of regional and dialect source texts for the 'frightful jumble' is indicated by the underlined word 'Sea', which is positioned at the head of notesheet 17.[190] Of the seafaring slang Joyce garnered from FitzGerald, only the terms 'armstrong halloring', 'Horry war', and 'query', are subsumed in some form in the 'frightful jumble' at the end of 'Oxen'.[191] A further cluster of dialect words and phrases from another literary source with a coastal setting are derived from the dialogue presented in the first few pages of *Cap'n Eri*. Lincoln himself was descended from a long line of seafarers and he set his bestselling verse and fiction along the Cape Cod shoreline. *Cap'n Eri*, his first novel, is a simple, humorous tale about the lives of three former sea captains who have given up long voyages

---

[188] *JJA* XII 39.

[189] For a semi-diplomatic transcription and detailed source list, see Van Mierlo, '"Oxen of the Sun": Notesheet 17: Commentary and Annotations with a New List of Sources, and Transcriptions, or Oxtail Soup: The Ingredients'. For an expanded discussion of these sources, see Davison, 'Oxtail Soup'.

[190] *N* 17.1.

[191] 'All off for a buster, armstrong, hollering down the street' (*U* 14.1440), see 'armstrong halloring' (*N* 17.2) and 'Arm in arm, "they came hallorin' down the street *Armstrong*"' (Edward FitzGerald, 'Sea Words and Phrases from the Suffolk Coast', in *East Anglian, or, Notes and Queries on Subjects Connected with the Countries of Suffolk, Cambridge, Essex, and Norfolk*, vol. 3 (1869), 207); 'Horryvar, mong vioo' (*U* 14.1522), see 'Horry war' (*N* 17.8) and FitzGerald, who notes that the word 'Horrywaur' is 'Au revoir' mispronounced (FitzGerald, 'Sea Words', 217); 'Query' (*U* 14.1465), see 'query' (*N* 17.9), also in FitzGerald, 'Sea Words', 219. For further details see Beck, 'Edward FitzGerald at Sea: Oxen notesheet 17'.

A 'BAWD OF PARODIES' 225

and are adjusting to life on land. The captains speak in a bracing Cape Cod dialect (represented through non-standard spelling, dropped consonants, and substituted vowels), enriched with maritime slang. It was this non-standard dialect that caught Joyce's attention as he took notes on the novel. Evidently, it was such a good source of vocabulary that Joyce returned to the text because a further three sequences of notes from *Cap'n Eri* appear on 'Oxen of the Sun' notesheet 20, which faces notesheet 17.[192] Joyce was particularly attracted to nautical terminology ('abaft', 'catch aholt', 'ship long of me') and ejaculations ('Thunderation', 'By gum'), but there is precious little that would firmly anchor the expressions he has gathered from *Cap'n Eri* to their source.[193] Joyce simply treated Lincoln's work as a lexicon that conveniently gathered examples of American coastal slang from the eastern seaboard. And it appears, as is so often the case with Joyce's source texts, that more of *Cap'n Eri* made its way into 'Oxen' than appeared on the notesheets, as there is an echo of the wording of the final chapter 'Dime-Show Bus'ness' when Alexander J Christ Dowie proclaims 'The Deity aint no nickel dime bumshow. I put it to you that He's on the square and a corking fine business proposition.'[194]

The importance of the sea as a zone with its own distinctive oral culture is emphasized by the subtitle of another of Joyce's primary sources for the tail of 'Oxen'—*Londinismen (Slang und Cant): Wörterbuch der Londoner Volkssprache sowie der Üblichsten Gauner-, Matrosen-, Sport- und Zunftausdrücke; mit Einleitung und Musterstücken; ein Supplement zu allen Englisch-Deutschen Wörterbuchern* [a dictionary of London vernacular and the most common criminal-, sailor-, and sports-guild expressions; with introduction and samples; a supplement to all English-German dictionaries]. Joyce took notes on many choice examples of cockney slang and cant that were glossed for German readers in the discursive introduction to *Londonismen* (in which many of the notable words and expressions discussed have been taken from popular English ballads and poems through the ages) and also the 'Wörterbuch der Londoner Volkssprache' (an alphabetized dictionary of popular speech). For instance, Joyce noted down the phrase 'of they sailors' from 'I be of they sailors who think 'tis no lie' by Charles Dibdin, whose sentimental, patriotic songs of the sea were officially appropriated for the use of the British navy during the Napoleonic wars, and are freighted with the history of British conquest overseas.[195] Joyce then

---

[192] *JJA* XII 38, 39.

[193] 'Abaft there!' (*U* 14.1452), see 'abaft' (*N* 17.37), which appears in Joseph Crosby Lincoln, *Cap'n Eri: A Story of the Coast* (New York: Burt & Co., 1912), 7; 'Catch aholt' (*U* 14.1493), see 'catch aholt' (*N* 20.1) and 'Catch a-holt now' (Lincoln, *Cap'n Eri*, 354); 'Sign on long o' me' (*U* 14.1572), see 'ship long of me' (*N* 20.102) and 'ship 'long of me' (Lincoln, *Cap'n Eri*, 243); 'Thunderation!' (*U* 14.1462), see 'thunderation' (*N* 20.58), which appears as 'Thunderation!' (Lincoln, *Cap'n Eri*, 307); 'Gum. I'm jiggered' (*U* 14.1509), see 'by gum' (*N* 20.103) and 'By gum!' (Lincoln, *Cap'n Eri*, 256).

[194] Lincoln, *Cap'n Eri*, 7, 376–97; *U* 14.1585–7.

[195] *N* 17.61; Baumann, *Londinismen*, xxvi. Dibdin will be familiar to readers of 'Eveline' in *Dubliners*, which contains an allusion to his popular song 'The Lass That Loves a Sailor' (a sailor who is cheerful, loyal, and loving).

226   MODERNIST PARODY

echoed Dibdin's phrasing in 'Oxen' in the line 'You larn that off of they there Frenchy bilks?'[196] In addition to seafaring slang, other lexical fields that particularly caught Joyce's attention as he canvassed *Londonismen* pertain to gambling, drinking, and swearing, all of which are germane to central topics in 'Oxen' (and *Ulysses*).

North's discussion of maritime language in *The Dialect of Modernism* contains a series of observations that help to explain why Joyce beachcombed works for examples of far-flung regional dialects and sea slang. As North points out, 'The early propaganda for the OED spoke confidently of "the race of English words which is to form the dominant speech of the world".'[197] However, 'the first linguists (from the Portuguese *linguoa*) were sailors who had learned to work with languages by living with a polyglot crew and traveling the globe'.[198] Mariners, 'with their insight into the infinite fungibility of language, are the embodied antithesis of a standard language. They are also, almost by definition, racial outsiders, suspended between the races, languages, and cultures they translate'.[199] Not only does North's assessment enable a connection to be made between Bloom as a racial outsider and Odysseus as the great mariner who navigates the ports and coastal landmarks of the Mediterranean, but it also says something about the special linguistic condition of coastal settlements. When sailors come ashore, they bring their language to a community that is already on the periphery of national culture. To approach English from its geographical margins, and to search for seafaring slang, was a primary move in decolonizing the language and resisting the idea that the 'dominant speech of the world' was the pure product of the English as a race.

The determination to view English from an outsider's perspective helps to explain why Joyce decided to consult a German authority like Baumann's *Londinismen* to access the slang and cant that percolated through England's imperial metropolis. As a reference work, *Londinismen* emphasizes how many different subcultures contribute to the dialect spoken in a single area and foregrounds the linguistic creativity of the communities that live on the geographical or social margins, such as sailors, gamblers, and thieves. It reveals that the English spoken in London is not the pure product of any one dominant group or race, but a series of dialects with diverse origins. The same is true of *Limehouse Nights: Tales of Chinatown*, from which Joyce noted examples from Burke's presentation of the lisping pronunciation and pidgin English of the Chinese characters. Snippets from Burke that appear in the final paragraphs of 'Oxen' and come via the notesheets are 'Malligold, lou shall not go. Lou shall stay with Tai Ling. Oh, lou'll have evelything beautiful, all same English lady' and 'Sung Dee be heap good sailor, heap

---

[196] *U* 14.1503.
[197] North, *Dialect of Modernism*, 49.
[198] North, *Dialect of Modernism*, 50.
[199] North, *Dialect of Modernism*, 50.

A 'BAWD OF PARODIES' 227

good servant, all same slave', which are amalgamated in the line 'Lou heap good man. Allee same dis bunch'.[200]

Limehouse Nights is not the only work that Joyce canvassed for dialogue between linguistic outsiders and native populations. The focus on sea words and coastal slang is supplemented by vocabulary and phrases from geographical locations where native and non-native speakers interact. In addition to works that explore the linguistic melting pots that are capital cities and coastlines, where the dialects that circulate tell of trade, immigration, and the rise and fall of empires, Joyce also raided Bret Harte's *Tales of the West* for examples of the Englishes spoken on the American frontier. The tales include a series of short stories set in the Wild West that focus on the lives of outsiders, among them Cherokee Indians, rednecks, orphans, drinkers, and gamblers, whose dialogue provides a ready store of regional and racial dialect. The only fragment from Harte's *Tales of the West* to appear in the final text of 'Oxen' in a guise that resembles a deliberate allusion is the exclamation 'Eternally dog-gone my skin ef this aint the puttiest chance yet', which is reworked as 'Tarnally dog gone my shins if this beent the bestest puttiest longbreak yet'.[201] This splendid piece of doggerel comes from the one story from *Condensed Novels* that caught Joyce's notice as he was canvassing *Tales of the West*: 'Muck-a-Muck: A Modern Indian Novel, after Cooper', a merciless parody of James Fenimore Cooper, satirizing Cooper's stilted style and the falsity of his characters and plots by replaying episodes from *The Pioneers* (1823), a portrait of life on the American frontier. It relays the unlikely meeting, courtship, and broken engagement of Genevra, the genteel daughter of a judge, and Natty Bumpo, the uncouth Pike Ranger of Donner Lake, who saves her from simultaneous assault by a grizzly bear, a Californian lion, a wild cat, a buffalo, and a wild Spanish bull. The farcical skit is named after 'Muck-a-Muck', an Indian Chieftain, who is shot in error by Bumpo (who sees his fiancée's hairpiece in his hand and wrongly concludes that she has been scalped). The fact that Joyce made an unusually extended note on an exaggerated parody of American speech by a character as unbelievable as Bumpo and distorted it further still before transplanting it into the tailpiece of 'Oxen', speaks of a determination to exaggerate linguistic markers of national difference to comic and parodic effect.

When Joyce answered Georg Goyert's appeal for help with the task of translating the 'Oxen of the Sun' episode into German in a letter dated 6 March 1927, Joyce emphasized his deliberate use of exaggeratedly stereotyped dialect.

---

[200] The following three consecutive notes were taken from Burke: 'lou'll' (*N* 17.34), 'all same' (*N* 17.35), and 'heap good' (*N* 17.36). Thomas Burke, 'The Father of Yoto', *Limehouse Nights: Tales of Chinatown* (London: Grant Richards, 1917), 50; Burke, 'The Bird', *Limehouse Nights*, 184 (compare 'heap good' (*N* 17.36)); *U* 14.1448.
[201] Compare 'Tarnally dog gone my shins if this aint the puttiest chance yet' (*N* 17.92–3); Bret Harte, 'Muck-a-Muck', *Tales of the West* (London: Nelson & Sons, n. d.), 149; *U* 14.1541–2.

228   MODERNIST PARODY

Towards the end of the chapter, there is a fragmentary burst of language purporting to be black American patois:

> Ludamassy! Pore piccaninnies. Thou'll no be telling me thot, Pold veg! Did ums blubble bigsplash crytears cos fren Padney was took off in black bag? Of all de darkies Massa Pat was verra best.[202]

Joyce glossed these offensive lines for Goyert, explaining that 'The English is quite unconvincing and meant to be so'.[203] The same could be said of Harte's depictions of red-neck and Native Indian American English in 'Muck-a-Muck'. In the case of the lines from 'Oxen' quoted above, the references to 'piccaninnies' and the stock character 'Massa Pat' make it clear that it is a parody of black American speech. The topic under discussion is Bloom's response to Paddy Dignam's funeral. The brief transformation of a dead Irishman into a black American suggests that racial and national identities as represented in dialect become fundamentally interchangeable in the linguistic melting pot that is the end of 'Oxen'.

The snippets of regional dialects from Britain and America on notesheets 17 and 20 mingle indiscriminately with loan words from other languages such as Indian American ('squaws and papooses'), interjections in French, German, Latin, Spanish ('*Caramba!*'), mock Yiddish ('Vyfor you no me tell?'), and *faux* French too ('Horryvar, mong vioo').[204] The dialect and loan words that appear in the tailpiece assert that the English language is no longer the preserve of England's national history and culture but is instead invigorated from without. Joyce actively sought works that would demonstrate this transition, for instance *Change: A Glamorgan Play in Four Acts*, which received wide publicity when it was awarded the Lord Howard de Walden prize (1912), a competition that aimed to establish a Welsh National Theatre. As the American theatre critic Montrose J. Moses explained in his introduction to the American edition of *Change*, the play received this award because it constituted a 'powerful call for a new order of things' and marked the entrance of Welsh drama on the international stage:

> So that it is only now, when Wales seems on the verge of social and industrial upheaval, that drama declares itself a force, without any native tradition, without any evolutionary history to trace. Full grown, it declares itself with modern technique in such a play as *Change*.[205]

---

[202] *U* 14.1555–7.

[203] Joyce's letter to Goyert is reproduced and transcribed in Alan M. Cohn, 'Joyce's Notes on the End of "Oxen of the Sun"', *James Joyce Quarterly* 4(3), translation issue (spring 1967), 199.

[204] *U* 14.1483, 14.1470, 14.1525, 14.1522.

[205] John Oswald Francis, *Change: A Glamorgan Play in Four Acts* (New York: Doubleday, Page & Co., 1914), v, vii.

A 'BAWD OF PARODIES'   229

The presence of a sequence of notes from *Change* on 'Oxen of the Sun' notesheet 17, albeit brief, suggests that Joyce was actively looking for works that signalled the growing status—and, crucially, the modernity—of the regions and their literatures, which far from being parochial, were now achieving increased global recognition. Interestingly enough, no snippets from Welsh literature make an appearance in the episode's re-enactment of the evolutionary history of English prose until the tailpiece, where Francis's epithet 'Meredith the bread' is reworked twice: first in the name 'Meredith' and then in 'Bartle the Bread we calls him'.[206] There is a sense in which the 'frightful jumble' at the end of 'Oxen' marks the moment when the idea of English literature as something monolithic is challenged by voices from beyond England's national boundaries.

The decision to canvass works such as *Change* was not only motivated by a desire to acquire examples of regional dialect, but also the will to use these linguistic curios towards an articulation of the 'modern spirit' of unrest that was then percolating in the literatures of outlying, recently developed regions. By opening up the language to the distinctive dialects of peripheral regions of the British Isles and the United States, Joyce strikes against the concept of Standard English that is modelled on the highest classes of London society and instead asserts the vitality of the linguistic formations that are generated on the cultural margins. The implication is that regional literatures and oral cultures will rise to displace the 'pure' English that has been institutionalized through accepted literary canons and become part of the mainstream. The form of 'Oxen' asserts that the future of English is not only to be found in parodic stylizations of canonized authors. It is also to be found in the non-standard Englishes of the outlying regions that were awakening to a restive modern spirit and asserting distinctive local identities; in metropolitan melting pots like London, where the language is invigorated by interactions between communities of locals and immigrant populations; in the realms beyond England's borders, the sea, coastal settlements; and, crucially, in America. In the same way that Joyce constellated the outlying linguistic cultures of the British Isles as he prepared notesheet 17 (Francis in the west, FitzGerald in the east, and *Londinismen* and Burke in the south), he reached across the American continent, selecting examples of regional and racial dialect from two authors who wrote about opposite sides of the country—Lincoln on the eastern seaboard and Harte in the Wild West. Joyce canvassed these American sources with a view to gesturing to the fringe Englishes that were developing at the extremities of a rising nation, a former colony that would soon eclipse England on the world stage, as suggested by the culminating soap-box sermon delivered by Alexander J Christ

---

[206] Francis, *Change*, 102; see 'Meredith the bread' (*N* 17.15); *U* 14.1486, 14.1550.

230 MODERNIST PARODY

Dowie at the episode's end, who claims to have already 'yanked to glory most half this planet from Frisco beach to Vladivostok.'[207]

By connecting the Englishes spoken in different regions and by different races to the future of the language, Joyce decentres and decolonizes English and remakes the language as a mode of liberation of race itself that transcends the national. The final paragraphs of 'Oxen' declare that English words no longer form the dominant speech of the world. Instead, English as a *lingua franca* encompasses sea slang, pidgin, and cant from communities whose dialects cross national boundaries, such as the English spoken by Chinese immigrants, Welsh nationals, and Native Indians. The 'oxtail soup' Joyce serves to readers at the end of the 'Oxen' is seasoned with maritime and coastal slang. It asserts that the future of the language lies beyond England's shores. As 'Oxen' makes clear, it rests in the hands of the parodist of world history who can invoke the breadth of his literary and linguistic heritage and transform it in ways that undermine received histories and facilitate historicized understanding of present-day concerns. In doing so, 'Oxen' establishes the agenda for Joyce's future conquest of English, pointing forward to the supra-national, polyglot, and profoundly parodic language of *Finnegans Wake*.

The sense of parody as something that could be orgiastic or onanistic, pleasurable for its own sake, but not necessarily resulting in fertile issue, was clearly signalled in *Ulysses* by Buck Mulligan's masturbatory play-text in 'Scylla and Charybdis' and the stylistic backdrop to Bloom's activities in 'Nausicaa'. 'Oxen' by contrast demonstrated that parody could give birth to revolutionary styles and take originality to unachieved heights. Woolf recorded a conversation with Eliot in her diary entry for 26 September 1922 in which he praised *Ulysses* for having 'destroyed the whole of the 19th century' and commented 'It left Joyce himself with nothing to write another book on. It showed up the futility of all the English styles.'[208] Eliot meant this as the highest compliment, a reflection of the ways in which no style could ever be sufficient for the purposes of true mimesis, since all are laden with prior associations that intervene in the precarious interplay of substitutions that constitutes signification. Making the problem that words and phrases ultimately refer to prior usage before they refer to things of the world visible through parody provided Joyce with the leverage to return styles to more precise usage and make them comment on the historical contingencies through which they are defined. 'Oxen of the Sun' is a parable of the 'phenomena of artistic conception, artistic gestation and artistic reproduction' for which Stephen sought 'a new terminology and a new personal experience' in *Portrait*.[209] 'Oxen' stages the modernist experience of entering a recently codified literary tradition and enacts

---

[207] *U* 14.1584–5.
[208] Virginia Woolf, *Diary of Virginia Woolf, Volume 2, 1920–1924*, ed. Anne Olivier Bell and Andrew McNeillie (London: Hogarth Press, 1978), 203.
[209] Joyce, *A Portrait of the Artist as a Young Man*, 176.

the process by which the author himself becomes modern precisely by becoming a parodist of history. The *aube-de-siècle* search for a style, enacted in the early work of modernist writers such as Pound, Eliot, and Joyce, discovers in the act of searching that the modern age is without a style, save the style that consists in the search, the ceaseless odyssey through the methods and resources of literature to understand the present in relation to its past. To be a parodist of history was the surest way to be original (and contemporaneous) in 1922.

7

Parodists of History

Ford Madox Ford, Virginia Woolf, Wyndham Lewis, and James Joyce

So far, this book has told the story of parody's formative role in modernist experimentation up to and including the *annus mirabilis* of 1922. However, the parody that was central to high modernism exerted an influence on later modernist writing, which, as Tyrus Miller has noted, 'appears a distinctly self-conscious manifestation of the aging and decline of modernism, in both its institutional and ideological dimensions'.[1] In particular, Joyce's exhilarating mastery over English prose styles in 'Oxen of the Sun' had shown how the literature of the future might be sustained through parody. As Eliot recognized in conversation with Woolf, *Ulysses* had become *incontournable*. It was not so much the case that *Ulysses* 'left Joyce himself with nothing to write another book on'; Joyce pushed his practice of parody further still in *Finnegans Wake*, contriving even to parody the sense-making structures of language itself.[2] But *Ulysses* certainly created a problem for other authors who felt compelled to match its achievement, even if they doubted their ability to exceed it. And in this sense, the parody that the high modernists set into motion persisted in later writings, either as a deliberate effect or an unintended consequence of less accomplished imitation of established modernist techniques. In the years after 1922, modernist writers practised parody self-consciously to reflect on the business of modernist writing, its formulaic techniques, as well as its position in the marketplace and within literary history, and to respond to the parody that was already a feature of the most celebrated high modernist texts. This final chapter surveys the practices of authors who, in their different ways, present parody as constitutive of the literature of their modern age by framing their own writing as the culminating product of its parodies of previous literatures.

Ford Madox Ford responded with brio to the new fashion for writing parodic histories of English in his surreal, farcical, and fragmentary book-length dramatic poem *Mister Bosphorus and the Muses, or A Short History of Poetry in Britain, Variety Entertainment in Four Acts, Words by Ford Madox Ford, Music*

---

[1] Tyrus Miller, *Late Modernism: Politics, Fiction, and the Arts between the World Wars* (Berkeley: University of California Press, 1999), 7.

[2] Woolf, *Diary of Virginia Woolf, Volume 2, 1920–24*, 203.

Modernist Parody. Sarah Davison, Oxford University Press. © Sarah Davison (2023).
DOI: 10.1093/oso/9780192849243.003.0008

by Several Popular Composers, with Harlequinade, Transformation Scene, Cinematograph Effects, and Many Other Novelties, as well as Old and Tried Favourites, Decorated with Designs Engraved on Wood by Paul Nash (1923). *Mister Bosphorus* is a 'Circe'-style fantasia, heavily influenced by music hall and, of course, 'Oxen of the Sun', and Joyce's play with parodic stylization in *Ulysses* more broadly, as well as *The Waste Land* and Pound's career up to *Hugh Selwyn Mauberley* (1920). Ford conceived of *Mister Bosphorus* as his '*Dunciad*', by which he meant a mock-epic poetic satire on the mainstream literary culture that officially approved of banal Victorian pastiche and left true and original talents unrecognized in their own time.[3] As Max Saunders notes, it was written at a time when Ford was feeling 'cut off and neglected'.[4] *The Marsden Case* (the novel Ford had been working on) had been turned down by Macmillan, he had been unable to interest Liveright in *The Marsden Case*, a volume of poems, or the history of English literature he was then writing, and he was thoroughly fed up with living in the isolated hamlet of Bedham, West Sussex, having endured a hard winter.[5] These dissatisfactions all feed into *Mister Bosphorus*, a text that with no small irony has itself received little in the way of the critical attention it deserves.[6]

In Act I, the starving poet Poore B. Bosphorus is visited by the Northern Muse in his garret and blunders in his attempts to make 'An income in the Great Victorian mode'.[7] Initially, his mind is set 'On imitating [Coventry] Patmore and Lord Tennyson,/As the fashion is to-day'.[8] Then, failing that, he turns to Arthurian Legend, producing *faux* Middle English verses, so '*flippant and lecherous*' that 'Queen Victoria/Would have turned purple pale if Tennyson/Had read to her verse like that'.[9] Unable to write the derivative and vacant lyrics that bring commercial success in his age without succumbing to irreverent parody, Bosphorus devotes himself to *vers libre*, loses the patronage of the Northern Muse, and resigns himself to the workhouse. In Act II, Bosphorus and Bulfin (one of the poem's many dunces) sit in the workhouse talking in front of a screen on which is projected:

From

Birth-place

to

---

[3] Ford Madox Ford to Joseph Conrad, 8 November 1923, *Letters of Ford Madox Ford*, ed. Richard M. Ludwig (Princeton, NJ: Princeton University Press, 1965), 157.

[4] Max Saunders, *Ford Madox Ford: A Dual Life, Volume II: The After-War World* (Oxford: Oxford University Press, 1996), 121.

[5] Saunders, *Ford Madox Ford*, 119.

[6] In addition to the commentary in Saunders, *Ford Madox Ford*, there have been two articles to date on *Mister Bosphorus*: Colin Edwards, 'City Burlesque: The Pleasures of Paranoia in Ford's *Mister Bosphorus and the Muses*', *International Ford Madox Ford Studies* 4 (2005), 93–109 and Robert E. McDonough, '"Mister Bosphorus and the Muses": History and Representation in Ford's Modern Poem', *International Ford Madox Ford Studies* 3 (2004), 155–62.

[7] *MB* 18.

[8] *MB* 18.

[9] *MB* 28, Ford's italics.

234   MODERNIST PARODY

> Museum
>> How
> Poets Live
>> FEAT
> Uring Mr. BOSPHORUS and
>> MUSA POORE
> (Rotten Films Ltd.)[10]

When Bulfin detects an echo of *A Midsummer Night's Dream*, Bosphorus laments 'Without a doubt, Verses all heard before/Make up our great tradition of to-day', restating Ford's own position on the secondhand nature of literary production.[11] The film provides the background story of Mr Bosphorus's life, to which he responds by vamping a song at the piano to the tune of 'It's a Long Way to Tipperary':

> Poets who cannot sell their manuscripts
>> Must Hope ! Hope ! Hope !
> Poisons are costly and to hand yourself
>> Needs rope ! Expensive rope !
> Summer flow'rs are coming and for rhyme they give much scope !
> So ! If there's no money in sham Tennyson
>> Try Pope ! Pope ! Pope ![12]

Bulfin responds 'That isn't Poetry. That's modern .... Here ! What's wrong with me ? I'm changing !' And Bosphorus, damningly, says 'You are changed !/You have become a critic'.[13] But although the 'sham Tennyson' is poor art because it is vapid pastiche, Ford's ironic point is that parody infused with the edgy spirit of music hall is 'modern', albeit bathetic, because the mordant comedy excludes the sentimentality popularly attributed to poetry.

In Act II, scene ii, Bosphorus endures a torturous conversation between a male chorus of nine naysaying Bulfins and a female chorus of muses, conducted in 'The Classic Modes' (which is to say rhyming verse approximating a range of poetic styles from ancient Greece to the eighteenth century, including a truly excruciating burst of sub-Spenserian pastiche).[14] The assembled choruses figure Bosphorus as a poet of all times but chide him for falling from classical standards and no longer singing of his love for them, regretting that his plays go unperformed and verses go unsung.

[10] *MB* 40, Ford's capitals.
[11] *MB* 44.
[12] *MB* 46.
[13] *MB* 46.
[14] *MB* 53.

PARODISTS OF HISTORY 235

Acts III and IV are set in the future year MCMLX. Bosphorus remains in the workhouse, now known only by a number to reflect the rationalization of the projected future society where true poetry is not prized. He dreams of the lecture he will give to the Orthodox Intelligentsia entitled '*The Poetry of the Prose Age*', espousing a viewpoint that is fully endorsed by Ford but deemed mad by his Labour Master, who seeks to have him put to death:

> Poetry is immortal because it is the endless chain of the linked expressions of the souls of man. This being a prose age, poetry has taken refuge in prose. The poem that we are living to-day, here and now ... [15]

The venal Northern Muse (now in the guise of the duchess, a jilted mistress) extracts a hundred words of deliberately indifferent pastiche from Bosphorus with a view to selling them to an American senator (who resembles that great collector of modern manuscripts John Quinn). But she is outwitted when the words fade as soon as they are written, for Bosphorus has used invisible ink. Bosphorus then escapes with the Southern Muse, who accompanies him on his journey to Elysium. Buried in Poet's Corner in Westminster Abbey, Bosphorus's works are 'only priced and prized ... in America', with 'not one word in manuscript or print/Of this great poet ... lives to call forth/The maiden's blush, in England'.[16] Ford signs off with the words 'SUSSEX: October 1992—TARASON: June 1923', a parody of Joyce's parting words '*Trieste–Zürich–Paris/1914–1921*', signalling Ford's own departure south from England's miasmic climate and tawdry culture to the continent that nourished the talent he freely admired and imitated.[17]

Mister Bosphorus is very much a product of the modernism that uses parody to articulate and thereby move beyond the historically determined conditions of the stagnant mainstream literature culture it criticizes. As Saunders notes, it turns Ford's 'near-paranoid anxiety about an orchestrated obliteration of his reputation into a celebratory fantasy of escape and regeneration'.[18] In doing so, *Mister Bosphorus* refuses to be part of the dystopian future imagined for a literature that public taste confines to dutiful but weak pastiche of hackneyed styles. When Joseph Conrad wrote to congratulate Ford and thank him for sending a copy of *Mister Bosphorus* on 20 November 1923, saying 'I had no idea that your versatile genius could master so well the comic spirit/both so grim and so ferociously gay', he summarized the attitude of the poem very precisely.[19] The ferocity and gaiety with which Ford presents Bosphorus as he tries on, puts on, and takes off different cos-

---

[15] *MB* 75, Ford's italics, 85–6.
[16] *MB* 122.
[17] *MB* 126, Ford's capitals; *U* 18.1609–10, Joyce's italics.
[18] Saunders, *Ford Madox Ford*, 124.
[19] Quoted in Saunders, *Ford Madox Ford*, 124.

236 MODERNIST PARODY

tumes of the past is in keeping with the spirited but derisive revelry Nietzsche foretold, whereby the only originality still possible is as 'a parodist of world history', or in this case as the author of a 'Variety Entertainment' that masquerades as 'A Short History of Poetry in Britain'.

Virginia Woolf too parodied the progress of literary history in *Orlando: A Biography* (1928), a spirited romp through the annals of English literature prepared by her youthful habit of practising the styles of admired Elizabethan writers in her copybooks. She later returned to reconsider what Ford described as 'the endless chain of the linked expressions of the souls of man' with sober urgency in *Between the Acts* (1941), in which she reflects on the construction of literary canons and their capacity to sustain communities and identities at a moment when the future itself was imperilled. Woolf was no fan of *Ulysses*: she considered it to be indecent, 'pretentious', and 'underbred ... in the literary sense', on the grounds that 'A first rate writer ... respects writing too much to be tricky; startling; doing stunts'.[20] And yet, Eliot's assessment that *Ulysses* was 'the most important expression which the present age has found; it is a book to which we are all indebted, and from which none of us can escape' applied painfully to Woolf, who was profoundly influenced by Joyce's achievement almost in spite of herself.[21] Her indebtedness included the conscious recapitulation of venerated canons to reflect on literary authority and artistic inheritance to challenge received historical narratives and reconfiguring the literary culture of the present.

Orlando is a fantastical biography of Vita Sackville-West, who—in the guise of Orlando—lives through five centuries in two genders. The book is also a composite biography of the aristocratic Sackville family through history. Woolf uses parody to laugh at the conventions of life writing, unsettling the foundational principle that subjects have a stable identity and knowable history that is faithfully recorded by the biographer, revealing historiography to be a department of fiction. The conceit that Orlando's life extends from the Elizabethan age to the present day provides a pretext to incorporate occasional parodies of historical literary styles into the narrative. She also rewrites 'A Note of household stuff sent by Symondes to Knole the 28th July 1624', a genuine item from the Sackville archives, with lavish hyperbole.[22] The frost fair on the Thames is presented after the manner of Thomas Dekker's *The Great Frost* (1608); the description of Orlando's descent into the family vaults in the seventeenth century segues into a parody of Sir Thomas Browne's *Hydrotaphia: Urne Buriall* (1658); and her rapid engagement to Marmaduke Bonthrop Shelmerdine, Esquire, who rescues her after a fall during a country walk, burlesques Marianne's first encounter with Willoughby in *Sense and Sensibility*

---

[20] Woolf, *Diary of Virginia Woolf*, 199.
[21] T. S. Eliot, '*Ulysses*, Order and Myth', *Dial* LXXV (November 1923), 480.
[22] Vita Sackville-West, *Knole and the Sackvilles* (London: William Heinemann, 1922), 95–6; *O* 66.

(1811).[23] Orlando's compositions are likewise presented as parodies of the dominant literary modes of the periods in which s/he lives. As a hot-headed young man in the reign of Elizabeth I, Orlando writes 'Æthelbert: A Tragedy in Five Acts' ('Vice, Crime, Misery were the personages of his drama; there were Kings and Queens of impossible territories; horrid plots confounded them; noble sentiments suffused them').[24] Under the aegis of the nineteenth century, the female Orlando produces 'the most insipid verse'.[25] Orlando's culminating masterpiece is 'The Oak-Tree', a poem that grows and develops through time. It functions as a proxy for Sackville-West's Hawthornden prize-winning poem *The Land* (1926), a hymn to her beloved Kent countryside, which sings the cycles of rural life and preserves its historical traditions.[26]

In the final chapter, Orlando encounters her old friend and fellow poet Nick Greene (first an avatar for the Elizabethan pamphleteer and dramatist Robert Greene, who attacked Shakespeare in *A Groats-Worth of Wit* (1592), now transformed by his entry into the nineteenth century as the most influential critic of the Victorian period). Greene salutes the 'giants' and 'heroes' of bygone ages, Marlowe, Shakespeare, Jonson, Dryden, Swift, and Addison, all representatives of an overwhelmingly male literary tradition, before opining 'the great days are over. We live in degenerate times. We must cherish the past; honour those writers—there are still a few left of 'em—who take antiquity for their model and write, not for pay but—'.[27] Orlando very nearly completes the sentence for him, for 'she could have sworn that she had heard him say the very same things three hundred years ago'.[28] Her disappointment in discovering that 'literature was an elderly gentleman in a grey suit', having 'thought of literature all these years (her seclusion, her rank, her sex must be her excuse) as something wild as the wind, hot as fire, swift as lightning; something errant, incalculable, abrupt', results in the spontaneous unfastening of the upper part of her dress from which falls 'The Oak Tree'.[29] The poem reminds Greene favourably of 'Addison's *Cato*' and 'Thomson's *Seasons*':

> There was no trace in it, he was thankful to say, of the modern spirit. It was composed with a regard to truth, to nature, to the dictates of the human heart, which was rare indeed, in these days of unscrupulous eccentricity. It must, of course, be published instantly.[30]

---

[23] *O* 16–17, 35–6; Thomas Dekker, *The Great Frost, Cold Doings in London, except it be at the Lotterie* (London: Henry Gosson, 1608); *O* 41–3; Thomas Browne, *Hydriotaphia, Urne-Buriall* (London: Henry Brome, 1658); *O* 162; Jane Austen, *Sense and Sensibility*, ed. James Kinsley, intro. Margaret Anne Doody, and notes Claire Lamont (Oxford: Oxford University Press, 2004).

[24] *O* 5.

[25] *O* 154.

[26] Vita Sackville-West, *The Land* (London: William Heinemann, 1926).

[27] *O* 182.

[28] *O* 182.

[29] *O* 183.

[30] *O* 183.

238   MODERNIST PARODY

His compliments are double-edged, for the poem's real-life counterpart *The Land* was after all a celebrated product of the modern age but one that was deeply rooted in the pastoral tradition.

Orlando resolves to understand the nineteenth-century literary marketplace better. Having previously only had experience of manuscript culture, she places an order with a bookseller to send her everything of importance. She requests not only the works of authors but also 'works about other works' by critics of likes of Sir Nicholas, 'whom, in her ignorance, she supposed ... to be very great writers too', availing herself to the archive of turn-of-the-century literature and criticism that was, incidentally, the subject of 'Oxen of the Sun'.[31] Sitting in Hyde Park, Orlando wonders how to formulate thoughts in the face of powerful influences in an age where the institution of literature itself is defined by stalwarts like Greene and Sir Nicholas, who are so mired in their reverence for the past that they are unable to understand new work except in relation to a masculine succession of greats. Orlando's review of the appalling mass of Victorian literature highlights its corpulence, dryness, and the fragility of its geniuses. The narrator's description of many lectures 'on the Influence of this upon that; the Classical revival; the Romantic survival, and other titles of the same engaging kind' mocks the same species of historical criticism that made modern writers keenly conscious of the ways in which they were belated and that created the culture where powerful influence must be consciously overcome for an author to feel truly original.[32]

At the end of the long nineteenth century, Orlando is quickly delivered of her first-born son in a gesture that presents obvious parallels to 'Oxen of the Sun', for, straight after, the modern age bursts upon the scene. On the eleventh of October 1928, at ten o'clock in the morning, Orlando enters 'the present moment' itself.[33] In the course of that day, she fulfils her own literary destiny and receives a prize for 'The Oak Tree'.[34] The poem is a work in her authentic voice, written in dialogue with nature, with which she has a deep affinity, consisting in 'the stammering answer she had made all these years to the old crooning song of the woods, and the farms and the brown horses standing at the gate, neck to neck, and the smithy and the kitchen and the fields, so laboriously bearing wheat, turnips, grass, and the garden blowing irises and fritillaries'.[35] Far from showing 'the futility of all the English styles', Woolf parodied English styles in *Orlando* to express her genuine affection for literature that she loved while simultaneously showing her irritation with the age-old critical culture that had institutionalized an androcentric canon in a way that conspired to deprive literature of its rightful vitality, wildness, and errancy. Woolf herself adds to its liveliness, reanimating works by admired writers through

---

[31] *O* 185–6.
[32] *O* 190.
[33] *O* 193, 195.
[34] *O* 203–4.
[35] *O* 213.

her own performance as a parodist of history, literature, and biography, placing a writer who has lived in two genders as the celebrated product of the present moment, one who has a feeling for the vitality of past literatures even to the extent that they are lived experiences, but nevertheless achieves self-expression in a way that is authentic and sensitive to historical contingencies and present-day realities. In this sense, Orlando's 'The Oak Tree' is a resolutely 'modern' text, a characteristic production of its own age, and no other, even though it is pastoral and romantic.

The parodic literary history staged in *Between the Acts* conspicuously lacks the élan of *Orlando* or 'Oxen'. *Between the Acts* began to take shape early in 1938, in a time of imminent war. Unable to envisage a future, for herself or the nation, Woolf probed the possibilities for the continuity of common literary heritage by depicting a village community on the day it stages a pageant-play. The play itself presents a potted version of the history of England, from 'England in the time of Chaucer' via parodies of Elizabethan drama, Restoration comedy, and Victorian melodrama before arriving at the present moment.[36] Pageant-plays were frequently banal affairs celebrating rural ideas of Englishness, and this play is no different, as the chatter from the villagers who are sitting on the grass watching makes clear.[37] Although Woolf made light of the rank amateurism, wretched dialogue, and homespun costumes of this parochial entertainment, she nonetheless took a serious interest in the genre's community ethos and the un-grandiose importance of an indigenous literary tradition that seemed, at that time, to be in great peril. In 'The Leaning Tower' (1940), Woolf proposed that 'English literature will survive this war and cross the gulf—if commoners and outsiders like ourselves make that country our own country, if we teach ourselves how to read and write, how to preserve and how to create'.[38] The pageant-play in *Between the Acts* indicates the difficulties that must be surmounted, recollecting a 'skimble-skamble' history for villagers whose common knowledge of national literature is dim and fragmentary.[39] Under Miss La Trobe's direction, the villagers on the stage assume identities from other historical periods:

> From behind the bushes issued Queen Elizabeth—Eliza Clark, licensed to sell tobacco. Could she be Mrs. Clark of the village shop? She was splendidly made up. Her head, pearl-hung, rose from a vast ruff. Shiny satins draped her. Sixpenny brooches glared like cats' eyes and tigers' eyes; pearls looked down; her cape was made of cloth of silver—in fact swabs used to scour saucepans. She looked the age in person.[40]

---

[36] *BTA* 73.
[37] See Joshua D. Esty, 'Amnesia in the Fields: Late Modernism, Late Imperialism, and the English Pageant-Play', *English Literary History* 69 (2002), 245–76.
[38] Virginia Woolf, 'The Leaning Tower', *Collected Essays*, vol. 2 (London: Hogarth Press, 1966), 181.
[39] *BTA* 85.
[40] *BTA* 76.

240   MODERNIST PARODY

But while the villagers are confident of identities as apparently fixed in the past, content to see Eliza Clark in costume as the personification of the Elizabethan age in the popular imagination (albeit with wire wool substituted for spun silver cloth), they are unable to conceive of their own place within that rudimentary anthropology. They have no idea how Miss La Trobe will present their own age, reflecting: 'But what could she know about ourselves? The Elizabethans yes; the Victorians, perhaps; but ourselves; sitting here on a June day in 1939—it was ridiculous.'[41]

Miss La Trobe's innovation is to confront her audience with present-day reality by presenting the spectators with their reflections in mirrors carried by the players, still dressed in their historical costumes, who simultaneously declaim 'some phrase or fragment from their parts':

> I am not (said one) in my perfect mind ... Another, Reason am I .. And I? I'm the old top hat ... Home is the hunter, home from the hill ... Home? Where the miner sweats, and the maiden faith is rudely strumpeted ... Sweet and low; sweet and low, wind of the western sea ... Is that a dagger that I see before me? ... The owl hoots and the ivy mocks tap-tap-tapping on the pane ... Lady I love till I die, leave they chamber and come ... Where the worm weaves its winding sheet ... I'd be a butterfly. I'd be a butterfly ... In thy will is our peace ... Here, Papa, take your book and read aloud ... Hark, hark, the dogs do bark and the beggars ... [42]

Among the mélange are snatches from *King Lear*, Robert Louis Stevenson's 'Requiem', Tennyson's *The Princess*, *Macbeth* (misquoted), and Dante's *Paradiso*.[43]

Miss La Trobe attempts to prompt the audience into realizing that although their era seems to be without a style of its own, it is, as Robert Graves and Alan Hodge quoted Noël Coward as saying in *The Long Week-End: A Social History of Great Britain 1918–1939* (1940), 'a "period" period, without a style of its own any longer, but with full liberty to borrow from any wardrobe of the past'.[44] In this age of costumes, all speech acts, all social performances, are composed of multiple echoes, fragmentary and fleeting. To be modern is to be supremely conscious of the way that the past contours the present. What the audience for the play (and, beyond that, the wider audience for Woolf's book) will make of this collective history hangs in the balance, and with it that sense of continuity that has the potential to overcome differences and consolidate a sense of belonging and community extending beyond the parochial.

---

[41] *BTA* 160.

[42] The effect is comparable to that of the 'Vortoscope', the photographic machine invented by the photographer Alvin Langdon Coburn, and named by Pound, that used mirrors to create shattered portraits, reflecting Pound's understanding of modern man as a 'bundle of broken mirrors' (see Pound, 'Near Perigord', *Lustra* (London: Elkin Mathews, 1916), 103). *BTA* 166, Woolf's italics and ellipses.

[43] See Frank Kermode's notes for further details (*BTA* 202).

[44] Quoted in Robert Graves and Alan Hodge, *The Long Week-end: A Social History of Great Britain 1918–1939* (London: Faber & Faber, 1940), 147.

PARODISTS OF HISTORY 241

Whereas Ford and Woolf parodied history to arrive at a more nuanced understanding of the present as a process in the production of their own original literary work, Lewis parodied his modernist contemporaries to insist that they were without art, sham innovators who lacked the original creative agency to effect real change, which is to say mere apes of god, rather than godlike creators. In the wake of the First World War, in an era of far-reaching change, Lewis recognized that society had entered a new epoch that demanded artists move beyond the earlier avant-garde position that technically innovative art has a 'purely "revolutionary" value' in and of itself.[45] Disgusted by the cultish elevation of work that presented itself as ground-breaking but in fact just recycled old styles as a fashionable commodity (along the lines of Miss Mouse's chic party invitations in *Vile Bodies* that Johnny Hoop adapted from the once revolutionary *Blast*), Lewis was preoccupied with the problem of how true art was to survive and once again become a creative force with the agency to make the necessary interventions in the course of civilization without capitulating to accepted ways of writing and thinking that were platitudinous and bore no relation to reality. In *Men without Art* (1934), Lewis argued that the true artist must be sensible of the gulf between the past and the present, a circumstance highlighted by the inadequacy of the derivative art that then passed for a fashionable commodity, which was in fact a sign of a civilization in its death throes:

> But there is no being 'Elizabethan', or being 'Georgian', any more, for the man who is in fact an artist. All *that* is over except as a pretty period-game. An artist who is not a mere entertainer and money-maker, or self-advertising gossip-star, must today be penetrated by a sense of the great discontinuity of our destiny. At every moment he is compelled to be aware of that different scene, coming up as if by magic, behind all that has been familiar for so long to all the nations of the Aryan World. Nothing but a sort of Façade is left standing, that is the fact: before which fustian property (labelled *The Past*, a cheap parody of *Ancien Régime*, with feudal keeps in the middle distance), the Gossip-column Class bask in enormous splashy spot-lights of publicity. It is what is behind the Façade alone that can be of any interest in such a pantomime.[46]

This sense of rupture with the past was so strong that, in Lewis's view, it was no longer worth seeking to reinterpret or even interrogate great traditions. Society had disintegrated beyond a point where those grand narratives had real relevance, presenting a mere façade that must be seen through and laughed at. For these reasons, Lewis concluded his reflections with a Nietzschean comment on the necessity of farce:

---

[45] Lewis, *Time and Western Man*, 56.
[46] Wyndham Lewis, *Men without Art* (London: Cassell, 1934), 126, Lewis's italics.

242 MODERNIST PARODY

All these things hang together—it is the end of history, and the beginning of historical pageant and play. But we are all compelled, to some extent, to enter into the spirit of the comedy—that is the humble message of this book.[47]

Parody is the enemy of true creativity when it is unwitting but when its laughter is knowing and its satire is barbed it may be the solution too.

To depose the discourses that uphold platitudinous and outmoded cultural ideologies and renew art as a truly revolutionary force that can intervene in society, Lewis became an active parodist of recent history, destroying clichés and tired styles from the inside, and scorning the salon culture that produced mere pretenders such as entertainers, money-makers, and gossip stars. His *roman-à-clef* *The Apes of God* (1930) is a torrential satire on the '*societification*' of London's artistic culture.[48] It expressed Lewis's intense contempt for the coteries of moneyed bohemians who treated art as 'a very large club for the well-to-do' and so made 'a sort of cult of the *amateur*—the child artist—in short any imperfectly equipped person' at the expense of true genius, by firing salvos at the Bloomsbury group and the Sitwells.[49] In *The Apes of God* the battle between debased mimicry and original experimentation is no longer staged in abstract terms. Instead, Lewis makes parasites of his peers, asserting (what he saw as) the failings of their unimaginatively imitative writing through brutal *ad hominem* parody and caricature.

The action is framed by the grotesque spectacle of the formidable Lady Fredigonde, an ex-gossip-column belle immobilized by extreme old age. She thinks in stuttering Steinese, a sub-Joycean mode of interior monologue that functions as a sign of her decrepitude:

> Sometimes she would Stein away night and morning to herself, making patterns of conversations, with odds and ends from dead disputes, and cat's cradles of this thing and that—a veritable peasant industry, of personal chatterboxing and shortsighted nonsense.[50]

As Lewis explained in a letter to Aldington of 30 July 1930, 'The Ulyssean "thought-stream" method is only appropriate to the depiction of children, morons, and the extremely infirm (Fredigonde)'.[51] The novel opens with Fredigonde's morning toilette and closes with the drama of her timely death, which is played out against the backdrop of the General Strike (1926), an event that foreshadows the passing of the old social order of which she is an emblem.

---

[47] Lewis, *Men without Art*, 204.
[48] *AOG* 131, Lewis's italics.
[49] *AOG* 127, 132.
[50] *AOG* 18, Lewis's italics.
[51] W. K. Rose, *The Letters of Wyndham Lewis* (London: Methuen, 1963), 191.

PARODISTS OF HISTORY   243

The main plot concerns the exploits of the trickster Horace Zagreus, a homo-sexual man in his sixties, who is engaged to marry Fredigonde for her money. He mockingly parodies the cult of the amateur child artist by initiating Dan Boleyn, a handsome 19-year-old naïf with only one slender poem to his name, into fashionable Chelsea, Mayfair, and Bloomsbury circles. The salons Boleyn enters at Zagreus's behest are populated by apes, that is, 'shabby Bloomsbury potentates', sham artists whose amateurish, derivative works parody divine creation.[52] As he attempts to assemble an anatomy of the apes under Zagreus's tutelage, Boleyn's picaresque adventures reveal that the apes' aesthetic sensibilities are ultimately conditioned by animalistic sexual desire and financial self-interest. Zagreus mocks Bloomsbury's talentless (and tasteless) artists for their apery, but he is no less apish. His master is the absent, inscrutable, godlike Pierpoint, who coolly surveys society from the perspective of a deity and sits in devastating judgement. Pierpoint blasts society artists as *'preposterous mountebanks who alternately imitate and mock at and traduce those figures they at once admire and hate'* but does so from a vantage point that is hopelessly removed from contemporary reality.[53] The apes of Lewis's novel are unwitting parodists, who express themselves through shabby imitations of the now formulaic techniques of high modernism. Zagreus antagonizes fashionable society artists by broadcasting Pierpoint's pronouncements word for word, revelling in the irony that he is no less a parasitic imitator than those he seeks to scourge.

What separates Zagreus from the society artists he goads is that he is a *knowing* ape, who is highly conscious of his parody as performance, as demonstrated by his self-reflective commentary and the magic tricks he performs at Lord Osmund Finnian Shaw's Lenten Party, a grotesque society event that degenerates into carni-valesque mayhem. The Finnian Shaws, who are described by Pierpoint as 'a family of "great poets" (each of them upon a little frail biographical family pedestal) where all the exultations of labour, a passionate experience, and probably a straightened life, issuing in works of great creative art, are thinly parodied at great expense', are, of course, Osbert, Sacheverell, and Edith Sitwell, writers who were already famil-iar targets for literary parody for having jumped on the modernist bandwagon and turned eccentricity into a publicity exercise.[54] As Mark Perrino notes, 'To a degree, Zagreus is a vehicle for the satire of youth-impresarios like Pound, but more importantly he himself deliberately parodies this role. He is the apotheo-sis of Apery and at the same time the instrument of its deconstruction.'[55] In this respect, Zagreus, like Lewis himself, can be seen as an original parodist, whose apery goes beyond mere imitation to towards complex cultural critique.

---

[52] *AOG* 67.
[53] *AOG* 131, Lewis's italics.
[54] *AOG* 122; for examples of parodies of the Sitwells, see Diepeveen, *Mock Modernism*, 91–100.
[55] Mark Perrino, *The Poetics of Mockery: Wyndham Lewis's 'The Apes of God' and the Populariza-tion of Modernism* (London: W. S. Maney & Sons for the Modern Humanities Research Association, 1995), 77.

244   MODERNIST PARODY

Lewis's highly energized prose convulses with multiple parodies of contemporary writers as it presents grotesque caricatures of literary types who bear passing resemblance to various members of the literati. While these caricatures are *ad hominem*, they often also implicate more than one figure. For instance, Boleyn is usually taken to have been modelled on Stephen Spender, but as Andrzej Gąsiorek memorably points out he resembles 'a mentally stillborn Stephen Dedalus even more'.[56] Zagreus is part Poundian impresario and part Horace de Vere Cole style prankster (the man behind the Dreadnought Hoax of 1910). Likewise, Lewis's *ad hominem* parodies of enemy authors' styles are often applied to different characters, with a view to mimicking and maligning the echo chamber that is coterie modernism. Julius Ratner is a viciously anti-Semitic caricature of John Rodker, the publisher, who contributed to *transition* (the little magazine that published instalments of Joyce's *Work in Progress*) and knew Joyce's works well. Ratner keeps 'a highbrow bookshop' J. Ratner & Co. that publishes a little magazine called '*Man X*' and he goes by a number of names that are indicative of his split personality and his overt interest in Joyce ('Joo', 'Jimmie', and various other plays on the words 'Jew', 'Julius', and 'James').[57] Ratner is a prime example of what Lewis calls 'The Split-Man', someone who is fundamentally divided from himself, that is, a feeble imitator with no authentic expression of his own.[58] Not only is the summary of Ratner's life and work textured with references to Trieste and 'Tristan and Isolde' (a key intertext of *Work in Progress*), but it also accuses Ratner of stealing outfits from the wardrobe of the past, and thereby appropriating that most of Joycean of techniques, 'stolentelling':[59]

> This highbrow-sub-sheik of the slum had been the triste-est Tristan tricked out in the dirtiest second-hand operatic wardrobe ... the eternal imitation-person in a word, whose ambition led him to burgle all the books of Western romance to steal their heroes' expensive outfits for his musty shop—the split-man of another tale.[60]

The Apes of God is populated with many such imitation persons who are second-hand even to the extent that their interior lives are but parodies of other writers' works.

A case in point is Matthew Plunkett, who is self-evidently a savage caricature of Lytton Strachey. Plunkett mills around Bloomsbury, muses about 'Eminent Victorian giants', and seduces the boyish Betty Bligh (Dora Carrington) on the advice

---

[56] Andrzej Gąsiorek, *Wyndham Lewis and Modernism* (Tavistock: Northcote House, 2004), 66.
[57] *AOG* 161.
[58] *AOG* 151.
[59] *FW* 424.35.
[60] *AOG* 153–4.

of his psychoanalyst.[61] When Plunkett contemplates his collection of shells, the narrative descends into his interior monologue, which is rendered in Woolfian prose:

> The Bloomsbury square with its museum of much-etched, and then untidily painted, Victorian trees, untidily posing, sluttish and sly, came to life (at Matthew Plunkett's emergence as he stepped boldly out) with a terrible explosion, between the wheels of a Shell-van full of petrol-tins, nosing its way round the railings. Vans simply farted and passed on he thought, as he jumped up a little, as though he were shot, and his pulse clanged in his heart upon the second step. SHELL IS SO DIFFERENT![62]

Woolf's techniques are expertly aped, from her ductile use of free indirect discourse to her habit of rendering scenes in impressionistic daubs, and her tendency to embed parenthetical updates on protagonist's movements within scenes, but the contents are bathetic. Unlike Septimus Smith, who is shell-shocked and therefore genuinely disturbed by the 'violent explosion' that emanates from the motor car that also arrests Clarissa Dalloway's interior monologue in *Mrs Dalloway* (1925), Plunkett is only mildly perturbed.[63] He observes 'Vans simply farted' ('simply' being one of Woolf's pet words) before proceeding to experience an epiphany that is none too bright but appears so startling to Plunkett that it is rendered in capital letters. The parody expresses Lewis's preference for hard, exteriorized form, what he called 'the shield of the tortoise, or the rigid stylistic articulations of the grasshopper', over the internal method, the formless, chaotic, inward voicings he likened to 'the jelly-fish that floats in the centre of the subterranean stream of the "dark" Unconscious'.[64]

Lewis returned to the episode in *Mrs Dalloway* when the motor car that onlookers assume contains either the Prime Minister or the Queen backfires in *Men without Art*, in which he pooh-poohed the popular estimation of Woolf as an originator and railed against her use of 'stream of consciousness', a 'so-called Bloomsbury technique' and a product of the fashionable time-cult practised by shallow imitators of Joyce:

> often the incidents in the local 'masterpieces' are exact and puerile copies of the scene in his Dublin drama (cf. The Viceroy's progress through Dublin in *Ulysses* with the Queen's progress through London in *Mrs. Dalloway*—the latter is a sort of undergraduate imitation of the former, winding up with a smoke-writing in the

---

[61] *AOG* 59. Lytton Strachey's brother James translated Sigmund Freud for the Hogarth Press.
[62] *AOG* 66–7, Lewis's capitals.
[63] Virginia Woolf, *Mrs Dalloway*, ed. David Bradshaw (Oxford: Oxford University Press, 2000), 12.
[64] Lewis, *Men without Art*, 120.

246 MODERNIST PARODY

sky, a pathetic 'crib' of the firework display and the rocket that is the culmination of Mr. Bloom's beach-ecstasy).[65]

Lewis subsequently defended his vicious attack on Woolf's originality in a letter to the editor of the *Spectator* of 2 November 1934, comparing her unfavourably to Eliot and Pound, who at least did not disguise their imitative methods:

> Mr. Ezra Pound—a literary figure as much esteemed as Mrs. Woolf has, for example, never disguised the fact that he is mainly a translator—an adapter, an arranger, a *pasticheur*, if you like. And Mr. T. S. Eliot has even made a virtue of developing himself into an incarnate Echo, as it were (though an *original* Echo, if one can say that).[66]

Mocked on her own terms, and for her proximity to Joyce, Woolf's individual talent is questioned; her characteristic style is asserted to be not only derivative but a readily reproducible effect. Lewis stated that his 'criticisms were rather a writer's than a reader's. It is the internal creative *machinery* that I expose.'[67] That critical exposure of 'the internal creative *machinery*' of now formulaic modernism and its imitative methods is shown by the contrast between the inimitable style of Lewis's spasmodic, abundantly energized, satirical prose in *The Apes of God* and the charges of belatedness and diluted imitation that he levels at the artists he parodies and caricatures.

As the progenitor of the '"thought-stream" method' that Lewis loathed, and a number of other widely imitated techniques and conceits besides, Joyce looms large in Lewis's fiction as an opponent whose aesthetics and person are vigorously and extensively rebutted. As Scott W. Klein notes, 'Lewis's most important fictions ... are in large part parodic responses to Joyce.'[68] In *The Fictions of James Joyce and Wyndham Lewis: Monsters of Nature and Design* (1994), Klein characterizes *The Apes of God* as 'a kind of anti-*Ulysses*, which attempts to put into fictional practice a revisionary theory of modernist representation, satirizing Joyce's achievements and deflating the pretensions of Bloomsbury'.[69] He points out that Lewis's earlier novel *The Childermass* (1928) 'adds a share of *ad hominem* criticism to literary parody' through the character of James Pullman, who 'had taught at the Berlitz in Trieste, breaks his glasses when pushed over, and "never looks at the objects of his solitude but busies himself in the abstract"', and also the 'gnome-like and authoritarian antagonist, the Bailiff, [who] spouts paragraphs of pseudo-Wakean

---

[65] Lewis, *Men without Art*, 168.
[66] Rose, *Letters of Wyndham Lewis*, 224.
[67] Rose, *Letters of Wyndham Lewis*, 223, Lewis's italics.
[68] Scott W. Klein, *The Fictions of James Joyce and Wyndham Lewis: Monsters of Nature and Design* (Cambridge: Cambridge University Press, 1994), 3, 8.
[69] Klein, *Fictions*, 8.

PARODISTS OF HISTORY   247

nonsense as part of his erratic rule of the other world'.[70] As Klein proceeds to show, Joyce gave Lewis every bit as good as he got, retaliating with numerous 'biographical squibs, echoing *Time and Western Man*, and parodying Lewis's and Joyce's personal interactions' in *Finnegans Wake* (in which he recast 'his one-time friend as a significant component of Shaun').[71] The two men's recourse to parody as a mode of literary criticism and personal attack is indicative of the competitive dynamics of modernist experimentation, where aesthetic differences are met with displays of one-upmanship, and also the intensity of modernism's inward gaze.

There is a sense in which *Ulysses* was a precursor too strong for anyone but Joyce to overcome. Reflecting on the process of 'endless interpolation' by which Joyce exponentially expanded successive drafts of the *Wake*, Clive Hart observes that Joyce 'seems to have felt compelled to turn on himself and parody his own achievement' so that the text also exhibits 'a kind of endless regress of self-parody'.[72] This regress is clearly shown through punning play on the titles of Joyce's previous works. The secondary meaning of *Chamber Music* is made explicit in the 'Sirens' episode of *Ulysses*, which invites readers to come to an ironic interpretation of Joyce's early verse when Bloom muses 'Chamber Music. Could make a kind of pun on that. It is a kind of music I often thought when she. Acoustics that is. Tinkling'.[73] Joyce's interest in 'shamebred music' found its correlative in the loving debasement of his own juvenilia.[74] To reconcile his sentimental attachment to his previous work, and to prevent it from ossifying and retaining a fixed form in either his imagination or that of his readers, Joyce came to parody his own writing in a continuous cycle, a practice made conspicuous by punning play with earlier titles in *Finnegans Wake* such as 'chambermade music', 'a poor trait of the artless', and 'usylessly unreadable Blue Book of Eccles'.[75]

Finnegans Wake did not just parody the work of Joyce's contemporaries, or his own compositions, but strove to encompass all human history in parody so profound that it extended even the sense-making structures of language itself. The parodic language of the *Wake* is 'nat language at any sinse of the world', but it everywhere refers back to its prime model, the English language, without which no sense of the word or the world of the *Wake* can be made.[76] Joyce explained this principle in a letter to Weaver of 27 June 1924:

> If ever I try to explain to people now what I am supposed to be writing I see stupefaction freezing them into silence. For instance Shaun, after a long absurd

---

[70] Klein, *Fictions*, 8; Klein refers readers to Wyndham Lewis, *The Childermass* (London: John Calder, 1965), 26, 99.
[71] Klein, *Fictions*, 168, 3.
[72] Clive Hart, *Structure and Motif in Finnegans Wake* (London: Faber & Faber, 1962), 41–2.
[73] *U* 11.979–81.
[74] *FW* 164.15–16.
[75] *FW* 184.4, 114.32, 179.26–7.
[76] *FW* 83.12.

248 MODERNIST PARODY

and rather incestuous Lenten lecture to Izzy, his sister, takes leave of her 'with a half a glance of Irish frisky from under the shag of his parallel brows'. These are the words the reader will see but not those he will hear.[77]

Joyce distorts familiar words and phrases, so that the parodied original(s) might be inferred through imagined audition, thus mingling the meanings of many gestured words. In the example he gave to Weaver the implied auditory sense underlying the words on the page is unusually clear. Joyce's coining 'paraidiotically', silly synthetic Greek for 'almost privately' (παρά + ιδιωτικά), is expressive of the many private meanings known only to Joyce, implicit in his parodies of sense-making language.[78]

Joyce frequently reverted to parody to make the process of writing *Work in Progress* accessible and intelligible to initiates, and also to disseminate the nature of his work to the general public. In a letter to Weaver of 16 November 1924 Joyce likened the difficult task of linking sections of his writing to teams of men tunnelling through a mountain, comparing the sound of the tunnelling 'gangs . . . hammering on all sides' to a hail of cannon fire in a parody of Tennyson's 'The Charge of the Light Brigade' (1854):

> Complications to right of me, complications to left of me, complex on the page before me, perplex in the pen beside me, duplex in the meandering eyes of me, stuplex on the face that reads me.[79]

Joyce's parody alludes to the presence of Tennyson's poem in his work, but it is also a statement about the writing of the *Wake* and the way its language signifies. The iteration 'complex . . . perplex . . . duplex . . . stuplex' enacts the protean, ever-proliferating complexity of Wakean language and also registers the readers' bafflement, as well as Joyce's growing problems with his sight. Joyce's endlessly mutable language reveals transformation to be *the* theme. Joyce's career as a writer culminates in the most extreme parody—parody not just of literature, but of language itself—to express what 'cannot be rendered sensible by the use of wideawake language, cutanddry grammar and goahead plot'.[80] When Joyce broke into a parody of Tennyson in his letter to Weaver, he seized on the most apposite vehicle to convey the basic compositional principle of *Finnegans Wake*, where the formal patternings of the English language undergo progressive distortion and transformation to the extent that parody is by no means a secondary form, but writing itself. The *Wake* commands its readers to 'listen to the mocking birde to micking

[77] *LJJ* I 216.
[78] *FW* 615.5–6.
[79] *LJJ* I 222; Tennyson, 'The Charge of the Light Brigade', *Poems*, 225–6.
[80] *LJJ* III 146.

barde making bared', announcing that paying attention to the narrator's mimicking mockery will lay bare the book's making.[81]

Parody, being transformative, is always an invitation to further transformation, and thus has endless generative potential. Accordingly, the *Wake* is 'parapilagian', ever parodying material pillaged from other texts, and the parody is so vast that it encompasses all language, literature, and human history.[82] This uninhibited exploration of parody identifies the qualitative difference between Joyce's practice and that of his modernist contemporaries. The echo of the Pelagian heresy here, the belief that Adam's sin did not taint human nature, figures and negates the concept of parody as a form of linguistic heresy. This association is reinforced by the repeated puns on 'sinse' (sense and sins) and 'parodies' and 'paradise', where 'parody' is a consequence and linguistic marker of lost paradise. Readers are told, after all, that it was 'Hoddum and Heave, our monsterbilker' (fallen Tim Finnegan heaving his builder's hod and Adam and Eve in heaven) who 'balked his bawd of parodies'.[83] When Muta asks Juta whether language that is 'twyly velleid' (truly and two-ly, valid and veiled) 'is thus then paridicynical' (paradisiacal or cynically parodic), Juva replies 'Ut vivat volumen sic pereat pouradosus!' [That the book may live let paradise be lost!][84] Paradise and the purity of prelapsarian language must be sacrificed to the endlessly iterative deformations of parody for the book *Finnegans Wake* to exist. In the symbolic order of the *Wake*, the Genesis story is also the story of parody, which likewise makes a subject of its own textual genesis. It is no coincidence then that Shem the Penman, one of Joyce's many semi-ironic doubles, learned '*with stolen fruit* how cutely to copy all their various styles of signature so as one day to utter an epical forged cheque on the public for his own private profit'.[85] Joyce profits by counterfeiting other authors' works, passed off as his own, and by the advantages he gains over a stupefied reading public, who are to persevere with a parodic language they can only partially comprehend.

Joyce's recourse to parody as a technique that explicates the genesis of the text and sheds light on his writing processes is manifest in the parodies that he concocted of 'Ride a Cock Horse' and 'Humpty Dumpty' to sell Faber's editions of *Anna Livia Plurabelle* (1930) and *Haveth Childers Everywhere* (1931):

> Buy a book in brown paper
> From Faber & Faber
> To see Annie Liffey trip, tumble and caper.
> Sevensinns in her singthings,

---

[81] *FW* 251.35.
[82] *FW* 387.5–6.
[83] *FW* 296.6–7.
[84] *FW* 610.14–16.
[85] *FW* 181.14–17, my italics.

250 MODERNIST PARODY

> Plurabelle on her prose,
> Seashell ebb music wayriver she flows.[86]

> Humptydump Dublin squeaks through his norse,
> Humptydump Dublin hath a horriple vorse
> And with all his kinks english
> Plus his irismanx brogues
> Humptydump Dublin's grandada of all rogues.[87]

These rhymes advertise the 'kinks english' and 'irismanx brogues' distinctive to *Work in Progress* and convey the fluidity and fallen nature of his principal characters Anna Livia Plurabelle (ALP) and Humphrey Chimpden Earwicker (HCE). As parodies they recall their models, drawing parallels between ALP and the fine lady of folklore and HCE and Humpty Dumpty, gesturing to the 'centuple celves' of the characters that populate the *Wake* and to its macaronic linguistic potpourri.[88] Of course, the figure of Humpty Dumpty is evoked many times in the *Wake*. The most famous version of the nursery rhyme appears in chapter 6 of *Through the Looking-Glass and What Alice Found There*, in which Humpty Dumpty explains the portmanteau neologisms in 'Jabberwocky' that provide the most obvious model for Joyce's punning deformations of the English language.[89]

Parody is doubly appropriate for introducing ALP and showing how she came into being. ALP developed out of the dream of Molly Bloom that Joyce wrote up for Gorman.[90] Initially Joyce worked it into a parody '(To the tune of "Molly Brannigan")'.[91] Here Molly morphs into a very preliminary sketch of ALP, at that time 'Annie Levy Blumenthal'.[92] Accordingly, the first time we encounter ALP in the *Wake* she is a 'parody's bird', pecking at spoiled goods for her 'nabsack'.[93] We leave her 'Alma Luvia, Pollabella' ('pollo' being Italian for 'chicken') reading the postscript to the letter and are told 'And she's about fetted up now with nonsery reams'—fattened up by and fed up with reams of non-serious nursery rhymes—before her soliloquy flows out to sea.[94]

Crawley, Faber's sales manager, hesitated over what to do with Joyce's rhymes, feeling something of Pound's anxieties about low verse and its proximity to high modernism. 'In the end', as Richard Ellmann notes:

> the verses were used only on a mimeographed publicity release, to which was prefixed a note: 'The sales department, puzzled as such departments are wont

[86] *LJJ* III 247, n. 1.
[87] *LJJ* III 247, n. 1.
[88] *FW* 49.33.
[89] Carroll, *Through the Looking Glass and What Alice Found There*, 113–36.
[90] Herbert Gorman, *James Joyce* (New York: Farrar & Rinehart, 1939), 283n and Ellmann, *James Joyce*, 549–50.
[91] Ellmann, *James Joyce*, 549–50.
[92] Ellmann, *James Joyce*, 549–50.
[93] *FW* 11.9, 11.19.
[94] *FW* 619.16–18.

to be, have sought some light on the two James Joyce contributions to Criterion Miscellany ... the explanations [the parodies] offered are passed on that you may be able to derive similar enlightenment.' Joyce was annoyed.[95]

It was quite understandable that Joyce should be peeved by the Faber sales department's indifference to his limericks. Crawley's offhand publicity release showed a general failure to appreciate the thematic and literary appropriateness of comic 'advt rhyme' to Joyce's work. Although Crawley was uncomprehending, seeing no publicity value in Joyce's 'nonsery reams' and sneering at their explanatory powers, the parodies of the literatures by which children first encounter language in fact shed the clearest light on the process of writing the *Wake* and Joyce's status as a 'bawd of parodies': a bard whose works are promiscuously parodic and also a bird of paradise, 'a parody's bird', who shows his borrowed plumes in ritual display.[96]

In an age when the storeroom of history was full to bursting with costumes, none of which fitted, the most original writers did indeed time and again discover 'the realm of their *invention*' in parody, just as Nietzsche foretold. In parody, the modernists found a ready mode of enquiry into origins, a method of origination that was fundamentally oppositional, from which they could construct genealogies that were also re-evaluations. Their laughter was 'spiritual' in the highest sense, in that it constituted a mode of epistemological enquiry that contrived to transcend history. It was also spirited, an exuberant means of self-assertion that provided a carnivalesque corrective to solemnity, romanticism, and other kinds of folly.

The parody and self-parody that made modernism encompassed many historical guises. Speaking very broadly, the modernists could be characterized as inheritors of Bakhtin's 'Second Stylistic Line', descendants of writers such as Rabelais, Swift, and Sterne for whom parody assumed the function of artistic representation in its own right. But the modernists took these practices to new extremes, taking inspiration from the European avant-garde, seeking to surpass the already written and discover new modes of expression and invention that might comprehend and thereby even overcome the movement's temporal predicament. While modernist parody was carnivalesque, overturning old orthodoxies and hierarchies, blurring the lines that divided high culture from low, it was also invested with a new and acutely self-conscious awareness of its own situatedness in history and responsibilities to its contemporary moment. It was a mode of composition that required authors to reflect on the value and purpose of writing in their time and through the ages, but most of all in the civilization they sought to interrogate, remake, and renew.

---

[95] *LJJ* III 247, n. 1. No publicity releases survive from this period in Faber's history in the Faber archive. 'Criterion Miscellany' is the series title for *Anna Livia Plurabelle* (1930) and *Haveth Childers Everywhere* (1931).
[96] *FW* 296.7, 11.9.

252 MODERNIST PARODY

Parody stimulated the modernist imagination. It was a basic compositional technique that was creative yet critical. Concerned with origins as much as originality, tempered by an acute sense of historicity and the ways in which the present must necessarily be constructed by reference to the past, parody as practised by the modernists was profoundly palimpsestual. Modernist parodists made a drama out of their own creative processes, placing the emphasis not on 'what is written but what is in the writing', to use Bradbury's phrase. This emphasis on process requires that their readers take account of how texts were written and then use this knowledge to interpret new works by the light of their relations to the material(s) they transform. In complex works where sources are multiple and references are dense, the doubleness of focus that parody introduces (whereby comparisons are invited and the criticism cuts both ways) creates texts that are profoundly dialogic and radically unstable in their potential proliferation of meaning, making strenuous demands on readers' critical faculties. In its most serious manifestations, modernist parody points to the constructedness of all discourses with a view to making critical interventions in the cultural ideologies they uphold, all the while showing language's tenuous grip on felt reality. It never concedes secondary status for itself (though it often assigns secondary status to the material it mocks). Instead, it presumes its own masterful primacy as an originally creative force.

Irreverent, spirited, and critically engaged, parody proved a creative means for realizing the objectives of modernism. It issued invigorating challenges to conventions of representation and undermined neoclassical standards of taste, allowing a double exposure of how the past is reconfigured in the present just as much as the present is an inflected development of the past. It provided a method for modernists to apprentice themselves to their crafts, come to terms with individual talents, learn the tricks of their trade, achieve saturation, and sift the durable from the apparent. It was one of the modernists' most intuitive literary-critical reflexes, a mechanism for registering their immediate response to new works, processing new techniques, and determining their future value. It offered a means to swat pretenders, best rivals, or inform mentors that their influence had been outgrown. In private, the modernists could let down their guard and indulge in one of writing's most self-consciously literary pleasures. In public, the assured transformation of luminous fragments from literary history into modernist masterpieces was achieved through finely controlled parodic inflection that renewed old styles and enlarged their discursive possibilities. Directing parodic scrutiny onto their own strategies of literary innovation spurred the modernists to produce yet more forcefully experimental and original art.

For all that Lewis was right that certain kinds of modernist writing had atrophied through imitative methods that had become automatic and that others had dissipated their force through their enduring fixation on the achievements of the past, parody remained at the heart of modernist greatness. From their apprentice experiments to the masterpieces of high modernism and beyond, the modernists' self-fashioning vitally depended on parody, as they discovered the realm of their own invention as parodists of world history and its literatures, and eventually even as parodists of modernism itself.

Bibliography

Manuscripts

Eliot, T. S., 'Parodies of Publisher's "Blurbs" Composed by T. S. Eliot for the Firm of Faber & Faber', typescript (1937), Papers of the Hayward Bequest of T. S. Eliot Material HB/P9, King's College, Cambridge.

Eliot, T. S., 'Old Possum's Book of Practical Cats &c. Typescript by the Author' [T. S. Eliot] with Early Drafts of Two Poems, & Unpublished Material, Including His Old Possum's Letter to the Publishers and Parodies of Readers' Reports Ascribed to Members of the Firm of Faber & Faber Ltd.', typescript, n.d., Papers of the Hayward Bequest of T. S. Eliot Material HB/V9, King's College, Cambridge.

James, Henry, *Terminations* (London: William Heinemann, 1895), Max Beerbohm's copy, Beerbohm Collection 3.62, Merton College, Oxford.

Pound, Ezra, 'In Praise of the Masters', typescript, n.d., Ezra Pound Papers, Yale Collection of American Literature, Beinecke Rare Book and Manuscript Library, Yale University, YCAL MSS 43, box 86, folder 3712.

—— 'Med', typescript, n.d., Ezra Pound Papers, Yale Collection of American Literature, Beinecke Rare Book and Manuscript Library, Yale University, YCAL MSS 43, box 89, folder 3809.

—— 'Mr. K', typescript, n.d., Ezra Pound Papers, Yale Collection of American Literature, Beinecke Rare Book and Manuscript Library, Yale University, YCAL MSS 43, box 89, folder 3809.

—— 'Pagentry', typescript, n.d., Ezra Pound Papers, Yale Collection of American Literature, Beinecke Rare Book and Manuscript Library, Yale University, YCAL MSS 43, box 88, folder 3778.

Printed Works

Blast: Review of the Great English Vortex I (20 June 1914).

'Comments and Responses', *Little Review* VIII(2) (spring 1922), 33–5.

'Dada Soulève Tout', *Little Review* VII(4) (January–March 1921), 62–3.

Glebe I(5), Des Imagistes—An Anthology (February 1914).

'Initial Manifesto of the "Fatuists" to the Public', *New Age* X(22) (28 March 1912), 524.

'An Introduction to Ultra-Violet Poetry', *Wisconsin Literary Magazine* (January 1917), 111–12.

'Notes and Announcements', *Poetry: A Magazine of Verse* I(2) (November 1912), 65.

Others III(5), The Spectric School (January 1917).

'Pathology des Dommagistes', *Chapbook* 23 (May 1921), 21–4.

'Sir Owen Seaman on "Parody": Lecture to English-Speaking Union', *Times* 45365 (20 November 1929), 12.

'Sir Owen Seaman on Parody: A Form of Literary Criticism', *Times* 46439 (9 May 1933), 12.

BIBLIOGRAPHY   255

'Abel Sanders' [Ezra Pound], 'The Poems of Abel Sanders', *Little Review* VIII(1) (autumn 1921), 111.
— 'The Reader Critic: Mr. Lindsay', *Little Review* IV(9) (January 1918), 54–5.
— 'The Reader Critic: This Approaches Literature!', *Little Review* IV(6) (October 1917), 39.
— 'Sculpshure [*sic*]', *Little Review* VII(4) (January–March 1921), 47.
Ackroyd, Peter, *T. S. Eliot* (London: Hamilton, 1984).
Adlard, John, *Owen Seaman: His Life and Work* (London: Eighteen Nineties Society, 1977).
Aldington, Richard, 'Anti-Hellenism: A Note on Some Modern Art', *Egoist* I(2) (15 January 1914), 35–6.
— 'Blast', *Egoist* I(14) (15 July 1914), 272–3.
— *Life for Life's Sake: A Book of Reminiscences* (New York: Viking, 1941).
— 'Penultimate Poetry: Xenophilometropolitania', *Egoist* I(2) (January 1914), 36.
'Alice Morning' [Beatrice Hastings], 'Impressions of Paris', *New Age* XVI(12) (21 January 1915), 308–9.
'Alfred Venison' [Ezra Pound], *Alfred Venison's Poems; Social Credit Themes by the Poet of Titchfield Street* (London: Stanley Nott, 1935).
Alter, Robert, *Partial Magic: The Novel as a Self-Conscious Genre* (Berkeley: University of California Press, 1975).
Ames, Christopher, 'The Modernist Canon Narrative: Woolf's *Between the Acts* and Joyce's "Oxen of the Sun"', *Twentieth Century Literature* 37(4) (1991), 390–404.
Apollinaire, Guillaume, 'L'Antitradizione Futurista', *Lacerba* (15 September 1913), 202–3.
Ardis, Ann, *Modernism and Cultural Conflict, 1880–1922* (Cambridge: Cambridge University Press, 2002).
— 'The Dialogics of Modernism(s) in the *New Age*', *Modernism/Modernity* 14(3) (September 2007), 407–34.
Atherton, J. S., 'The Peacock in the Oxen', *Wake Newslitter* 7 (1970), 77–8.
— 'Still More Peacock in the Oxen', *Wake Newslitter* 8 (1971), 53.
Auden, W. H., *The Orators: An English Study* (London: Faber & Faber, 1932).
— 'The Poet and the City' (1962), *The Dyer's Hand and Other Essays* (London: Faber & Faber, 1963), 72–89.
Austen, Jane, *Northanger Abbey, Lady Susan, The Watsons, Sandition*, ed. John Davie (Oxford: Oxford University Press, 1990).
— *Sense and Sensibility*, ed. James Kinsley, intro. Margaret Anne Doody, and notes Claire Lamont (Oxford: Oxford University Press, 2004).
Bakhtin, M. M., *The Dialogic Imagination: Four Essays by M. M. Bakhtin*, ed. and trans. Michael Holquist and Caryl Emerson (Austin: University of Texas Press, 1981).
— *Problems of Dostoevsky's Poetics*, ed. and trans. Caryl Emerson (Minnesota and Manchester: University of Minneapolis Press, 1984).
— *Rabelais and His World*, trans. Hélène Iswolsky (Bloomington, IN: Indiana University Press, 1984).
Barnett, Annie, and Lucy Dale, *An Anthology of English Prose (1332–1740)*, pref. Andrew Lang (London: Longmans, Green & Co., 1912).
Barth, John, 'The Literature of Exhaustion', in Malcolm Bradbury, ed., *The Novel Today: Contemporary Writers on Modern Fiction* (Manchester: Manchester University Press, 1977), 70–83.
Baudelaire, 'À une passante', *Les fleurs du mal*, in *Œuvres complètes*, vol. 1, ed. Claude Pichois (Paris: Gallimard (Bibliothèque de la Plèia), 1975), 93.

256 BIBLIOGRAPHY

Baumann, Heinrich, *Londinismen (Slang und Cant), Wörterbuch der Londoner Volkssprache sowie der Üblichsten Gauner-, Matrosen-, Sport- und Zunftausdrücke; mit Einleitung und Musterstücken; ein Supplement zu allen Englisch-Deutschen Wörterbuchern* (Berlin-Schoneberg: Langenscheidtsche Verlagsbuchhandlug, n.d. (c. 1902).

Beach, Sylvia, and James Laughlin, *Shakespeare and Company*, 2nd edn (Lincoln, NE: University of Nebraska Press, 1991).

Beaumont, Francis, and John Fletcher, *The Maid's Tragedy*, ed. T. W. Craik (Manchester: University of Manchester Press, 1988).

Bechhöfer, C. E., 'Pastiche', *New Age* XV(13) (30 July 1914), 308.

Beck, Harald, 'Edward FitzGerald at Sea: Oxen Notesheet 17', *James Joyce Online Notes* (2013), www.jjon.org/.

Bede, Cuthbert, *Medley* (London: Blackwood & Sons, 1856).

Beerbohm, Max, *Around Theatres* (London: Hart-Davies, 1924).

—— *A Christmas Garland* (London: William Heinemann, 1912).

—— 'A Defence of Cosmetics', *Yellow Book: An Illustrated Quarterly* I (April 1894), 65–82.

—— *Last Theatres*, 1904–1910 (London: Hart-Davis, 1970).

—— 'A Letter to the Editor', *Yellow Book: An Illustrated Quarterly* II (July 1894), 281–4.

—— *Letters of Max Beerbohm*, 1892–1956, ed. Rupert Hart-Davies (Oxford: Oxford University Press, 1989).

—— *Max Beerbohm: Collected Verse*, ed. J. G. Riewald (Hamden, CT: Archon Books, 1994).

—— 'Savonarola Brown', *Seven Men* (London: William Heinemann, 1919).

—— *The Works of Max Beerbohm, with a Bibliography by John Lane* (London: John Lane/Bodley Head, 1896).

Behrman, S. N., *Conversations with Max* (London: Hamish Hamilton, 1960).

Bell, Clive, *Old Friends, Personal Recollections* (London: Chatto & Windus, 1956).

—— *Since Cézanne* (New York: Harcourt Brace & Co., 1922).

Bergson, Henri, *An Introduction to Metaphysics* (1903), trans. T. E. Hulme (Indianapolis: Bobbs-Merrill, 1949).

—— *Laughter: An Essay on the Meaning of the Comic*, trans. Cloudesley Brereton and Fred Rothwell (London: Macmillan, 1911).

Bloom, Harold, *The Anxiety of Influence: A Theory of Poetry* (New York: Oxford University Press, 1997).

Boileau Despréaux, Nicolas, *Boileau's Lutrin a Mock-heroic Poem. In Six Canto's, Render'd into English Verse. To Which Is Prefix'd Some Account of Boileau's Writings, and This Translation*, trans. N. Rowe (London: Printed for R. Burrough and J. Baker; E. Sanger and E. Curll, 1708).

Bornstein, George, ed., *Ezra Pound among the Poets: Homer, Ovid, Li Po, Dante, Whitman, Browning, Yeats, Williams, Eliot* (Chicago: University of Chicago Press, 1985).

Boswell, James, *The Life of Samuel Johnson*, ed. R. W. Chapman (Oxford: Oxford University Press, 2008).

Bradbury, Malcolm, 'An Age of Parody: Style in the Modern Arts', *No, Not Bloomsbury* (London: Deutsch, 1987), 46–64.

—— ed., *The Novel Today: Contemporary Writers on Modern Fiction* (Manchester: Manchester University Press, 1977).

Breunig, Le Roy C., 'F. S. Flint, Imagism's 'Mâitre d'Ecole', *Comparative Literature* 4 (1952), 118–36.

Brodsky, Horace, 'The Lewis–Brzeska–Pound Troupe', *Egoist* I(14) (15 July 1914), 272.

Brooker, Jewel Spears, ed., *T. S. Eliot: The Contemporary Reviews*, American Critical Archives 14 (Cambridge: Cambridge University Press, 2004).

BIBLIOGRAPHY 257

Browning, Robert, *Fifine at the Fair, and Other Poems* (Boston: James R. Osgood & Co., 1872).

Budgen, Frank, *James Joyce and the Making of 'Ulysses', and Other Writings* (London: Oxford University Press, 1972).

Burke, Thomas, *Limehouse Nights: Tales of Chinatown* (London: Grant Richards, 1917).

Burney, Fanny, *Camilla, or, A Picture of Youth*, ed. Edward A. Bloom and Lillian D. Bloom (Oxford: Oxford University Press, 2009).

— *Cecilia, or Memoirs of an Heiress*, ed. Peter Sabor and Margaret Anne Doody (Oxford: Oxford University Press, 2008).

Burns, Christie L., *Gestural Politics: Stereotype and Parody in Joyce* (Albany, NY: State University of New York Press, 2000).

Burns, Robert, 'Is There for Honest Poverty', in James Kinsley, ed., *Poems and Songs of Robert Burns*, vol. 2 (Oxford: Clarendon Press, 1968), 762–63.

Bush, Ronald, *T. S. Eliot: A Study in Character and Style* (Oxford: Oxford University Press, 1983).

— *The Genesis of Ezra Pound's Cantos* (Princeton, NJ: Princeton University Press, 1976).

Butcher, S. H., *Aristotle's Theory of Poetry and Fine Art with a Critical Text and Translation of the Poetics*, 4th edn (London: Macmillan, 1927).

Byron, Lord, *The Vision of Judgment*, in *Lord Byron: The Complete Poetical Works, Volume 6, 1821–22*, ed. Jerome J. McGann and Barry Weller (Oxford: Oxford University Press, 1991), 309–45.

Caesar, Terry, 'Betrayal and Theft: Beerbohm, Parody, and Modernism', *Ariel* 17(3) (July 1986), 23–37.

— '"I Quite Forget What—Say a Daffodilly": Victorian Parody', *English Literary History* 51(4) (1984), 795–818.

Calverley, C. S., *Fly Leaves* (Cambridge: Deighton, Bell & Co., 1872).

— *Verses and Translations* (Cambridge: Deighton, Bell & Co., 1861).

— *Verses and Translations by Charles Stuart Calverley, with an Introduction by Owen Seaman*, 17th edn (London: Blackie & Son, 1905).

Carpenter, Humphrey, *A Serious Character: The Life of Ezra Pound* (London: Faber & Faber, 1988).

Carr, Helen, *The Verse Revolutionaries: Ezra Pound, H. D. and the Imagists* (London: Jonathan Cape, 2009).

Carroll, Lewis, *Alice's Adventures in Wonderland* (London: Macmillan, 1866).

— *The Letters of Lewis Carroll*, ed. Morton N. Cohen, vol. I (New York: Oxford University Press, 1979).

— *Through the Looking Glass and What Alice Found There* (London: Macmillan, 1872).

Carter, Huntly, 'Art and Drama in Paris', *New Age* X(19) (7 March 1912), 443.

Caws, Mary Ann, ed., *Manifesto: A Century of Isms* (Lincoln, NE: University of Nebraska Press, 2001).

Cervantes Saavedra, Miguel de, *Don Quixote De La Mancha*, trans. Charles Jarvis, ed., and intro. E. C. Riley (Oxford: Oxford University Press, 1998).

Chambers, Robert, *Parody: The Art that Plays with Art* (New York: Peter Lang, 2010).

'Charles Brookfarmer' [C. E. Bechhöfer], 'Futile-Ism. Or, All Cackle and No Osses', *New Age* XV(7) (18 June 1914), 154.

Chinitz, David, 'T. S. Eliot and the Cultural Divide', *PMLA* 110(2) (March 1995), 236–47.

— *T. S. Eliot and the Cultural Divide* (Chicago: University of Chicago Press, 2003).

258 BIBLIOGRAPHY

Chipchase, Paul, rev., Linda Hutcheon, *A Theory of Parody* (1985), in *Tempo* 154 (1985), 41–3.

Clare Local Studies Project, *The Celtic Times: Michael Cusack's Gaelic Games Newspaper*, foreword Micheál Ó Muircheartaigh, pref. Breandán Mac Lua, intro. Marcus De Búrca (Ennis, Co. Clare: CLASP, 2003).

Clearfield, Andrew, 'Pound, Paris, and Dada', *Paideuma* 7 (spring and fall, 1978), 113–40.

Cohn, Alan M., 'Joyce's Notes on the End of "Oxen of the Sun", *James Joyce Quarterly* 4(3), Translation Issue (spring, 1967), 194–201.

Coleridge, Samuel Taylor, *The Collected Works of Samuel Taylor Coleridge*, ed. H. J. Jackson and J. R. de. J. Jackson, vol. 11 (Princeton, NJ: Princeton University Press, 1995).

Connolly, Cyril, 'Gertrude Stein', *Previous Convictions* (London: Hamish Hamilton, 1963), 283–4.

Connolly, Thomas E., *The Personal Library of James Joyce: A Descriptive Bibliography*, 2nd edn (Buffalo, NY: University of Buffalo Press, 1957).

Cooper, John Xiros, *T. S. Eliot and the Ideology of 'Four Quartets'* (Cambridge: Cambridge University Press, 2008).

Cork, Richard, *Vorticism and Abstract Art in the Machine Age, Volume 1: Origins and Development* (London: Gordon Fraser, 1976).

Crowley, Ronan, 'Earmarking "Oxen of the Sun": On the Dates of the Copybook Drafts', *Genetic Joyce Studies* 18 (2018).

Csengeri, Karen, ed., *The Collected Writings of T. E. Hulme* (Oxford: Clarendon Press, 1994).

Cummings, E. E., 'Untitled Parody of *The Waste Land*' (Houghton MS Am 1892.5 (736)), in J. Alison Rosenblitt, *E. E. Cummings' Modernism and the Classics: Each Imperishable Stanza* (Oxford: Oxford University Press, 2016), 301.

Danson, Lawrence, *Max Beerbohm and the Act of Writing* (Oxford: Clarendon Press, 1989).

Davidson, John, *John Davidson: A Selection of his Poems, with a Preface by T. S. Eliot*, ed. Maurice Lindsay (London: Hutchinson, 1961).

Davison, Sarah, 'An "Atmosphere of Parody": Ezra Pound and Imagism', in Catherine Morley and Alex Goody, eds., *American Modernism: Cultural Transactions* (Newcastle: Cambridge Scholars Publishing, 2009), 143–64.

—— 'Joyce's Incorporation of Literary Sources in "Oxen of the Sun"', *Genetic Joyce Studies* 9 (2009), www.geneticjoycestudies.org/.

—— 'Max Beerbohm's Altered Books', *Textual Cultures* 6(1) (spring 2011), 48–75.

—— 'Oxtail Soup: Dialects of English in the Tailpiece of the 'Oxen of the Sun' Episode of *Ulysses*', *Genetic Joyce Studies* 14 (2014), www.geneticjoycestudies.org/.

—— 'Trenchant Criticism: Joyce's Use of Richard Chenevix Trench's Philological Studies in "Oxen of the Sun"', *Joyce Studies Annual* (2014), 164–95.

—— '"The True-Born Englishman" and the Irish Bull: Daniel Defoe in the "Oxen of the Sun" Episode of *Ulysses*', *New Quotatoes: European Joyce Studies* 25 (2016), 111–40.

Dekker, Thomas, *The Great Frost, Cold Doings in London, except it be at the Lotterie* (London: Henry Gosson, 1608).

Deming, Robert, ed., *James Joyce: The Critical Heritage: Volume 1: 1907–27* (London: Routledge & Kegan Paul, 1970).

Denisoff, Dennis, *Aestheticism and Sexual Parody 1840–1940* (Cambridge: Cambridge University Press, 2001).

Diepeveen, Leonard, *The Difficulties of Modernism* (New York: Routledge, 2003).

—— *Mock Modernism: An Anthology of Parodies, Travesties, Frauds, 1910–1935* (Toronto: University of Toronto Press, 2014).

—— *Modernist Fraud* (Oxford: Oxford University Press, 2019).

Dobrée, Bonamy, 'T. S. Eliot: A Personal Reminiscence', in Allen Tate, ed., *T. S. Eliot: The Man and His Work* (New York: Dell, 1966), 65–77.

Dobson, Austin, *Eighteenth Century Studies* (London: Dent, 1914).

Dostoevsky, Fyodor, *The Village of Stepanchikovo: and Its Inhabitants: from the Notes of an Unknown*, rev. edn, trans. and intro. Ignat Avsey (London: Penguin, 1995).

Downing, Gregory, 'Joyce's "Oxen of the Sun" Notesheets: A Transcription and Sourcing of the Stylistic Entries, A Compilation of the Existing Transcriptions and Sourcings, Supplemented by New Sourcing Work: first installment: notesheet 1 and the left-hand column of entries on notesheet 2', *Genetic Joyce Studies* 2 (2002), www.geneticjoycestudies. org/.

Dowson, Ernest, 'In Tempore Senectutis', *The Poems of Ernest Dowson, with a Memoir by Arthur Symons, Four Illustrations by Aubrey Beardsley and a Portrait by William Rothenstein* (London: John Lane/Bodley Head, 1905), 50–1.

Dryden, John, *Mac Flecknoe*, in James Kinsley, ed., *The Poems of John Dryden*, vol. I (London: Oxford University Press, 1958), 265–71.

Edgeworth, Maria, *Belinda*, ed. Linda Bree (Oxford: Oxford University Press, 2019).

Edwards, Colin, 'City Burlesque: The Pleasures of Paranoia in Ford's *Mister Bosphorus and the Muses*', *International Ford Madox Ford Studies* 4 (2005), 93–109.

Eliot, T. S., *After Strange Gods: A Primer of Modern Heresy* (New York: Harcourt Brace, 1934).

—— *The Complete Prose of T. S. Eliot: The Critical Edition, Volume 1, Apprentice Years, 1905–1918*, ed. Jewel Spears Brooker and Ronald Schuchard (Baltimore: Johns Hopkins Press, 2014).

—— *The Complete Prose of T. S. Eliot: The Critical Edition, Volume 2, The Perfect Critic, 1919–1926*, ed. Anthony Cuda and Ronald Schuchard (Baltimore: Johns Hopkins Press, 2014).

—— *The Complete Prose of T. S. Eliot: The Critical Edition, Volume 7, A European Society, 1947–1953*, ed. Iman Javadi and Ronald Schuchard (Baltimore: Johns Hopkins Press, 2018).

—— 'Dante', *Selected Essays, 1917–1932* (New York: Harcourt Brace, 1932), 205–30.

—— *Ezra Pound, His Metric and Poetry* (New York: Knopf, 1917).

—— 'John Dryden', in Anthony Cuda and Ronald Schuchard, eds., *The Complete Prose of T. S. Eliot: The Critical Edition, Volume 2, The Perfect Critic, 1919–1926* (Baltimore: Johns Hopkins Press, 2014), 350–61.

—— 'In Memoriam: Marie Lloyd', *Criterion* I(2) (January 1923), 192–5.

—— *The Letters of T. S. Eliot: Volume 1: 1898–1922*, rev. edn, ed. Valerie Eliot and Hugh Haughton (New Haven, CT: Yale University Press, 2011).

—— *The Letters of T. S. Eliot: Volume 3, 1926–1929*, ed. Valerie Eliot and John Haffenden (New Haven, CT: Yale University Press, 2012).

—— 'London Letter', *Dial* LXXI(4) (October 1921), 452–5.

—— *On Poetry and Poets* (London: Faber & Faber, 1957).

—— *Poems* (New York: Knopf, 1920).

—— *The Poems of T. S. Eliot: Volume I, Collected and Uncollected Poems; Volume II, Practical Cats & Further Verses*, ed. Christopher Ricks and Jim McCue (London: Faber & Faber, 2015).

260 BIBLIOGRAPHY

Eliot, T. S., *Poems Written in Early Youth* (London: Faber & Faber, 1967).
— 'Reflections on Contemporary Poetry', *Egoist* VI(3) (July 1919), 39–40.
— 'Reflections on Vers Libre', in Jewel Spears Brooker and Ronald Schuchard, eds., *The Complete Prose of T. S. Eliot: The Critical Edition, Volume 1, Apprentice Years, 1905–1918* (Baltimore: Johns Hopkins Press, 2014), 511–18.
— *The Sacred Wood* (London: Methuen, 1920).
— *Selected Essays, 1917–1932* (New York: Harcourt Brace, 1932).
— 'Sweeney Erect', *Poems* (New York: Knopf, 1920).
— *Noctes Binanianae: Certain Voluntary and Satyrical Verses and Compliments as Were Lately Exchang'd between Some of the Choicest Wits of the Age: Collected with the Greatest Care and Now Printed without Castration after the Most Correct Copies* (London: Lund Humphries & Co., 1939).
— *To Criticize the Critic* (London: Faber & Faber, 1965).
— '*Ulysses*, Order and Myth', *Dial* LXXV (November 1923), 480–3.
— 'What Dante Means to Me', in Iman Javadi and Ronald Schuchard, eds., *The Complete Prose of T. S. Eliot: The Critical Edition, Volume 7, A European Society, 1947–1953* (Baltimore: Johns Hopkins Press, 2018), 482–92.
Eliot, Valerie, ed., *The Waste Land: A Facsimile & Transcript of the Original Drafts including the Annotations of Ezra Pound* (London: Faber & Faber, 1971).
Ellmann, Richard, *The Consciousness of Joyce* (London: Faber & Faber, 1977).
— *James Joyce*, rev. edn (Oxford: Oxford University Press, 1982).
Erkkila, Betsy, *Walt Whitman among the French: Poet and Myth* (Princeton, NJ: Princeton University Press, 1980).
Esty, Joshua D., 'Amnesia in the Fields: Late Modernism, Late Imperialism, and the English Pageant-Play', *English Literary History* 69 (2002), 245–76.
'F. M.' [Vivien Eliot], 'Letters of the Moment—II', *Criterion* II(7) (April 1924), 360–4.
Felstiner, John, *The Lies of Art: Max Beerbohm's Parody and Caricature* (New York: Knopf, 1972).
Fiedler, Leslie, 'Pound as Parodist', in *Ezra Pound: The Legacy of Kulchur*, ed. Marcel Smith and William A. Ulmer (Tuscaloosa, AL: University of Alabama Press, 1988), 128–44.
Fielding, Henry, *The History of the Adventures of Joseph Andrews, and of his friend Mr. Abraham Adams, and An Apology for the Life of Mrs Shamela Andrews*, ed. Douglas Brooks-Davies, rev. edn, intro. Thomas Keymer (Oxford: Oxford University Press, 1999).
— *Tom Jones*, ed. John Bender (Oxford: Oxford University Press, 1998).
FitzGerald, Edward, 'Sea Words and Phrases from the Suffolk Coast', *East Anglian, or, Notes and Queries on Subjects Connected with the Countries of Suffolk, Cambridge, Essex, and Norfolk*, vol. 3 (1869).
Flanell Friedman, Donald, ed. and trans., *An Anthology of Belgian Symbolist Poets* (New York: Peter Lang, 2003).
Flint, F. S., 'Book of the Week: Recent Verse', *New Age* III(11) (11 July 1908), 212–13.
— 'Contemporary French Poetry', *Poetry Review* I(8) (August 1912), 355–414.
— 'Imagisme', *Poetry: A Magazine of Verse* I(6) (March 1913), 198–9.
Ford, Ford Madox, *The Face of the Night* (London: John McQueen, 1904).
— *Letters of Ford Madox Ford*, ed. Richard M. Ludwig (Princeton, NJ: Princeton University Press, 1965).
— *The March of Literature, from Confucius' Day to our Own*, intro. Alexander Theroux (Illinois: Dalkey Archive Press, 1998).

BIBLIOGRAPHY 261

—— *Mister Bosphorus and the Muses, or A Short History of Poetry in Britain, Variety Enter-tainment in Four Acts, Words by Ford Madox Ford, Music by Several Popular Composers: with Harlequinade, Transformation Scene, Cinematograph Effects, and Many Other Nov-elties, as well as Old and Tried Favourites, Decorated with Designs Engraved on Wood by Paul Nash* (London: Duckworth & Co., 1923).

—— *Return to Yesterday* (London: Victor Gollancz, 1931).

Francis, John Oswald, *Change: A Glamorgan Play in Three Acts*, intro. Montrose J. Moses (New York: Doubleday, Page & Co., 1914).

Freytag-Loringhoven, Else von, 'Poems': 'Irrender König'; 'Klink—Hratzvenga (Death-wail)'; 'Nari—Tzarissamanili (He is Dead!)', *Little Review* VI(10) (March 1920), 10–12.

—— 'Thee I call "Hamlet of the Wedding Ring", Criticism of William Carlos William's "Kora in Hell" and Why . . . Part I', *Little Review* VII(4) (January–March 1921), 48–55; Part II, *Little Review* VIII(1) (autumn 1921), 108–11.

Gallup, Donald, *T. S. Eliot & Ezra Pound, Collaborators in Letters* (New Haven, CT: H. W. Wenning/C. A. Stonehill, 1970).

Gammel, Irene, *Baroness Elsa: Gender, Dada, and Everyday Modernity—A Cultural Biog-raphy* (Cambridge, MA: MIT Press, 2002).

Gardner, Helen, *The Art of T. S. Eliot* (London: Cresset Press, 1949).

—— *The Composition of 'Four Quartets'* (London: Faber & Faber, 1978).

Gates, Norman T., ed., *Richard Aldington: An Autobiography in Letters* (Pennsylvania: Pennsylvania State University Press, 1992).

Genette, Gérard, *Palimpsests: Literature in the Second Degree*, trans. Channa Newman and Claude Dubinsky (Lincoln, NE: University of Nebraska Press, 1997).

Gibson, Andrew, *Joyce's Revenge: History, Politics, and Aesthetics in 'Ulysses'* (Oxford: Oxford University Press, 2002).

Gibson, Mary Ellis, *Epic Reinvented: Ezra Pound and the Victorians* (Ithaca, NY: Cornell University Press, 1995).

Gifford, Don, *'Ulysses' Annotated: Notes for James Joyce's 'Ulysses'*, 2nd rev. edn (Berkeley: University of California Press, 2008).

Gilbert, Stuart, *James Joyce's 'Ulysses': A Study*, rev. edn (New York: Vintage, 1955).

Gilbert, W. S., *Patience, or Bunthorne's Bride!* (London: Chappell & Co., 1881).

Gill, Jonathan, 'Protective Colouring: Modernism and Blackface Minstrelsy in the Bolo poems', in John Xiros Cooper ed., *T. S. Eliot's Orchestra: Critical Essays on Poetry and Music* (New York: Garland, 2000), 65–84.

Gilman, Sander L., *Nietzschean Parody: An Introduction to Reading Nietzsche*, 2nd edn (Aurora: Davies Group, 2001).

Goethe, Johann Wolfgang von, *Goethe's Faust*, ed. and trans. Walter Kaufmann (New York: Doubleday & Co, 1961).

—— *Wilhelm Meisters Lehrjahre, Ein Roman* (Berlin: Bey Johann Friedrich Unger, 1795).

Gogol, Nikolai, *Selected Passages from Correspondence with Friends*, trans. Jesse Zeldin (Nashville, Tenn.: Vanderbilt University Press, 1969).

Goldsmith, Oliver, *The Vicar of Wakefield* (London: George Routledge & Sons, 1886).

Gordon, Lyndall, *T. S. Eliot: An Imperfect Life* (London: Vintage, 1998).

Gorman, Herbert, *James Joyce* (New York: Farrar & Rinehart, 1939).

Gourmont, Remy de, 'Litanies de la rose', *Le Pèlerin du Silence* (Paris: Société du Mercure de France, 1896), 203–16.

Graves, C. L., ed., *Owen Seaman: A Selection* (London: Methuen, 1937).

262 BIBLIOGRAPHY

Graves, Robert, and Alan Hodge, *The Long Week-end: A Social History of Great Britain 1918–1939* (London: Faber & Faber, 1940).

Green, Malcolm, ed. and trans., *The Dada Almanach* (London: Atlas Press, 1993).

Grieve, Thomas F., *Ezra Pound's Early Poetry and Poetics* (Columbia; London: University of Missouri Press, 1997).

Groden, Michael, *'Ulysses' in Progress* (Princeton, NJ: Princeton University Press, 1977).

H. D., *End to Torment: A Memoir of Ezra Pound, With the Poems from 'Hilda's Book' by Ezra Pound*, ed. Norman Holmes Pearson and Michael King (New York: New Directions, 1979).

—— 'Three Poems', *Poetry: A Magazine of Verse* I(4) (January 1913), 118–22.

H. M., 'Comments and Reviews: Give Him Room', *Poetry: A Magazine of Verse* VI(2) (May 1915), 81–84.

Haeckel, Ernst, *The Riddle of the Universe at the Close of the Nineteenth Century*, trans. Joseph McCabe (New York: Harper & Brothers, 1900).

Hále, W. G., 'Correspondence: Pegasus Impounded', *Poetry: A Magazine of Verse* XIV(1) (April 1919), 52–5.

Hall, Donald, interview with T. S. Eliot, 'The Art of Poetry, I: T. S. Eliot', *Paris Review* 21 (spring/summer, 1959), 47–70.

Hamilton, Scott, *Ezra Pound and the Symbolist Inheritance* (Princeton, NJ., Princeton University Press, 1992).

Hamilton, Walter, ed., *The Aesthetic Movement in England* (London: Reeves & Turner, 1882).

—— *Parodies of the Works of English and American Authors*, 6 vols. (London: Reeves & Turner, 1884–9).

Hannoosh, Michele, *Parody and Decadence: Laforgue's 'Moralités legendaires'* (Columbus, OH: Ohio State University Press, 1989).

Harmer, J. B., *Victory in Limbo: Imagism 1908–1917* (London: Secker & Warburg, 1975).

Hart, Clive, *Structure and Motif in 'Finnegans Wake'* (London: Faber & Faber, 1962).

Harte, Bret, *Tales of the West* (London; New York: T. Nelson & Sons, Ltd. n.d.).

Hassan, Ihab, 'From Postmodernism to Postmodernity: The Local/Global Context', *Philosophy and Literature* 25(1) (2001), 1–13.

—— *The Postmodern Turn: Essays in Postmodern Theory and Culture* (Columbus, OH: Ohio State University Press, 1987).

—— 'POSTmodernISM: A Paracritical Bibliography', *New Literary History* 3(1) (1971), 5–30.

Hastings, Beatrice, *The Old 'New Age' Orage—and Others* (London: Blue Moon Press, 1936).

Haughton, Hugh, ed., *The Chatto Book of Nonsense Poetry* (London: Chatto & Windus, 1988).

Heine, Heinrich, *Buch der Lieder* (Hamburg: Hoffmann und Campe, 1847).

Henderson, Alice Corbin, 'Baiting the Public', *Poetry: A Magazine of Verse* XII(3) (June 1918), 169–71.

Herring, Phillip F., 'More Peacock in the Oxen', *Wake Newslitter* 9 (1971), 51–3.

Hewlett, Maurice, *The Forest Lovers: A Romance* (London: Macmillan 1898).

—— *A Masque of Dead Florentines* (London: J. M. Dent & Co., 1895).

—— 'Prelude to 'The Man on the Hill', *Westminster Gazette* (18 October 1913).

—— *The Song of the Plow: Being the English Chronicle* (London: William Heinemann, 1916).

Hichens, Robert, *The Green Carnation* (London: William Heinemann, 1884).

BIBLIOGRAPHY   263

Höfele, Andreas, *Parodie und literarischer Wandel: Studien zur Funktion einer Schreib-weise in der englischen Literatur des ausgehenden 19 Jahrhunderts* (Heidelberg: Winter, 1986).

Hoffenstein, Samuel, 'The Moist Land—A Parody of Eliot's Poem', *New York Tribune* (28 January 1923), 24.

Hogg, James, *Poetic Mirror, or The Living Bards of Great Britain* (London: Printed for Longman, Hurst, Rees, Orme, and Brown, 1816).

Holley, Horace, 'Correspondence. Imagists', *Egoist* I(12) (15 June 1914), 236.

Homberger, Eric, ed., *Ezra Pound: The Critical Heritage* (London: Routledge, 1972).

Hosty, Matthew, *Batrachomyomachia (Battle of the Frogs and Mice): Introduction, Text, Translation, and Commentary* (Oxford: Oxford University Press, 2019).

Householder, Fred W., 'ΠΑΡΩΙΔΙΑ', *Classical Philology* 39(1) (1944), 1–9.

Howarth, Herbert, *Notes on Some Figures Behind T. S. Eliot* (London: Chatto & Windus, 1965).

Hueffer, Ford Madox, *Collected Poems* (London: Max Goschen, 1916).

—— *High Germany* (London: Duckworth, 1911).

Huelsenbeck, Richard, ed., *Dada Almanach* (Berlin: Erich Reiss, 1920), 3–9.

Hulme, T. E., 'The Complete Poetical Works of T. E. Hulme', *New Age* X(13) (25 January 1912), 307.

—— 'A Lecture on Modern Poetry', in Karen Csengeri, ed., *The Collected Writings of T. E. Hulme* (Oxford: Clarendon Press, 1994), 49–56.

Hutcheon, Linda, *Narcissistic Narrative: The Metafictional Paradox* (London: Methuen, 1984).

—— *The Politics of Postmodernism*, 2nd edn (New York: Routledge, 2002).

—— *A Theory of Parody: The Teachings of Twentieth-Century Art Forms* (London: Methuen, 1985).

Huxley, Aldous, 'Eclecticism', in Robert S. Baker and James Sexton, eds., *Aldous Huxley: Complete Essays—Volume 1, 1920–1925* (Chicago: Ivan R. Dee, 2000), 341–3.

Huyssen, Andreas, *After the Great Divide: Modernism, Mass Culture, Postmodernism* (Bloomington, IN: Indiana University Press, 1986).

Jackson, Thomas H., *The Early Poetry of Ezra Pound* (Cambridge, MA: Harvard University Press, 1968).

James, Henry, *The Wings of the Dove*, vol. II (New York: Scribner's, 1902).

Jameson, Fredric, 'Postmodernism, or The Cultural Logic of Late Capitalism', *New Left Review* 1(146) (1984), 53–92.

Janusko, Robert, 'Another Anthology for "Oxen": Barnett and Dale', *James Joyce Quarterly* 27(2) (1990), 257–81.

—— 'Further Oxcavations: Joyce's "Oxen": Notes from Swift, Steele, Goldsmith, Landor and De Quincey', *Genetic Joyce Studies* 2 (2002), www.geneticjoycestudies.org/.

—— 'Grave Beauty: Newman in "Oxen"', *James Joyce Quarterly* 28(3) (spring 1991), 617–21.

—— *The Sources and Structures of James Joyce's 'Oxen'* (Epping: Bowker 1983).

—— 'The Sources and Structures of the "Oxen of the Sun" Episode of James Joyce's Ulysses', diss., Kent State University Dissertation, 1967.

—— 'Yet Another Anthology for "Oxen": Murison's Selections', *James Joyce Annual* 1 (1990), 117–31.

Jefferson, Ann, rev., 'Margaret A. Rose, *Parody//Metafiction* (1979)', *Poetics Today* 3(3) (summer 1982), 231–2.

264   BIBLIOGRAPHY

Jencks, Charles, *The Language of Post-Modern Architecture* (New York: Rizzoli International, 1977).

Jerrold, Walter, *A Century of Parody* (London: H. Milford/Oxford University Press, 1913).

'jh' [Jane Heap], 'Dada—', *Little Review* VIII(2) (spring 1922), 46.

J. H. [Jane Heap], 'The Reader Critic: The Hoax of the "Spectrics"', *Little Review* V(2) (1 June 1918), 53–4.

Johnson, Lionel, *Poetical Works of Lionel Johnson*, ed. Ezra Pound (London: Elkin Mathews, 1915).

Johnson, Loretta, 'Feeling the Elephant: T. S. Eliot's Bolovian Epic', *Journal of Modern Literature* 37(4) (summer 2014), 109–29.

Jonson, Ben, *Every Man in His Humour*, ed. Gabriele Bernhard Jackson (New Haven, CT: Yale University Press, 1975).

—— 'Song to Celia', *Ben Jonson*, vol. 8, ed. C. H. Herford and Percy and Evelyn Simpson (Oxford: Clarendon, 1947), 106.

Joyce, James *Dubliners*, ed. Terence Brown (London: Penguin, 1992).

—— *Finnegans Wake*, ed. Seamus Deane (London: Penguin, 1992).

—— *Joyce's 'Ulysses' Notesheets in the British Museum*, ed. Phillip F. Herring (Charlottesville: University Press of Virginia, 1972).

—— *Letters of James Joyce*, vol. I., ed. Stuart Gilbert (London: Faber & Faber, 1957); vols. II and III, ed. Richard Ellmann (London: Faber & Faber, 1966).

—— *Occasional, Critical, and Political Writing*, ed. Kevin Barry and trans. Conor Deane (Oxford: Oxford University Press, 2008).

—— *Poems and Shorter Writings*, ed. Richard Ellmann, A. Walton Litz, and John Whittier-Ferguson (London: Faber & Faber, 1991).

—— *A Portrait of the Artist as a Young Man*, ed. Jeri Johnson (Oxford: Oxford University Press, 2008).

—— *Stephen Hero*, ed. J. Slocum and Herbert Cahoon (New York: New Directions, 1955).

—— *Ulysses*, ed. Hans Walter Gabler, Wolfhard Steppe, Claus Melchior, afterword by Michael Groden (London: Bodley Head, 2002).

—— 'Ulysses: Episode 12: part I', *Little Review* VI(7) (November 1919), 38–54.

—— *Ulysses: Notes & 'Telemachus'—'Scylla and Charybdis': A Facsimile of Notes for the Book & Manuscripts & Typescripts for Episodes 1–9*, ed. Michael Groden, James Joyce Archive, vol. XII (New York: Garland, 1978).

—— *Ulysses 'Oxen of the Sun' & 'Circe': A Facsimile of Drafts, Manuscripts, and Typescripts for Episodes 14 & 15 (Part I)*, ed. Michael Groden, James Joyce Archive, vol. XVI (New York: Garland, 1977).

—— *Ulysses: The 1922 Text*, ed. Jeri Johnson (Oxford: Oxford University Press, 1993).

Joyce, Stanislaus, *The Dublin Diary of Stanislaus Joyce*, ed. George. H. Healey (London: Faber & Faber, 1962).

—— *My Brother's Keeper: James Joyce's Early Years*, 1st edn (New York: Viking Press, 1958).

Kenner, Hugh, *Dublin's Joyce* (London: Chatto & Windus, 1955).

—— *Flaubert, Joyce and Beckett: The Stoic Comedians* (Boston: Beacon Press, 1962).

—— *Joyce's Voices* (Rochester, NY: Dalkey Archive Press, 2007), 59–60.

Killeen, Terence, *'Ulysses' Unbound: A Reader's Companion to James Joyce's 'Ulysses'* (Bray, Co. Wicklow: Wordwell, National Library of Ireland, 2005).

King, Julia, and Laila Miletic-Vejzovic, *The Library of Leonard and Virginia Woolf: A Short-title Catalogue* (Pullmann: Washington State University Press, 2003).

Kipling, Rudyard, *Barrack-Room Ballads* (London: Methuen, 1892).

BIBLIOGRAPHY 265

Kiremidjian, David, *A Study of Modern Parody: James Joyce's 'Ulysses', Thomas Mann's 'Doctor Faustus'* (New York: Garland, 1985).

Kitchin, G., *A Survey of Burlesque and Parody in English* (London: Oliver & Boyd, 1931).

Klein, Scott W., *The Fictions of James Joyce and Wyndham Lewis: Monsters of Nature and Design* (Cambridge: Cambridge University Press, 1994).

Knoepflmacher, U. C., 'Revisiting Wordsworth: Lewis Carroll's "The White Knight's Song"', *Victorians Institute Journal* 14 (1986), 1–20.

Koestenbaum, Wayne, *Double Talk: The Erotics of Male Literary Collaboration* (New York: Routledge, 1989).

Kristeva, Julia, *The Kristeva Reader*, ed. Toril Moi (Oxford: Basil Blackwell, 1986).

Lawrence, Karen, *The Odyssey of Style in 'Ulysses'* (Princeton, NJ: Princeton University Press, 1981).

Leavis, F. R., 'Mirrors up to Art', *The Spectator* 6967 (5 January 1962), 13.

Lee, Hermione, *Virginia Woolf* (London: Vintage, 1997).

Lee, Vernon, *Miss Brown: A Novel*, 3 vols. (London: Blackwood & Sons, 1884).

Leick, Karen, *Gertrude Stein and the Making of American Celebrity* (New York: Routledge, 2009).

—— 'Popular Modernism: Little Magazines and the American Daily Press', *PMLA* 123(1) (January 2008), 125–39.

Leopardi, Giacomo, *Paralipomeni della Batracomiomachia* (Parigi: Libreria Europa di Baudry, 1842).

Levenson, Ada, 'The Advisability of Not Being Brought up in a Handbag: A Trivial Tragedy for Wonderful People', *Punch* (2 March 1895), 107.

Lewis, Wyndham, *The Apes of God* (London: Penguin, 1965).

—— *Blasting and Bombardiering* (London: Eyre & Spottiswoode, 1937), 2nd rev. edn (Berkeley: University of California Press, 1967).

—— *The Childermass* (London: John Calder, 1965).

—— *Men without Art* (London: Cassell, 1934).

—— *Time and Western Man* (London: Chatto & Windus, 1927).

Liddell, Henry George, and Robert Scott, *Greek–English Lexicon*, 9th rev. edn, ed. Henry Stuart Jones (Oxford: Clarendon Press, 1968).

Lincoln, Joseph Crosby, *Cap'n Eri: A Story of the Coast* (New York: Burt & Co., 1912).

Lokke, Kari Elise, '*Orlando* and Incandescence: Virginia Woolf's Comic Sublime', *Modern Fiction Studies* 38(1) (1992), 235–52.

McCue, Jim, 'Editing Eliot', *Essays in Criticism* 56(1) (January 2006), 1–27.

—— 'Vivien Eliot in the Words of TSE', *Review of English Studies* 68(283) (February 2017), 123–64.

McDonough, Robert E., '"Mister Bosphorus and the Muses": History and Representation in Ford's Modern Poem', *International Ford Madox Ford Studies* 3 (2004), 155–62.

Macherey, Pierre, *A Theory of Literary Production*, trans. Geoffrey Wall (London: Routledge & Kegan Paul, 1978).

MacShane, Frank, ed., *Ford Madox Ford: The Critical Heritage* (London: Routledge, 1972).

Mallock, W. H., *Every Man His Own Poet* (Oxford: Shrimpton & Son, 1872).

—— *The New Republic: Or Culture, Faith, and Philosophy in an English Country House* (London: Chatto & Windus, 1877).

Malory, Thomas, *Selections from Malory's Morte D'Arthur, edited, with introduction, notes, and glossary*, ed. A. T. Martin (London: Macmillan, 1896).

Mandeville, Sir John, *The Travels of John Mandeville* (London: Macmillan, 1905).

266   BIBLIOGRAPHY

Manning, Frederic, 'Kore', *Poems* (London: John Murray, 1910), 38–9.

Mansfield, Katherine, and Beatrice Hastings, 'Letters to the Editor: A P. S. A.', *New Age* IX(4) (25 May 1911), 95.

March, Richard, and Tambimuttu, eds., *T. S. Eliot: A Symposium from Conrad Aiken and Others* (London: Frank & Cass Co., 1948).

Marinetti, F. T., 'Let's Murder the Moonlight' (11 April 1909), in Lawrence Rainey, Christine Poggi, and Laura Wittman, eds., *Futurism: An Anthology* (New Haven, CT: Yale University Press, 2009), 54–61.

— 'Technical Manifesto of Futurist Literature' (11 May 1912), in Lawrence Rainey, Christine Poggi, and Laura Wittman, eds., *Futurism: An Anthology* (New Haven, CT: Yale University Press, 2009), 119–25.

— 'The Variety Theatre' (29 September 1913), in Lawrence Rainey, Christine Poggi, and Laura Wittman, eds., *Futurism: An Anthology* (New Haven, CT: Yale University Press, 2009), 159–64.

Martin, Theodore, and William Edmonstoune Aytoun, *The Book of the Ballads* (London: W. S. Orr, 1845).

Martin, Theodore, *Memoir of William Edmonstoune Aytoun* (London: Blackwood & Sons, 1867).

Materer, Timothy, ed., *Pound/Lewis: The Letters of Ezra Pound and Wyndham Lewis* (New York: New Directions, 1985).

—+ *The Selected Letters of Ezra Pound to John Quinn, 1915–1924* (Durham, NC: Duke University Press, 1991).

Matthiessen, F. O., *The Achievement of T. S. Eliot: An Essay on the Nature of Poetry* (New York: Oxford University Press, 1958).

M. C. A. [Margaret C. Anderson], 'Discussion: William Carlos Williams' "Kora in Hell" by Else von Freytag-Loringhoven', *Little Review* VII(3) (September–December 1920), 58–9.

— 'The Reader Critic: Note', *Little Review* IV(3) (July 1917), 29.

Mellow, James R., *Charmed Circle: Gertrude Stein & Company* (New York: Praeger, 1974).

Miller, Tyrus, *Late Modernism: Politics, Fiction, and the Arts Between the World Wars* (Berkeley: University of California Press, 1999).

Milton, John, 'L'Allegro', in Roy Flannagan, ed., *The Riverside Milton* (Boston: Houghton Mifflin, 1998), 65–71.

M. M. B., '"The Imagists", A Talk with Mr. Ezra Pound, Their Editor', *Daily News and Leader* (18 March 1914), 14.

Monroe, Harriet, *A Poet's Life: Seventy Years in a Changing World* (New York: Macmillan, 1938).

Moody, David, *Ezra Pound: Poet; A Portrait of the Man & His Work, Volume 1: The Young Genius 1885–1920* (Oxford: Oxford University Press, 2007).

Morgan, Emanuel, and Anne Knish, *Spectra: A Book of Poetic Experiments* (New York: Mitchell Kennerley, 1916).

Morgan, Emanuel, 'Opus 96', *Little Review* IV(3) (July 1917), 25.

Morrisson, Mark, *The Public Face of Modernism: Little Magazines, Audiences, and Reception 1905–1920* (Madison, WI: University of Wisconsin Press, 2000).

Münsterberg, Margarete, ed. and trans., *A Harvest of German Verse* (New York: Appleton & Co., 1916).

Murison, A. F., *Selections from the Best English Authors (Beowulf to the Present Time)* (London: W. & R. Chambers, 1901).

BIBLIOGRAPHY 267

Nadel, Ira B., 'Ezra Pound: Two Poems', *Journal of Modern Literature* 15(1) (summer 1988), 141–5.

Nagy, N. Christopher de, *The Poetry of Ezra Pound: The Pre-Imagist Stage* (Bern: Francke, 1960).

Naumann, Francis M., *New York Dada, 1915–1923* (New York: Abrams, 1994).

Nevinson, C. R. W., 'Vital English Art', *New Age* XV(7) (18 June 1914), 160–2.

Nietzsche, Friedrich, *Beyond Good and Evil: Prelude to a Philosophy of the Future*, ed. and trans. Walter Kaufmann (New York: Vintage, 1989).

—— *The Gay Science: With a Prelude in Rhymes and an Appendix of Songs*, ed. and trans. Walter Kaufmann (New York: Random House, 1974).

Nolan, Emer, *James Joyce and Nationalism* (London: Routledge, 1995).

North, Michael, *The Dialect of Modernism: Race, Language and Twentieth-Century Literature* (New York: Oxford University Press, 1994).

O'Grady, Standish James, *History of Ireland: Critical and Philosophical*, vol. I (London: Sampson Low & Co., 1881).

Ormond, Leonée, *George Du Maurier* (London: Routledge & Kegan Paul, 1969).

Painter, George D., *Marcel Proust: A Biography*, vol. 2 (London: Chatto & Windus, 1965).

Palmer, Herbert, *Cinder Thursday* (London: E. Benn, 1931).

Peacock, William, *English Prose from Mandeville to Ruskin* (London: Grant Richards, 1903).

Perrino, Mark, *The Poetics of Mockery: Wyndham Lewis's 'The Apes of God' and the Popularization of Modernism* (London: W. S. Maney & Sons for Modern Humanities Research Association, 1995).

Phiddian, Robert, 'Are Parody and Deconstruction the Same Thing?', *New Literary History* 28(4) (1997), 673–96.

—— *Swift's Parody* (Cambridge: Cambridge University Press, 1995).

Poe, Edgar Allan, 'The Murders in the Rue Morgue', in Patrick F. Quinn and G. R. Thompson, eds., *Edgar Allan Poe: Poetry, Tales, & Selected Essays* (New York: Library of America, 1996), 397–431.

—— 'The Raven', *The Raven and Other Poems* (New York: Wiley & Putnam, 1845), 1–5.

Poirier, Richard, *The Performing Self: Compositions and Decompositions in the Languages of Contemporary Life* (London: Chatto & Windus, 1971).

Pondron, Cyrena, 'H. D. and the Origins of Imagism', in Susan Stanford Friedman and Rachel Blau DuPlessis, eds., *Signets: Reading H. D.* (Madison, WI: University of Wisconsin Press, 1990), 85–109.

Pope, Alexander, *The Dunciad*, in John Butt, ed., *The Poems of Alexander Pope: A One Volume Edition of the Twickenham Text with Selected Annotations* (London: Methuen, 1963), 709–805.

—— *The Rape of the Lock*, in John Butt, ed., *The Poems of Alexander Pope: A One Volume Edition of the Twickenham Text with Selected Annotations* (London: Methuen, 1963), 217–42.

Pound, Ezra, *ABC of Reading* (London: Faber & Faber, 1991).

—— 'Alf's Second Bit', *Personæ, Collected Shorter Poems of Ezra Pound* (New York: New Directions, 1952), 266.

—— 'The Approach to Paris: I', *New Age* XIII(19) (4 September 1913), 551–2.

—— 'The Approach to Paris: II', *New Age* XIII(20) (11 September 1913), 577–8.

—— 'The Approach to Paris: III', *New Age* XIII(21) (18 September 1913), 607–9.

—— 'The Approach to Paris: IV', *New Age* XIII(22) (25 September 1913), 631–3.

—— 'The Approach to Paris: V', *New Age* XIII(23) (2 October 1913), 662–4.

268   BIBLIOGRAPHY

Pound, Ezra, 'The Approach to Paris: VI', *New Age* XIII(24) (9 October 1913), 694–6.

—— 'The Approach to Paris: VII', *New Age* XIII(25) (16 October 1913), 726–8.

—— *The Cantos of Ezra Pound*, rev. edn (London: Faber & Faber, 1975).

—— *Canzoni* (London: Elkin Mathews, 1911).

—— *Collected Early Poems of Ezra Pound*, ed. Michael John King (London: Faber & Faber, 1977).

—— 'Contemporania', *Poetry: A Magazine of Verse* II(1) (April 1913), 1–12.

—— *A Draft of XVI Cantos of Ezra Pound* (Paris: Three Mountains Press, 1925).

—— *Ezra Pound: Selected Poems*, ed. T. S. Eliot (London: Faber & Gwyer, 1928).

—— 'A Few Don'ts by an Imagiste', *Poetry: A Magazine of Verse* I(6) (March 1913), 200–6.

—— *Gaudier-Brzeska: A Memoir* (London: John Lane/Bodley Head; New York: John Lane Company, 1916).

—— 'Homage to Sextus Propertius', *Personae: Collected Shorter Poems of Ezra Pound* (London: Faber & Faber, 1952), 215–39.

—— 'Homage to Sextus Propertius', *Quia Pauper Amavi* (London: The Egoist, 1919).

—— *Hugh Selwyn Mauberley* (London: Ovid Press, 1920).

—— 'How I Began', *T.P.'s Weekly* (6 June 1913), 707.

—— 'I Gather the Limbs of Osiris: I. The Seafarer', *New Age* X(5) (30 November 1911), 107.

—— 'I Gather the Limbs of Osiris: II', *New Age* X(6) (7 December 1911), 130–1.

—— 'I Gather the Limbs of Osiris: III. Five translations from "The Sonnets and Ballate of Guido Cavalcanti"', *New Age* X(7) (14 December 1911), 155–6.

—— 'I Gather the Limbs of Osiris: VI', *New Age* X(10) (4 January 1912), 224–5.

—— 'I Gather the Limbs of Osiris: V. Four Early Poems of Arnaut Daniel', *New Age* X(9) (28 December 1911), 201–2.

—— 'Kongo Roux', *391*, No. 16, Le Pilhaou-Thibaou (10 July 1921), 10, reprinted in Andrew Clearfield, 'Pound, Paris, and Dada', *Paideuma* 7 (spring and fall, 1978), 135.

—— 'Letters to the Editor: Vorticism', *New Age* XVI(13) (28 January 1915).

—— 'A List of Books: "Others"', *Little Review* IV(11) (March 1918), 56–8.

—— *Literary Essays of Ezra Pound*, ed. T. S. Eliot (London: Faber & Faber, 1954).

—— *A Lume Spento, and Other Early Poems* (New York: New Directions, 1965).

—— *Lustra* (London: Elkin Mathews, 1916).

—— *Lustra* (New York: Knopf, 1917).

—— 'Paris Letter', *Dial* 71(4) (October 1921), 456–63.

—— *Personae* (London: Elkin Mathews, 1909).

—— *Personæ, Collected Shorter Poems of Ezra Pound* (New York: New Directions, 1952).

—— 'Poems', *Poetry: A Magazine of Verse* III(2) (November 1913), 53–60.

—— 'Poems from the Propertius Series: I–IV', *Poetry: A Magazine of Verse* XIII(6) (March 1919), 291–9.

—— 'Prolegomena', *Poetry Review* I(2) (February 1912), 72–6.

—— *A Quinzaine for this Yule: Being Selected from a Venetian Sketch-book, 'San Trovaso'* (London: Pollock & Co., 1908).

—— 'A Rejoinder', *Poetry: A Magazine of Verse* VI(3) (June 1915), 157–8.

—— *Ripostes of Ezra Pound: Whereto Are Appended the Complete Poetical Works of T. E. Hulme, with Prefatory Note* (London: Stephen Swift & Co., 1912).

—— *Selected Poems, with an Introduction by T. S. Eliot* (London: Faber & Gwyer, 1928).

—— *Selected Prose: 1909–1965*, ed. William Cookson (New York: New Directions, 1973).

—— 'The Serious Artist: I', *New Freewoman* I(9) (15 October 1913), 161–3.

—— 'The Serious Artist: III', *New Freewoman* I(10) (1 November 1913), 194–5.

BIBLIOGRAPHY 269

— *The Spirit of Romance: An Attempt to Define Somewhat the Charm of the pre-Renaissance Literature of Latin Europe* (London: J. M. Dent & Sons, 1910).

— *Sonnets and Ballate of Guido Cavalcanti, with Translation of them and an Introduction by Ezra Pound* (London: Stephen Swift & Co., 1912)

Pound, Ezra, et al, *Des Imagistes: An Anthology* (New York: Albert and Charles Boni, 1914).

Pound, Omar, and A. Walton Litz, eds., *Ezra Pound and Dorothy Shakespear: Their Letters 1910–1914* (London: Faber, 1985).

Power, Arthur, *Conversations with James Joyce*, ed. Clive Hart (Chicago, University of Chicago Press, 1982).

Priestman, Judith, 'The Age of Parody: Literary Parody and Some Nineteenth Century Perspectives', diss., University of Kent, 1980.

Proust, Marcel, *Pastiches et mélanges* (Paris: Gaston Gallimard, 1919).

— *Time Regained*, trans. Stephen Hudson (London: Chatto & Windus, 1931).

Quintilian, Marcus Fabius, *Institutio Oratoria*, vol. IV, trans. H. E. Butler (Cambridge, MA: Harvard University Press, 1921).

Rabelais, François, *The Works of the Famous Mr. Francis Rabelais, Doctor in Physick Treating of the Lives, Heroick Deeds, and Sayings of Gargantua and His Son Pantagruel: to Which Is Newly Added the Life of the Author*, trans. Sir Thomas Urquhart (London: printed for R.B., 1664).

— *The Works of Rabelais*, trans. Sir Thomas Urquhart, illust. Gustave Doré (Nottingham, n.d.).

Rachewiltz, Mary de, A. David Moody, and Joanna Moody, eds., *Ezra Pound to His Parents, Letters 1895–1929* (Oxford: Oxford University Press, 2010).

Radcliffe, Ann, *The Mysteries of Udolpho*, new edn, ed. Bonamy Dobrée, intro. and notes Terry Castle (Oxford: Oxford University Press, 1998).

Rainey, Lawrence, *The Annotated Waste Land with Eliot's Contemporary Prose* (New Haven, CT: Yale University Press, 2005).

— *Institutions of Modernism: Literary Elites and Public Culture* (New Haven, CT: Yale University Press, 1998).

— *Revisiting 'The Waste Land'* (New Haven, CT: Yale University Press, 2005).

Rainey, Lawrence, Christine Poggi, and Laura Wittman, eds., *Futurism: An Anthology* (New Haven, CT: Yale University Press, 2009).

'R. C. H'. [A. R. Orage], 'Readers and Writers', *New Age* XIV(2) (13 November 1913), 50–2.

— 'Reader and Writers', *New Age* XV(10) (9 July 1914), 229.

— 'Readers and Writers', *New Age* XV(11) (16 July 1914), 253.

— 'Readers and Writers', *New Age* XVII(14) (5 August 1915), 332–3.

Read, Forrest, ed., *Pound/Joyce: The Letters of Ezra Pound to James Joyce, with Pound's Essays on Joyce* (New York: New Directions, 1967).

Richardson, Mrs. Herbert, *Parody*, The English Association Pamphlet 92 (London: Milford/Oxford University Press, 1935).

Rickword, Edgell, 'A Fragmentary Poem', *Times Literary Supplement* 1131 (20 September 1923), 616.

Rochester, Lord [John Wilmot], 'To all Curious Criticks and Admirers of Metre', *The Works of the Earls of Rochester, Roscommon, Dorset, &c. In Two Volumes. Adorn'd with Cuts*, 4th edn (London: printed for E. Curll, at the Dial and Bible against St. Dunstan's Church in Fleet-Street, 1714).

Rose, Margaret A., *Parody: Ancient, Modern, and Post-Modern* (Cambridge: Cambridge University Press, 1993).

270 BIBLIOGRAPHY

Rose, Margaret A., *Parody//Meta-Fiction: An Analysis of Parody as a Critical Mirror to the Writing and Reception of Fiction* (London: Croom Helm, 1979).

Rose, W. K., *The Letters of Wyndham Lewis* (London: Methuen, 1963).

Rosenblitt, J. Alison, *E. E. Cummings' Modernism and the Classics: Each Imperishable Stanza* (Oxford: Oxford University Press, 2016).

Rossetti, Dante Gabriel, *Poems by Dante Gabriel Rossetti* (Leipzig: Bernhard Tauchnitz, 1873).

Rossetti, W. M., *Swinburne's Poems and Ballads: A Criticism* (London: John Camden Hotten, 1866).

Russell, Leonard, ed., *Parody Party* (London: Hutchinson, 1936).

Rutter, Frank, 'Pastiche: Art and Artists', *New Age* XV(4) (28 May 1914), 92.

Sackville-West, Vita, *Knole and the Sackvilles* (London: William Heinemann, 1922).

—— *The Land* (London: William Heinemann, 1926).

Saintsbury, George, *A History of English Prose Rhythm* (London: Macmillan, 1912).

Sassoon, Siegfried, *Memoirs of a Fox-Hunting Man* (London: Faber & Gwyer, 1928).

Saunders, Max, *Ford Madox Ford: A Dual Life, Volume II: The After-War World* (Oxford: Oxford University Press, 1996).

Scarron, Paul, *Le Virgile travesty en vers burlesques* (Paris: Chez Toussaint Quinet, 1648).

Schuchard, Ron, *Eliot's Dark Angel: Intersections of Life and Art* (Oxford: Oxford University Press, 1999).

Scott, Thomas L., and Melvin J. Friedman, with Jackson R. Bryer, eds. *Pound/Little Review: The Letters of Ezra Pound to Margaret Anderson: Little Review Correspondence* (New York: New Directions, 1988).

Seaman, Owen, *Horace at Cambridge* (London: A. D. Innes & Co., 1895).

—— 'The Rhyme of the Kipperling', *Punch* (13 January 1894), 13.

Shakespeare, William, 'Sonnet 98', in Colin Burrow, ed., *The Complete Sonnets and Poems* (Oxford: Oxford University Press, 2002), 577.

—— *The Tragedy of Anthony and Cleopatra*, ed. Michael O'Neill (Oxford: Oxford University Press, 1994).

Shallcross, Michael, *Rethinking G. K. Chesterton and Literary Modernism: Parody, Performance, and Popular Culture* (New York: Routledge, 2018).

Sherry, Vincent, *Ezra Pound, Wyndham Lewis, and Radical Modernism* (Oxford: Oxford University Press, 1993).

—— *Ulysses* (Cambridge: University of Cambridge, 1994).

Shklovsky, Victor, 'Sterne's Tristram Shandy: Stylistic Commentary', *Russian Formalist Criticism: Four Essays*, trans. Lee L. Lemon and Marion J. Reis (Lincoln, NE: University of Nebraska Press, 1965), 25–57.

Sieburth, Richard, 'Dada Pound', *South Atlantic Quarterly* 83 (winter 1984), 44–68.

Silvestre, Armand, 'Preface pour Les Pays du Mufle' (1891), in Laurent Tailhade, *Poèmes aristophanesques* (Paris: Société Mercure de France, 1904), 173–6.

Smith, James, and Horace Smith, Preface, *Rejected Addresses: Or the New Theatrum Poetarum*, 18th edn (London: John Murray, 1833).

Smith, William Jay, *The Spectra Hoax* (Middletown, CT: Wesleyan University Press, 1961).

Sontag, Susan, *Against Interpretation and Other Essays* (New York: Farrar, Straus and Giroux, 1966).

Southam, B. C., *A Student's Guide to the Selected Poems of T. S. Eliot*, 5th edn (London: Faber & Faber, 1991).

BIBLIOGRAPHY 271

Southey, Robert, *A Vision of Judgement*, in Tim Fulford and Lynda Pratt, eds., *Robert Southey: Later Poetical Works, 1811–1838*, vol. III, *Poems from the Laureate Period*, (London: Pickering & Chatto, 2012), 533–605.

Squire, J. C., ed., *Apes and Parrots: An Anthology of Parodies* (London: Herbert Jenkins, 1928).

—— *Collected Parodies* (New York: George H. Doran Co., 1921).

—— 'Editorial Notes', *London Mercury* XVIII(106) (August 1928), 342.

—— 'Imaginary Speeches', *New Age* VI(7) (16 December 1909), 151; *New Age* VI(8) (23 December 1909), 175; *New Age* VI(9) (30 December 1909), 199; *New Age* VI(10) (6 January 1910), 222; *New Age* VI(11) (13 January 1909), 247; *New Age* VI(12) (20 January 1909), 272.

—— 'The Man Who Wrote Free Verse', *London Mercury* X(56) (June 1924), 121–37.

—— 'The Sort of Poems Modern Poets Write', *New Age* VII(21) (22 September 1910), 500–1; *New Age* VII(24) (13 October 1910), 562; *New Age* VII(26) (27 October 1910), 605.

—— *Tricks of the Trade* (London: Martin Secker, 1917).

Stayer, Jayme, 'The Short and Surprisingly Private Life of King Bolo: Eliot's Bawdy Poems and Their Audiences', in John Morgenstern, ed., *The T. S. Eliot Studies Annual* (Clemson, SC: Clemson University Press, 2017), 3–30.

Stephen, J. K., *Lapsus Calami* (Cambridge: Macmillan & Bowes, 1891).

Sterne, Laurence, *The Life and Opinions of Tristram Shandy, Gentleman*, ed. Melvyn New and Joan New (London: Penguin, 1997).

Stock, Noel, *The Life of Ezra Pound* (London: Routledge & Kegan Paul, 1970).

Stone, Christopher, *Parody* (London: Martin Secker, 1914).

Stones, Graeme, and John Strachan, eds., *Parodies of the Romantic Age*, 5 vols, I: The Anti-Jacobin, II: Collected Verse Parody, III: Collected Prose Parody, IV: Warreniana, V: Rejected Articles (London: Pickering & Chatto, 1999).

Swift, Jonathan, *A Tale of a Tub, The Battle of the Books and other Satires* (London: J. M. Dent & Sons, 1916).

Swinburne, A. C., *The Heptalogia, or, the Seven against Sense: A Cap with Seven Bells* (London: Chatto & Windus, 1880).

Symons, Arthur, *The Symbolist Movement in Literature*, 2nd edn (London: Archibald Constable & Co., 1908).

Tagore, Rabindranath, 'Poems', *Poetry: A Magazine of Verse* II(3) (June 1913), 81–91.

Tailhade, Laurent, *Poèmes aristophanesques*, 3rd edn (Paris: Mercure de France, 1910).

Taylor, Bert Leston, *Chicago Tribune* (17 April 1913), 6.

—— *Chicago Tribune* (18 April 1913), 8.

Tennyson, Alfred Lord, *Poems* (London: George Bell & Sons, 1905).

'T. K. L'. [Beatrice Hastings], 'All Except Anything', *New Age* XIII(25) (16 October 1913), 733–4.

—— 'Aristophanes or Tailhade?', *New Age* XIII(24) (9 October 1913), 702–3.

—— 'Clear Tongue Plus Pindarism', *New Age* XIII(22) (25 September 1913), 636–7.

—— 'Humanititism and the New Form', *New Age* XIII(23) (2 October 1913), 669–70.

—— 'Ride a Cock Pegasus', *New Age* XIII(27) (30 October 1913), 794–5.

—— 'The Way Back to America', *New Age* XIII(21) (18 September 1913), 604–5.

Tracey, Daniel, 'Investing in "Modernism": Smart Magazines, Parody, and Middlebrow Professional Judgement', *Journal of Modern Periodical Studies* 1(1) (2010), 38–63.

Trench, Herbert, *New Poems: Apollo and the Seaman, The Queen of Gothland, Stanzas to Tolstoy, and Other Lyrics* (London: Methuen, 1907).

272 BIBLIOGRAPHY

Trench, Richard Chenevix, *English, Past and Present*, 14th edn, rev. and ed. A. L. Mayhew (London: Kegan Paul, Trench & Co., 1889).

— *On the Study of Words*, 21st edn, rev. and ed. A. L. Mayhew (London: Kegan Paul, Trench & Trübner, 1890).

Trotter, David, *The English Novel in History: 1895–1920* (London: Routledge, 1993).

Tynianov, Yuri, 'Dostoevsky and Gogol: Towards a Theory of Parody'; part I in Priscilla Meyer and Stephen Rudy, ed. and trans., *Dostoevsky and Gogol: Texts and Criticism* (Ann Arbor: Ardis, 1979), 101–17; part II in Victor Erlich, ed. and trans., *Twentieth-Century Russian Literary Criticism* (New Haven, CT: Yale University Press, 1975), 102–16.

Tzara, Tristan, 'Dada Manifesto', in Mary Ann Caws ed., *Manifesto: A Century of Isms* (Lincoln, NE: University of Nebraska Press, 2001), 297–304.

— 'Memoirs of Dadaism', reprinted in an appendix to Edmund Wilson, *Axel's Castle* (New York: Scribner's 1931), 304–5.

— *Vingt-cinq poèmes*, illustrated by Jean Arp (Zurich: Collection Dada, 1918).

Untermeyer, Louis, *And Other Poets* (New York: Holt & Co., 1916), 55–7.

Upward, Allen, 'Correspondence. The Discarded Imagist', *Egoist* II(6) (1 June 1915), 98.

Van Mierlo, Chrissie, 'Joyce and Malory: A Language in Transition', *New Quotatoes: European Joyce Studies* 25 (2016), 88–110.

— '"Oxen of the Sun" Noteshet 17: Annotations and Commentary with A New List of Sources, and Transcriptions, or Oxtail Soup: the ingredients', *Genetic Joyce Studies* 14 (2014), www.geneticjoycestudies.org/.

Verhaeren, Emile, *Poems*, trans. and intro. Will Stone, pref. Patrick McGuinness (Todmorden: Arc Publishing, 2014).

Ward, Christopher, 'The Dry Land', *The Triumph or the Nut, and Other Parodies* (New York: Henry Holt & Co., 1923), 170–8.

Waugh, Evelyn, *Vile Bodies* (London: Penguin, 2000).

Waugh, Patricia, *Metafiction: The Theory and Practice of Self-Conscious Fiction* (London: Routledge, 2003).

Weeks, Leroy Titus, 'Correspondence: The New Beauty', *Poetry: A Magazine of Verse* VI(1) (April 1915), 48–51.

Wells, Carolyn, *A Parody Anthology* (New York: Scribner's, 1904).

Wetherwell, J. E., *Later English Poems: 1901–1922* (Toronto: McClelland & Stewart, 1922).

Whitman, Walt, *Leaves of Grass* (London: G. P. Putnam's Sons/Boston: Small Maynard and Co., 1897).

Wilhelm, James, *Ezra Pound in London and Paris, 1908–1925* (Pennsylvania: Pennsylvania State University Press, 1990).

Williams, Ellen, *Harriet Monroe and the Poetry Renaissance: The First Ten Years of Poetry, 1912–22* (Urbana: University of Illinois Press, 1977).

Williams, William Carlos, *Kora in Hell: Improvisations* (Boston: Fours Seas Company, 1920).

— 'Improvisations I–III', *Little Review* IV(6) (October 1917), 19.

— 'Improvisations I–IV', *Little Review* IV(9) (January 1918), 1–9.

— 'Improvisations I–III', *Little Review* VI(2) (June 1919), 52–9.

Witemeyer, Hugh, 'Clothing the American Adam: Pound's Tailoring of Walt Whitman', in George Bornstein, ed., *Ezra Pound among the Poets: Homer, Ovid, Li Po, Dante, Whitman, Browning, Yeats, Williams, Eliot* (Chicago: University of Chicago Press, 1985), 81–105.

— *Poetry of Ezra Pound: Forms and Renewals* (Berkeley: University of California Press, 1969).

BIBLIOGRAPHY 273

— *Diary of Virginia Woolf, Volume 2, 1920–1924*, ed. Anne Olivier Bell and Andrew McNeillie (London: Hogarth Press, 1978).

— *Diary of Virginia Woolf, Volume 3, 1925–1930*, ed. Annie Olivier Bell and Andrew McNeillie (London: Hogarth Press, 1980).

Woolf, Virginia, *Between the Acts*, ed. Frank Kermode (Oxford: Oxford University Press, 1998).

— *Mrs Dalloway*, ed. David Bradshaw (Oxford: Oxford University Press, 2000), 12.

— *Orlando: A Biography*, intro. Peter Ackroyd and Margaret Reynolds (London: Vintage, 2000).

— 'The Leaning Tower', in *Collected Essays*, vol. 2 (London: Hogarth Press, 1966), 162–81.

— 'The Modern Essay', *The Common Reader*, vol. 1 (New York: Harcourt, Brace & Co., 1925), 293–307.

— 'Parodies', *Times Literary Supplement* 790 (8 March 1917), 112.

— 'The "Sentimental Journey"', in *Collected Essays by Virginia Woolf*, vol. 5, ed. Stuart N. Clarke (London: Hogarth Press, 2009), 401–10.

Worthen, William B., 'Eliot's *Ulysses*', *Twentieth Century Literature* 27(2) (summer 1981), 166–77.

Yeats, W. B., 'The Cap and Bells', *The Wind Among the Reeds* (New York: John Lane/Bodley Head, 1899), 32–4.

— 'The Withering of the Boughs', *The Seven Woods: Being Poems Chiefly of the Irish Heroic Age* (New York: Macmillan, 1903), 21–4.

Zukovsky, Louis, 'Poem Beginning "The"', *Exile* 3 (spring 1928), 7–27.

Index

391 magazine 144

absurdity 7–8, 20, 90, 99–101, 166, 120–1, 125, 126, 138, 144
  see also Dada
Addison, Joseph 210
aestheticism 19 n.56, 23–5, 29–30, 49, 52, 70, 86, 98, 104, 108–9, 119–20
Aiken, Conrad 153–4, 157–8, 181
  The Charnel Rose 165
Aldington, Richard 79 n.9, 87, 97–103, 104, 105–6, 112, 117, 128–9, 134, 178, 242
  'Anti-Hellenism: A Note on Some Modern Art' 98
  Des Imagistes 104, 105–6
    'Au Vieux Jardin' 105
    'To Atthis' 106
    'Vates, the Social Reformer' 105
  'Penultimate Poetry' 97, 99–100, 103
    'Altruism' 100–1
    'Ancora' 99–100
    'Cantata' 99
    'Convicted' 100
    'Elevators' 99
    'Further Instructions' 99
    'Gitanjali' 100
    'Salvationists' 99
    'Songs of Innocence' 101
    'Tenzone alla Gentildonna' 98
Americanism 40, 69 n.99, 99, 135–6, 140, 142, 154
Anderson, Margaret 124, 139
Anti-Jacobin (newspaper) 18, 19 n.55, 122
Apollinaire, Guillaume: 'L'Antitradizione Futurista' 108–9
appropriation 32, 34, 35, 40, 57, 59, 99, 125, 146, 244
Aristophanes 84
Aristotle: *Poetics* 7
artifice 23, 25–6, 30, 161, 174
'atmosphere of parody' 5, 83, 85–7, 95, 116
Auden, W. H. 40
  'daydream College for Bards' 45
Austen, Jane
  Northanger Abbey 11–12
  Sense and Sensibility 236

avant-garde 2, 5, 36, 38, 80, 81–2, 95, 102, 105, 108–9, 112, 113, 118, 120–2, 125–7, 128, 130, 137–8, 140, 143, 144, 147, 159, 165, 241, 251
Aytoun, W. E.
  Book of the Ballads 19 n.55, 22
  'The Lay of the Lovelorn' 22

Bakhtin, Mikhail 14–18, 31, 69, 83–4, 147, 159, 194, 200, 203, 251
  The Dialogic Imagination 14–18, 194, 200 n.43, 203 n.64
  Rabelais and his World 200 n.43
  'Second Stylistic Line' 17, 147, 159, 203, 251
  stylization 14–18
Barnett, Annie: *An Anthology of English Prose* 213, 217, 218
Barth, John: 'The Literature of Exhaustion' 33
Baudelaire, Charles 82, 139
  'Éloge du maquillage' 26
  'À une passante' 73
Baumann, Heinrich 221
  Londonismen (Slang und Cant) 224, 225–6, 229
Beach, Sylvia 160
Beardsley, Aubrey 30, 82
Beaumont, Francis, and John Fletcher: *The Maid's Tragedy* 161
Bechhöfer, C. E. 112–15
  see also Brookfarmer, Charles
Beckett, Samuel 33, 38, 40
Beckford, William: *Azemia* 18
Beerbohm, Max 25–30, 32, 37, 43, 47, 51, 178
  'Carmen Becceriense' 43
  A Christmas Garland 27–9
    'The Mote in the Middle Distance' 27–9
  'A Defence of Cosmetics' 25–7
  'Diminuendo' 30
  'Savonarola Brown' 65
  The Works of Max Beerbohm 80–1
Bell, Clive 46, 153
  Since Cézanne 154
belletristic entertainment 18, 19 n.55, 22
Bergson, Henri: 'Introduction to Metaphysics' 79
Berners, Lord 217

INDEX 275

blackface minstrelsy 147, 154–8, 160
Blackwoods (magazine) 19
Blake, William 49, 170
Blast 5, 102, 108–15, 129, 153, 159, 241
  parodies of *Blast* 112–15, 158–9
Bloomsbury group 126, 242, 243, 244, 245, 246
Boileau, Nicolas: *Le Lutrin* 8
Bomberg, David 131
Borges, Jorge Luis 33
Boswell, James 13
Bradbury, Malcolm: 'An Age of Parody, Style in
  the Modern Arts' 38–9, 252
Breton, André: *Littérature* 140
Brodsky, Horace 129
Brookfarmer, Charles [C. E. Bechhöfer]:
  'Futile-Ism. Or, All Cackle and No
  Osses' 131
Browne, Maurice 121
Browne, Sir Thomas 209
  Hydrotaphia: Urne Buriall 236
Browning, Robert 52, 53, 54, 56–7, 58–60, 61,
  63, 64, 76, 99
  Balaustion's Adventure 53
  'Fifine at the Fair' 60
  'Mesmerism' 59
  Sordello 60
Budgen, Frank 207, 209–11, 216–17, 221, 223
buffoonery 1, 2, 3, 55, 111, 138, 143, 153,
  158, 160
Burke, Thomas: *Limehouse Nights: Tales of
  Chinatown* 224, 226–7, 229
burlesque 8, 10, 22, 27, 30, 40, 124, 127,
  178–9, 198
Burnard, F. C. 23
Burney, Fanny
  Camilla, or, A Picture of Youth 12
  Cecilia, or Memoires of an Heiress 12
Burns, Robert: 'Is There for Honest Poverty' 68,
  104, 184 n.154
Bynner, Witter 120–7, 128
  see also Morgan, Emanuel
Byron, Lord 17, 18, 21–2
  Childe Harold 17
  Don Juan 17
  'The Vision of Judgment' 21–2

Caesar, Terry 20, 30 n.99
Calverley, C. S. 37, 44
  Fly Leaves 19 n.55, 37
  Verses and Translations 19 n.55, 46 n.17
Cambridge Review 44
caricature 23, 69, 158, 162, 164, 172–3, 193–4,
  204, 242, 244–5, 246
Carlyle, Thomas 221, 223

Carroll, Lewis
  Alice's Adventures in Wonderland 20
  *Through the Looking-Glass and What Alice
    Found There* 20, 250
Catullus 84
Cavalcanti, Guido 50, 53, 61, 64, 74–5
Cervantes, Miguel de 9–10, 13, 14, 55, 85,
  147, 199
  Don Quixote 9–10, 13
Chambers, Robert: *The Art that Plays with
  Art* 41
Chapbook: A Monthly Miscellany 117, 182
  'Pathology des Dommagistes' 117
Chaucer, Geoffrey 23, 54, 58, 133, 220, 239
Chesterton, G. K. 32, 39, 40 n.141, 45, 64, 130
Chicago Tribune 95–6
classicism 78, 85, 88, 131
Coleridge, Samuel Taylor 18, 21
  Biographia Literaria 18
comedy 7, 11, 12, 35, 40, 45, 82, 153, 154, 158,
  190, 200, 234, 239
Connolly, Cyril 128
Conrad, Joseph 233 n. 3, 235
Cooper, James Fennimore: *The Pioneers* 227
Corbière, Tristan 82
Corbin Henderson, Alice 97, 123
Courtney, W. L. 58
Coward, Noël 240
Cowley, Abraham 174–5, 217
Cowper, John 53
Cravens, Margaret 81
Crawley, W. J. (Faber sales manager) 187, 250–1
Criterion 153, 177, 179
Cubism 96, 118, 131
Cummings, E. E. 134, 183

Dadaism/Dadaists 2, 3, 36, 38, 137–46, 148, 152,
  165, 166–70, 250
  see also Huelsenbeck, Richard; and Tzara,
    Tristan
Dadaphone 140
'Dada Soulève Tout' [Dada Excites
  Everything] 137–8
Dale, Lucy: *An Anthology of English Prose* 213,
  217, 218
Daniel, Arnaut 74
Dante 61, 75, 93, 113, 139
  Inferno 164, 167
    Canto XV 188
    Canto XXVI 171
  Paradiso 240
  Purgatorio 63, 168
    Canto III 63
Darwin, Erasmus: *The Loves of the Plants* 122

276 INDEX

Davidson, John 72
 'Thirty Bob a Week' 72 n.112
Day, John: *The Parliament of Bees* 175–6
Deacon, William: *Warreniana* 18–19
decadence/decadents 26–7, 30, 40, 49, 62, 63–4,
 70, 72, 84 n.34, 191, 194
deconstruction 35–7, 38, 145, 149
Defoe, Daniel 210, 213 n.103, 217, 221
 Colonel Jack 217
 Moll Flanders 217
Dekker, Thomas: *The Great Frost* 236
Denisoff, Denis: *Aestheticism and Sexual Parody
 1840–1940* 24
De Quincey, Thomas: 'Levana, or our Ladies of
 Sorrow' 215
Des Imagistes: An Anthology 4, 104–7, 122
Dial (magazine) 95, 97, 145, 177
Dibdin, Charles: 'I be of they sailors who think
 'tis no lie' 225–6
Dickens, Charles 17
 Our Mutual Friend 163
Diepeveen, Leonard 119–20
 *Mock Modernism: An Anthology of Parodies,
 Travesties, and Frauds* 40–1, 119–20,
 135 n.73, 243 n.54
 Modernist Fraud: Hoax, Parody, Deception 41,
 183 n.149
 The Difficulties of Modernism 126, 183 n.149
directness 74, 107, 109
distortion 17, 39, 191, 248
Dobson, Austin: *Eighteenth Century
 Studies* 214–16
doggerel 49, 119, 137, 158–9, 210, 223, 227
Doolittle, Hilda
 see H. D.
Dostoevsky, Fyodor: *The Village of
 Stepanchikovo* 14
double-coding 32, 121
double-voiced discourse 15
Dowson, Ernest 57 n. 50, 63, 72
Dryden, John 5, 8–9, 177, 217, 237
 Drydenesque parody 148, 164, 174–5, 177,
 181, 185
 Mac Flecknoe 8–9, 164, 174–5
Duchamp, Marcel 38, 138
 Nude Descending a Staircase 96
Dynamistes 79, 92

Eastman, Max: 'A Dramatic Career in Modernist
 Art' 118
Edgeworth, Maria: *Belinda* 12
Egoist (magazine) 97–8, 102–10, 128–9,
 165, 170

Eliot, T. S. 5, 30 n.100, 32, 40 n.141, 41, 43–4, 64,
 72 n.112, 73, 80, 137, 139, 146, 147–89,
 190, 230, 231, 232, 236, 246
 After Strange Gods 157
 Ash Wednesday 188
 'Ballade pour la grosse Lulu' 159
 'Brilliants' 5, 147, 156
 'Burbank with a Baedecker: Bleistein with a
 Cigar' 160
 'The Columbiad' 156 n. 44, 156–60
 'A Cooking Egg' 160
 'Dante' 164, 179
 'Dirge' 170
 'East Coker' 189
 'Effie the Waif' 5, 147, 155–6
 'Elegy' 170
 'Exequy' 170
 Ezra Pound: His Metric and Poetry 73
 Ezra Pound: Selected Poems 178–9
 Four Quartets 184–5, 188–9
 Gideon Seymour Lecture 185
 'He do the Police in Different Voices' 163
 'Humouresque' 44
 King Bolo verses 5, 147, 156–60
 'The Love Song of J. Alfred Prufock' 152
 'A Lyric' 43
 Noctes Binanianae 187–8
 Old Possum's Book of Practical Cats 187
 'Parodies of Publisher's "Blurbs"' 185–7
 'Reflections on Contemporary Poetry' 165–6,
 169
 'Reflections on *Vers Libre*' 177
 The Rock 188
 'Sweeney Erect' 160–2, 171, 176
 'Tradition and the Individual Talent' 164, 177
 'The Triumph of Bullshit' 159
 The Waste Land 33, 40, 41, 146–8, 155,
 159–60, 162–85, 233
 Part I: 'The Burial of the Dead' 163, 170,
 172–3
 Part II: 'A Game of Chess' 163, 173–4,
 177, 180
 Part III: 'The Fire Sermon' 163, 175–6
 Part IV: 'Death by Water' 163–4, 171–2,
 180
 Part V: 'What the Thunder Said' 164,
 166–70
 Pound's editorial interventions 147–50,
 154, 156–7, 160, 162, 164–5, 170,
 172–3, 176–7, 179–80, 183, 185, 189
 'Notes to *The Waste Land*' 175, 181–5
 'What Dante Means to Me' 152

INDEX   277

Eliot, Valerie 156 n.45, 163
   The Waste Land: A Facsimile & Transcript of the Original Drafts including the Annotations of Ezra Pound 163
Eliot, Vivien 156, 179–80
   see also 'F. M.'
Elyot, Sir Thomas 217
English Review 136
Epstein, Jacob 98, 131
evaluative parody 64

'F. M.' [Vivien Eliot]: 'Letters of the Moment – II' 179–80
Faber, Geoffrey 187
Faber & Faber 187
feminist parody 40
Ficke, Arthur Davison 120–7, 128
   see also Knish, Anne
Fielding, Henry 9–11, 14, 17
   The History of Tom Jones: A Foundling 10–11
   Joseph Andrews 9–10
   Le Figaro 47
   Shamela 9
Fisher, Saint John 218
FitzGerald, Edward 229
   Rubaiyat of Omar Khayyam 48
   'Sea Words and Phrases from the Suffolk Coast' 224
Flaubert, Gustave 40, 46, 82, 199
Flint, F. S. 79, 80, 87, 94–5, 104
   'Contemporary French Poetry' 80, 83–4
   'Imagisme' 81 n.16, 94 n.77, 107 n. 28
Florio, John 217
Ford, Ford Madox 6, 71–2, 104, 105–6, 107, 232–6, 241
   'Canzone a la Sonata (To E. P.)' 72
   Collected Poems 71–2
   Des Imagistes 105–6
   'Fragments Addressed by Clearchus H. to Aldi' 105–6
   High Germany 105
   'Süssmund's Address to an Unknown God' 105
   'In the Little Old Market-Place' 104
   The March of Literature 106
   The Marsden Case 233
   Mister Bosphorus 232–6
   The Saddest Story 114
Francis, John Oswald: *Change: A Glamorgan Play in Four Acts* 224, 228–9
Francis, Sir Philip: *Letters of Junius* 214
Fraser's (magazine) 19, 22
free indirect style 194, 196, 197, 206–8, 245
French post-Symbolists 86, 87, 93, 131, 165

French Symbolists 143, 147, 152
Freytag-Loringhoven, Elsa von 137–8, 139–40, 146
   'Irrender König' 142
   'Klink-Hratzvenga (Deathwail)' 142
   'Nari-Tzarissamanili (He is Dead!)' 142
   'Thee I call "Hamlet of the Wedding Ring", Criticism of William Carlos Williams's "Kora in Hell" and why...' 137, 139–40, 142
Fu I 112
Futurism/Futurists 38, 80, 81–2, 86, 92, 97, 108, 118, 119, 121, 130, 135, 138

Gautier, Théophile 160
Genette, Gérard 35 n.121, 37
gestural parody 39
Gibbon, Edward: *The History of the Decline and Fall of the Roman Empire* 215
Gilbert, Stuart 197
Gilbert, W. S.: *Patience* 24
Glebe (magazine) 122
Gogarty, Oliver St John 192
Gogol, Nikolai: *Selected Passages from Correspondences with Friends* 14
Golding, Arthur 75
Goldsmith, Oliver: *The Vicar of Wakefield* 181–2
Goncourt, Edmund de 47
Gosse, Edmund 29, 182
   The Life of Algernon Charles Swinburne 61
Gourmont, Remy de: 'Litanies de la rose' 132
Goyert, Georg 227–8
Granta (university newspaper) 44
Gray, Thomas: *Elegy* 20
Greene, Robert: *A Groats-Worth of Wit* 237
Greville, Fulke 217
Groden, Michael: *'Ulysses' in Progress* 196–7, 202–3, 204 n.66, 222

H. D. 79 n.9, 82–3, 87, 89, 90, 95, 99, 100, 104
   'Hermes of the Ways' 82–3
   'Oread' 110
Hakluyt, Richard 46, 218
Hale, William Gardner 150–1
Hamilton, Walter
   The Aesthetic Movement in England 23
   Parodies of the Works of English and American Authors 20
Hannoosh, Michelle 36
   Parody and Decadence: Laforgue's 'Moralités légendaires' 39
Harte, Bret 224, 229
   'Condensed Novels' 224, 227
   Tales of the West 224, 227–8

278 INDEX

Hassan, Ihab 33–4, 38
  'POSTmodernISM: A Paracritical
    Bibliography' 33
Hastings, Beatrice 129–30, 131–4
  see also 'Alice Morning'; 'T. K. L.'
Hayward, John 186–9
Heap, Jane 123–4, 143–4
Heine, Heinrich 17, 69–71, 84
Hellenism 101, 105–6
Henderson, Alice Corbin 97, 123
Herrick, Robert 191–2
Herriman, George: *Krazy Kat* 153
Herring, Phillip F.: *James Joyce's Notesheets in*
    the British Museum 212
  see also Joyce, James: *Ulysses*
heteroglossia 15–17, 223
Hueffer, Ford Madox, see Ford Madox Ford
Huelsenbeck, Richard 3
Hewlett, Maurice 62
  The Masque of the Dead Florentines, A 50
  'Prelude' to the 'Man on the Hill' 133
Hichens, Robert: *The Green Carnation* 24
high modernism 25, 30, 32, 34, 39, 118, 148,
    184, 193, 232, 243, 253
Hinkley, Eleanor 155
history of parody 7–42
Hoffenstein, Samuel: 'The Moist Land – A
    Parody of Eliot's Poem' 183
Holinshed, Raphael 217
Holley, Horace: 'The Mice' 129
Homer 198, 199, 201
  Iliad 86, 199
  Odyssey 171, 195–8, 201, 209
Horace 67
Housman, A. E.: 'A Shropshire Lad' 67–8
Hulme, T. E. 64, 78–81, 82, 104, 129
  The Complete Poetical Works of T. E.
    Hulme 78–9, 80, 130
Hutcheon, Lynda
  The Politics of Postmodernism 32
  A Theory of Parody: The Teachings of
    Twentieth-Century Art Forms 32, 41
    n.151
Huxley, Aldous 25
Huyssen, Andreas 117

Ibsen, Henrik 17, 192–3
Imagism/Imagists 66, 74, 76, 77, 79–83, 87, 94,
    98, 103–8, 110, 117, 120, 128–9, 165
  see also *Des Imagistes*; Aldington, Richard:
    'Penultimate Poetry'; and the Spectra
    hoax
imitation 7, 8, 9–10, 32, 34, 36, 43, 139, 180, 232,
    243, 244, 245, 246

aestheticism 23
Beerbohm, Max 26
  debased 8
Eliot, T. S. 43, 139, 147, 165, 171, 180, 189
Fielding, Henry 9–10
Joyce, James 191–2
  neoclassical 32
  pastiche 34, 46
Pound, Ezra 48, 50–3, 56, 63–4, 67, 69, 85,
    104, 110, 139, 147, 151, 165
Quintilian, Marcus Fabius 43
reception theorists 17
Swinburne, Algernon Charles 23–4
transformative writing 7
Impressionism 118
insane parody 33, 38
interior monologue 196–7, 200, 206–8, 242, 245
intertextuality 31, 32, 35, 219–20, 221–2
  see also Joyce, James: *Ulysses*, 'Oxen of the Sun'
irony 8, 15, 17, 26, 32, 35, 44, 48, 66, 69, 77, 85,
    109, 110, 112, 137, 147–50, 152, 153,
    154, 162, 174, 187, 191, 194–5, 204,
    234, 243, 247, 249

James, Henry 27–9
  'The Death of the Lion' 37
  The Wings of the Dove 27
Jameson, Fredric 34–5
  blank parody 34–5
  'Postmodernism, or The Cultural Logic of
    Late Capitalism' 34
Janusko, Robert: *The Sources and Structures of*
    James Joyce's 'Oxen' 211, 212 n. 103
Japanese poetry 94–5, 101, 120
Jencks, Charles 32
Jepson, Edgar: 'The Western School' 136
Johnson, Samuel 13
Jonson, Ben 7–8, 43, 55, 57, 237
  Every Man in His Humour 7
  'Song to Celia' 43
Joyce, James 3, 5–6, 25, 30 n.99, 32, 33, 38,
    39–40, 41, 104, 147, 157, 160, 170, 171,
    172, 183–4, 190–231, 232–3, 235, 236,
    242, 244, 245, 246–51
  'Anna Livia Plurabelle' 249–50
  Chamber Music 191–2, 247
  Dubliners 190, 193–4
    'A Little Cloud' 190
  Finnegans Wake 5, 6, 184, 190, 230, 232,
    246–51
  'Haveth Childers Everywhere' 249–50
  'I Hear an Army' 104
  'James Clarence Mangan' 222
  'The Mirage of the Fisherman of Aran' 202

'Moods' 191
A Portrait of the Artist as a Young Man 191,
 194–5, 223, 230
'Shine and Dark' 191
'The Twilight turns from Amethyst' 191
Ulysses 3, 5–6, 25, 33, 39–40, 41, 127, 136,
 146, 160, 170, 171, 190, 191, 195–231,
 232–3, 235–6, 245, 246, 247
 'Aeolus' 143, 196
 'Circe' 160, 170, 172, 196, 203
 'Cyclops' 5–6, 191, 197–207
 'Eumaeus' 160, 170
 'Hades' 196
 'Lotus Eaters' 196
 'Nausicaa' 5–6, 41, 191, 197, 206–9, 230
 'Oxen of the Sun' 3, 5–6, 40, 160, 170–1,
  191, 196–7, 209–31, 232, 233, 238, 239
  notesheet 1 217
  notesheet 2 217, 218, 219
  notesheet 3 217, 221
  notesheet 6 217
  notesheet 7 218, 219–20
  notesheet 8 218
  notesheet 14 218
  notesheet 15 218, 220
  notesheet 16 214–16
  notesheet 17 221, 224, 225, 227, 228–30
  notesheet 19 221
  notesheet 20 221, 225, 228
  see also Herring, Phillip F.: *James Joyce's
   Notesheets in the British Museum*
 'Scylla and Charybdis' 196, 211, 230
 'Sirens' 199, 207, 247
 'Telemachus' 196
 'Wandering Rocks' 196
'Villanelle of the Temptress' 195
Work in Progress 244, 248
Joyce, Stanislaus 191, 192, 193, 194, 213 n.104

Keats, John 67, 72, 74
Kenner, Hugh 39–40, 190–1
 Dublin's Joyce 39, 190–1
 *Flaubert, Joyce, Beckett: The Stoic
  Comedians* 40
Kipling, Rudyard 44, 50–1, 135
 Barrack Room Ballads 50
 'The Rhyme of the Three Sealers' 44
 'The Young British Soldier' 51
Kitchin, George: *A Survey of Burlesque and
  Parody in English* 30, 127–8
Knish, Anne [Arthur Davison Ficke] 121–4
 Spectra: A Book of Poetic Experiments 121–2
Kreymborg, Alfred 122

Kristeva, Julia 31
Kyd, Thomas: *The Spanish Tragedy* 168

Lacerba (magazine) 108
Laforgue, Jules 5, 39, 44, 145, 147–9, 152, 160,
 180, 182
Lamb, Charles 18
Landor, Walter Savage 210
Lane, John 80–1
Larbaud, Valery 198
late modernism 45, 232
Leavis, F. R. 28–9
Lee, Vernon: *Miss Brown* 24
Leopardi, Giacomo 65
 Paralipomeni alla Batracomiomachia 85, 86
Levenson, Ada: 'Advisability of Not Being
  Brought up in a Handbag: A Trivial
  Tragedy for Wonderful People' 24
Lewis, Wyndham 3, 5, 6, 40 n.141, 82, 108–9,
 111–15, 129, 151, 153, 157, 158–9,
 241–7, 252
 The Apes of God 3, 242–6
 The Childermass 246
 Enemy of the Stars 114–15
 Men Without Art 241–2, 245–6
 Time and Western Man 111, 241 n.45, 247
Linati, Carlo 197
Lincoln, Joseph Crosby 224–5, 229
 Cap'n Eri: A Story of the Coast 224–5
Lindsay, Vachel 135–6
Li Po: 'Epitaphs' 112
little magazines 117–46
Little Review 120, 122, 123–4, 135–6, 137–8,
 139–44, 170, 184 n.154, 196, 202
Little Tich 153
Liveright, Horace 177, 185, 233
 Poems 152
Lloyd, Marie 153, 164
Lockhart, John Gibson 221
logopoeia 148–53, 160, 162, 171, 174, 180
London Mercury 45, 127
Longfellow, Henry Wadsworth 20, 40
 'Excelsior' 20
Lovelace, Richard 191
Lowell, Amy 104, 107–8, 124
 'In a Garden' 107
 Some Imagist Poets 108
Loy, Mina 138, 149
Lucretius 43

McAlmon, Robert 171
Macdonald Alden, Raymond. 95
Macherey, Pierre 31
Mackail, J. W.: *Latin Literature* 150

280 INDEX

Maeterlinck, Maurice 95, 139
Mallarmé, Stéphane 87
Mallock, W. H.
   Every Man His Own Poet 19 n.55
   The New Republic 24
Malory, Sir Thomas 209, 214, 217, 219–20
Mandeville, Sir John 209, 213, 217, 218–20, 223
Mann, Thomas 32, 39
Mansfield, Katherine 129–30
Marinetti, F. T. 38, 80, 81–2, 86, 92, 108, 115,
   128 n.49, 130–1, 135, 137
   'Let's Murder the Moonlight' 82
   'Vital English Art' (lecture) 131
   'Technical Manifesto of Futurist Literature' 81
Martin, A. T.: *Selections from Malory's Le Morte
   d'Arthur* 214, 217, 219–20
Martin, Theodore
   The Book of the Ballads 22
   'The Lay of the Lovelorn' 22
Marvell, Andrew: 'To His Coy Mistress' 175–6
Masters, Edgar Lee 122, 136
Mathews, Elkin 68
Maurier, George du 23
medieval revivalism 64
melopoeia 74, 148
Melville, Herman: *Moby Dick* 33
Mercure de France 199
metafiction 31, 35, 40
Milton, John 67, 113
   L'Allegro 67
mimesis 3, 5, 30, 35, 118, 190, 191, 197, 230
mimicry 29, 34, 35, 110, 146, 147, 154, 156, 158,
   160, 163, 165, 189, 242
mockery 12, 22, 72–3, 85–6, 87, 91, 98, 107–9,
   112, 115–16, 120, 122, 128, 147, 154,
   156, 159
mock heroic 7, 8, 10, 147, 164, 175, 195, 198,
   201–3, 218
Monroe, Harriet 80 n.10, 82–4, 87, 95–7, 100,
   106, 117, 122, 123, 135, 150–1, 152
   A Poet's Life 72 n.114, 96, 121 n.13
Moore, Marianne 138, 149, 150
More, Sir Thomas 218
Morgan, Emanuel [Witter Bynner] 121–5
   'Opus 6' 122
   'Opus 96' 123–4
   'Opus 102' 122
   Spectra: A Book of Poetic Experiments 121–2
Morley, Frank 187, 188
   'T. S. Eliot as a Publisher' 187
Morning, Alice [Beatrice Hastings]: 'Impressions
   of Paris' 134
Morris William 72, 74
Moses, Montrose, J.: *Change* 228–9

Murison, A. F.: *Selections from the Best English
   Authors (Beowulf to the Present
   Time)* 212 n.103, 214, 221
Murray, John Middleton 180
music halls (inspiration from) 147, 153, 158,
   160, 163, 164, 180, 190–1, 201, 233–4

Nabokov, Vladimir 33
Nerval, Gérard de: '*El Desdichado*' 168
New Age (magazine) 45, 73, 78, 84 n.30–1, 92
   n.66, 94, 112–13, 129–34
New English Weekly 137
New Statesman 177
New Yorker 118
Newman, John Henry 210
Nietzsche, Friedrich 1–3, 17, 65, 206, 236,
   241, 251
North, Sir Thomas 218
Nouvelle Revue Française 92

O'Grady, Standish James 204–5
Orage, A. R. 112–13, 133–4, 151
orientalism 99
originality 3, 27, 30, 36, 52, 165–6, 169, 180, 192,
   230–1, 236, 246, 252
Others (magazine) 122, 149
Ovid: *Metamorphoses* 168
Oxford Magazine 44

pageant-play 239
palimpsestual parody 37, 196
Palmer, Henry: *Cinder Thursday* 184–5
paraphrasing 43
Parker, Dorothy 119
parodic stylization 14–18, 24, 46, 47, 84, 85, 86,
   95, 115, 116, 147, 233
   Eliot, T. S. 147, 159, 162
   Joyce, Joyce 5, 190, 194, 197–8, 200, 205, 208,
   211, 218, 220, 223, 229, 233
   see also Bakhtin, Mikhail
passéism 86
pastiche 24, 32, 34–5, 57, 88, 93, 95, 111, 144,
   147, 233–5, 236, 246
   Dobson, Austin 214, 216
   Eliot, T. S. 152, 160–2, 165, 171, 173, 174,
   176, 187–9, 246
   Ford, Ford Madox 233–5
   Joyce, James 190, 194
   Pound, Ezra 4, 43–77, 152, 165, 189, 246
   Proust, Marcel 46–7

INDEX   281

Swinburne, Algeron Charles 24
Woolf, Virginia 46, 246
Pater, Walter 26, 30, 195, 210
Patmore, Coventry 233
Patmore, P. G.: *Rejected Articles* 18–19
Peacock, William: *English Prose from Mandeville to Ruskin* 212 n. 103, 213–14, 217–18
pedagogical parody 45, 48
Phiddian, Robert 35–6, 149
   'Are Parody and Deconstruction Secretly the Same Thing?' 35
   Swift's Parody 36
Phoenix Society 179
Picabia, Francis 138, 143–5, 152
plagiarism 8, 12, 38, 48, 86, 174, 185
Poe, Edgar Allen: 'Murders in the Rue Morgue' 162
Poetry: A Magazine of Verse 81, 82, 87, 97, 100, 102–5, 107, 123, 128, 150
Poetry Review 51, 80
Poirier, Richard
   'The Literature of Waste' 33
   'The Politics of Self-Parody' 33
Pope, Alexander 5, 8–9, 17, 147, 149, 163, 177–80, 234
   The Dunciad 8–9, 233
   The Rape of the Lock 8, 163, 178
post-Impressionists 79, 80, 81, 90, 95, 97
postmodernism 31–5, 38, 41
post-Symbolists 80, 83, 86, 87, 92, 93, 131, 147, 165
Pound, Ezra 3, 4–5, 30 n.99, 32, 40, 42, 43–104, 106–13, 121, 124, 128–9, 131–52, 154, 157, 159–60, 162–5, 170–3, 176–83, 185, 189, 192, 199, 200, 233, 243, 244, 246, 250
   ABC of Reading 48–9
   'Further Tests' 48, 49, 64, 101–2
   'How to Read' 61, 149 n
   'A Few Don'ts by an Imagiste' 107
   'Affirmations' 134
   'The Approach to Paris' 83–5, 131–2
   Blast
      'Monumentum Aere, Etc' 111
      'Fu I' 112
      'Li Po' 112
      'Salutation the Third' 110–11
      'Vortex. Pound' 109–10
   Cantos 60, 62, 111, 144, 145, 146, 151
   Canzoni 3, 4, 64–72, 77, 78, 95, 104
      'Aria' 65–6
      'Ballad of the Goodly Fere' 64
      'Canzon: The Yearly Slain (written in reply to Frederic Manning's "Korè")' 65

   'The Decadence' 62
   'Donzella Beata' 60–1
   'Her Monument, the Image Cut thereon/From the Italian of Leopardi' 65
   'L'Art" 66–7
   'A Prologue' 65
   'Redondillas, or Something of that Sort' 69
   'Song in the Manner of Housman' 67, 69
   'Translations from Heine' 69–70
   'Und Drang' 70–1
   'Victorian Eclogues' 65
   'Contemporania' 4, 83, 87–98, 102, 104, 110–11
      'Commission' 91, 95
      'The Condolence' 88–9
      'Dance Figure' 89
      'The Garden' 89, 100
      'The Garret' 89
      'In a Station of the Metro' 94, 101
      'Ortus' 89
      'A Pact' 93
      '*Pax Saturni*' 91, 93
      'Salutation' 89–90, 96
      'Salutation the Second' 90, 93, 95
      'Tenzone' 87–8, 96, 98
   Des Imagistes 104
      'To Hulme (T. E.) and Fitzgerald (A Certain)' 68, 104
      see also 'Contemporania': 'In a Station of the Metro'
   Exultations 63, 73
   Gaudier-Brzeska: A Memoir 63
   'Have I Not, O Walt Whitman' 56
   Hugh Selwyn Mauberley 171, 233
   'I Gather the Limbs of Osiris' 73–5, 129
      'The River Merchant's Wife: A Letter' 129
      'The Seafarer' 129
      'The Song of the Bowmen of Shu' 129
   'In Praise of the Masters' 56, 58
   'James Joyce et Pécuchet' 199
   'Kongo Roux' 144–6, 152
   Literary Essays of Ezra Pound
      'Cavalcanti' 75–6
      'Irony, Laforgue, and Some Satire' 148
      'A Retrospect' 78–9
      'Swinburne versus His Biographers' 61, 73
   A Lume Spento 58, 60, 62–3, 73, 104
      'Fifine Answers' 60
      'La Fraisne' 58
      'In Tempore Senectutis (*An Anti-stave for Dowson*)' 63

282 INDEX

Pound, Ezra (*Continued*)
'Mesmerism' 58–60
'Salve O Pontifex!/To Swinburne: an hemichaunt' 61–2
'Scriptor Ignotus' 62
'Sestina: Altaforte' 64
A Lume Spento and Other Early Poems 72
Lustra 62, 68, 91 n.64, 97
'Ancient Music' 68
'Med' 50–1
'Mr. K.' 50
'Pagentry' 53–5
'Paris Letter' 145
Pavannes and Divisions 79 n.9
Personae 63, 73
'Piccadilly' 73
'Revolt: Against the Crepuscular Spirit in Modern Poetry' 63
Personæ: Collected Shorter Poems of Ezra Pound 150 n.10
'Alf's Second Bit' 137
'The Poems of Abel Sanders' 137, 140–3
'Poems': *Poetry: A Magazine of Verse* III(2) (November 1913)
'April' 99
'Ancora' 99
'Gentildonna' 98
'Lustra' 98
'Xenia' 98, 99, 101
Poetical Works of Lionel Johnson 44
'Prolegomena' 51–2
Quia Pauper Amavi 151–2
'Homage to Sextus Propertius' 148, 150–2
'Langue d'Oc' 151–2
'Moeurs Contemporaines' 151
A Quinzaine for this Yule 55, 63
'Histrion' 55
Ripostes of Ezra Pound: Whereto Are Appended the Complete Poetic Works of T. E. Hulme, with Prefatory Note 78–80, 104
'The Return' 78
'The Seafarer' 74, 78
see also Hulme, T. E
'Sage Homme' 159
'San Trovaso Notebook' 57
'Piazza San Marco' 57
'The Serious Artist' 82, 88
The Sonnets and Ballate of Guido Cavalcanti 74–5
The Spirit of Romance 49, 88–9, 91–2
'To R. B.' 52–3
'Vorticism' 63, 94
'What I Feel about Walt Whitman' 93

see also Sanders, Abel; Venison, Alfred; Eliot, T. S.: *The Waste Land*, Pound's editorial interventions
Power, Arthur 208
Pre-Raphaelites 52, 56, 64, 70, 71, 72
Priestman, Judith: 'The Age of Parody: Literary Parody and Some Nineteenth Century Perspectives' 19
Proust, Marcel 32, 46–7, 57, 93
In Search of Lost Time 47
Lemoine Affair 47
Pastiches et mélanges 47
Time Regained 47
Punch 19–20, 23, 24, 44, 178, 182, 188, 193

Quinn, John 62, 136, 199, 235
Quintilian, Marcus Fabius: *Institutio Oratoria* 43

Rabelais, François 12, 13, 14, 17, 84, 147, 198–200, 201, 205, 251
The Life of Gargantua and Pantagruel 12–13, 198–200
Radcliffe, Ann: *The Mysteries of Udolpho* 11
Raleigh, Sir Walter 217
Ransom, John Crowe 181–2
Read, Herbert: *Naked Warriors* 165–6
realism 17, 39, 192–3, 199, 217
reception theorists 17
Reedy's Mirror 122, 124
regional dialects and slang 223–30
Rembrandt 56
Reynolds, John Hamilton: *Peter Bell* 18
Rice, Wallace 95, 97
Richards, Grant 193
Richardson, Samuel: *Pamela* 9
Rickword, Edgell 181–2
ridicule 8, 15, 16, 20, 22, 32, 82, 84, 85, 99, 102, 109, 116, 130, 134, 136, 138, 175, 183
Rochester, Lord: 'To all Curious Criticks and Admirers of Metre' 11
Rodker, John 244
Romains, Jules 92, 94, 95
L'Armée dans la Ville 94
La Vie unanime 92
romanticism 2, 19, 85, 88, 98, 104, 251
Rose, Margaret A. 31 n.103, 35, 41 n.151
Parody: Ancient, Modern and Post-Modern 35
Rossetti, Dante Gabriel 46, 56, 58, 60–1, 63, 70, 74–5, 76
'The Blessed Damozel' 60–1
Rossetti, William Michael 23
Ruskin, John 221
Russian formalists 13–14, 31

INDEX 283

Sackville-West, Vita 236–7
  The Land 237
Saintsbury, George: *A History of English Prose*
    Rhythm 213–15, 217–18, 220–3
Sanders, Abel [Ezra Pound] 135–7, 140–3, 159
  'Committee for the Increase of
      Population' 136
  'The Poems of Abel Sanders' 140–3
  'The Reader Critic: Mr. Lindsay' 135–6
Sappho 81, 106
satire 9, 18, 21–2, 32, 47, 78, 81, 84, 89, 107–8,
      112, 117–18, 123, 130–1, 138, 174, 177,
      190, 193, 242
  Eliot, T. S. 180, 186, 187
  Eliot, Vivien 177
  Ford, Ford Madox 233
  Joyce, James 190–1, 193, 194
  Lewis, Wyndham 242–3
  political 9
  Pound, Ezra 49, 51, 64, 68–9, 76–7
saturation 166, 169, 171, 180, 252
Saturday Review 29
Scarron, Paul: *Le Virgile travesty en vers*
    burlesques 8
Schelling, Felix 148, 151–2
Schiff, Sydney 170, 180
Scriblerians 9
Seaman, Owen 25, 27 n.87, 44–5, 50
  Horace at Cambridge 44
  'The Rhyme of the Kipperling' 44, 50
self-mockery 32, 68, 91, 112, 115, 122, 147
self-parody 17, 23, 33, 86, 102, 108, 120, 122,
      128, 147, 251
  Beerbohm, Max 29
  Dada 137–8
  Eliot, T. S. 5, 147, 152, 188–9
  Futurism 86
  Joyce, James 33, 191, 192, 194, 247
  Imagism 80
  Nabokov, Vladimir 33
  Pound, Ezra 47, 61, 68, 69, 95, 152
  Proust, Marcel 47
  Swinbrune, Algernon Charles 61–2
  Vorticism 108
  Whitman, Walt 92
sexual parody and camp 24
Shadwell, Thomas 9
Shakespear, Dorothy 64
Shakespeare, William 55, 57, 67, 133, 179,
      201–2, 237
  Antony and Cleopatra 163, 173–4
  King Lear 240
  'Sonnet 98' 57
Shelley, Percy Bysshe 18, 56, 66–7, 186, 221
  Peter Bell the Third 18

Shklovsky, Viktor 13–14
Sidney, Sir Philip 217
Silvestre, Armand 85
Sitwell family 242, 243
Skeat, William Walter: *Etymological*
    Dictionary 219
Smith, James and Horace: *Rejected Addresses* 18,
      19 n.55, 22
Southey, Robert: *A Vision of Judgement* 21–2
Spectra hoax 120–7
Spectrism 122–3
Spenser, Edmund 54, 57, 133, 234
Squire, J. C. 44–6, 67–8, 120, 125–7, 182–3
  Apes and Parrots: An Anthology of Parodies 30
      n.101, 127
  'Imaginary Speeches' 45
  'The Man Who Wrote Free Verse' 120, 125–7,
      183
  'The Sort of Poems Modern Poets Write' 45
  Tricks of the Trade: Parodies in Verse and
      Prose 45–6
Stein, Gertrude 116, 118, 128, 242
  'Miss Furr and Miss Skeen' 118
Stephen, J. K.: *Lapsus Calami* 19 n.55, 37, 45,
      46 n.17
Steele, Sir Richard 210
Sterne, Lawrence 12–14, 17, 147, 210, 251
  Life and Opinions of Tristram Shandy 12–13,
      14
Stevenson, Robert Louis: 'Requiem' 240
Stevens, Wallace 138
Stone, Christopher 25
Stones, Graeme: *Parodies of the Romantic*
    Age 18–19
Storer, Edward 129
Strachan, John: *Parodies of the Romantic*
    Age 18–19
Strachey, Lytton 244
Stravinsky, Igor: *The Rite of Spring* 176
stream of consciousness 245
Swift, Jonathan 9, 17, 109, 210, 217, 218 n.144,
      220–1, 237, 251
  Polite Conversation 217
  A Tale of a Tub 9, 36, 217
Swinburne, A. C. 23–4, 52, 58, 61–2, 63, 64, 73,
      74, 75
  Poems and Ballads 23–4
  Specimens of Modern Poets: The Heptalogia or
      the Seven Against Sense 24
  'Nephelidia' 24, 61–2
Symbolists 80 n.11, 82, 84 n.34, 94, 98, 143,
      147, 169
  see also post-Symbolists
Symons, Arthur: *The Symbolist Movement in*
    Literature 147

284 INDEX

Tagore, Rabindranath 87, 100
Tailhade, Laurent 83–6, 132
  Au Pays du Mufle 85
  'Place des Victoires' 84
  Poèmes aristophanesques 83, 86
  presentative method 84
  Virgo fellatrix 85
Tait's (magazine) 19
Taylor, Bert Leston 95–6
Tennyson, Alfred Lord 22, 72, 73, 137, 168, 171,
    233–4, 240, 248
  'The Charge of the Light Brigade' 248
  Idylls of the King 73
  'Locksley Hall' 22
  The Princess 168, 240
  'Ulysses' 171
Thackeray, William Makepeace 17, 43
theory of parody 7–42
'T. K. L.' [Beatrice Hastings] 131–4
transcontextualization 32, 35
transition (magazine) 244
travesty 7–8, 22, 25, 30, 40, 106, 147
Trench, Herbert: 'Apollo and the Seamen' 37
Trench, Richard Chenevix 213, 217–20
  English Past and Present 213 n. 104, 219
  On the Study of Words 213, 217, 219
Tynianov, Yuri: 'Dostoevsky and Gogol: Towards
    a Theory of Parody' 14
Tzara, Tristan 5, 138, 140, 165–6, 168–9
  'Dada Manifesto' 138, 169
  Vingt-cinq poèmes 165–6, 169
  see also Dada

Ultra-Violets 122–3
Unanimistes 79, 80, 93, 94, 98
university newspapers 44
Upward, Allen 104, 107, 129

Vanity Fair (magazine) 118
Vega, Lope de 55, 88–9, 95
Venison, Alfred [Ezra Pound] 136–7, 159
  *Alfred Venison's Poems: Social Credit Themes
    by the Poet of Titchfield Street* 137
Verhaeren, Emile: 'Fleur Fatale' 169
Verlaine, Paul 139, 175–6
  Parsifal 175–6

Vidal, Peire 58
Villon, François 54, 55, 58, 61, 71, 80, 81, 82, 84
Vorticism 82, 108–12, 129, 131, 144, 165

Wallace, Nellie 153, 164
Ward, Christopher: 'The Dry Land' 183
Watts-Dunton, Theodore 62
Waugh, Evelyn: *Vile Bodies* 115, 241
Weaver, Harriet Shaw 170, 183, 196–7, 211,
    247–8
Weeks, Leroy Titus 103, 178
  'Tommy Rot' 103
Western School 136, 143
West, Rebecca: 'Indissoluble Matrimony' 112,
    114
Whistler, James 23
Whitmanisme 80, 92
Whitman, Walt 40, 56, 69, 91–5, 97, 98, 104, 191
  Leaves of Grass 69, 91
Wilde, Oscar 23, 24, 26, 39 n.137, 108
  trials 108
Williams, William Carlos 104, 137–42
  'Improvisations' 137–9
  Kora in Hell 137, 139–40
Woolf, Virginia 3, 6, 13, 29, 30 n.99, 40, 45–6,
    187, 230, 232, 236–40, 241, 245–6
  Between the Acts 3, 236, 239–40
  'The Leaning Tower' 239
  'The Modern Essay' 29
  Mrs Dalloway 245
  Orlando: A Biography 40, 236–9
  'Parodies' 45–6
  'The Sentimental Journey' 13
  'Tragedy in a Duckpond' 46
Wordsworth, William 18, 20, 72, 151
  'Resolution and Independence' 20
Wycliffe, John 220

Yeats, W. B. 52, 58, 71, 78, 100, 104, 151, 191
  'The Cap and Bells' 71
  In the Seven Woods 58
  Tuatha Dé Danan 151
  'The Withering of the Boughs' 151
Yellow Book 25

Zukovsky, Louis: *Poem Beginning 'The'* 183